THE VICTORIA AND ALBERT MUSEUM

THE VICTORIA AND ALBERT MUSEUM

The history of its building

John Physick

Victoria and Albert Museum
London

To the memory of Sir Henry Cole (1808–1882)

This book was designed and produced by
The Oregon Press Limited, Faraday House,
8–10 Charing Cross Road, London WC2 0HG

Editor: Mary Anne Sanders
Designer: Gail Engert
Reader: Raymond Kaye
Index: Myra Clark

0 905209 25 7

Filmset by SX Composing Limited, Rayleigh, England
Printed by Westerham Press Limited, Westerham, Kent
Bound by Robert Hartnoll Limited, Bodmin, Cornwall

Acknowledgments

Material from the Royal Archives at Windsor Castle
is quoted by gracious permission of H.M. the Queen.
I am also greatly indebted to Mr Anthony Burton and
Miss Jennifer Brain for the invaluable assistance that
they have given in the latter stages of this book, and to
the enthusiasm and encouragement of Mr Nicky Bird,
the Museum's Publication Officer; also to Mrs Cyn-
thia Dutnall and Mrs Elizabeth Bonython for their
permission to use the papers of Sir Henry Cole in the
National Art Library, the Keeper of the Public Records
for his permission to reproduce material in his care,
the executors of the late H. G. Wells for permission to
quote from *Love and Mr. Lewisham*, and those copy-
right holders who were not traced. I am grateful to
colleagues and friends who have given me information
and help, among them Miss Elizabeth Aslin, Mr Peter
Bezodis, Mrs Shirley Bury, Mr David Church, Dr
Michael Darby, the late Charles Gibbs-Smith, Miss
Caryl Stanley and Miss Sarah Wray, and to my wife
Eileen who has for many years endured a house full of
thousands of sheets of paper.

Whoever is interested in the history of the Victoria
and Albert Museum's building and of the Department
of Science and Art, owes a special debt of gratitude
not only to the photographers from 1856 to those of
the present day who helped, from Charles Thurston
Thompson, Sergeant Benjamin Spackman, Corporal
Milligan and Corporal Church to Messrs. Peter Mac-
donald, Stanley Eost, Kenneth Jackson, Stephen
Heritage, Philip Spruyt de Bay, Miss Sally Chappell
and Miss Christine Smith – but also to the many
anonymous clerks who kept such a comprehensive
series of press-cutting albums from 1852 to the end of
the 19th century, relating to all the activities of the
Department and its officers. This history was written
at the request of Sir John Pope-Hennessy, the Director
1967–73, and was completed by 1975. That it is not
being published until 1982, in a reduced form, is I
suppose a result of the difficult economic situation
that we have all found ourselves in.

J.P.
Meopham, Kent
Easter 1982

HALF-TITLE *Line engraving of the 1851 Exhibition medal
designed by William Wyon (1795–1851)*

Contents

Foreword

We have almost lost the idea of a museum being a work of art in its own right. Instead, in this century, it has become a complex machine for the presentation and display of objects. For the interior decoration of a museum to be anything other than subservient to the artefacts it displays has come to be regarded almost as a crime. But is it? The history of the Victoria and Albert Museum tells one otherwise. Like all great building projects it was full of stops and starts, muddle and maladministration, dramas and disagreements, but it was held together by a vision that we are now not only trying to rediscover and restore, but to revive in the terms of today. The Museum can and should be such a work of art in its own right.

Visitors to the V&A in the last decade must have become acutely aware of our search for a new strategy to recover and reinstate the original articulation and decoration of the building as it appeared when it opened in 1909 but, at the same time marry those objectives to fulfilling all the demands made upon the Museum in the late 20th century. It is a formidable challenge and inevitably a long process. Total restoration, as far as is possible, is almost the easiest part of the exercise. We have put back the William Morris Room with its painted panelling, its stencilled ceiling and strange, dim chandeliers. The old restaurant and grill room were scheduled for demolition as late as the 1960's. Now they provide the Museum with a setting for events when, lit by the light of a hundred flickering candles, these rooms evoke gasps from the visitor astonished at the soaring Minton columns or the Kate Greenaway charm of Sir Edward Poynter's ceramic panels of the months. One of the two great Cast Courts opened in the 1870s now delights every visitor to the Museum with its sculptural phantasmagoria, giving us the quintessence of Victorian eclecticism of taste as the triumphant procession encircling Trajan's column stands side by side with Germain Pilon's sinuous maidens bearing the urn contain-

ing the heart of Henri II. These are complex but straightforward essays in putting the clock back. More daunting is the task of re-establishing the former axes of the Museum, those gracious vistas and airy arcaded openings that must have made it a place of enchantment to visit as the eye was led up flight after flight of marble stairs or layer after layer of column and arch.

It is a miracle that so much actually still remains for the inroads made upon the interior, especially in the aftermath of the Second World War, were significant. For a generation it achieved a surface effect of modernity that is now removable. It was the illusory prosperity of the sixties that did real damage for it is certain that the mezzanine inserted in the room immediately beyond the great central concourse area ought never to have been built. It has damaged not quite irreparably but substantially one of Aston Webb's greatest concepts, a sweeping perspective through from the main entrance to the greenery of the quadrangle beyond.

The Victorian revival of the sixties was totally fomented in the V&A but we have moved on and I believe that we are now in for a radical reassessment of Sir Aston Webb's status. More and more for me he becomes the architectural Elgar of his age. Although the foundation stone of the V&A was laid by the great Queen herself in 1899, the Museum opened its doors in the reign of Edward VII. We tend to forget that the V&A substantially belongs also to the Edwardian age, the sunset apogee of our optimism. Like Elgar's music the sweep, thrust and movement of Webb's architecture speaks of solemnity, grandeur and security, but always tinged with a certain poignancy, a hidden sadness that all this was not to last. This book sets out to tell that story.

Sir Roy Strong
Director, Victoria and Albert Museum
August 1982

7

Notes to the text

Report . . .   *Report[s] of the Science and Art Department,* from 1853.

Decorations   *Decorations of the South Kensington Museum 1862–1874* (1875), unpublished.

Survey   *Survey of London,* Vol. XXXVIII, 1975, the Museums Area of South Kensington and Westminster (published for the GLC).

Select Committee 1860   *Report from the Select Committee on the South Kensington Museum,* 1860, (with Minutes of Evidence).

Select Committee 1897 [1898]   *Report from the Select Committee on Museums of the Science and Art Department* (with the proceedings of the Committee), 1897 and 1898.

PRO, Ed. 84   Public Record Office; papers of the Department of Science and Art and Board of Education relating to the Museum.

PRO, Works 17   Public Record Office; papers of the Office of Works relating to the Museum's building.

PRO, Works 33   Drawings by Aston Webb and his office for the Museum's building.

Introduction

The Victoria and Albert Museum is, to a very large extent, the result of an experiment, both as a huge collection of decorative and fine art objects, and as a vast, labyrinthine building covering 12 acres of land in London. It began in the most humble manner, as an assemblage of plaster casts for an art school (which later became the Royal College of Art). Gradually, to these casts were added specimens of ornamental art, mostly contemporary.

When the art school and its instructive collection moved from Somerset House to Marlborough House in 1852, the art collections became the focus as the Museum of Practical Art, the art school becoming subordinate. Under dynamic leadership, the Museum of Ornamental Art (as it had become) expanded and moved in 1857 into a temporary iron building at Brompton, while the art school had to be satisfied with wooden huts.

At Brompton, the Museum became part of the South Kensington Museum and was crammed into the iron building with a miscellaneous collection of British sculpture, architectural casts, animal products, food, models and patented inventions, educational aids, the nucleus of the National Art Library, a circulating art library, and construction and building materials. The temporary iron structures established the floor level for the permanent building. This remains, although the iron sheds were dismantled during the 1860s and reassembled at Bethnal Green.

A select committee of the House of Commons in 1860 confirmed that the creation of the Museum had been a success, and recommended that the government should provide money for the permanent Museum buildings which had been designed, not by an architect, but by a Royal Engineer, Captain Francis Fowke. It is at this point, then, that the second experimental stage began, which lasted for about the next twenty years, producing a building, many parts of which were considered objects in the Museum's collections, as much as the thousands of artifacts which were housed in it.

The officers of the Museum were, at the same time, the controlling officials of its parent body, the Department of Science and Art, which at first was a division of the Board of Trade, but later came under the auspices of the Privy Council Committee of Education. Departmental and Museum activities were, in the main, inextricably mingled as a result, whether concerned with planning or building the 1862 Exhibition, or the Royal Scottish Museum, or decorating the buildings at South Kensington.[1]

These officials were all keen on experimenting with, and reviving the use of, mosaic in glass and ceramic, tile, terracotta and mural paintings, and had, of course, a plentiful supply of art students to hand, whose training could be put to practical use in their own building.

Fowke's South Kensington complex comprised Museum, art school, and later a science school, refreshment rooms, a lecture theatre for both museum and art school use, houses and offices. All these became an integral part of the section of the Museum of which Fowke was in charge, the Museum of Construction and Building Materials, until his early death in 1865.

The Museum of Construction, as it soon became known, contained: 'samples of building stones and marbles, specimens of all the best cements and asphalts, examples of the numerous applications of ceramic manufacture to the purpose of construction, more especially in this country and in France; such as tiles for roofing and flooring of the newest and most approved form and clays; bricks hollow, solid, and moulded, of various sorts, examples of many ingenious applications of these materials which are made in France, such as lintels, jambs, exterior and interior cornices, mouldings, window dressings &c.; specimens of French fire-

---

1. The history of the Department, Art School and Museum will be found in *The Nationalisation of Culture*, Janet Minihan, 1977.

1, 2. (above and left) Testing the strength of Colonel Scott's 'newly invented' cement, 9 July 1861, for the Museum of Construction, in the South Court

proof floors for private houses ... To this list may be added ornamental tiles for interior wall decoration from England, France, and Spain, and a great variety of hip and ridge tiles and crest ornaments, principally intended for edifices in the Gothic style. Some bricks decorated after the manner of majolica, and samples of enamelled slate and other imitations of marble, may be classed with this description of material.'[2]

As public interest in this practical and permanent exhibition grew, to it were added models of then new buildings, as well as specimens of such ordinary items as drainpipes and gutters, but always as examples of modern techniques. The Museum, for example, conducted experiments on a cement *1, 2* newly invented by another Royal Engineer officer, Henry Scott, in order to test the 'crushing weight of an archway of 10 feet span, two feet thick, and

2. Museum of Construction, *Catalogue*, 1862, p. 5.

on the crown nine inches deep',[3] as well as on 'the crushing weight of one of the [terracotta] columns employed by Captain Fowke for the south portion of the ornamental arcades surrounding the gardens of the Royal Horticultural Society'.[4] Scott's cement had entered the collection in 1858 as an example that gave 'a material almost equal to Portland cement at little more than half price'.[5] It was used throughout the buildings.

However, neither Fowke, nor his superior, Henry Cole, head of both the Museum and the Department of Science and Art, was content to have these examples simply displayed and labelled. The buildings were used as practical examples, sometimes funded as part of the building costs, or otherwise paid for as objects of the Construction Museum. This enabled the visitor, having seen isolated, mute, specimens, subsequently to wander round the South Kensington Museum to see them in use, during the various phases of building activity.

There was much to see. Floor tiles, exhibited by Maw & Co., of Shropshire, and the Architectural Pottery Co. of Poole, Dorset, were laid as a 'large piece of ornamental tile pavement' in the Museum,[6] or 'white glazed tiles, or slabs for wall linings, &c., were also purchased from French and English manufacturers. These have been applied to several purposes in the new buildings of the Science and Art Department. A notable feature of this application has been made in the new porte-cochère entrance to the Department, where they have been used for the ceiling under the fire-proof flooring, on Messrs. Fox and Barrett's system, of the new board room. These white glazed tiles or slabs, which produce an agreeable and light effect, were manufactured by M. M. Ergel and Tremblai, of Paris.'[7] 'Ornamental enamelled iron sheets or plaques have also been similarly suggested for ceilings under fire-proof floors, and these seem to be a very useful and important application thus opened, in the matter of fire-proof ceilings'.[8] It was not long before such enamelled iron plates were fixed to the ceiling of the Refreshment Room, where they still are.

Experiments for ornamental pavements were carried out in Cromwell Road. Areas each 20 feet by 12 feet, one including a vitreous material, known as 'terra metallic', were laid to see how they stood up to public traffic.[9] They have long since been swept away by later improvements.

Much remains, though a lot has been covered up since the Second World War, notably the South Court, with its ironwork bronzed by the Parisian, M. Oudry's, recently invented paint,[10] or the mosaics in the same court.[11] The most conspicuous material is the terracotta of the quadrangle and the Henry Cole Building. Whole chunks of this, including the arches of the Lecture Theatre, were duplicated and dispatched to the 1867 Paris Exhibition, as well as one of the ceramic columns in the Gamble Room.[12] The Report of the Museum of Construction for 1865 states: 'It may here be worthy of remark, that in order to obtain some idea of the relative cost of wrought stone and terra cotta decorations for external use, the Department procured from Messrs. Smith & Taylor a copy in wrought Portland stone of one of the ornamental blocks in terra cotta, designed by Godfrey Sykes, Esq., and executed by Messrs. Blanchard & Co., Blackfriars Road, for the façades of the new buildings of the Museum. The original terra cotta and the copy in wrought stone are exhibited side by side for comparison. The cost of the former was £2 3s, while that of the latter was £5 8s, or nearly three times the cost of the terra cotta.'[13]

The activity was intense: Minton's had to set up a manufactory near the Albert Hall; students were painting ceilings, modelling majolica, or engraving layers of coloured cement on the abyss-like east wall of the Henry Cole Building. Henry Cole

3. *8th Report of The Department of Science and Art 1861* (1862), Museum of Construction, p. 125.

4. Ibid. These experiments were photographed.

5. *6th Report of the Department of Science and Art 1858* (1859), Museum of Construction, p. 33.

6. *8th Report of the Department of Science and Art 1860* (1861), Museum of Construction, p. 139.

7. *16th Report of the Department of Science and Art 1868*, 1869, Museum of Construction, p. 383.

8. Ibid.

9. *13th Report of the Department of Science and Art 1865* (1866), Museum of Construction, p. 229.

10. *12th Report of the Department of Science and Art 1864* (1865), Museum of Construction, p. 224.

11. Ibid., pp. 223, 224. *13th Report of the Department of Science and Art 1865* (1866), Museum of Construction, p. 228, which also refers to the acquisition of the Minton ceramic portrait of Prince Albert for the Prince Consort's Gallery (Room 110).

12. *15th Report of the Department of Science and Art 1867* (1868), Museum of Construction, p. 252, and 201, 202. 'The use of majolica or glazed earthenware in the decoration of the new columns designed by Mr. Gamble ... excited much attention ...'

13. *12th Report of the Department of Science and Art 1864* (1865), Museum of Construction, p. 223.

created a ladies' mosaic class, into which he pressed members of his family to cope with all the work in the Museum and the Albert Hall, and even lady convicts at Woking were making mosaic floors.

But most of this do-it-yourself design, creation and manufacture came to an end after 1870 when Acton Smee Ayrton,[14] First Commissioner of Works, insisted that the Office of Works, and not the Department of Science and Art, had control of the South Kensington Museum buildings. After the last of the early buildings, the National Art Library, was completed, the architect, Major-General Henry Scott (who had succeeded Fowke in 1865), was dismissed by the Office of Works: he died within a year of this humiliation.

For many years the gaunt buildings remained incomplete, the subject of constant criticism. In 1891, selected architects were invited to compete for the final phase, the Cromwell Road and Exhibition Road façades. The assessor, Alfred Waterhouse, recommended Aston Webb's design, but it was not until 1899 that work began on the ten-year long construction.

During the eighteen years from first plans to completion, the architect was not only barely adequately briefed, but the future use of the building was constantly changing. At one moment, half of it was to be given over to science; at another, the entire top floor was to be devoted to the Royal College of Art. The central tower, therefore, was planned as its library and bookstacks. The decision being reversed, the tower has since remained an empty shell. One of the firm requirements of the competition was a main staircase leading directly from the entrance to the first floor and the Library. For an undetermined reason, this was abandoned by the Board of Education. As a result, the building is now divided by a huge entrance which allows no direct communication from the galleries on the western side to those on the eastern, except on the top floor – if one ever finds it. Webb was not asked to provide any offices until after the building was finished, when the 1908 Committee

of Re-arrangement required them. Poor Webb – much of the criticism of the inadequacies of the building is laid at his feet, totally unjustifiably. He can, however, be blamed for the extremely inconvenient changes in floor levels. For some reason, he took as his ground level that of General Scott's cast courts, the only rooms with a basement and, as a result, raised above any of the others at the time.

When, at last, the extension opened, there was a new Director, Sir Cecil Smith, formerly a Keeper in the British Museum and chairman of the Committee of Re-arrangement. He determinedly set about to obliterate as much of the internal decoration as he could – stained glass was removed, ceilings painted over, majolica columns hacked down – but the public outcry was such that his hands were stayed as they were set to attack the Ceramic Staircase just before the First World War. At least something survived this, and subsequent disfavour and neglect. The link with the Royal College of Art has been revived and the new iron gates by Douglas Coyne and Christopher Hay, in Exhibition Road were the result of a direct commission to the College.

Perhaps the Victoria and Albert Museum is the only museum in the world housed in a building which to a great extent itself was meant to be one of its own museum exhibits.[15]

---

14. '... a notoriously ignorant bully ...'. H. S. Goodhart-Rendel, in a lecture at the Victoria and Albert Museum, 1952, reprinted in *Victorian Architecture*, ed. Peter Ferriday, 1963, p. 99.

15. Until 1939, at least, apprentice bricklayers were brought to the quadrangle to study the quality of the bricklaying of the Lecture Theatre façade. (Information give to the author, *c.* 1949, by Harry Rogers, lately Restorer in the Department of Conservation.) 'Congratulations to the Victoria and Albert Museum on the newly refurbished Cast Courts opened last month. These rooms have been restored in their original colours with most of the original casts collected in the 19th century ... Sir Roy Strong ... has shown again how perceptive and enterprising he is as Director ... By capitalising on the Museum's architectural advantages and restoring more of its original rooms he has enhanced its appeal as a living museum ...' The Victorian Society, April 1982; Programme and Newsletter no. 15.

CHAPTER I

The genesis of the Museum

The Victoria and Albert Museum, which until 1899 was known as the South Kensington Museum, opened on its present site, in temporary buildings, in 1857. During the next half-century the buildings it occupies today developed as a result of a tortuous and elaborate construction programme. An embryonic form of the Museum, however, was in existence before 1857. Its history had begun some twenty years earlier.

In 1836, a committee of the House of Commons investigated the subject of the promotion of art in Britain. In their report,[1] the members of the committee adverted

> ... with regret to the inference they are obliged to draw from the testimony they have received, that from the highest branches of practical design, down to the lowest connexion between design and manufacturers, the arts have received little encouragement in this country. The want of instruction in design among our industrious population; the absence of public and freely-open galleries containing approved specimens of art; the fact that only recently a National Gallery has even been commenced among us, have all combined strongly to impress this conviction on the minds of the members of the Committee.

This lack of facilities was not observable in many 'despotic countries', France in particular, and it was therefore all the more important that in England, a great manufacturing country, there should be a much stronger connection between art, design, and manufacture.

The committee made two chief recommendations: that schools of design should be established to afford suitable instruction in the application of art to industry and that encouragement should be given to the 'formation of open public galleries, or museums of art, in the various towns willing to undertake a certain share in the foundation, and to continue the maintenance of such establishments'. Other countries were much better off, especially France, where the larger towns were

... generally adorned by such institutions; in this country we can scarcely boast of any; our exhibitions (where they exist) are usually periodical. A fee is demanded for admission, and modern works only exhibited. From such exhibitions, the poor are necessarily excluded....

The committee went on to suggest that these museums, once set up, should contain examples not only of ancient art, but also of 'the most approved modern specimens, foreign as well as domestic, which our extensive commerce would readily convey to us from the most distant quarters of the globe'.

The Schools of Design

As a result of this enquiry the president of the Board of Trade, C. Poulett Thomson, called a meeting with C. R. Cockerell RA, C.L. Eastlake RA, Alderman Copeland MP, H. Bellenden Ker, and Apsley Pellatt at the Treasury on 19 December 1836 to discuss the foundation of a School of Design in Ornamental Art. Two committees were then formed – one to decide on a course of instruction, the other to determine what books, plaster casts, and other equipment would be needed. By the middle of May 1837, all these points had been settled sufficiently for the opening day of the School to be fixed for Thursday 1 June. It was to be accommodated at Somerset House, in the three rooms on the top storey which had previously been occupied by the Royal Academy, and which have occasionally been reopened for exhibition purposes in recent years.

The School of Design – after its transference to South Kensington referred to as the Art School or the Art Training School – survives to this day, in a much altered form, as the Royal College of Art. Its history was closely linked with that of the Museum at South Kensington until it achieved

---

1. Quoted in Select Committee 1860, para. 29.

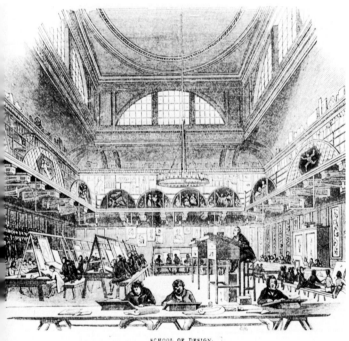

SCHOOL OF DESIGN.

3. *(top) The Royal Academy Room, Somerset House, 1787. Engraving by P. A. Martini after H. Ramberg*

4. *(above) The Royal Academy Room, Somerset House, occupied by the School of Design, 1843*

independent status in 1949. During the nineteenth century, students from the School were often employed on the interior decorations of the Museum buildings.

By 1841 the original number of students had doubled to 38 day students and 92 evening students. Two years later, in 1843, the numbers had increased to 76 day students and 220 evening students, as well as 45 women students, who were taught separately. In 1845, however, numbers declined, partly as a result of disputes among the staff.

In its early years the School was beset by changes of management and curriculum. It 'went through five or six changes of government, all of which, however, were of the nature of *dilettanti* government, and irresponsible'.[2] There were shifts of emphasis between the study of various branches of practical design and the mastery of basic fine art techniques. The students displayed 'a deficiency in that early elementary knowledge of Drawing requisite for making satisfactory progress in Ornamental Art'.[3]

2. Ibid., para. 55.
3. *Second Report of the Royal Commissioners of the Exhibition of 1851* (1852), p. 32.

4 In 1841 the government also set up seventeen local schools of design, in manufacturing towns such as Birmingham, Sheffield, Manchester, and Coventry. Their needs soon led to the provision of classes for teachers at the central school and by 1852 the central school had become almost exclusively a teacher-training establishment, under Richard Burchett, an ex-student. Its fortunes had declined to such an extent that in 1849 it was felt necessary to set up another select committee of Parliament to investigate it. Nonetheless, it was here, in the government School of Design, that the Victoria and Albert Museum had its origin.

During 1838 £1,500 had been spent on purchases for the School of examples of contemporary art from Paris; other purchases had been made in the following years; a reference library was begun, which developed into the National Art Library; and an art circulating library was formed in 1843. By 1852, however, the collection of casts and works of ornamental art was stored in the cellars of Somerset House, and everything was in confusion. Milner Gibson, chairman of the 1849 select committee that investigated the School, noted in his report that

> Complaints have been made as to the want of accommodation at Somerset House, as well as the house temporarily hired in the Strand for the female pupils. The collection of casts and other beautiful and instructive works of art in the school is thereby rendered useless, and the development of the institution is, in several respects, seriously retarded.

'It was in that stage of the matter that I was asked to join the School of Design, and see if I could do any good with it.'[4] These are the words of Henry Cole (1808–82), a young civil servant who had already shown a conspicuous talent for getting things done. A soldier's son, Cole went from his school, Christ's Hospital, into the Civil Service: when he retired he was able to look back with pride on fifty years of public work, and the official biography by his son took that title. Cole's mind was formed, not by a university education, but by mixing with a group of 'philosophical radicals', including Thomas Love Peacock, John Stuart Mill, Charles Buller, and George Grote, and from them he derived his lifelong commitment to the reform of the institutions in which he worked. He was first employed by the Public Records Commission, and was instrumental in the agitation that led to the establishment of the Record Office in Chancery Lane. He moved on to use his talents for manipulating public opinion in favour of postal reform, and was employed at the Treasury to implement the reforms for which he had campaigned. In private life he became interested in the improvement of artistic taste, and under the cheerful name 'Felix Summerly' started a firm which produced tea services and children's books in good taste. In 1846 he carried this interest into the public arena, becoming a member of the Society of Arts, and playing a major part in the Society's attempts to promote exhibitions of industrial art. These culminated in the Great Exhibition of 1851. Cole served on the executive committee, where his dynamic energy singled him out and won him the special approbation of Prince Albert.

Cole's interest in art secured for him a place on the 1849 select committee that investigated the School of Design, but he was not able to have an influence on the School at this stage since his energies were at once diverted to the Great Exhibition. After the Exhibition was over, however, he was the obvious man to reform the School, and he took over as General Superintendent in 1852. He transformed the School utterly: by the end of his career he had set up a national system of vocational education, and had founded the internationally renowned museum which is now the Victoria and Albert.

His first act as Superintendent was to create new classes in various practical arts, with the intention that the students should become either qualified designers or practitioners. By 1859 a system of instruction had been drawn up by Richard Redgrave RA (1804–88), whose first appearance at the School had been as temporary headmaster in 1845, and who was to become Cole's chief ally throughout his career at South Kensington.[5]

---

4. Select Committee 1860, para. 58, where the preceding passage from the Select Committee, 1849, is quoted. Cole diary, 16 November 1871: 'To Ascot to visit Sir J. Shaw Lefevre. It was he who first introduced me officially to reform Schools of Design in about 1847-8.'
5. After hearing of the death of the surveyor of the Queen's Pictures, Thomas Uwins RA, on 29 August 1857, Cole lost no time in writing to Prince Albert's secretary, General Grey, recommending Redgrave as his successor. The 'very fittest of the R.A.S to carry out the artistic inspection with knowledge and zeal will be Mr. Redgrave.' Cole correspondence. Redgrave was consequently appointed to the post.

5. Marlborough House. Engraving by Le Pettit after Shepherd

Redgrave divided the artistic curriculum into twenty-three stages, grouping these as a basis for awarding certificates.

Cole's second step in 1852 was to turn his attention to the problem of accommodation. As early as February he went to see Prince Albert, who was then meditating an ambitious scheme for a national institution concerned with the arts. The Prince asked Cole if he was 'in earnest about the Sch. of Design – would I want to connect it with his proposed institute? – He wd. assist in lending Marlborough House.'[6] Cole took advantage of this offer: the plaster casts were taken from Somerset House in April, and the 'Museum of Manufactures' first opened at Marlborough House in May 1852, for two months, and then permanently in September after re-arrangement. In 1853 the Treasury requisitioned the rooms occupied by the School in Somerset House, so the School itself also moved to Marlborough House,

being accommodated in two wooden huts erected in the courtyard. Marlborough House thus became the headquarters of both the School of Design and its attached Museum. School and Museum, together with the network of schools in the provinces, formed a Civil Service unit first called the Department of Practical Art, controlled by the Board of Trade.

On 25 February 1856, the Department was renamed the Department of Science and Art, and was placed under the control of a Privy Council committee on education, along with the Education Department. The latter department was concerned with awarding grants to elementary schools teaching the three Rs; the former with vocational education in the network of science and art schools. Henry Cole soon emerged as the Secretary

5

---

6. Cole diary, 19 February 1852.

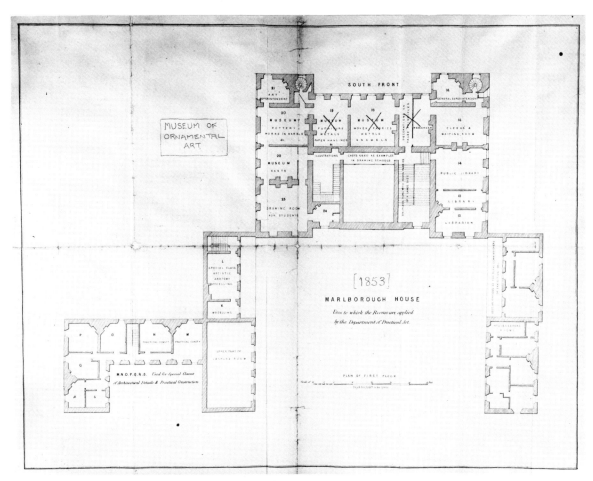

6. *Plan of the Museum of Ornamental Art, Marlborough House*

of the Department of Science and Art, with a large degree of independence: his superiors (who play a part in the ensuing story from time to time) were the Vice-President of the Committee of Council on Education and, above him, the Lord President of the Council.

Marlborough House

Shortly after the move to Marlborough House, the School of Design received one of the most important commissions ever to come its way. The Duke of Wellington died on 14 September 1852 and Marlborough House was asked to design his funeral car. It was not an unqualified success. The enormous bronze construction was so heavy that it sank into the ground while crossing Horse Guards Parade. Writing from the Department of Practical Art on 5 January 1853, someone (perhaps Cole himself) complains that 'owing to the pressure of time at the last moment, no opportunity was afforded to us to judge of the Effect of the Car. The parts were brought together for the first time a few hours before the Procession started, and finally the Car was used in an imperfect state.'[7] To his diary Cole confided that the 'D of Cambridge thought the car a complete failure'.[8]

The Museum of Manufactures at Marlborough House was, on the other hand, comparatively successful. In 1852 it was open on 54 free days, during which time 42,134 visitors were admitted. On the 47 days when an admission charge was made the visitors numbered 3,426. The next year, some 125,000 members of the public were admitted. This figure dropped to 104,523 in 1854, and fell even further in 1855 to 78,427, but rose sharply in 1856 to 111,768.

The catalogue of exhibits at Marlborough

7. Cole correspondence, anonymous letter, 5 January 1853.
8. 2 November 1852.

17

House, in its fifth edition in 1853, explained that the use of the house was only temporary, 'until more suitable premises' were provided. The public was admitted without charge on Monday and Tuesday of each week, and also during the Easter and Christmas weeks. On Wednesdays, Thursdays and Fridays:

> Persons not Students are admitted on payment of 6d each; and any single example on payment of an additional 6d, or any number of examples in one portfolio, on payment of 1s additional each person, may be removed and copied. Manufacturers and others, by payment of an annual subscription of £1. 1s may obtain a ticket, transferable to any member of their firm, or any person in their employ.

The students, however, had free admission on each day and did not have to pay any fee for the privilege of examining and copying the exhibits. In all cases, stated the rules, a member of the Museum staff had to be present, and visitors had to wash their hands before being allowed to handle any object.

The original collection, which had been accumulated since 1838, was greatly enlarged by purchases from the Great Exhibition of 1851. A Treasury grant of £5,000 was made for this purpose, and the objects were selected by Cole, the Gothic Revival architect and designer, A. W. N. Pugin, and others. Further purchases followed in 1852–3, including pottery and porcelain from the Bandinel Collection, and in 1854 items of pottery, porcelain, majolica, glass, and metalwork were bought from the collection of Mr R. Bernal MP. Furthermore, a number of people, headed by Queen Victoria, made gifts or temporary loans to the Museum.

A feature of the new museum, typical of its evangelizing spirit, was (as the catalogue put it) a

> collection of articles such as are of daily production, which are only remarkable from their departure from every law and principle, and some even from the plainest common sense, in their decoration.

These objects were subjected to forthright criticism in the catalogue. A glass goblet, for example, was denounced as being of a 'form unfitted for use', while another was of a 'coarse form, the transparency of the material sacrificed to imitate alabaster'. A French scent bottle was found to have a 'total disregard of utility; the handle incapable of being grasped; the base resting on points of metal', and a lamp, which was also made in France,

> in all its parts, without exception, illustrates some false principle. Its constructive line is bad – the heavy top totters upon an insubstantial base; it rests upon the points of leaves, which seem ready to give way under the load; these leaves are direct but bad imitations of nature...

A gas burner was also condemned because it was designed to have the 'gas flaming from the petal of a convolvulus! – one of a class of ornaments very popular, but utterly indefensible in principle'. Despite the underlying seriousness of these catalogue entries, Cole and Redgrave must have had a great deal of fun writing them. One can picture, too, the fury of firms thus castigated.

This 'chamber of horrors', however, filled only the first room of the Museum, the rest being devoted to objects much more in tune with the principles of decorative art as laid down by Cole and Redgrave. It was their hope that the public who came to the Museum would create a demand for 'improvements in the character of our national manufactures'. This aspiration received only lukewarm support from the Curator of the Museum, appointed in 1853. John Charles Robinson (1824–1913) had been an art teacher at the School of Design at Hanley, in the Potteries, but he was to become the greatest English connoisseur and art scholar of his time. It is owing to his taste and enterprise that the Victoria and Albert Museum's outstanding holdings of medieval and Renaissance art were assembled. Robinson did not get on well with his doctrinaire chief, and the parting of the ways for him and Cole came in 1867. He played little part in the history of the building, but was the principal architect of the collections which it was to house.

As these grew, space at Marlborough House was becoming restricted, and by 1854 Cole and Redgrave were both hopeful that more suitable premises could be found.

CHAPTER II

The establishment of the Museum at South Kensington

Of all the influences that led to the foundation of what was eventually to become the Victoria and Albert Museum, the single most important factor was the Great Exhibition of 1851. Not only did purchases made there form the nucleus of the Museum's early collections, but the profits from the Exhibition made it possible to establish the Museum on a secure site. Moreover, a scrutiny of the lists of organizers of the Exhibition reveals that many of them, from Prince Albert downwards, eventually became involved with the Museum at South Kensington. Foremost, after the Prince Consort, was Henry Cole, through whose enterprise the whole Exhibition had come into being; it was a project he had pursued with the Prince since 1849. Prince Albert recognized Henry Cole's worth, and a close liaison was maintained between the two men from that time until the Consort's death ten years later.

Among others who played more minor parts in the organization of the Exhibition were Sir William Cubitt, a member of the Royal Commission for the Exhibition; Owen Jones, a member of the Building Committee, who was responsible for the decoration; and Richard Redgrave RA. While the Exhibition was being assembled, G. F. Duncombe was in charge of correspondence; George Wallis, superintendent of Class IX, Cotton Textiles, and Class XVIII, Woven Textiles; Richard A. Thompson, superintendent of Class XXI, Cutlery; his brother Charles Thurston Thompson, superintendent of Class XXVI, Furniture, and Class XVIII, Animal Manufactures, as well as being in charge of all the photographic arrangements; and Second Lieutenant E. F. Du Cane, was a member of one of the two companies of Royal Engineers and Sappers and Miners, whose men acted as clerks, storemen, modelmakers, sweepers, and firemen. All these officials eventually became members of the staff of, or

were closely connected with, the South Kensington Museum. They were a ready-made team.

When the Exhibition closed triumphantly at a ceremony attended by Prince Albert on Wednesday 15 October, it had attracted 6,039,195 visitors, who had paid £256,808 in entrance fees, mainly at a shilling a time. When all the bills had been settled, it was found that the Exhibition accounts had a surplus of just over £186,000, a fact that was grandly certified by none other than the Governor and Deputy Governor of the Bank of England.

It was decided that the Royal Commission that had been established to supervise the preparation and administration of the Exhibition should remain in being to dispose of the surplus money. Queen Victoria confirmed a Supplemental Charter on 2 December 1851; the money, invested for educational purposes, is still in use; and the Royal Commission for the Exhibition of 1851 remains an active organization today.

Prince Albert was the president of the Commission, and he – aided to some extent by Cole – had far-seeing plans as to how the money should be spent. His proposal was to centralize the existing learned and artistic societies of Britain on a site south of Hyde Park. Numerous suggestions and applications by interested parties were made for the disposal of the surplus funds, but Prince Albert[1] and his fellow commissioners 'did not feel themselves to be in a position to comply with proposals which involve the surplus being applied to purposes of a limited, partial, or local character'.[2] They held the view that the country needed one institution which should 'serve to increase the means of Industrial Education, and extend the

---

1. The Prince wrote a long memorandum on the subject, dated 10 August 1851 (Royal Archives, F25/1.).
2. *Second Report of the Royal Commissioners of the Exhibition of 1851* (1852), p. 11.

influence of Science and Art upon Productive Industry'. London was felt to be the best place for such an institution, and links should be maintained with India and the colonies by scholarships and other means.

The commissioners noted that the public already owned much material that could be united into a proper collection to support their aims. In addition to the Marlborough House collection, there were other suitable specimens in the British Museum; the Museum of Practical Geology possessed examples of ceramic and glass manufactures; and the Commission itself owned many valuable objects of the same character.

To lend weight to their argument that this proposed institution, together with a complex of purpose-built premises to rehouse existing learned institutions, should be constructed on one site, the commissioners reviewed the limitations of space that were impeding the development of existing learned bodies in Britain. Besides the National

Gallery, the collections of which were currently dispersed in 'separate buildings at some distance from each other', the Royal Society, the newly founded School of Mines, the College of Chemistry, the Royal Academy, the British Museum, and the School of Design itself, with its attached museum, were all experiencing difficulties of one kind or another resulting from lack of space. It was clear to the 1851 commissioners that a substantial area of land must be purchased.

The estate of the 1851 commissioners

In respect of land purchase, the hands of the commissioners were to some extent forced. In August 1851 the report of an enquiry into the question of a new site for the National Gallery recommended that a site should be selected in the neighbourhood of Hyde Park, not only because of the 'dry nature of the soil', but because there would be fewer smoky chimneys in the area. For this purpose the Gore House Estate had become the subject of a

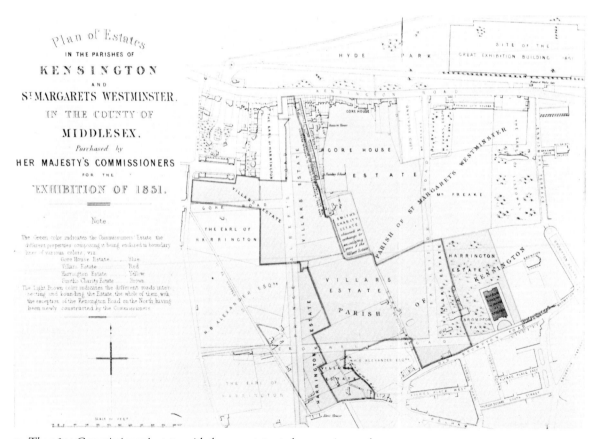

7. *The 1851 Commissioners' estate, with the present street plan superimposed*

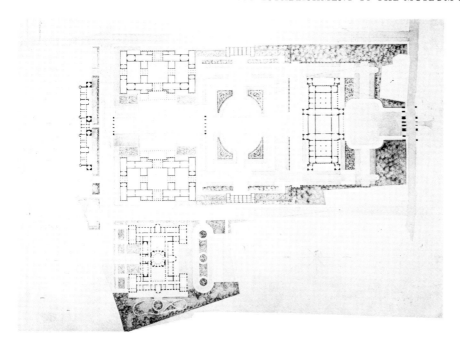

8. *Sir James Pennethorne's design for the development of the 1851 Commissioners' estate*

proposed government purchase, but for some reason negotiations had been broken off. The estate was of approximately 20 acres, with a frontage of between 500 and 600 feet to the south side of the Park, on the open ground between Kensington and Brompton. The commissioners quickly stepped in, and, through 'the zealous and disinterested instrumentality of Mr. Kelk, the builder, we have obtained possession of the land for which the Government had been treating'.[3] The cost of the estate was £60,000.

It was apparent, however, that 20 acres would be insufficient. Since the area was as yet undeveloped, and the land price was still comparatively low, the commissioners were eager to make further purchases as soon as possible. They had insufficient money themselves to buy all the land they wanted, but they resolved to spend up to £153,000, if the government would contribute the same amount. The government agreed and the commissioners bought an estate of 48 acres owned by Baron de Villars, adjoining Gore House, for £153,000. After a series of complicated negotiations they acquired a block of land totalling 86 acres.[4] Cole noted in his diary that 'Cobden expressed a high opinion of the Prince's sagacity in the purchase of the land, saying "H.R.H. would have made his fortune as a land agent."'

Running diagonally across the commissioners'

lands from Kensington Gore to Brompton was Gore Lane, on which were a few small houses. During 1854, the commissioners obtained an Act of Parliament to authorize 'stopping up Lanes and Footways between Kensington and Brompton . . . and for otherwise facilitating the formation of a Site for Institutions connected with Science and Art'. Between 1853 and 1856, Cromwell Road, Exhibition Road, and Queen's Gate (at first known as Prince Albert's Road) were constructed by William Jackson for £17,980, two-thirds of the cost of which was borne by the commissioners.

No firm decision had yet been reached about how the lands were to be used. In 1854, in an attempt to advance the proceedings, Cole and Redgrave, who were running very short of space at Marlborough House, produced their own plans for development. As Alan Cole wrote in his father's biography:

A complete plan showing how the whole of the estate might be laid out as a public garden, surrounded and crossed with buildings for the National Gallery, the Collections and Normal Schools of the Science and Art Department, a Museum of Patented inventions, the Society of Arts, the University of

3. Ibid., p. 36.
4. The story of the commissioners' estate is given in great detail in *Survey*, Ch. 4.

7

London, and the Royal Academy of Music, was prepared in 1854 by Mr. Cole and Mr. Redgrave, and submitted to His Royal Highness.[5]

In addition, Cole and Redgrave proposed an industrial School for Youth and a large 'boarding house' for students.[6]

Cole emphasized that the buildings were so planned that they could be erected in sections, as required, without spoiling the general effect. (Construction by stages was precisely the procedure that was eventually carried out, although the designs were by then totally different.) A little later, the architects James Pennethorne and T. L. Donaldson also submitted plans. The principal feature of Donaldson's plan was a large central building for a picture gallery, with gardens to its north and south. Pennethorne, on the other hand, proposed four relatively small galleries, with extensive gardens between them.[7]

Meanwhile, there were constant delays in the negotiations for the removal of the National Gallery to the new site, which it never eventually occupied, but where it was intended to form a centrepiece. The partial financing of the land purchase by the government had resulted in the commissioners and the government becoming partners in the development enterprise. Certain holders of political office became ex-officio members of the Commission: those nominated were the Lord President of the Council, the First Lord of the Treasury, the Chancellor of the Exchequer, the President of the Board of Trade, and the First Commissioner of Works. Governmental indecision caused further delays and eventually the 1851 commissioners were to lose patience. The partnership between them and the government was to be dissolved by Act of Parliament in 1858, when the commissioners became sole owners of the estate. They repaid £181,379 4s 2d to the government, less £60,000 for the actual site on which the Museum was by now being built. Thus the freehold of the Museum site remains with the 1851 commissioners to this day.

For the moment it seemed that the great hopes of the Prince Consort had been frustrated. Later, Cole recalled that 'the Prince met with many disappointments, and his idea of using the land for public institutions of Science and Art, was received with hostility and opposition'.[8]

It was intended to place the National Gallery in the main rectangle of the estate, now occupied by the Natural History Museum and the Science Museum. While the National Gallery's fate remained unresolved, part of the estate was leased to the Horticultural Society, and another area was set aside as a site for the proposed exhibition of 1861. The Prince therefore turned his attention to a parcel of land of about 12 acres in the south-eastern corner of the estate, but cut off from the rest by Exhibition Road. This area, which adjoined the churchyard of Holy Trinity Church, Brompton, had been bought from the Earl of Harrington. (The church, a plain Gothic building, was erected in 1826–9, and now lies obscured behind the huge Italianate bulk of the Roman Catholic church of the Brompton Oratory built in the 1880s.) On this parcel of land in rural and out-of-the-way Brompton was Brompton Park House (originally built for Queen Anne's gardener, Henry Wise), by then divided into four rambling and rotting empty dwellings, of which the most recent inhabitants had been Mr Greenwood, of Cox and Greenwood, Sir Cresswell Cresswell, Lord Talbot, and the actress Madame Celeste.[9] The Brompton Park House Estate was to become the site of the Victoria and Albert Museum.

During February 1854, Cole had been to Buckingham Palace to discuss the Prince's plan to erect buildings on this site which could be used as temporary galleries for the Marlborough House and other collections. The Prince made a sketch on blotting paper to show the kind of thing he had in mind: 'the buildings should be somewhat on the plan of the Palais Royale – shops with a colonnade, and residences above'.[10] He asked the architect Gottfried Semper to prepare plans, for which he himself was willing to pay.[11]

Semper produced plans and a model made of

5. Cole, *Fifty Years of Public Work*, vol. i, p. 319. 'The Prince will be most anxious to see your plans, he will be glad to see you and Mr. Redgrave any morning ...' Cole correspondence, Grey to Cole, 9 February 1854.

6. Cole, diary, 11 December 1853, 'Considering plans at Kensington it seems to me that the College of Science & Art should be connected with its Museum and built towards the south'.

7. Layout suggestions by Prince Albert, T. L. Donaldson, and C. R. Cockerell, are illustrated in *Survey*, pp. 82, 83. A photograph of the proposals by Cole and Redgrave is in the V&A guard books, No. 2510.

8. Cole, *Fifty Years of Public Work*, vol. i, p. 322.

9. The history of Brompton Park House is given in *Survey*, pp. 6, 7. A view, from Thurloe Square, is Pl. 4b in the same work.

10. Cole correspondence, 24 February 1854.

11. Cole, *Fifty Years of Public Work*, vol. i, p. 322.

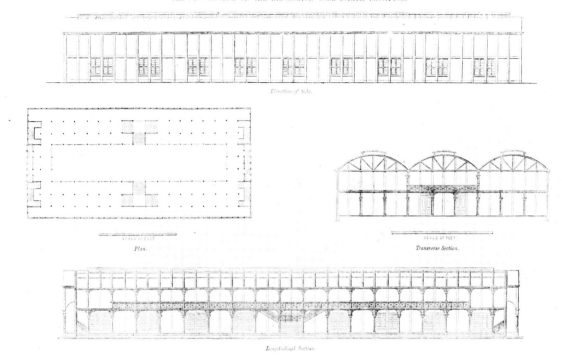

Elevation of Side.

Plan.

Transverse Section.

Longitudinal Section.

9. *Plan, sections and elevation of the proposed Iron Museum*

painted cardboard, which for some years was exhibited in the Museum, but unfortunately seems now to have disappeared.[12] The plan has not survived either, so it is impossible to ascertain how ambitious Semper had been. After careful scrutiny of the scheme it was concluded to be financially impracticable, 'very much I believe to the Prince's disappointment',[13] as Redgrave later reported to Cole.

It is ironical that Semper's connection with the Department of Science and Art should have been so brief, since his later influence in Germany was very great. His writings provided a theoretical basis for the study of the decorative arts, and dominated German work on the subject from the mid-century until the rise of the Vienna school of art historians at the end of the century; and as an architect, he himself designed several museum buildings, most notably the influential Gemälde-galerie at Dresden.

Even while discussions were going on with Semper about one proposal, Prince Albert was developing yet another scheme, this time for a temporary building only. On 14 June 1855 he proposed the erection of an 'iron house' on the Brompton Park Estate.[14]

The Iron Museum

Four days after the Prince's suggestion, the firm of Charles Young, of Great George Street, sent to the 1851 commissioners the specification of an iron building. The proposed building was 266 feet long, 126 feet wide, and about 30 feet high, to the eaves. It was to be iron-framed, and covered by sheets of corrugated iron. Inside there were to be three galleries, each 42 feet wide. For economy and ease of construction Charles Young planned that the building should be constructed in bays 14 feet square (see Appendix 1).

Charles Young and Company specialized in 'iron structures for Home and Abroad'. They supplied iron houses, hospitals, barracks, and other buildings to the British colonies and America, as well as to places in Britain. That they were selected as builders of the Museum may (as the *Builder*,[15]

9

12. *Catalogue* of the Museum of Construction, South Kensington, 1876, No. 54 Y. See also, Gert Reising, 'Kunst, Industrie und Gesell-schaft. Gottfried Semper in England', in Zürich, E. T. H., *Geschichte und Theorie der Architektur*, No. 18 [Symposium, 1974], 1976, pp. 50–66.

13. Cole correspondence, 30 June 1855.

14. Cole, *Fifty Years of Public Work*, vol. i, p. 323.

15. *Builder*, 24 January 1857.

10. *Building the Brompton Boilers, from the north, 1856*   11. *The Brompton Boilers (upper floor), 1856*

the leading architectural journal of the day, subsequently hinted) have had something to do with the fact that their London offices chanced to share the same address with that of the civil engineer Sir William Cubitt, who was one of the 1851 commissioners. The *Builder* regretted that no professional architect had been consulted about the Museum building.

The commissioners liked the proposed iron building. In a letter to the Chancellor of the Exchequer, applying for funds to build it, they drew attention to its merits:

> Irrespective of its simplicity and cheapness, and the remarkable facility with which it can be constructed, it enjoys the great advantage from a pecuniary point of view, of being designed of a material which possesses a permanent pecuniary value, to which the cost of the labour employed in its construction bears only a small proportion. While, therefore, it could on the one hand be at any time taken down and re-erected, if necessary, on another site, or in another form, at a very trifling expense, it could, on the other, be re-sold . . .[16]

The commissioners reminded the Chancellor that Marlborough House had only been lent to the Department of Science and Art on a temporary basis. It was to become the residence of the Prince of Wales when he attained his eighteenth birthday,

a date that was now approaching. They further supported their arguments in favour of new premises by listing other collections besides their own that were in need of a home. There were items from an exhibition on the subject of education, which had been held at St Martin's Hall in 1855 under the auspices of the Society of Arts, now intended to form the nucleus of a permanent museum. There was a collection of models formed by the Commissioners of Patents. A Trade Museum was being formed; the government had established the Museum of Economic Geology for mineral produce, and the Kew Museum for vegetable produce. (Animal produce was not yet represented, although a small collection had been formed.) The result of this argument was that when the new iron museum was completed and opened, it housed an astonishing variety of collections besides those originally based at Marlborough House.

The Treasury approved of the proposed iron structure. An application was made to Parliament, and a sum of £15,000 was eventually voted for the construction of the new Museum.

---

16. Letter to the Chancellor of the Exchequer, 30 June 1855, quoted in *Third Report of the Royal Commissioners of the Exhibition of 1851* (1856), Appendix T, p. 265.

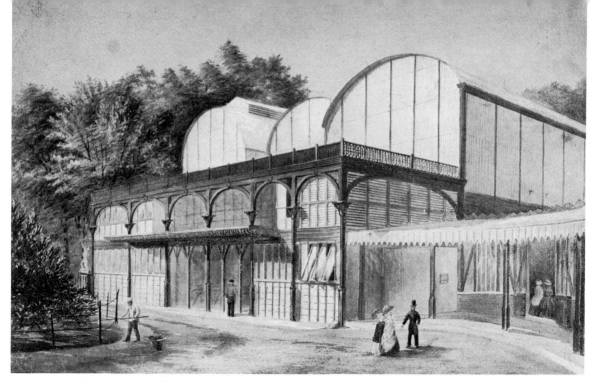

12. *Exterior of the Brompton Boilers, 1863. Watercolour by J. C. Lanchenick*

Work began on the iron building early in 1856. By mid-April the structure was well advanced and was beginning to attract the notice of the press. The *Builder*[17] complained that our rulers at times found strange ways of demonstrating the value they attached to art in industry – one had only to look at the inartistic iron building being erected on the Kensington Gore Estate to house the Marlborough House art collections. The journal was crushingly hostile and unkind to the half-formed building:

> Its ugliness is unmitigated: never was a beautiful sward, where daisies blossom and trees and shrubs put forth their leaves and branches and flowers in forms of beauty unapproachable by man, so vilely disfigured. . . . If the Marlborough House authorities retain their Chamber of Horrors – their examples of 'what to avoid', when they get to their new quarters – Mr. Cole's first act must be to have a model made of this Museum itself. . . .

It was clearly in this report in the *Builder* that the Museum's nickname originated: the report observed that the building 'is in three equal spans, all at the same height from the ground, like huge boilers placed side by side'. The journal returned to this theme a month later, by which time the building had advanced a stage further. 'We did our simile of the boiler some injustice for saying

so, for it is filled in externally with corrugated iron, and is therefore all the more like a threefold monster boiler.'[18] Thereafter the Museum was known as 'the Brompton Boilers'.

An attempt was made to enhance the appearance of the building by painting it in green and white stripes, and a portico with light iron pillars was added at the south end. This, no doubt, was the 'architectural front, for about £1,000', mentioned in Charles Young's original estimate for the iron building, submitted on 18 June 1855. Other drawbacks, however, besides the building's appearance, revealed themselves before it even opened. It leaked. On 22 September 1856 Cole counted twenty-one places where the rain was coming through.[19] This problem had not been solved by the following June, shortly before the opening, when Cole observed that the rain had come in through the roof and 'by the sides of the walls',[20] and on 1 July there was 'a deluge of rain which flowed through the museum'.[21] Even after the opening the problem remained, and 'in a

17. *Builder*, 19 April 1856.
18. *Builder*, 10 May 1856.
19. Cole diary, 22 September 1856.
20. Cole diary, 8 June 1857.
21. Cole diary, 1 July 1857.

heavy shower, the attendants are obliged to hasten with oil skin and tarpaulin, and put them over the objects where the rain drips in'.[22] Subsequently,

> the leakage in the roof was lessened to a certain extent by altering the colour of the roof; ... the roof had been caulked with oakum and pitch, and painted a dark colour, and the heat of the sun brought the pitch out of the joints; by painting it white, we got rid of the sun's powerful action upon it.[23]

The drainage of rain water was also poor, as twenty pipes, each 5 inches in diameter, all discharged into a single pipe 6 inches in diameter.

Condensation dripping from the roof was another problem, which came to light in November 1856, only two months after the discovery of the leaks. The condensation was caused by extreme variations of temperature inside the building, which in themselves constituted yet another problem. The temperature variations were alleviated by the addition of vertical partitions and plaster ceilings, and by cutting away part of the gallery floors to increase ventilation. Unfortunately this had the effect of increasing the risk of fire. It had originally been hoped that the building would be fireproof. The *Builder*, in consequence, was triumphant:

> We impressively warned the public against the contemplated erection when the design was in progress: the appeal was disregarded; our contemporaries gave no aid, and here we have the result, the Brompton Boilers, a loud-speaking disgrace to the Country.[24]

Cole was unable to utter any defence, for he privately agreed. He summarized the building's disadvantages to General Charles Grey, Prince Albert's Secretary:

> All its ugliness is laid upon my department, which knew nothing about it until Redgrave and I returned from Paris and found the columns fixed. The public laugh at its outside ugliness and us ... The light is so bad below the wide galleries, that nothing can be exhibited well there. Above the galleries, the angle of light is quite wrong for pictures. The iron produces excess heat in summer, and cold in winter. It offers virtually no protection against fire, which will burn the contents and prevent ready succour from the outside.[25]

Two further imperfections became apparent later. The floors in the upper part of the building, intended for the display of the Architectural Museum's collection of plaster casts, proved insufficiently strong to carry the weight; and within three years of the building's completion parts of the roof had nearly corroded through.

Despite these defects, however, the Boilers remained in position until 1866, when they were partially dismantled. The parts taken down were removed in 1867–8 and re-erected to form the framework of the Bethnal Green Museum. What was left was demolished in 1899.

Other temporary buildings

It had been decided that the School of Design as well as the Museum should be moved to the Brompton site. The School was to be housed 13 partly in the four old houses already on the site, and partly in the wooden buildings from the courtyard at Marlborough House. A temporary linking building, or 'junction', was to be erected between the old houses and the Boilers. The junction would contain a library and lecture theatre for the Design School, and also administrative offices. These buildings, together with a planned refreshment room, were to comprise all the temporary structures on the site. Work on these buildings proceeded concurrently with the construction of the Boilers.

In July 1856 Cole inspected Brompton Park House with a view to renovating it. He was accompanied by Redgrave, and a captain in the Royal Engineers, Francis Fowke. Cole had discovered the value of the army as a labour force while engaged in the organization of the Great Exhibition, and he had obtained a detachment of sappers to clear the ground at Brompton. They remained on the site, even constructing the Museum's new buildings, until the Office of Works took over in 1870. Many of the names associated with early work on the Museum construction are those of Royal Engineers officers.

The remarkable Fowke, born in Belfast in 1823, was commissioned in the Royal Engineers, and 14

---

22. Select Committee 1860, para. 421.
23. Select Committee 1860, para. 2270.
24. *Builder*, 24 January 1857.
25. Cole, *Fifty Years of Public Work*, vol. i, p. 323, letter of August 1856.

13. *(right) Brompton Park House : the eastern portion used by the Art Schools, photographed in 1899*

14. *(centre) Brompton Park House, with the Royal Engineers detachment, c. 1860*

15. *(below) Wooden huts used by the Art Schools, transferred from Marlborough House, 1863. Watercolour by Anthony Stannus*

his early service was spent in Bermuda where the Governor was Sir William Reid, later to become one of the executive committee of the 1851 Exhibition, and subsequently Secretary for the Paris Exhibition of 1855. In 1854 Reid asked Fowke to superintend the Machinery Department of the Paris Exhibition, and Fowke later succeeded Reid as the Secretary of the British Commission for the Exhibition. At the end of his work in Paris, for which he was appointed a Chevalier of the Legion of Honour, Fowke was made an Inspector on the staff of Henry Cole's Department of Science and Art, in 1856, later becoming its architect and engineer. He designed several buildings for the army, as well as the Great Conservatory of the Horticultural Society, the 1862 Exhibition Building, the Royal Albert Hall, the Scottish Industrial Museum, the Dublin National Gallery, and the Prince Consort Library at Aldershot; and he won the competition for the Natural History Museum at South Kensington, though this was not built to his design. An inventive man in many fields, he perfected a collapsible pontoon for the army, a portable bath, an umbrella, and a vacuum cleaner, and devised the camera bellows. He also contrived the special camera needed to support the 3 feet square glass negatives used by Thurston Thompson, the Museum photographer, when he made the first photographs of the Raphael cartoons. Obviously ready to turn his hand to many things, he was the ideal man to be associated with Henry Cole and the development of South Kensington.

Fowke superintended the alterations and renovation of the old houses, carried out by Kelk for £1,500. Roofs and windows were mended, lavatories were installed, and communicating doorways made between the houses. In January 1857 the *Builder* reported on the results.

Some of the attics are even picturesque, and the apartments of the female school have a look of

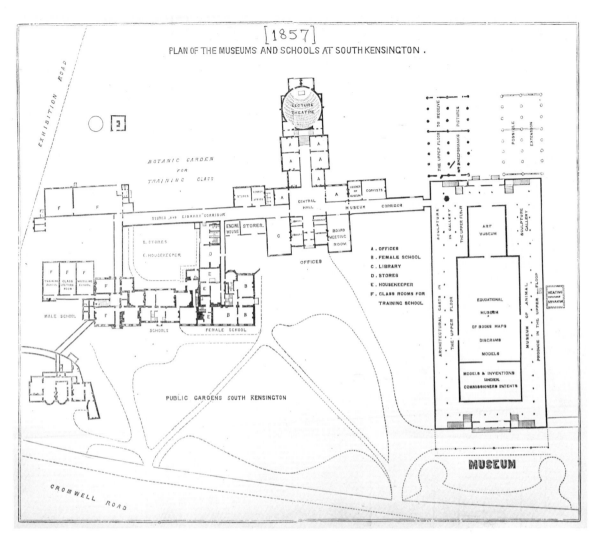

16. (above) Plan of the South Kensington Museum, 1857

17. (left) Sir James Pennethorne's office building (the 'junction') in 1863, after the erection behind it of the Residences. Watercolour by Anthony Stannus

18. *Moving a tree outside the Brompton Boilers and the Refreshment Rooms, c. 1863*

19. *The First Lecture Theatre, from the north-west*

comfort which has very properly been made an object. A sage green colour in the painting and paper, under the direction of Mr. Redgrave has been adopted throughout.

By this time the wooden buildings from Marlborough House had been erected at the western end of the Brompton site, and the school was in residence.

It had originally been intended to build the junction between the old houses and the Boilers in iron, but by the middle of 1856 Cole and his colleagues were becoming disenchanted with iron buildings, perhaps partly as a result of the early onslaughts by the *Builder* on the half-constructed Boilers. Brick was now felt to be more suitable, a preference shared by Prince Albert, who was kept closely informed of all developments. The architect James Pennethorne was therefore commissioned to design a temporary brick building, which he did in four days, the Board approving the plans on 12 July 1856. The layout of the junction as designed by Pennethorne can be seen in a plan of the Museum buildings in 1857. It was a long, low, single-storey building running from east to west, mainly a corridor, from which, in the centre, were projections on the north (including a lecture theatre) and south sides.[26]

Kelk estimated £5,500 for building the junction, which was considered very reasonable. Construction proceeded apace and by January 1857 the *Builder* was able to report on the completed appearance of the building:

Externally, it is true, the design, for a plain brick building, has some degree of effect. The projections from the front, forming the library and boardroom, have gabled ends, with roofs of low pitch, and windows arch-headed with red brick. Internally, however, the rooms are low, and in some cases dark. The library, as first completed, was deficient in wall-space, and otherwise inconvenient . . .

Shortly afterwards, however, some of the library windows were blocked up to give more wall-space, and a skylight was inserted. The Lecture Theatre was decorated by Andrew MacCallum for £50, in only four weeks. No illustrations of the Lecture Theatre have survived, except for photographs taken immediately before its demolition some years later.[27]

In the years to come, the administrative offices were very cramped. Henry Cole described the situation in 1860, beginning with the room of

. . . the Assistant Secretary, Mr. MacLeod, the next to that is devoted to the general superintendent of the Museum, who sits there with a clerk. Then in a little room opposite sit two clerks who conduct the correspondence with the art schools; then the next room is my own, in the next room sit two other clerks, the head clerk and another. Then, coming downwards, there is a room where the three in-

26. A view of Pennethorne's link building is shown in a watercolour, 1872, by C. E. Emery (Print Room 7927) reproduced in *Survey*, pl. 36.

27. *Survey*, pl. 12c. shows the demolition.

spectors frequently sit who inspect the Art Schools. The Inspector General for Art occupies the next room; the other room is used for occasional purposes from time to time; the room opposite the inspector's room, coming down, is occupied as a drawing office for clerks employed in making drawings about the buildings; the next room is occupied by four messengers; the next room is the engineer's office, Captain Fowke. Then the room opposite is occupied by the inspector for science and his clerk; the other is used as an examination room and for miscellaneous purposes. On the other side is the storekeeper's office, with three or four persons employed in keeping the stores; then there are two rooms which contain the various examples sent from the country, prize drawings, prizes sent out and so on. On the opposite side is the entrance where the stores come in.

There were 16 rooms on a single floor into which, Cole sourly commented, 'we are packed as close as pigs at present'.[28] *Plus ça change*. The whole of this temporary block was to be pulled down after 1866 to make room for the new developments.

20

The other temporary building constructed on the Brompton site in the period 1856–7 was the Refreshment Rooms. The provision of refreshment rooms, first suggested by the commissioners, was a daring innovation. As always, Cole discussed the plan with the Prince Consort at a meeting on 29 December 1856, at Windsor.[29] Prince Albert was in favour of it. Cole and Fowke acted with their usual speed, and on New Year's Eve they were both at Windsor again, with plans by Fowke, which the Prince approved.[30] The new

21

Museum thus became the first in the world to provide such an amenity, which it has retained ever since, though not on the same site.

The site chosen for the Refreshment Rooms was on the eastern edge of the land, immediately adjoining the buildings of the Brompton Oratory (the present church was not built until many years afterwards). In such a position the new buildings, which quickly began to rise,[31] were quite prominent, and before long the public was alerted by the newspaper *Lloyds* to this new architectural abomination. On 29 March 1857, the paper declared that:

In addition to the hideous corrugated iron structure already erected, and described by the press as a railway shed, or hospital for decayed railway carriages, another building is being erected close by, and, from what we see of it, when finished, it will harmonise with its larger neighbour, in as much that it will be hideously ugly, and will not, we fear, say much for the art of design as practised at headquarters. It is being constructed of common brick, and will form a contrast to the yellow and green striped erection with which it is so immediately associated. Its chimneys are terminated by villainous-looking red clay chimney-pots, as plain as a pike-staff.

This building was finished by May, when, to a certain extent, its brick construction had been

---

28. Select Committee 1860, para. 466.
29. Cole diary, 29 December 1856.
30. Ibid., 31 December 1856.
31. Ibid., 14 February 1857: Cole reports that the timbers of the refreshment rooms were above ground.

20. *The first Refreshment Rooms, adjacent to the Brompton Oratory, 1863. Watercolour by Anthony Stannus*

21. In Town, with Art. –
At the South Kensington
Museum: *caricature of the
Refreshment Rooms*

masked by an unconvincing half-timbered mock-Tudor veneer. In July 1857 the Board agreed to pay Octavius Hudson the sum of £25 for the decoration of the Refreshment Rooms.[32]

These Refreshment Rooms[33] were to remain in use until 1868, when new rooms were opened in the main building. Throughout the Museum's history the catering has always been contracted out. The first manager of the Refreshment Rooms was Mr G. Withers, 'the respectable confectioner in Baker Street'.[34] He paid the Department of Science and Art a percentage of his takings, £47 in the first year. At first the rooms were unlicensed, but a licence was soon granted. Cole stated later that he considered the venture an entire success, and was satisfied that the visiting public much preferred tea or coffee to gin, of which they hardly drank 'a thimbleful',[35] only one person ever being ejected from the Museum for walking unsteadily.

The ugly appearance of the building, and the howls of derision that greeted it on completion, were a source of embarrassment to the commissioners, who were threatened by the Office of Works with legal proceedings for an infringement of building regulations. Cole soon found a solution to the problem. It was at this time that the 1851 commissioners were in the process of breaking off their partnership that had been formed with the government for the purpose of land purchase. The partnership was dissolved by Act of Parliament in 1858. The Refreshment Rooms were immediately presented to the government,[36] which was exempt from building regulations.

Henry Cole always avoided referring to the estate or the Museum by the name of Brompton. He preferred the term 'South Kensington', which he appears to have invented himself. On 1 December 1856 he proposed the name South Kensington Museum to the Prince Consort, and this title was formally accepted by the Board on 21 May 1857. The Museum remained the South Kensington Museum until 1899, when it was renamed the Victoria and Albert Museum.

Entries in Henry Cole's diary in 1856–7 bear witness to the astonishing energy with which he master-minded all aspects of the foundation of the Museum. He was frequently on the site, inspecting the progress of the new buildings. (On 1 August 1856 conditions must have been almost unbearable for the workmen encased inside the iron building, for Cole's diary records that the temperature rose to 98° F in the shade, 120° F in the

32. PRO, Ed. 84/35, Board minute, précis, 30 July; and earlier, on 19 March, the Board had sanctioned a M. Lawson being appointed as draughtsman to prepare working drawings for the new building at £1 5s a week.

33. A contemporary interior photograph is in *Survey*, pl. 6c.

34. *Middlesex Advertiser*, 18 March 1858.

35. Select Committee, 1860, para. 527. To the Select Committee on Public Institutions on 1 March 1860, Cole gave evidence that none of the visitors to the Museum had been removed for drunkenness. During February of that year 20 bottles of wine, 5 of brandy, 6 quarts of ale, 71 pints of stout, 80 gallons of draught ale, and 20 gallons of porter had been drunk. As there had been 45,354 visitors during the month, the average amount consumed by each person had been 15/25 drops brandy, 2½ drops of wine, or 10½ drops of bottled ale; but there had also been a 'large consumption of tea and coffee'.

36. The Treasury accepted it on the same day that the offer was made. PRO Ed. 84/54, 12 May 1858.

22. *The north side of Pennethorne's office building, c. 1861, with Sappers exercising in the water tank*

one sapper each month in the operation of photography, thus effectively giving him an assistant.[40]

22

The sappers were proving invaluable in other ways. Their duties included fire prevention, for which purpose there was a small reservoir in the Museum grounds; an early photograph shows them rowing a boat on it. Early in the morning of 17 March 1857 Cole was woken at 5 a.m. with the alarming news that the painting room of the Schools had gone up in flames. The sappers, however, were able to extinguish the fire before the firemen arrived. Cole later recorded the comment of Mr Braidwood, the Superintendent of the London Fire Brigade, that he 'had never seen a fire stopped so prettily in his life; and that he would not have attempted it himself; the sappers did it unscientifically, according to firemen's notions'.[41] No doubt the excitement made Cole less alert than usual later in the day: he set off for Hastings, but, as he confessed in his diary, he 'rode with Ld. G. Lennox and went on to Brighton by mistake'.

In Henry Cole's diary of 31 July 1856 there is an early hint of a matter of some excitement and far-reaching consequence to the Museum. Cole records that he, Fowke, and Redgrave had called on John Sheepshanks, who had indicated that 'he wd make the offer of his collection to the Nation'. A week later, Cole strolled from his country cottage at Shere in Surrey to Abinger church, where he met Redgrave, who had just received a letter from Sheepshanks offering his valuable collection of pictures by Landseer and other notable contemporary painters to 'our department'. Although the formalities had yet to be settled Cole at once began to plan a picture gallery.

sun.) He worked tirelessly behind the scenes, 'pulling the wires of government', as Sir Joseph Paxton remarked.[37] Initial contacts were made with numerous individuals who were to feature in the later history of the Museum. Besides Francis Fowke, Cole also met Henry Scott,[38] another Royal Engineer who was to succeed Fowke as architect of the new buildings at South Kensington in 1865, after the latter's untimely death. He also visited his friends Richard and Charles Thurston Thompson, and proposed that a department of photography should be established at the Museum, with Charles Thurston Thompson as its superintendent.[39] Thurston Thompson was to produce an invaluable photographic record of the early development of the Museum, the earliest such record of a major public building in the world; many pictures from his studio are reproduced in this book. He became very overworked, so Cole suggested that he should train

---

37. Cole diary 19 February 1856.
38. Cole diary, 15 January 1857.
39. Ibid., 20 July 1856. C. T. Thompson was appointed superintendent on 29 July 1856; see J. Physick, *Photography and the South Kensington Museum*, 1975.
40. Ibid., 23 December 1857.
41. Select Committee 1860, para. 505.

PLATE I *(opposite above) Marlborough House, 1856. Watercolour by W. Casey*

PLATE II *(opposite below) Brompton Park House, 1863. Watercolour by Anthony Stannus*

CHAPTER III

Fowke's first permanent buildings

In the period 1856–61 the first permanent structures were built on the South Kensington site. The earliest, the Sheepshanks Gallery, was under construction at the same time as the temporary buildings described in the last chapter; and in 1857 the upper floor of it, which housed the Sheepshanks collection of paintings, was opened, together with the iron building. The gallery below it was opened in 1858. The Turner and Vernon Galleries, followed by further galleries for paintings, were constructed in 1857–61.

The Sheepshanks Gallery

v For some years John Sheepshanks had been considering presenting to the nation his collection of paintings, mainly by contemporary artists, such as William Etty, Sir Edwin Landseer, William Mulready, and C. R. Leslie. In 1852 he had suggested to Henry Cole that parts of the 1851 Exhibition building might be used as a gallery.[1] Cole describes the terms on which John Sheepshanks eventually made the gift.

> Mr. Sheepshanks has an abhorrence of trustees; he dislikes the noise and crowd and clatter and dirt of Trafalgar-square, and he gave those pictures on three conditions: first, that there should be an individual responsible personally for their management, and that they should not be under a Board of trustees; secondly, that a decent building should be

PLATE III *(opposite above) Brompton Park House, 1862; in the background, the dome of the 1862 Exhibition. Watercolour by Anthony Stannus*

PLATE IV *(opposite centre) The Brompton Boilers and the entrance to the Patent Museum, 1863. Watercolour by J. C. Lanchenick*

PLATE V *(opposite below) The western side of the Sheepshanks Gallery, 1861: Prince Albert, Henry Cole and Francis Fowke inspecting John Durham's model of the 1851 Exhibition memorial. Watercolour by Anthony Stannus*

erected before he gave them, feeling that the Vernon and Turner pictures had been shabbily used [at the National Gallery]; and his third condition was, that they should be exhibited in the neighbourhood of the parks. Upon those terms Lord Palmerston accepted them.[2]

The deed of gift stipulated that a 'well-lighted and otherwise suitable' gallery should be erected near to the buildings of the Science and Art Department on the South Kensington site. It was also stipulated that the building should be completed within twelve months of the date on which the offer was made.

Upon the government's acceptance of the Sheepshanks gift in 1856, Parliament voted £3,500 for a building to be erected expressly to house the paintings. Other money might also be available from the £10,000 voted to finance the move from Marlborough House. It was decided to build in brick, and, although the gallery was originally intended to be temporary, it still stands today, and is discernible internally as Rooms 26 and 29 on the ground floor and Rooms 83, 84, 91, and 92 on the floor above. The wall on the west side, however, the only outside wall which has not subsequently been built against, and which now faces into the Quadrangle, has been pulled down and rebuilt to a new alignment, so that the galleries now taper inwards towards the north.

The gallery was designed by Captain Francis Fowke. Its position, at the north end of the western span of the Boilers, was to affect the whole future structural development of the Museum, by establishing the direction in which all the early buildings grew. (Its position relative to the Boilers is shown in illustration 34.) As Fowke explained,

> ... the proportions of the building were necessarily much governed by its connexion with the main Museum [i.e. the Boilers]. The principal conditions

1. Cole diary, 3 April 1852.
2. Select Committee, 1860, para. 201.

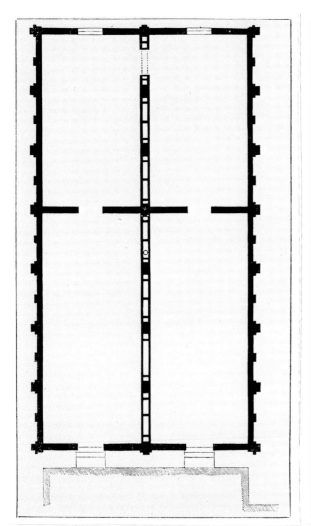

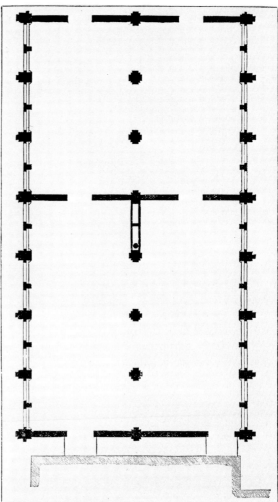

23. *(above left) The Sheepshanks Gallery, first floor plan*

24. *(above right) The Sheepshanks Gallery, ground floor plan*

25. *(left) Building the Sheepshanks Gallery, west side, 1857*

26. *(opposite) The Sheepshanks Gallery, section*

laid down previous to its being designed were that its width should equal that of one of the three iron vaults or spans which constitute that building, viz., 42 feet; that its two floors should also be on a level with the corresponding Museum floors . . .[3]

Thus the level of the first floor of the present museum building round the Quadrangle, and the width and height of the galleries on the ground floor and the first floor on the eastern side, were determined by the Brompton Boilers, which were themselves removed over a century ago.

Other conditions listed by Fowke were that fire risks should be minimized by keeping a small space between the new building and the Boilers, by using non-combustible materials for the floor and other parts of the building, and by avoiding iron columns and supports; that the upper, or picture gallery floor should be lighted from above, and the lower 'should have as much light as possible, and should be open from side to side'; and that the building should easily be capable of extension at any future period.

23
24
25
The building was to be of two storeys, externally about 87 feet long and 50 feet wide, 36 feet from the ground to the eaves, and 50 feet to the roof ridges. It was 4 feet away from the north end of the most western section of the iron building, and linked to it by two bridges. The long walls were constructed in seven bays, and the interior on both storeys was subdivided by a cross wall into two unequal portions, with four bays in the

northern section and three in the southern. The upper floor was also subdivided by a wall longitudinally. The lower floor had a corresponding row of brick piers down the centre, still to be seen.

26
The construction was begun by Kelk on 25 November 1856 (Cole noted in his diary that it began to snow on the following day). The next January it was first noticed, with surprise, by the *Builder*.[4] By then it had advanced with astonishing speed, and was ready to be roofed in. A year later the *Builder*'s report described the completed building, which was by now open to the public:

> The materials used in the construction are the best grey stock bricks, faced with an ornamental brickwork of Suffolk cream-coloured, Staffordshire blue, and Surrey red, bricks. Internally, the walls are coloured a sage green; the walls and dado are painted in three shades of grey. Names of painters are introduced in the cornice.[5]

27
The report in the *Builder*, which is of some length, describes various innovations observable in the new building. The most notable was the daring introduction of gas illumination. It seems that in this, as in many other things, South Kensington was among the first in the field. The gas lighting enabled Cole to carry out a cherished scheme for opening the gallery in the evenings, even in the winter, when it was dark early. The painting galleries were open until 10.00 p.m. on Mondays, Tuesdays, and Wednesdays. The newspaper *Lloyds* hoped that other museums would soon follow suit, to lure the working man from the public house.

> The anxious wife will no longer have to visit the different taprooms to drag her poor besotted husband home. She will seek for him at the nearest museum, where she will have to exercise all the persuasion of her affection to tear him away from the rapt contemplation of a Raphael.[6]

A commission consisting of Professors Faraday, Hofmann, and Tyndall, together with Redgrave and Fowke, was appointed by the Lords of the Committee of Council on Education to investigate the possibly deleterious effect of gas lighting

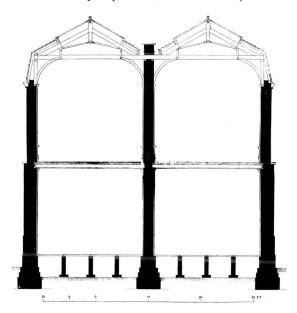

3. *5th Report . . . 1857* (1858) pp. 56, 61.
4. *Builder*, 24 January 1857, p. 46. Cole diary, interior scaffolding removed 9 May, plastering finished by 23 May, painters still there on 6 June.
5. *Builder*, 27 February 1858, pp. 137, 139.
6. *Lloyds*, 5 July 1857.

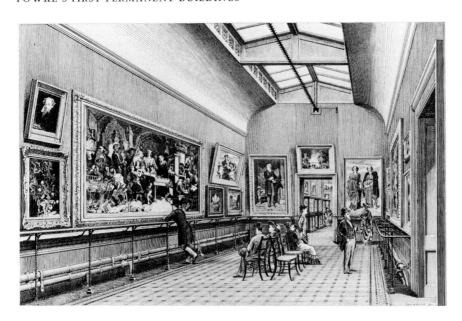

27. *The Sheepshanks Gallery, interior, c. 1876, after the Sheepshanks collection had been moved elsewhere*

upon pictures. The report, delivered on 20 July 1859 (by which time gas lighting was installed in the newly built Turner and Vernon Galleries as well), is interesting as an early attempt at scientific analysis of the museum environment, and it is worth quoting here.

> There is nothing innate in coal gas which renders its application to the illumination of Picture Galleries objectionable ... Coal gas may be free from sulphuretted hydrogen compounds, and in London is so at the present time. But it has not yet been cleansed from sulphide of carbon, which, on combustion, yields sulphuric acid gas capable of producing $22\frac{1}{2}$ grains of sulphuric acid per 100 cubic feet of present London coal gas. It is not safe to permit this product of the combustion to come into contact with pictures painted either in oil or water-colours.

The commissioners were emphatically of the opinion that any gas-lighted picture gallery should be equipped with adequate ventilation to carry away the products of combustion. The ventilation of the Sheepshanks Gallery fulfilled these requirements. Furthermore, the lighting of the gas did not cause a temperature increase of more than one degree Fahrenheit. Further experiments had also been carried out.

> Certain colour tests, consisting of surfaces covered with white lead, or with vegetable and mineral oils (especially the more fugitive ones), and in which also boiled linseed oil, magylp, and copal varnish

were employed as vehicles, had been prepared, and were, when dry, covered one-fourth with mastic varnish, one-fourth with glass, one-fourth with both mastic varnish and glass, and one-fourth left uncovered. Sixteen of these have been placed for nearly two years in different situations, in some of which gas has been used, in others not. They give no indications respecting the action of coal gas (except injury from heat in one placed deliberately very near to and above the burners), but seven of them show signs of chemical change in the whites, due to either a town atmosphere or want of ventilation. The most injured is that from the National Gallery, Charing Cross; and the next is from a country privy; the third much less changed is from the House of Commons; the fourth is from the Barber Surgeons' Hall; the fifth from the Bridge-water Gallery, the sixth from the Royal Society's Rooms, Burlington House; the seventh from the British Museum.

Among the remaining eight samples, none of which was damaged, was the one that hung in the Sheepshanks Gallery.

Besides the lighting of the gallery by night, much thought had gone into its daytime illumination, by the skylight, so that glitter and reflection from the glass on the painting was eliminated.[7] The heating was 'a modification of the arrange-

---

7. Francis Fowke in *5th Report ... 1857* (1858), pp. 62, 63; Richard Redgrave, RA, 'Construction of Picture Galleries', a lecture given at the Museum, *Builder*, 28 November, 1857, pp. 689, 690.

ment patented by Mr. Gurney, whereby the air is damped as well as heated . . .'[8]

Ventilation was considered to be particularly important, both because of the gas lighting mentioned above, and because large numbers of people were expected to crowd into the room. There were ventilation shafts in the hollow walls, and access to these from the lower rooms was achieved by means of a perforated ornamental frieze of terracotta, which ran all round the tops of the rooms. This was the first appearance in the Museum of terracotta, a material which was to be much used in the later buildings, and which formed part of the so-called South Kensington style of architecture. (The designer Godfrey Sykes, who undertook much of the decorative work at South Kensington, worked frequently in terracotta, and further influenced Fowke in his later use of this medium for external decoration. He had previously been considering Portland stone. Henry Cole also came to support the continued use of terracotta, which he saw used in a newly discovered ancient tomb in Rome in 1859. This was of fine brickwork, with mouldings and ornamental parts of light buff. Another building he noted had pilasters of red brick and capitals of yellow, 'not cut but moulded before they were baked. I hope we shall adopt this system at Kensington, eschewing the use of stone, except where stone, would be decidedly best.)'[9]

v   For the external decoration of the gallery Fowke chose another technique which was also to appear in the later Museum buildings. This was 'a species of surface decoration approaching fresco painting, and known in Italy by the name of sgraffiatto, of which many old examples may be seen in Florence, and a modern example, by Professor Semper, at Hamburg.'[10]

The sgraffito work appeared on the upper storey of the long west wall, in the fourteen recesses which corresponded to the windows in the lower storey. It was achieved by applying first a dark layer of cement, then a thin, pale grey layer; then, while the cement was still wet, lines were cut through the pale layer to expose the dark layer below. Thirteen medallions at £5 each, containing portraits of artists such as Reynolds, Gibbons, Opie, and Barry, with dates and names of their work, were carried out in sgraffito by Andrew MacCallum, who had previously decorated the interior of the Lecture Theatre in

the junction.

The entire cost of the building was

Construction, including heating and ventilating	£4,500. 0. 0.
Minton's floor tiles	132. 13. 0.
Artists' designs for, and execution of decorated panels	140. 0. 0.
Gas fittings	81. 0. 0.
Terracotta casing for girders and open work cornice	95. 0. 0.
	£4,948. 13. 0.

On 13 February 1857, Cole visited Sheepshanks with W. F. Cowper, the vice-president of the Committee of Council on Education, and several others. They persuaded Sheepshanks to return with them to South Kensington to place a tablet in the brickwork. 'He rather flinched from doing so, but as it was, very unostentatiously consented.'[12] Presumably the tablet had an inscription recording the gift. It does not survive.

The official opening

Everything was moving towards the opening day, now only four months away. Inside the iron building, colour experiments were going on,[13] and Prince Albert visited on two days, and 'went over almost every room in the offices and schools', and, with the Prince of Wales, inspected the Sheepshanks Gallery.[14] Objects were being taken into the Museum, and Cowper spent one afternoon watching the plaster legs of the cast of Michelangelo's *David* being erected, an undertaking that was, as Cole remarked, 'not without jeopardy'.[15]

By now, the Museum comprised nine different sections, some of which had come from the Museum of Marlborough House, or had been presented to the new Museum, others that had been offered temporary display space there. The sections were as follows: 1. the Sheepshanks paintings; 2. a collection of modern sculpture donated by the Sculptors' Institute; 3. the collection of Ornamental Art, which had formed an important

8. *Builder*, 27 February 1858.
9. Cole diary, 7 June 1859.
10. *Builder*, 27 February 1858, p. 139.
11. Ibid.
12. Cole diary, 13 February 1857.
13, 14. Cole diary, 18, 19 February 1857.
15. Ibid., 21 February 1857.

part of the collection at Marlborough House, and which was now divided into seventeen subsections; 4. collections of architectural casts and drawings, partly from Marlborough House, and partly the property of the Architectural Museum, removed from Cannon Row; 5. the circulating Art Library; 6. a collection of models and materials illustrative of building, obtained partly from the Paris Exhibition and partly from the Exhibition of 1851; 7. the collection of models, diagrams, and books from the Education Exhibition held in St Martin's Hall in 1855; 8. the collection of animal products which was the third section of the Trade Museum, of which the Museum of Economic Geology and the Kew Museum formed the other two sections, and which, with its exhibits of feathers, fur, bristles, human hair bought from Flemish girls, and so on, was to prove particularly popular; 9. the collection of models formed by the commissioners of Patents, which remained under independent management, and had its own catalogue and access from a different entrance. There was also the Art Reference Library.

The subdivisions of the Ornamental Art section were: 1. sculpture, including carvings in marble, alabaster, stone, wood, ivory, bronze, terracotta and models in wax; 2. painting, including wall decoration, paper-hanging, illuminations, painting, design; 3. glyptic and numismatic art; 4. mosaics; 5. furniture and general upholstery; 6. basketwork; 7. leatherwork; 8. japanned or lacquer work; 9. glass painting; 10. glass manufactures; 11. enamels; 12. pottery; 13. works in metal; 14. arms, armour, and accoutrements; 15. watch and clock-work; 16. jewellery; and 17. textile fabrics.

Plans went ahead for the royal opening on 20 June 1857. Cole wagered a hat with the decorator John Crace that more people would come to South Kensington in its first year than had visited Marlborough House in its final year.[16] At last the great day came. According to Cole, the

> ... Queen and Prince and Court came in the evening punctually at 9.30. Ld. Granville and Mr. Cowper not arrived but did so a few minutes afterwards ... The Queen expressed herself quite pleased with all the arrangements. Refreshments given to students etc.[17]

Today the Prince Consort's appearance is well-known – but apparently this was not so in 1857, for Cole records that when a student was asked during the royal visit to demonstrate an engraving

16. Ibid., 29 May 1857.
17. Ibid., 22 June 1857.

28. (left) Interior of the Brompton Boilers, 1859: the Educational Museum

29. (above) Interior of the Brompton Boilers, 1857: the Architectural Museum

tool for the Prince, he did not recognize him. The following Monday, 22 June, was the day appointed for the official opening, with a private view which was attended by about 2,500 people.

In spite of its disgust at the iron building, the *Builder* reported quite favourably on the new establishment, though it refused to acknowledge the existence of any district of South Kensington:

> General expressions of satisfaction have attended the opening of the Government Museum at Brompton. Few among the thousands who have already visited it were prepared to see so many departments of science and art illustrated so fully as are to be found there.[18]

The Sheepshanks collection proved popular. Cole recorded that owing to the density of the crowds round the pictures, when the viewers coughed or sneezed, saliva ran down the pictures and positively ate away the surface of them.[19]

The public continued to come to outlying Brompton in quite large numbers. Before the opening, Cole had had a visit from Mr Church of the General Bus Company, who agreed that an omnibus would call at the Museum once every half hour, but so great was the attendance that only a month after the opening the promoters of the South London Railway called on Cole to ask if he would like a railway brought to the Museum. Gladstone approved, but nothing came of this.

The year 1858 saw the completion of the ground-floor rooms below the Sheepshanks Gallery. They were inspected by Gladstone on 27 March, and opened by the Queen on 14 April. After all this intense activity Cole saw Sir J. Clark, his doctor, who said that Cole ought to have a rest for at least twelve months, and suggested that he should go to Italy. Cole agreed, and set off in July. He was not away for a full year, but was back at the office on 5 March 1859, when he plunged into the new work concerned with the Vernon and Turner Galleries, on which he had been kept informed, during his absence, by Redgrave.

The Vernon and Turner Galleries and their extension

Shortly after the completion of the Sheepshanks Gallery, there had arisen the question of housing

---

18. *Builder*, 27 June 1857, pp. 357, 358.

19. '... a minute inspection has satisfied me that danger is to be apprehended to those near the eye, and that many small spots have already been acted on and chemically changed by the acrid nature of the expectorations ... I have therefore commenced placing works near the eye under glass ...' R. Redgrave, *7th Report of the Science and Art Department, 1859* (1860), p. 124. See also 'Sightseeing and Sneezing', *Punch*, 6 April 1861, p. 139.

30. *(left) Visitors to the South Kensington Museum. Caricature by Sir John Tenniel*

31. *(above) The South Kensington Museum from the south-west, 1861–2*

the painting of J. M. W. Turner, and those in the collection of Mr Vernon. Turner had bequeathed his unsold paintings to the nation and, after much argument and a court case, it had been decided that they should go to the National Gallery. Owing to shortage of space, however, they had first been exhibited at Marlborough House. The Vernon collection was originally displayed in the basement of the National Gallery, but, as a result of public protest, it too was removed to Marlborough House. Both collections had remained there when the Department of Science and Art moved to South Kensington. But the Prince of Wales was due to move into Marlborough House after his eighteenth birthday on 9 November 1859, and so the building was scheduled for renovation in the spring of that year. The paintings would obviously need to be rehoused, but where should they go?

Sir Charles Eastlake, the Director of the National Gallery, favoured the adaptation of Carlton Ride, the riding school at Carlton House Terrace, to receive the pictures, since it was reasonably near to the National Gallery. The South Kensington officials, on the other hand, privately supported by Prince Albert, hoped to secure the pictures for their new site. They consequently conducted a rapid and forceful campaign to capture the collection, led by Cole himself until his departure to Italy, and then taken up by Redgrave.

Sir Charles Eastlake and the trustees of the National Gallery eventually agreed to the move, but constantly reiterated that it should be regarded as a temporary measure. They were determined that the collections, though housed at South Kensington, should be quite separate from the South Kensington Museum. They must be approached by a separate entrance, and any communicating doors between the new galleries and the South Kensington Museum should be kept locked; 10,000 feet of hanging space would be required for the Vernon and Turner collections, and Eastlake later asked for an extra 4,000 feet on which to hang other pictures for which there was insufficient room at the National Gallery. In their customarily precipitate manner, the officials at South Kensington had begun to build before all these arrangements were finalized.

32 The new galleries were designed by Fowke. The building housing the Turner and Vernon collections, below which the Art Museum and Art Library were to be located, was attached to the north end of the Sheepshanks Gallery and extended northwards in line with it, reaching the northern edge of the site. It was 150 feet long and was slightly wider than the Sheepshanks Gallery. The building to house the extra pictures from the National Gallery (now Room 94) extended eastwards at right angles to it, from the northern end of its east wall. It was a single gallery, 30 feet wide and 110 feet long. The lower rooms of this building were to house the Female Art School, currently occupying the decayed houses in the grounds. The Turner and Vernon Galleries were still intended to be temporary, but it was necessary to make the building permanent 'as far as the first floor, because that floor was to be a fireproof floor, and it was impossible to carry a fireproof floor upon a temporary building', as Fowke stated later. 'Above that,' he added, 'I consider the building temporary.' However, in his view, since they were carefully built 'in cement', the buildings were likely to stand for at least a century.[20] They are now well past that age. The long east–west gallery was of a more substantial construction and 'the upper storey of that building is good, and the roof is such as might be allowed to remain'.[21]

Cole held the view that 'nature had given Captain Fowke a sluggish and indolent temperament',[22] but he admitted that Fowke could be roused to prompt action when the occasion demanded it. Such an occasion was the building of these picture galleries. When the Treasury gave its sanction for them, as Cole recorded later,[23] Fowke was staying at Hatfield with the Marquis of Salisbury. That evening, Salisbury told Fowke that work could start. The next morning, at breakfast, the Chancellor of the Exchequer, also on a visit, asked Captain Fowke when the works would begin. ' "They are begun already." "How so? You only knew last night at twelve." Captain Fowke replied, "I was at the telegraph office, at Hatfield, as soon as it was open, I ordered the works to begin, and I have received an answer that the foundations are being dug." "I call that work!" said Mr. Disraeli.'

The buildings went up at an almost incredible

20. Select Committee 1860, paras. 2284–2292.
21. Ibid., para. 2294.
22. Henry Cole, *Fifty Years of Public Work*, 1884, vol. ii, p. 351.
23. *Loc. cit.*, p. 352.

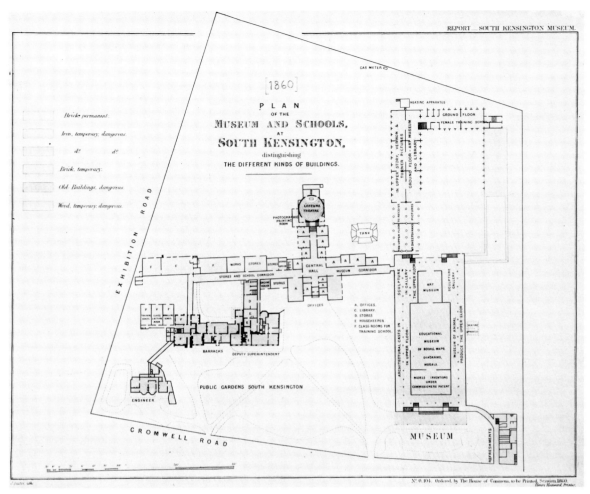

[1860]

PLAN
OF THE
MUSEUM AND SCHOOLS,
AT
SOUTH KENSINGTON,
distinguishing
THE DIFFERENT KINDS OF BUILDINGS.

32. Plan of the South Kensington Museum, 1860

rate. Just before Christmas Redgrave wrote to Cole, who was still resting in Italy:

> Lord S. has talked the Treasury into sending the Vernon and Turner pictures down here and a very temporary building is going on at a great pace to receive them ... The whole was only settled on Friday morning last and already the foundations are in ... The building will be rough but I think Fowke and myself can make it a very handsome and appropriate gallery.[24]

Even at this stage the negotiations with the National Gallery had not been completed. The question of the extra 4,000 feet of wall space, which South Kensington was only too delighted to provide, and which necessitated the financing and construction of the additional gallery, was settled on Christmas Eve 1858, with Redgrave forcing the pace in a manner that Cole himself could not

have surpassed. The whole business is recorded in a series of letters that were rushed across London by messengers.[25]

Redgrave began at 10.30 on the morning of Christmas Eve. He wrote to Eastlake that Lord Salisbury, Lord President of the Council (and therefore South Kensington's political master) was with him, and would, at the meeting on that day of the Privy Council Committee on Education, support any requirements Eastlake might wish to make concerning the accommodation of his pictures at South Kensington. But Eastlake must reply by noon. The messenger bearing Redgrave's letter found Eastlake at home at Fitzroy Square, and Eastlake, timing his reply at 11 o'clock, undertook to send an estimate of wall

24. Cole correspondence, 20 December 1858.
25. *Printed Correspondence*, 24 December 1858.

33. (right) The Sheepshanks
and Turner Galleries,
exterior, west side

34. (below) Bird's-eye view
of the South Kensington
Museum

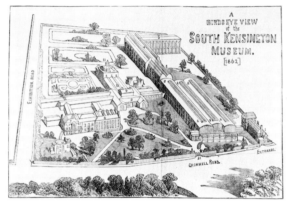

space before midday. Hotfoot on the heels of the returning first messenger, therefore, followed another less than an hour later, bearing a further letter from Eastlake, who had by then hastened to the National Gallery. He had come to the conclusion that extra space, beyond the 10,000 feet originally planned, would indeed be needed for the overflow of paintings, and – no doubt trying to give as good as he got from Redgrave – he also put in a request for a curator's residence.

Redgrave, anxious to get as much as possible settled before the matter became too public, sent a reply at midday on Christmas Eve. Lord Salisbury would not consider any residence, or anything else besides space for hanging pictures. He would, however, back the application for extra wall space. 'But this must be done at once, as our building flows out of the ground so fast, as to astonish even him.' Eastlake and his clerks at the National Gallery spent a busy afternoon measuring. That achieved, Eastlake replied to

Redgrave, stating that an additional 4,000 feet would be required; then he wrote to the Chancellor of the Exchequer, with a copy to Lord Salisbury, asking officially for the additional space. Returning home, Eastlake wrote yet again to Redgrave, telling him of his communications with Lord Salisbury and the Chancellor, and adding, with an air of pained exhaustion,

> You appear to attach much importance to the removal of the pictures to South Kensington, for reasons apparently independent of the safety or due exhibition of the works; and I gather from your notes that you wish to proceed with expedition and secrecy; for fear of opposition. This anxiety I do not comprehend; as regards opposition, I beg to assure you that it will not come from me. If the pictures are well provided for, the trustees treated with proper respect, and the establishment not unjustly neglected, I can have no objection to offer.

Despite his assurances, however, disagreements over the housing of National Gallery paintings at South Kensington were to continue. Looking back a year later, Henry Cole admitted that there was 'an instinctive jealousy between one government department and another; they always fancy that one is going to eat the other up, and our relations naturally began upon that footing'[26]; and it is only fair to say that the Department of Science and Art clearly did want to eat up the National Gallery's pictures.

Redgrave pressed ahead with the building works. Early in 1859, he informed Cole that

---

26. Select Committee 1860, para. 235.

33 ... the building for the T. & V. pictures if we get them is up to the level of the Sheepshanks gallery floor; it is of rough brickwork 2 stories high. It has been most favourable weather – has been pushed on at a tremendous pace – and will I think be completed in 8 weeks from the first brick laid ...[27]

Summing up the results of his Christmas Eve campaign, he told Cole on 15 January 1859, 'Lord S. has just sanctioned the erection of another Gallery 110 ft. long 30 ft. wide for more pictures [Room 94] and accepted an estimate and the work is in progress.' There was also good news for Cole about the Turner and Vernon Gallery, for this had 'the flag flying on its top – the ridge on – and the brick work completed. Lord S. even is quite astonished at the rapidity ... 300,000 bricks in 3 weeks and shall be ready in 3 weeks more.'

Norman MacLeod, assistant secretary in the Department of Science and Art reported to the Treasury

... The amounts at which the buildings have been contracted for, is as follows viz:—

1st. Building erected for the Vernon and Turner Collections, and containing 10,000 feet of wall space...	£3,783
2nd. Building to provide an additional space of 4,000 feet at the request of the Trustees of the National Gallery	2,997
Warming	312
	£7,092

35 I am to add that the wall space thus provided, extending as it does to 14,000 feet, will enable the Trustees to hang in a very satisfactory and sufficient manner, all the pictures for which they require temporary accommodation.[28]

MacLeod added that 'the proposed building has been constructed with a view to meet the wishes of the Trustees', aiming to 'secure to the public the freest and most convenient access to the collections...'

Provision had not, however, been made for a separate entrance, largely on the grounds of expense. This angered the trustees of the National Gallery, who protested that such an entrance was essential to preserve 'the separate character of the National Gallery', and to prevent visitors 'being distracted by the long lines of miscellaneous exhibitions, and impeded by the public crowd'

while entering by way of the South Kensington Museum.[29]

Faced with the National Gallery's tenacious demand for an entirely separate entrance, South Kensington began to flag. On 12 March, Henry Cole (just back from Italy) invited Eastlake to South Kensington to see Francis Fowke's designs for a staircase to form a separate entrance. Eastlake approved the design, but the Treasury refused to authorize the expenditure, for Kelk had estimated £2,538 for the construction. A further, less ambitious, design of Fowke's was later accepted. Unfortunately we do not know the details of either plan, and the staircase itself has not survived. Another staircase designed by Fowke during this period, however, remains to this day. This is the North Staircase, situated at the opposite end of Room 94 from the National Gallery entrance, in the north-west corner of the early building. It was completed and decorated at a later date, as described in Chapter VI: Other early work by Fowke, and further decoration.

The building of the separate National Gallery entrance did not resolve all the inter-departmental disputes over access. In August, when the walls of the new gallery were dried out, Ralph Nicholson Wornum, a former colleague of both Cole and Redgrave at Marlborough House, and now Keeper of the National Gallery, wrote to suggest that the pictures should be moved in, and the communicating doors between the new galleries and the Sheepshanks Gallery should be closed.[30] Cole replied that this was impossible, as the alternative access, via the new staircase, was not yet complete on account of a builders' strike.[31] Wornum then agreed to bring the pictures in through the doors from the Sheepshanks Gallery.

Meanwhile Cole and the Department of Science and Art had written to the Treasury protesting about the closing of the doors between the new galleries and the South Kensington Museum.

... visitors to the Turner and Vernon pictures will very generally desire to inspect, on the same occasion, the pictures given by Mr. Sheepshanks, as well as other objects in the Museum ...

35. *(top) The Turner and Vernon Galleries, looking east*

36. *(above) The Turner Gallery (Room 88), when a paintings gallery in 1910*

If the public were expected to leave the Turner and Vernon galleries by the separate entrance, and 'pass more than a thousand feet through the open air' before entering the Sheepshanks Gallery by way of the South Kensington Museum, 'it may be foreseen that the public will question the necessity for such an arrangement and complain ...'[32] The Treasury agreed, and eventually reason triumphed, and the National Gallery capitulated.

This group of buildings of 1858–9 was extremely plain; in fact, externally they were, and still are, quite unprepossessing. Fowke explained that they were erected in order to provide a good picture gallery as cheaply as possible:

> They were never meant to be an ornamental front; the building is at the back, looking into a mews and back yards. The back of a part of Somerset House is in the same way; the Mansion House is another case, and the National Gallery another. It would have been a great waste of money to have made the backs of these buildings anything more than they are.[33]

These buildings were thus quite different from the Sheepshanks Gallery, which was meant to be seen on both sides, and had an amount of external decoration. Cole supported Fowke:

36

32. Ibid., 20 August 1859.
33. Select Committee 1860, para. 2337.

If money were given for ornamentation, the interior of it might be made one of the most effective exhibition rooms in Europe. With respect to the exterior, I do not think people going to the Holy Trinity Church need bother themselves with the look of the building ... I maintain that it is as sightly as it ought to be, considering its situation.[34]

The Eastern Galleries

After the rapid construction of the rooms to house the National Gallery pictures, the momentum of building work at South Kensington did not slacken. The iron building was overcrowded and was proving to be so unsatisfactory for the housing and display of South Kensington's own art collections, that Cole and Fowke were anxious to build permanent galleries for them as soon as possible. The galleries so far built formed the east and north sides of a rectangle. The Boilers stood on the south side. Fowke planned to build a new range of galleries from the National Gallery entrance at the north-east corner, southwards down the east side. Already in Fowke's mind was a further plan to cover the resultant quadrangle to form the North and South Courts.

The building of the eastern range of galleries (now largely occupied by offices, and kitchens for the Museum restaurant on the ground floor, with the textile galleries above) is not well documented. It was built by Kelk, apparently in several stages. The first estimates were received in December 1859, and work began, but soon came to a halt, as funds had run out. In 1860 a select committee of the House of Commons was appointed to investigate the development of the South Kensington Museum. A plan included in their report shows that in August 1860 the gallery immediately south of the National Gallery entrance was in a very incomplete state, and that the extension to the south of it, opposite the Sheepshanks Gallery, was still in a rudimentary planning stage. The northern section of the eastern block was to form painting galleries for South Kensington's own collections; the ground floor of the southern section, which on the west side took the form of an open cloister, was to house the Indian, Chinese, and Japanese collections, while the

gallery above it was to become the National Competition Gallery.

The select committee was convinced by the arguments of Cole and Fowke, and agreed that '... additional space for the accommodation and exhibition of the Art Collection should be provided at once'.[35] Funds were therefore supplied, and work proceeded briskly. Kelk had already been given several contracts, for example: £976 for a building up to the first-floor level, agreed in December 1859; £815 for further buildings up to the first-floor level, 24 January 1860; £3,044 for an additional storey and roof, 4 April 1860.[36] The specification for completing the carcass of the new galleries south of the National Gallery is dated March 1860.[37] Later in the year we find the specifications and estimates for the southward continuation and completion of the range, to bring it opposite the Sheepshanks Gallery. The specification for the carcass of new galleries above, is dated October 1860. Estimates from Kelk accepted by Cole included £1,317 for erection of 'upper storey and roof of new gallery ... including the finishing of offices under new galleries, also the digging and concrete for wall of new court' (24 October 1860);[38] 'several works ... in finishing the offices under the new gallery opposite the Vernon gallery, £171' (26 October 1860); 'wrought iron joists etc. and concrete floor to upper storey of gallery opposite Sheepshanks ... £372' (25 October); and so on.

In the second half of 1860 work on the new buildings must have advanced with characteristic speed, because, by 25 February 1861, Kelk was able to send in an estimate for plastering all the walls and ceilings and asphalting the floors at £2,017. From this estimate, which is endorsed 'Recommended Francis Fowke Capt. R.E.'[39] we must presume that the most northerly of the range of buildings was virtually complete by the autumn of 1861.

34. Select Committee 1860, paras. 563, 567.
35. Select Committee 1860, Report para. 18.
36. PRO, Ed. 84/3.
37. PRO, Ed. 84/15.
38. PRO, Ed. 84/3.
39. PRO, Ed. 84/54.

CHAPTER IV

The construction of the North and South Courts

While grappling with the building extensions described in the previous chapter, Captain Fowke had also moved on to other things. The eastern galleries formed the third side of an open rectangle, of which the National Gallery formed the north and west sides. The north end of the Boilers, 4 feet away from the south end of the Sheepshanks Gallery, screened the open southern end of the rectangle by reaching most of the way across the opening. Even before the building of the eastern galleries, Fowke had had an imaginative, but perfectly logical idea, which he unveiled to the select committee of 1860. 'A simple and cheap way of obtaining space', he told them, 'would be to cover the quadrangle formed.' This could be done by a glass roof, and 'it is proposed, for the purposes of securing it from fire, to build a wall across the middle [of the quadrangle]; the north court would then be about 110 feet square, and the south court would be 120 feet by 90 feet'. He considered that a glass roof was essential, because rooms looking into the Quadrangle, such as the inner rooms of the Library, the repairing rooms, and the Female Art School, would be dependent on it for their light.[1]

The select committee endorsed Captain Fowke's suggestion of completing the Quadrangle and glazing it over.

> He estimates that this might be done for £17,000, and by doing so the Art collections now in the Iron Museum would be placed in safety, others not properly shown would be efficiently exhibited, whilst space would be provided in the Iron Museum to receive and exhibit the architectural casts procured as models for the Houses of Parliament, which at present lie unexhibited in buildings at Thamesbank, costing an annual rent of £490.[2]

As a result of the committee's report and recommendation, the Department was authorized to go ahead with the plan, beginning with the northern part. Anticipating formal permission, the Department had been inviting tenders, and on 6 December 1860 preliminary estimates had been received: £4,505 from Kelk for the North Court, and £5,070 from Grissell for the South Court.[3]

The North Court

Fowke had originally entertained the idea of covering the North Court with an octagonal dome up to 120 feet in height, which he regarded as 'a large glass case to contain beautiful objects'. If the 'foundations under the columns were perfect, and the ironwork were of a perfect character', there was no doubt that it would last as long as any building in the country.[4] Cole had private doubts about Fowke's octagonal dome supported on columns. He took Fowke and Redgrave to Oxford to see the new museum there – 'cast iron columns substituted for wrought iron. Diagonal roof of glass. Quite a muddle', thought Cole, and by 11 September 1860, the dome with its forest of columns was abandoned.[5] Fowke then modified his plans to achieve an iron and glass roof which, though simpler than the dome, was completely self-supporting, and left the 110 foot square floor space unimpeded by columns.

The North Court progressed very rapidly during 1861,[6] and it was opened on 30 April 1862.

37
38

39

---

1. Select Committee 1860, paras. 2301–2.
2. Ibid., Report, para. 18.
3. PRO, Ed. 84/3.
4. Select Committee 1860, para. 2326.
5. PRO, Ed. 84/35, Board minute précis, 17 June 1859. Cole diary, 7 September 1859, 14 June, 11 September 1860.
6. PRO, Ed. 84/35, Board minute précis, 9 May 1861 'T. W. Grover to superintend the erection of iron work in N. and S. Courts. To be paid £63 deducted from Fowke's salary.'

43. (opposite) The roof of the North Court

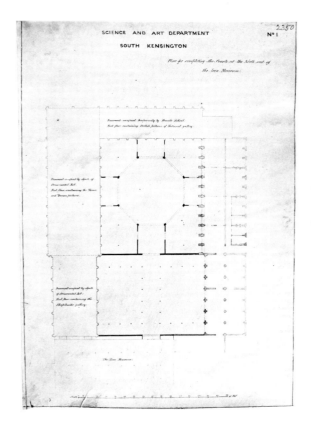

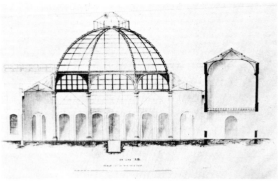

37. (left) Francis Fowke's first plan for the North and South Courts

38. (below left) Section through the proposed North Court, from the east

39. (bottom) Section through the North Court as built, from the west

Not unnaturally, Fowke was proud of his new construction. The 1861 Report of the Science and Art Department[7] contains his account of his aims and the manner in which he achieved them.

The objects sought to be attained in the construction of the court were:

1. That the amount of light should be the greatest possible, and at the same time,

2. That the light should be under the most perfect and immediate control.

3. That while it was thus manifestly necessary to have the roof mainly of glass that the access to all parts of that roof should be as ready as possible.

4. That the ventilation should be so perfect as not only to ensure equability of temperature, but also that the products of gas combustion, and the exhalations from large crowds of visitors, should be thoroughly and speedily carried off, while at the same time the deteriorating effects of a London atmosphere should be as much as possible avoided.

5. That the temperature should be as nearly equal as possible that, in spite of the great amount of glass

7. _10th Report . . . 1861_ (1862), Appendix K.

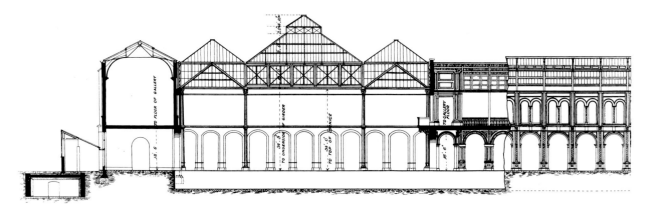

CIMABUE   GIOTTO   RAPHAEL   M·ANGELO

B·1240 D·1302   B·1276 D·1336   B·1483 D·1520   B·1474 D·1564

PLATE VIII *(opposite above)* The Industrial Arts in Time of Peace, *a design (not executed) by F. R. Pickersgill, for a lunette fresco in the South Court. Oil*

PLATE IX *(opposite below)* Silk Culture, *a design (not executed) by F. W. Moody for a mosaic in the North Court. Watercolour*

40. *(right) The roofs of the South and North Courts, 1 August 1873*

41. *(centre right) Building the North Court*

42. *(below right) A main roof girder of the North Court*

surface, nearly 18,000 square feet, it should be free from all extremes of heat and cold.

6. In addition to these it was necessary to provide for gas lighting in such a way that gas should illuminate the objects in the court as nearly as possible at the same angle as the daylight, that it should be capable of being lighted quickly without the use of rods, which might be dangerous to objects, and that the products of combustion should be thoroughly got rid of.

1. The greatest possible amount of light is obtained by constructing the entire roof of glass, and in the surrounding rooms by removing the windows and leaving open archways into the court. A light is thus obtained in the court but little inferior to that of the open air, while in the rooms the light is nearly the same as with the usual glazing through windows.

2. To control the quality of light at all times a system of interior blinds has been devised by which any blind can be raised or lowered in a few minutes, cords being attached and hoisted into position in a few minutes by one or more men on the roof.

3. The system of roofing adopted may be thus briefly described: the entire space to be covered, viz. 110 × 110, is spanned in each direction by two girders at 30 feet from each angle, leaving therefore 50 feet of the side of the square between their adjacent ends, these four girders intersecting each other, divide the whole area into a centre square of

40

41
42
43

49

50, four corner squares of 30 feet, and finally four rectangles of 50 × 30. These five squares are roofed by square pyramids at the level of the top flange of the girder, and by keeping the roofs of the remaining four rectangles at the level of the bottom of the girders, it will be at once understood that an upright space or clerestory [10 feet high] is obtained for ventilation . . .

Ventilation – The inlet of fresh air is provided by a sunk passage or tunnel 5 feet wide and 6 feet deep, which runs across the centre of the court in two directions, covered with an open iron grating, and which at each end is carried under the surrounding buildings, and terminates in an area open to the external air.

In this tunnel and close under the open grating are carried the hot-water pipes for warming the court, so that the fresh air in winter must pass over a considerable heated surface before being diffused through the court.

The area of entrance from the external air into this tunnel is about 100 square feet, and as it is dispersed into the court from a grating surface of 1,100 feet its gradual diffusion without current is ensured.

Heating – The heating is by means of hot water at a low temperature, but with a large heating surface (3,500 square feet), the furnaces are entirely removed from the building, and there is an ample supply of spare boiler power in case of accident or repair.[8]

Cleansing the Air – To guard against the influence of London atmosphere, an apparatus has been devised by which fresh air (previously passed through a screen and thoroughly cleansed), being forced into the court through the tunnels, shall so fill the interior as to ensure a constant set outwards from every opening, and entirely prevent the entrance of blacks or other impurities, rendering the air, in fact as free from mechanical impurity as in the open country.

The effect of the heating and ventilation systems was to achieve a remarkably equable temperature. In the first summer, Fowke recorded, the temperature in the North Court, day and night, remained between 55° and 75° Fahrenheit, except on one afternoon, when it rose to 77°, the temperature in the galleries at that time being 84° and 79° respectively. In the winter the temperature remained between 50° and 66°, while outside the thermometer ranged from 21° to 69°.

On 29 April 1862, before the opening, Cole held a private view in the North Court of objects from the Campana, Soulages, and other private collections, which were displayed in thirty cases.[9] A few

days later there was a party during the evening when 3,500 people saw the first illuminations of the Court by gas; Cole thought it 'very brilliant'.[10] *The Times* (4 June 1862) reported that there were 2,000 gas jets, and its readers were urged to go and see the 'curious little apparatus' that travelled along the line of gas burners for the purpose of lighting them.

At this time Cole had not made any decisions about the decoration of the Court, but even so, in the spring of 1863, he decided to ask for permission to exhibit there the wedding presents given to the Prince of Wales and Princess Alexandra.[11] The proposal was well received at Buckingham Palace, and the private view of the presents was held on 15 April 1863 when, according to Cole, some 4,900 people attended, which he considered 'too many'.[12]

The exhibition proved to be the first of South Kensington's successes. Open only between 16 April and 2 May, it had a larger attendance over the period of a fortnight than most exhibitions since. Visitors turned up in unprecedented numbers. On the first day the waiting time in the queue was at least one hour and a half, and 700 people an hour were passing through the gates.[13] Altogether just under 230,000 visitors to the Museum were recorded during the run of the exhibition; of these at least 180,000 saw the wedding presents, in addition to 1,349 members of both Houses of Parliament; and more than 25,000 catalogues were bought. These are impressive figures, which would make the organizers of many an exhibition today green with envy.

During 1865, J. C. Robinson, previously the Superintendent of the Art Collections at South Kensington, now the Art Referee, found much to criticize in the North Court, particularly concerning the heating and lighting. As Fowke subsequently pointed out, he had not intended the large area to be filled with small objects contained in glass cases, but had designed a space as far as

44

---

8. During 1861 Kelk contracted to provide 8 wrought-iron boilers in a new boiler-house, and to dig channels in the floors of the Female School, and the new courts, for £2,656. PRO, Ed. 84/3.
9. *Standard*, 30 April 1862.
10. Cole diary, 2 May 1862.
11. Ibid., 26 March 1863, 'To Windsor saw Phipps who arranged with the Prince of Wales for Exhibition of presents.'
12. Cole diary, 15 April 1863.
13. *Daily News*, 16 April 1862.

44. (above) The North Court, interior, 1864

45. (left) Interior of the North Court, when used by the Circulation Department, 1956, showing the main supports to the roof inserted in 1908

possible to represent the open air, in which would be large pieces 'that were originally placed in the open air, or in analogous positions'.[14] Not long afterwards the court became the home of such large architectural items as the cast of Trajan's Column and the model by Wren of St Paul's Cathedral, which was lent by the Dean and Chapter.

Many years later, towards the end of 1908, when Aston Webb's new building was almost complete, the large architectural objects were about to be moved into its various courts. One of these was the Santa Chiara chapel from Florence which at that time occupied the centre of the north wall of the North Court, and behind which was the Fernery. This and other such objects had been built into the walls, and it was thought that their removal might reveal weaknesses in the structure of the buildings, which were then more than fifty years old. Anxiety was expressed about the stability of Fowke's immense, unsupported glass roof[15] and inspection revealed that there was a real danger of its collapse. The Office of Works, therefore, inserted four stanchions at the points of intersection, to give support, at a cost of £600.[16]

Fowke's roof is still in position, although only

14. PRO, Ed. 84/54.
15. PRO, Ed. 84/68. The Fernery was a conservatory, on the site of the present Conservation block, which provided art students with a large variety of growing plants.
16. Ibid., 3 February 1908.

the centre of it is visible from the ground floor. A new gallery on the first-floor level was created in 1957 by building in the empty roof space of the court, leaving the centre light-well open. When the Museum was rearranged to fit Aston Webb's new building in 1909, the North Court became a gallery for temporary exhibitions (until 1939) and its adjacent rooms of the Circulation Department. This Department was closed in 1978, and in

1982 plans are in preparation to turn the North Court into galleries for the Oriental collections.

The decoration of the North Court, which was begun in 1863, and continued until the mid-1870s, is described in Chapter V.

The South Court

Grissell's work on roofing in the South Court began in the same year as that on the North Court,

45

47

46. *Clock in the North Court, the face painted by F. W. Moody, from the 1862 Exhibition*

but proceeded more slowly. The south side of the South Court took the form of a plain brick wall parallel with the north end of the Boilers, which had been built by Kelk in the autumn of 1861, for £445 6s. It was a temporary wall, to be demolished at the time of the South Court's planned extension. Iron doors led through this wall to the Boilers.[17] As it was felt that the North Court could satisfy the need for space for larger items, a different form of layout and roofing was planned for the smaller South Court. It was desirable to provide in this court first-floor galleries of communication. Besides, as Fowke reported, 'it was necessary to have a scheme of court that should be capable of extension whenever the time should come for the removal of the temporary iron building known as "the boilers"'.[18]

The South Court, also to be known as the Lord Presidents' Court, presented a completely different appearance from the North Court. It was an altogether more splendid and lavish affair: a structure of glass and cast iron, elaborately decorated, not unlike a train shed in one of the new stations of London – or rather, two train sheds. For the court, 110 feet by 94 feet, was divided down the centre into two smaller courts. Between them was an arcaded corridor, 20 feet wide, above which was the Prince Consort's Gallery. At the north end, this gallery ran into a similarly constructed transverse gallery, 10 feet wide, which linked the Sheepshanks Gallery with the newer eastern galleries. At the south end, the central gallery met the blank south wall. The later southward extension was to provide at the south end a gallery matching the one at the north end, but

wider. The central division created two equal courts 84 feet by 50 feet, which were roofed by semi-circular wrought-iron ribs supporting a plain, ridged glass roof with a continuous ventilator running the entire length. The gallery between the two courts was roofed with slate, with a ventilating clerestory on either side.[19]

A conspicuous feature of the South Court was its decorated cast- and wrought-iron work,[20] designed by Godfrey Sykes, which was described at length by the *Building News* in 1865.[21]

A continuous arcade ran all round both subdivisions of the court. Between each arch, standing out from the wall, rose an elaborate wrought-iron

---

17. PRO, Ed. 84/35, Board minute précis, 24 October 1862.

18. *10th Report . . . 1861* (1862), p. 130.

19. A perspective section (V&A Print Room E 1051 – 1927) is reproduced in *Survey*, Pl. 9a.

20. The wrought-iron work was made by the firms of Thomas Potter & Son, and George Smith & Co. 'Building with Fowke, did not like the Iron Columns in the S.C.: like bed posts', Cole, diary, 27 March 1862.

21. *Building News*, 24 February 1865.

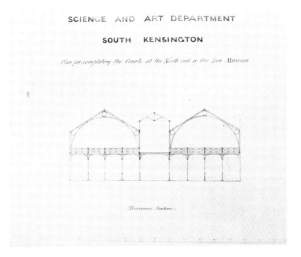

47. (right) *Francis Fowke's first scheme for the South Court, 1860*

48. (below) *Section through the South Court, from the south*

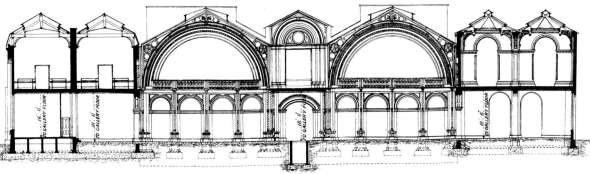

Building the South Court. 49. (above left) from the south; on the left is the east wall of the Sheepshanks Gallery. 50. (above right) east portion, north end. 51. (left) Ironwork

column with a twisted shaft and foliated cap. The rows of columns running down the long sides of the halls supported the semi-circular transverse roof trusses. Above the arcade and between the roof trusses the walls were further decorated at first-floor level: each bay of the arcade supported twin arched niches.

This arrangement, in which each arch on the ground floor supported two above, was based on the wall decoration of the Sheepshanks Gallery, for the eastern exterior wall of this gallery now formed the western interior wall of the South Court, and so its rhythms were taken up in the ironwork decoration. The twin niches at first-floor level were later filled with mosaic panels.

The South Court opened in June 1862 with a glittering special exhibition of works of art lent by many owners. The papers were somewhat critical of the bald title of the 'Loan Exhibition' as it was felt that this provided absolutely no 'gauge of the merits of the show'. Like most of the large exhibitions ever since, it was presented to the press (over a three-day period) in a state of some unreadiness and confusion: we are told of 'cases imperfectly arranged'. The exhibition, organized by J. C. Robinson, was a complete jumble – so much so, that comment was unanimous on the 'neglect of any system of classification, or attempt to separate the works of one age from those of another'.

52
53

54

But, whatever criticism there was of the exhibition, Captain Fowke's architecture was applauded. A visitor arriving by way of the despised iron building would have been impressed by its complete unexpectedness. As *The Times*[22] put it,

> he would have to ask himself where he was, since ... the place is new ... it is a great hall which has some pretensions to architectural merit. It is, in fact, the commencement of a new building, which is gradually to replace the 'boilers'. At the back of the edifice which has obtained this distinguished name, Captain Fowke has been rearing the first instalment of a permanent Art Gallery. How his work looks on the outside we have no means of judging, but internally it promises a complete success when the designs are fully accomplished ... We see but one-third of the new building which is suddenly cut short by an immense brick wall, though it is only a temporary one ...

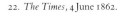

22. *The Times*, 4 June 1862.

52. *(above) The Sheepshanks Gallery, east side, c. 1858. Watercolour by an unknown artist*

53. *(below) Design from Francis Fowke's studio, with additions possibly by Godfrey Sykes for altering the east wall of the Sheepshanks Gallery for the South Court interior*

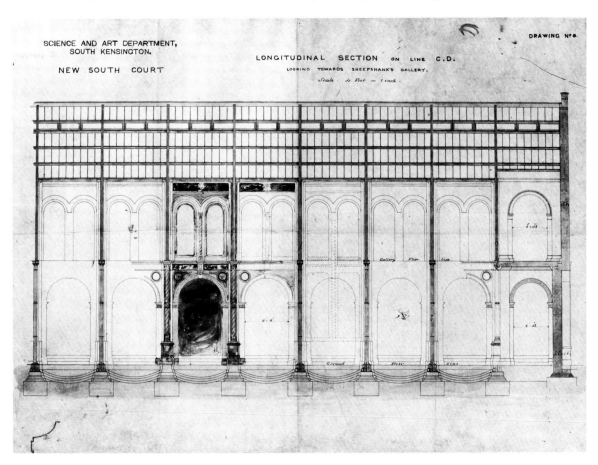

SCIENCE AND ART DEPARTMENT, SOUTH KENSINGTON.

NEW SOUTH COURT

LONGITUDINAL SECTION ON LINE C.D.
LOOKING TOWARDS SHEEPSHANK'S GALLERY.

DRAWING Nº 6.

As there was no public access to the grounds, the paper's contributor did not realize that there were no exterior elevations to the new courts, which had been formed by roofing over a quadrangle.

The extremely complicated decoration of the South Court, which is described in Chapter V, began at the end of 1862. The second of Lord Leighton's two frescos, which together represented the most ambitious element in the decoration, was not completed until after 1880. There are four huge semi-circular lunettes for frescos in the South Court, two at first-floor level on the north wall, behind the gallery, and two in the corresponding positions at the south end, in the extension, although those on the west side at each end remain empty to this day.

The extension of the South Court was undertaken in the autumn of 1869, by General Scott, Captain Fowke's successor, who maintained an extremely close adherence to Fowke's design, left unfinished on 18 October 1864. Most of the Boilers had been dismantled and moved to Bethnal Green before the extension was undertaken. In order that the builders could work without causing any interference with the exhibition in the court itself, Scott decided to build a screen across the whole southern end. This was constructed at night, and was of timber, covered with canvas and paper. Although it was 114 feet wide and 50 feet high, and standing 3 feet from the brick wall which had to be demolished, the workmen took only three weeks to do the whole work.[23] The extension itself was then built and was opened in 1871.

During the Second World War the South Court was used as a Royal Air Force mess; afterwards the eastern side of the South Court became the Museum restaurant. In 1949–50 a new ceiling was put in, which hides Fowke's glass roof, and the iron arcades were concealed behind walls and pillars. Now, a portion of the ironwork has been uncovered. The western half of the South Court (Room 38) is used as a gallery to show tapestries. Here the main lines of the roof are still visible.

54

55

56

54. *(top) The South Court used as an Royal Air Force canteen during the Second World War*

55. *(centre left) The South Court restaurant, as recast by the Ministry of Works, c. 1950*

56. *(above) The western portion of the South Court, when used as the medieval tapestry court.*

23. *17th Report . . . 1869* (1870).

CHAPTER V

The decoration of the North and South Courts

A museum director today would almost certainly decide that a new gallery should have no ornamental decoration; he would want it to serve as an inconspicuous and self-effacing background for the exhibits. In the nineteenth century, however, all public buildings were dignified with appropriate ornamentation, museums no less than churches, theatres, courts of justice, and banks. Indeed, art museums must have seemed especially to demand suitable artistic decoration. Several Continental museums had shown the way. In Paris, in the section of the Louvre known as the Musée Charles X (built 1827–33) a series of ceiling paintings depicted the civilizations of

57. Henry Cole, Francis Fowke, Godfrey Sykes and (?) John Liddell, outside the Residence, c. 1865

antiquity. In the Neues Museum at Berlin (1843–55) there were paintings of the Teutonic myths. And in Munich, the Alte Pinakothek (1826–36) had a gallery with frescos by Peter Cornelius depicting the history of European art in the Middle Ages and Renaissance; while the Neue Pinakothek (1843–54) had exterior frescos by Wilhelm von Kaulbach showing modern painters, sculptors, and architects.[1]

Whether Cole consciously tried to emulate these museums we cannot tell. The extent to which his taste, Prince Albert's taste, and that of their associates such as William Dyce, Sir Matthew Digby Wyatt, Owen Jones, and Gottfried Semper, contributed to the formation of a recognizable 'South Kensington' style has been pondered by Nicholas Taylor;[2] it remains largely a matter of speculation. What is undeniable is that Cole had his own architects, his own decorators, and his own labour force on the South Kensington site.

The architects (though they were not formally qualified) were Francis Fowke, whom we have already met, and Henry Scott, who enters the story after Fowke's death in 1865. To assist him with the decoration of the South Kensington Museum, Henry Cole called upon a young man still in his thirties,[3] Godfrey Sykes, a former pupil of Alfred Stevens. Sykes, whose work was much influenced by the style of his master, in turn had a team which carried on the Stevens tradition at South Kensington until almost the end of the century. Sykes had originally been employed in 1859 to assist Fowke with the decorative details of

57

---

1. Germain Bazin, *The Museum Age*, Brussels, 1967, p. 199.
2. See *Survey*, Ch. v.
3. Sykes's birth date has been given as 1825, but a manuscript note in the Museum copy of the *Dictionary of National Biography* records that his son stated that the year should have been 1824. Sykes had been recommended by the Board as drawing master at the Sheffield School of Art in 1856. PRO, Ed. 84/35, 29 July 1856.

the 1862 Exhibition, and the Horticultural Society's garden. His use of terracotta[4] in the various buildings had caused Fowke to change his mind about the decorative material to be used on his Museum buildings; he had previously been considering Portland stone. Sykes was so highly regarded that the Board decided that his 'views on questions of decoration [were] to be adopted in future', although there was the safeguard that, if it were thought necessary, Richard Redgrave was to be consulted.[5]

After Sykes's early death in 1866, his principal assistants, Reuben Townroe and James Gamble (both 1835–1911), were appointed to succeed him in planning and executing the decoration of the Museum, for which they relied to a large extent on the drawings, often slight sketches, that Sykes had left.

Another of Sykes's assistants was Frank W. Moody (1824–86), who joined the Department in 1863. He headed a team of students from the Art Schools, as the Schools of Design were now called, and was a 'frank and genial chief'.[6] Sykes's other associates were William Ellis, John B. Fidler, Lockwood Kipling, Matthew Eldon, and Gilbert Redgrave (Richard Redgrave's son).

The design team produced work in many media. Terracotta for external work was their speciality, and they achieved a bold yet sensitive and spontaneous style of modelling. Decorative constructional ironwork found its place in the South Court, while enamelled metalwork (one of Cole's bright ideas) was tried in the Refreshment Rooms. Sgraffito decoration in coloured cement covered expanses of the Quadrangle walls, and the back wall of the Science Schools. The South Kensington team were especially keen on ceramic decoration. Mosaic was extensively used for floors and for panels of wall decoration; many stained-glass windows were designed; patterns and pictures were both painted on tiles and modelled in relief in glazed and enamelled terracotta.

Most of the decoration was provided by the home team, but distinguished outsiders were also called in. Many contemporary painters designed figures for the 'Valhalla' in the South Court, where, also, Leighton painted frescos. Poynter designed tile panels for the Refreshment Rooms, and William Bell Scott designed the stained-glass windows. Many commercial firms were employed

to make the terracotta, iron, and ceramic decoration, and will be mentioned when they occur. The contribution of Minton, Hollins and Company is especially noteworthy: this firm, an offshoot of the Minton porcelain concern, was greatly admired by Henry Cole.

Although the total effect of the decoration must have been of incoherence, and much has been obscured in recent times, the decorative experiments at South Kensington were invariably enterprising, and some of the work of Sykes and Gamble is of excellent quality. Some of the recently restored decorations, notably in the Refreshment Rooms, have come as a revelation to modern eyes.

Decoration of the North Court

There is very little extant information on the colour scheme introduced into the North Court by Godfrey Sykes. The *Reader*[7] printed one of the few descriptions: the lower part of the court, up to the string course above the arches of the cloister, was painted a 'deep blood red', while above that was a 'cold purple grey'. The paper thought that the contrast between the two had a 'most savage and unpleasing effect'. Nevertheless, on the whole the North Court presented a most 'imposing aspect', though Fowke's great glass roof was, in the opinion of the reporter, 'more wonderful than beautiful'. It was thought that it would have been much cheaper to build if 'handsome columns' had been placed at the intersection of the iron girders.

Other details are provided by Henry Cole, who recorded in his diary[8] that he had settled the colour of the 'paper' that Sykes had designed, and later in the same month, Octavius Hudson, who had earlier decorated the temporary Refreshment Rooms, was paid £25 for suggestions and sketches that he had shown to Cole during August. Not long afterwards, Brucciani estimated £8 10s for making plaster casts to be used in a frieze.[9] These probably included the small angels placed

4. 'Godfrey Sykes to be engaged for £5 per week for 1 year to make designs for terra-cotta and sgraffiatura.' Ibid., 28 July 1859.

5. Ibid., 14 December 1865. The work by Sykes and his assistants, is discussed by Benedict Read, *Victorian Sculpture*, 1982, pp. 226–7.

6. Richard Lunn, 'Some recollections of the National Art Training School & the old Museum', *R.C.A. Students' Magazine*, vol. i (1911–12), pp. 61–3, 84–7.

7. *Reader*, 9 September 1865.

8. Cole diary, 10 August 1863.

9. PRO, Ed. 84/36, Board minute précis, 28 November 1863.

along the girders, which were visible until the painting galleries were built over the court in 1957.

In fact, of the original decorative schemes, it is only the floor that can be described with assurance, as the pavements still, to a great extent, exist. The tile pavement of the court itself was designed by Sykes, and made by Minton, Hollins and Company, at an estimated cost of £1,320.[10] In the cloisters on the east side, Maw and Company designed and produced a floor in buff octagonal and white square tiles for £210,[11] and on the north side were more buff and white tiles by Maw, and also a glass mosaic pavement in black, white, and red, with figures of birds, which was designed by Frank Moody, and made by Powell and Sons in 1873.[12] Another similar floor, the first in mosaic, had been made earlier in the same year by Jesse Rust, who said of it, and another, near the North Staircase,

> I take old glass of any description and fuse it with a large quantity of sand together with the colouring matter. I thereby get a material resembling marble, but which is much harder and will resist moisture. Any colour and shape can be made while in a fused state. I then press it into moulds, in the shape required either for geometric designs, or in squares to be broken up for mosaic.[13]

There is one other floor by Rust, which was in the west cloister, and which displayed a pattern of yellow diamonds intermingled with yellow stars.

There were two abortive schemes for decorating the walls of the North Court with mosaics. The first came from Henry Cole himself. The Raphael cartoons were brought to South Kensington from Hampton Court in 1865, and this inspired Cole with the idea that they might be copied and turned into full-size paintings or mosaics for the walls of the North Court. In May 1868, Sergeant Spackman, one of the Museum's sapper photographers, was given the job of projecting lantern slides of the cartoons onto strained cloth, and tracing the outlines.[14] Cole then set about getting estimates. Woods, a former National Scholar from the Art School, estimated that he could make a copy in tempera for £120, taking three days a week for ten months or a year. But Moody thought that one of his assistants, Wise, could do the job in seven months for £70. In August 1869 the firm of Simpson's informed Cole that they could supply tesserae for making mosaics of

Feed my Sheep, the *Miraculous Draught of Fishes*, and *St Paul at Athens*, for £1,200, and for a fourth cartoon at an additional £250. In 1871 Minton, Hollins estimated that they could provide four large mosaic copies at £1,800 each. The Department's comment was that 'This is a much *higher* rate than cheapest mosaic in South Court.'[15] Cole was unwilling to abandon the project, and wrote again to Minton, Hollins asking for a quotation in 'vitrified ceramic'. On 15 December 1871, the company replied that this would cost £3 a square foot. At this point Cole really did give up, and the project was abandoned.

The second scheme was for mosaics from designs by F. W. Moody. In 1873 the Board agreed that Moody should be asked to prepare 'designs in mosaic for decoration . . . and to be paid for them – £150 for each of the smaller panels, and £300 for that in the middle'.[16] Moody, after some prodding, submitted a design the following summer. On being shown the design by MacLeod, Assistant Secretary of the Department of Science and Art, Redgrave stated that

> . . . The Director of the Museum should in the first instance give his opinion as to this occupying so much available wall space, and Major Festing [Assistant Director, Works] as to the safety and stability of such a heavy mode of execution.
> . . . The sketch submitted Silk Culture is rich and picturesque. I think somewhat too picturesque if the same style of work is to be carried out round the whole court, as it would require greater variety on the lower parts below the picture – *and would attract the eye too much from the objects exhibited* – these objects being the first purpose of the museum.[17]

Redgrave estimated that £4,000 would be needed for the preparatory work. Richard Thompson, Assistant Director (Administration), was equally unenthusiastic. He considered that the total costs, including the completed mosaics and the incidentals such as carriage and fixing, would be in the region of £25,000.[18]

IX

---

10. PRO, Ed., 84/4, 20 June 1865.
11. PRO, Ed., 84/5, 30 January 1866.
12. *21st Report . . . 1873* (1874), p. 381.
13. *Decorations*, p. 2; *21st Report . . . 1873* (1874), states that these two floors by Rust were the 'first trials' in using mosaic.
14. See *17th Report . . . 1869* (1870), p. 318.
15. V&A Museum, Cartoon file.
16. PRO, Ed. 84/36, Board minute précis, 28 May 1873.
17. PRO, Ed. 84/67, 24 July 1874.
18. Ibid., 29 July 1874.

58. *Wood engraving of Godfrey Sykes's designs for the decoration of the South Court*

It is doubtful whether even the then recently retired Director, Cole, would have had the nerve to put forward such an expenditure to the Treasury; certainly the Board took fright. MacLeod told Moody that although there was no criticism of his design, the Board had decided that there was insufficient money for such an ambitious scheme.[19] Moody was annoyed, and, as on several other occasions, he composed a lengthy plea in defence of his proposal, during the course of which he remarked:

> I should much prefer not to send in any account for the work I have already done, the value of which I feel I cannot fairly estimate but to leave the matter of remuneration in the hands of their Lordships.

This letter was passed by MacLeod to Festing, and the case was eventually referred to Sir Francis Sandford, who by then had taken over from Cole as Secretary of the Department of Science and Art, and he curtly ordered 'Tender him £60.'[20] Presumably Moody accepted this sum. So ended the only attempts to provide the North Court with a lavish scheme of decoration to bring it into line with other areas of the Museum – a lucky escape, it might be thought, but there is still a great deal of Moody's work to be seen elsewhere.

Decoration of the South Court

Godfrey Sykes devised the elaborate scheme of decoration in the South, or Loan, Court, which was undertaken concurrently with that of the North Court. It is necessary to rely on written evidence for information about the colour scheme, since it was covered up during the 1940s, by which time it had become very dark. When the South Court was first opened, however, the prevailing tints were considered light and cool.

The overall impression was of brown, heightened with gold, with blue and white as relief. Above the series of niches round the upper part of the court, an extension of the pattern established by the outer wall of the Sheepshanks Gallery, was diapering in gold and grey, and the frieze of the cornice consisted of festoons of grey on a dark blue ground. The space between this and the glass roof was covered with hexagons in buff, brown, and gold. 'This part of the decoration has an unfortunate resemblance to a hearthrug', was one comment.[21]

The *Builder* reported in some detail on the colour

19. Ibid., 31 July 1874.
20. Ibid., 20 October 1874.
21. *Reader*, 9 September 1865.

59. (above), 60. (below) Godfrey Sykes's designs for
details of the decoration of the South Court

scheme.[22] The ironwork was painted a 'dark
yellowish brown', with gilding on the capitals and
bases of the columns, the heads of the rivets, and
the flanges of the ribs. 'The openwork ornamentation of the spandrels of the small arches is entirely
bronzed; whilst in the archivolts, the perforation,
in the form of leaves, is divided by medallions

bearing gilt pateras, or a monogram.'

The spandrels over the arches were filled with
monochrome paintings bearing some relation,
at the time of their execution, to the objects
exhibited.

> For instance, females occupied in spinning from the
> distaff, and in silk-winding; sculptors carving a
> Corinthian capital and a Gothic gargoyle: Smiths
> engaged on ornamental metal work; glass blowers;
> and boys painting on pottery fruit, flowers and
> foliage. The spandrels also exhibit ornamental ar-
> rangements of goldsmiths' work, etc. The friezes
> are decorated with figures and panels in mono-
> chrome: the figures hold tablets, inscribed Coins,
> Pottery, Enamels, Glass, Bronzes, Arms, Carvings,
> Gems, Fabrics, Mosaics, Medals, Inlays, Tapestry,
> Majolica, Niello, Seals, and Repoussé.[23]

If all these subjects were exhibited simultaneously
the court must have been a welter of bewilderment

---

22. *Builder,* 26 November 1864. Henry Sandham, Keeper of the
Museum of Construction, pointed out that L. Oudry, of Auteuil,
was the inventor of 'a valuable bronze paint, which has been very
extensively employed by the Department for bronzing the wrought
and cast ironwork used in the construction and decoration of the
South Courts of the Art Division ...' *12th Report ... 1864* (1865),
p. 224.

23. *Decorations,* p. 3.

to the visiting public. The decorative scheme was devised by Godfrey Sykes, and painted by his assistants Reuben Townroe and James Gamble.

In the eastern half of the court, the great roof spandrels were painted 'blue on the face; whilst the thickness of the leaves is coloured crimson'.[24] The *Builder* felt that the effect was inferior to that of the western half of the court, where the spandrels were the same colour as the ironwork, with gold outlines to the ornamental forms.

The *Builder* complained of 'the painted imitation of festoons' and 'substitutes ... for actual relief' observable in some places. The *Building News*[25] likewise disapproved of the festoons, the painting of which, it was felt, presented an almost

> deceptive appearance of projection. This very evil has proved so difficult to root out from our art manufacturers, that those who have to train designers for them might have been expected to give it a wide berth.

In all probability, however, these were designs intended for moulded majolica, by Minton, which were never realized.

The *Building News* approved of 'the constant change in the coloured ornament' which 'preserves the entire design from that appearance of monotony which the extensive use of cast iron often leads to'.

The tiled floor of the court was also designed by Godfrey Sykes,[26] and the tiles were made and laid down by Minton, Hollins and Company for £905.[27]

On the whole, the court was commended as showing skill and – what was thought even more important – a love for honest and commonsense construction.

61 To complete the decorative scheme, it was decided to insert full-size mosaic figures of well-known artists into the arcade niches that ran round the upper level of the South Court. Later another sequence, representing the Lords President of the Council, which thus gave its alternative name to the court, was installed in the cloister on the ground floor between the North and South Courts.

The 'Kensington Valhalla'

Work on the mosaics in the niches of the South Court continued from 1862 until 1871. A number of established contemporary artists were approached to produce designs on which to base the

mosaics, which were named the 'Kensington Valhalla' by the *Builder*. As early as January 1862, Daniel Maclise was offered a payment of £70, although his name does not figure among the artists whose work was eventually translated into mosaic. Holman Hunt and Ford Madox Brown[28] were among the artists invited to take part in the venture, although they never actually produced anything either. Others, fearful that their work might not be represented in such a prominent scheme, offered their services to Cole – among these were the Academicians Ward and Phillips. Phillips's design for Sir Joshua Reynolds eventually found a place among the mosaics, but Ward does not appear to have been successful. A notable absentee was Godfrey Sykes's former master, Alfred Stevens, but Cole had visited St Paul's Cathedral during August 1864 and had found Stevens's *Isaiah* mosaic 'a failure'[29] which may have influenced him against the artist.

The media used for the mosaics themselves were either glass, prepared by the Italian firm of Salviati (who received £140 for each mosaic), or the English Harland and Fisher, or Powell and Sons; or English ceramic, by Minton, Hollins and Company, or W. B. Simpson and Sons. Minton, Hollins and Powell and Sons sometimes subcontracted the work to female students from the Art School, a special mosaic class having been established for the purpose.[30] Among the members of the class were Letitia, Florence, and Mary Cole, members of Henry Cole's family. William E. Aldridge recorded the way in which the class worked:

> *1st* A tracing of the outline of the figure is made and divided into convenient portions. *2nd* Each portion or division of the outline is transferred to a flat piece

24. *Builder*, 26 November 1864.
25. *Building News*, 24 February 1865.
26. 'I have a note from Gamble this morning informing me that they have commenced putting down the large tile border in South Court. If not too late I should like it placing as I have shown on the enclosed sketch.' Sykes (at Weymouth) to Cole, 16 February 1865. Cole correspondence.
27. PRO, Ed. 84/4, 7 December 1864. Approved by H. A. Bruce, PRO, Ed. 84/36, Board minute précis, 22 December 1864.
28. PRO, Ed. 84/36, Board minute précis, 23 March 1865.
29. Cole diary, 11 August 1864.
30. The Board agreed, on 17 July 1862, that space was to be allocated within the Museum, 'to enable female students to witness, and themselves perform, process of laying wall pictures.' The class was to be formed of female students who had taken any prize, on payment of a fee of 2 guineas. PRO, Ed. 84/35, Board minute précis.

61. *Four mosaic portraits in position in the South Court:* Apelles, Pisano, Cimabue, Torel

62. *Wood engravings of mosaic portraits in the South Court*: Apelles, Giorgione, Cimabue, Raphael

63. *Wood engravings of mosaic portraits in the South Court*: Palissy, Inigo Jones, Nicolo Pisano, Benozzo Gozzoli

of paper, and the work commenced by fixing the tesserae on the paper face downwards according to the colours and shades in the picture. By this method several can work at the picture at the same time. *3rd* After all the portions of the picture are finished, they are laid flat and joined carefully on a slate larger than the picture, and the cement is laid on the back of sufficient thickness to make it strong. When the cement is set hard enough to bear moving it is turned over in one piece, and the mosaic stands the same way as the picture it is copied from. During the working and when laid for fixing, it is the reverse of the picture.[31]

A new process, vitrified ceramic enamel, which was invented by Colin Minton Campbell of Minton, Hollins, was first used in the mosaic of William Henry Fisks's design of Ghiberti. In the *18th Report of the Science and Art Department, 1870*, Henry Cole stated that Acton Smee Ayrton, the First Commissioner of Works, had suggested to Minton Campbell that he should experiment with painting on ceramic. A process had consequently been developed which 'obviates all the difficulties which have heretofore prevented the execution of large paintings on pottery; there being no limit in respect of size of picture in Mr. Campbell's new method...'. In connection with this new process, Minton, Hollins was given permission by the 1851 commissioners to build a studio on their land, provided that students were employed there in order that they might become proficient in the process.[32]

62
63
The mosaics, which were acquired as objects for the collections of the Museum of Construction,[33] were:

1. *Phidias*. Painted by Sir Edward Poynter and made in English glass mosaic by Harland and Fisher for £95.[34] It was finished in 1865.[35]
2. *Apelles*. Also painted by Poynter and made in Italian glass mosaic by Salviati. It was finished in 1865.[36]
3. *Nicolo Pisano*. Painted by Lord Leighton (who later undertook the huge South Court frescos) and made in Italian glass mosaic by Salviati, whose estimate was £120.[37] It was finished in 1865.[38]
4. *Cimabue*. Also painted by Lord Leighton and made in English ceramic (earthenware) mosaic by Letitia M. Cole, William E. Alldridge (both former students of the South Kensington Museum mosaic class), and Samuel Cooper, superintended by William E. Alldridge for Minton, Hollins and Company. It was finished in 1866.[39]
5. *William Torel*. Painted by Richard Burchett,[40]

31. *Decorations*, p. 5.
32. See Elizabeth Aslin and Paul Atterbury, *Minton 1798–1910*, V&A exhibition catalogue (1979), p. 67.
33. *13th Report ... 1865* (1866), Appendix D, p. 228. A detailed critique of this sequence of mosaics can be found in the *Builder*, 27 February 1875, and there is also comment in the *Reader*, 9 September 1865.
34. PRO, Ed. 84/36, Board minute précis, 29 October 1864. 'Mr Poynter called abt Mosaic designs & chose Phidias', Cole, diary, 16 February 1864.
35. *13th Report ... 1865* (1866), p. 167. Cartoon, V&A, Department of Paintings, 1761–1869.
36. Ibid. Cartoon, V&A Department of Paintings, 1760–1869.
37. PRO, Ed. 84/36, Board minute précis, 1 December 1864.
38. *13th Report ... 1865* (1866), p. 167. Cartoon, V&A Department of Paintings, 1139–1868.
39. *14th Report ... 1866* (1867), p. 185. Cartoon, V&A Department of Paintings, 1140–1869.
40. There are three designs by Burchett for this in the V&A Department of Paintings; 873–1868, 1141–1868, 1762–1869.

headmaster of the Art School, and made in English ceramic mosaic by W. B. Simpson and Sons. It was finished in 1869.

6. *Giotto*. Painted by John Calcott Horsley RA, and made in English glass mosaic by Florence Cole[41] and Mary Cole (of the mosaic class) for Powell and Sons, whose estimate of £120 was dated 8 March 1873.[42]

7. *William of Wykeham*. Painted by Richard Burchett and made in Italian mosaic by Salviati, whose tender was £180. He offered to reduce it if he did the Giorgione as well (£135), the price being £300 for the two mosaics.[43] *William of Wykeham* was finished in 1867.[44]

8. *Jan van Eyck*. Painted by F. W. Moody but not made in mosaic by 1875. There is some uncertainty as to whether it was ever made.[45]

9. *Fra Angelico*. Painted by Charles West Cope RA and made by Letitia M. Cole and Samuel Cooper, superintended by William E. Alldridge for Minton, Hollins. It was finished by 1866.[46]

10. *Ghiberti*.[47] Painted by William Henry Fisk and made in Colin Minton Campbell's new process of vitrified ceramic painting by Minton, Hollins for £120.[48]

11. *Donatello*. Painted by Richard Redgrave RA, the Inspector-General for Art, and made in English ceramic mosaic by Samuel Cooper, superintended by William E. Alldridge for Minton, Hollins. It was finished in 1867.[49]

12. *Benozzo Gozzoli*. Painted by Edward Armitage and made in Italian glass mosaic by Salviati. It was finished in 1865.[50]

13. *Luca della Robbia*. Painted by Frank Moody and made in English glass mosaic by Harland and Fisher. It was ordered on 28 March 1866 for £130 and was finished in 1867.[51]

14. *Andrea Mantegna*. Painted by Frederick Richard Pickersgill RA, and made in English ceramic mosaic by Florence H. Cole and Mary J. Jennings (of the mosaic class), superintended by Samuel Cooper for Minton, Hollins. It cost £120 and was finished in 1871.[52]

15. *Giorgione*. Painted by Valentine Prinsep and made in Italian glass mosaic by Salviati. It was finished in 1866.[53]

16. *Fra Beato Giacomo da Ulma*. Painted by N. H. J. Westlake and made in Italian glass mosaic by Salviati. It was finished in 1868.[54]

17. *Leonardo da Vinci*. Painted by Sir John Tenniel and made in English ceramic mosaic by Kate Clarke and Florence H. Cole, superintended by Samuel Cooper for Minton, Hollins. It was finished in 1869.[55]

18. *Raphael*. Painted by Frank Moody and made in English earthenware ceramic by Florence H. Cole and Mary J. Jennings, superintended by Samuel Cooper for Minton, Hollins. The estimate for the mosaic was £120. The *17th Report* of the Department records that Moody completed his design in 1870.[56]

19. *Torrigiano*. Painted by William Frederick Yeames and made in English ceramic mosaic by Samuel Cooper, superintended by William E. Alldridge for Minton, Hollins. Completed in 1867.[57]

20. *Peter Vischer of Nuremberg*. Painted by William Bell Scott,[58] and made by Kate Clarke, superintended by Samuel Cooper, for Minton, Hollins. The cost of the mosaic was less than £130[59] and it was finished in 1871.[60]

41. 'Florence Cole came to learn mosaic-making.' Cole diary, 15 January 1866.
42. PRO, Ed. 84/7. Horsley's design is V&A, Department of Paintings, 20–1874.
43. PRO, Ed. 84/5, 22 February 1866. PRO, Ed. 84/36, Board minute précis, 10 March 1866.
44. *15th Report ... 1867* (1868), p. 197. Cartoon, V&A, Department of Paintings P. 15–1934.
45. Moody told Henry Scott on 7 January 1871 that he had chosen Van Eyck as a subject, and asked for payment of £25 for the design, PRO, Ed. 84/7. Cartoon, V&A Department of Paintings, P.43–1937.
46. *14th Report ... 1866* (1867), p. 185. Cartoon, V&A, Department of Paintings, 1142–1868.
47. The cartoons for Ghiberti and Mantegna (No. 14) were originally painted by Edward Henry Wehnert (1813–36), but condemned. Wehnert's cartoons are both in the Department of Paintings, 1143, 1144–1868.
48. PRO, Ed. 84/7, 26 July 1870. Cartoon, V&A, Department of Paintings, 1181–1875.
49. *15th Report ... 1867* (1868), p. 197. Cartoon, V&A, Department of Paintings, 1707–1869.
50. *13th Report ... 1865* (1866), p. 167. Cartoon, V&A, Department of Paintings, 25–1871.
51. PRO, Ed. 84/5, 21 March 1866; *15th Report ... 1867* (1868), p. 197. Cartoon, V&A, Department of Paintings, 1758–1869.
52. PRO, Ed. 84/7; *18th Report ... 1870* (1871), p. 380. Cartoon, V&A, Department of Paintings, 28–1873.
53. *14th Report ... 1866* (1867), p. 185. Cartoon, V&A, Department of Paintings, 233–1870.
54. *16th Report ... 1868* (1869), p. 281. Cartoon, V&A, Department of Paintings, 1145–1868.
55. Cartoon, V&A, Department of Paintings, 33–1870.
56. *Reader*, 9 September 1865. Cartoon, V&A, Department of Paintings, 25–1873. A cartoon of the same subject by Godfrey Sykes, V&A, Department of Paintings, p.45–1937, was not used.
57. *15th Report ... 1867* (1868), p. 197. Cartoon, V&A, Department of Paintings, 506–1869.
58. Cartoon, V&A, Department of Paintings, 26–1871.
59. PRO, Ed. 84/36, Board minute précis.
60. *19th Report ... 1871* (1872), p. 388.

21. *Bernardino Luini.* Painted by Charles Rossiter and made by Florence H. Cole and Kate Baysford (of the mosaic class), superintended by Samuel Cooper, for Minton, Hollins. The firm's estimate of £120 was agreed by the Office of Works on 5 January 1871.[61]

22. *Hans Holbein.* Painted by William Frederick Yeames and made in English glass mosaic by Salviati. It was finished in 1868.[62]

23. *Maestro Giorgio of Gubbio.* Painted by Solomon Alexander Hart RA and made in English ceramic mosaic by Mary J. Jennings, superintended by Samuel Cooper for Minton, Hollins. The mosaic cost £120 and was finished in 1871.[63]

24. *Lancelot Blondeel.* Painted by F. W. Moody and made in English ceramic mosaic by Florence H. Cole and Mary J. Jennings, superintended by Samuel Cooper for Minton, Hollins.[64]

25. *Michelangelo.* Painted by Godfrey Sykes and made in English ceramic mosaic by Samuel Cooper, superintended by William E. Alldridge for Minton, Hollins. The Board approved Sykes's design on 22 December 1863, but the mosaic was not finished until 1869.[65]

26. *Jean Goujon.* Painted by H. A. Bowler, former student of the School of Art, and made in English ceramic mosaic by Florence H. Cole and Kate Baysford, superintended by Samuel Cooper for Minton, Hollins. It cost £120[66] and was finished in 1871.[67]

27. *Titian.* Painted by George Frederick Watts OM, RA, and made in English ceramic mosaic by Kate Clarke and Mary J. Jennings, superintended by Samuel Cooper for Minton, Hollins. It was finished in 1869.[68]

28. *Bernard Palissy.* Painted by Reuben Townroe and made in English glass mosaic by Jesse Rust. An estimate for £150 for the mosaic was approved in 1864.[69]

VII 29. *Inigo Jones.* Painted by Alfred Morgan, a former student at the School of Art, and made in English ceramic mosaic by W. B. Simpson and Sons. It was placed in position in 1868.[70]

30. *Velásquez.* Painted by Edwin Long RA and made in English ceramic mosaic by Florence H. Cole and Kate Baysford, superintended by Samuel Cooper for Minton, Hollins.[71] The design was received by the Department in 1871.[72]

31. *Grinling Gibbons.* Painted by J. D. Watson and made in English ceramic mosaic by Florence H. Cole and Amelia Gibbon, superintended by Samuel Cooper for Minton, Hollins. It was finished in 1870.[73]

32. *Sir Christopher Wren.* Painted by Eyre Crowe and made by Florence H. Cole and Amelia Gibbon, superintended by Samuel Cooper for Minton, Hollins. It was finished in 1869.[74]

33. *William Hogarth.* Painted by Eyre Crowe and made in English ceramic mosaic by W. B. Simpson.[75]

34. *Sir Joshua Reynolds.* Painted by Henry Wyndham Phillips and made in Italian glass mosaic by Salviati, for £140. It was finished in 1869.[76]

35. *William Mulready.* Painted by Frederick Bacon Barwell and made in English ceramic mosaic by Letitia M. Cole and Samuel Cooper, superintended by William E. Alldridge for Minton, Hollins. The mosaic was placed in position in 1868.[77]

The Valhalla includes many famous artists, but there are also one or two of startling obscurity. Phidias (1) and Apelles (2) were, of course, the pre-eminent sculptor and painter of the Greeks. The rest are European artists of the Middle Ages

61. PRO, Ed. 84/7. Cartoon, V&A, Department of Paintings, P. 44 – 1937.

62. *16th Report ... 1868* (1869), p. 281. Cartoon, V&A, Department of Paintings, 1149 – 1868.

63. PRO, Ed. 84/7. *19th Report ... 1871* (1872), p. 388. Cartoon, V&A, Department of Paintings, 46 – 1874.

64. PRO, Ed. 84/7. Cartoon, V&A, Department of Paintings, 1200 – 1872.

65. It was decided that Sykes was to be paid £12 a week, and that his drawings and sketches were to be the property of the Department. PRO, Ed. 84/36, Board minute précis, 22 December 1863. Cartoon, V&A, Department of Paintings, 1708 – 1869. Completion of mosaic recorded in *17th Report ... 1869* (1870), p. 317.

66. PRO, Ed. 84/7.

67. *19th Report ... 1871* (1872), p. 388.

68. *17th Report ... 1869* (1870), p. 317. Cartoon, V&A, Department of Paintings, 845 – 1870.

69. PRO, Ed. 84/36, Board minute précis, 1 December 1864, *14th Report ... 1866* (1867), p. 185. Cartoon, V&A, Department of Paintings, 1759 – 1869. The Board increased payment from £130 to £150 because of 'additional work'.

70. *16th Report ... 1868* (1869), p. 281. Cartoon, V&A, Department of Paintings, 505 – 1869.

71. Minton's estimated for three mosaics at £120 each on 17 February 1870; they were ordered on 20 January. PRO, Ed. 84/7.

72. *19th Report ... 1871* (1872), p. 388. Cartoon, V&A, Department of Paintings, 27 – 1873.

73. *18th Report ... 1870* (1871), p. 379. Cartoon, V&A, Department of Paintings, 27 – 1871.

74. *17th Report ... 1869* (1870), p. 317. Cartoon, V&A, Department of Paintings, 844 – 1870.

75. *14th Report ... 1866* (1867), p. 185. Cartoon, V&A, Department of Paintings, 1148 – 1868.

76. PRO, Ed. 84/36. Cartoon, V&A, Department of Paintings, 1710 – 1869.

77. *16th Report ... 1868* (1869), p. 281. Cartoon, V&A, Department of Paintings, 1709 – 1869.

and later. Most are painters. Some are sculptors: Nicolo Pisano (3), Ghiberti (10), Donatello (11), Luca della Robbia (13), who specialized in glazed and coloured terracotta sculpture, Michelangelo (25), and the English Grinling Gibbons (31). Jean Goujon (26) was a sixteenth-century French sculptor who worked on the earliest part of the Louvre. There are only three architects, and all, oddly, are English: William of Wykeham (7), who was in fact a patron of architects, not himself an architect, Inigo Jones (24), and Wren (32).

There are also three ceramic artists. Fra Beato Giacomo da Ulma (16) seems almost unknown in art history outside this Valhalla, but is said to have been a Dominican Friar (d. 1517) who painted on glass at Bologna. Better documented are the majolica painter Maestro Giorgio of Gubbio (23), and Bernard Palissy (28), the French potter of the sixteenth century, known for his enamelled earthenware encrusted with modelled reptiles. Three metalworkers might equally well be regarded as sculptors: William Torel (5), who made the bronze effigies of Henry II and Queen Eleanor in Westminster Abbey in the 1290s; Torrigiano (19), the Italian Renaissance sculptor (the man who broke Michelangelo's nose) who made the monument to Henry VII and his Queen in the Henry VII Chapel in Westminster Abbey; and Peter Vischer of Nuremberg (20), who made the bronze monument to St Sebald, in the church of St Sebald in Nuremberg.

Lancelot Blondeel (24), sculptor and painter of Bruges (1496–1561) and Jan van Eyck (8) are the only representatives of Netherlandish art. There are ten Italian painters of the Renaissance; one German, Hans Holbein (22); one Spanish, Velásquez (30); and three Englishmen, Hogarth (33), Reynolds (34), and Mulready (35). The inclusion of Mulready, who had died only a few years previously, among the array of significant artists, must undoubtedly be due to his friendship with Henry Cole, and perhaps also to the part he played in securing the Sheepshanks paintings for South Kensington.

At least two other mosaics were projected. A painting of Dürer by W. H. Fisk was submitted,[78] and it is recorded in a report of the unfinished decorations in 1876 that Holman Hunt had been invited to produce cartoons of Aholiab, or Bezaleel, or both. There would not, however, have been room for both if Fisk's Dürer had been in-

cluded. Before each mosaic was completed the full size cartoon, 104 inches by 34 inches, was exhibited in its place. The *Reader*[79] was unimpressed:

> With few exceptions these portraits do little credit to the English school. As one glances along the wall, and sees the common-place faces, the mean drawing, the crude colour, the total want of power and knowledge, we cannot but feel that by this exhibition, a blot has been exposed in our modern art education.

The paper hoped that the intention of executing the whole series in mosaic 'will not be persevered in'. The scheme went ahead, nonetheless, and the mosaics remained in place until 1949, when they were taken down and stored.

The Lords President

The cloister on the ground floor between the North and South Courts was the site of a second sequence of mosaics – a frieze of portrait heads of the Lords President of the Council, and their immediate predecessors, the Presidents of the Board of Trade. These mosaics have also been taken down and put into storage, and the western part of the cloister has been concealed in the Tapestry Court, although the eastern part is still visible at the north end of the present restaurant.

All the portraits, with the exception of the Marquis of Salisbury were painted by F. W. Barwell. They were as follows:

1. *Charles Edward Poulett-Thomson* (later Lord Sydenham) President of the Board of Trade, 1834. Executed by the South Kensington Museum mosaic class, the head by Letitia M. Cole, for Minton, Hollins and Company. Minton's tender for ten heads in mosaic at £25 each was accepted by the Board on 24 March 1870.[80]
2. *Henry Labouchère* (later Lord Taunton), President of the Board of Trade 1850–2. Made by the South Kensington Museum mosaic class, the head by Letitia M. Cole, for Minton, Hollins in 1869.[81]

78. PRO, Ed. 84/36. Cartoon, V&A, Department of Paintings, 848 – 1870. J. McN. Whistler must also have been approached as a design, pastel on brown paper, related to the South Court scheme, was No. 116 in the Arts Council Exhibition, 'Whistler', 1–24 September 1960. I am grateful to Miss Elizabeth Aslin for drawing this to my attention.

79. *Reader*, 9 September 1865.

80. PRO, Ed. 84/36, Board minute précis. Cartoon, V&A, Department of Paintings, 9 – 1873.

81. Cartoon, V&A, Department of Paintings, 749 – 1870.

64. *Earl Granville, a cartoon by F. B. Barwell for one of the series of mosaic portraits of Lords President of the Council in the South Court. Oil*

3. *Joseph Warner Henley,* President of the Board of Trade 1852–9. Executed by the South Kensington Museum mosaic class, the head by Letitia M. Cole, for Minton, Hollins. In February 1869 Barwell was given permission to exhibit his painting at the Royal Academy.[82]

4. *Edward Cardwell* (later Viscount Cardwell), President of the Board of Trade 1852–3. Executed by the South Kensington Museum mosaic class, the head by Kate Clarke, for Minton, Hollins. The artist received permission for the painting of this portrait also to go to the Academy exhibition in 1869.[83]

5. *Edward, 2nd Baron Stanley of Alderley,* President of the Board of Trade, 1855–8. Executed by the South Kensington Museum mosaic class, the head by Letitia M. Cole, for Minton, Hollins, in 1869.[84]

64 6. *2nd Earl Granville* KG, Lord President of the Council, 1852, 1855, 1859–66. Executed by the South Kensington Museum mosaic class, the head by Letitia M. Cole, for Minton, Hollins, in 1869.[85]

7. *2nd Marquis of Salisbury* KG, Lord President of the Council, 1858–9. Painted by J. Griffiths. Executed by the South Kensington Museum

mosaic class, the head by Letitia M. Cole, for Minton, Hollins.[86]

8. *6th Duke of Marlborough* KG, Lord President of the Council, 1867–8. Painted by F. W. Barwell. Executed by the South Kensington Museum mosaic class, the head by Letitia M. Cole, for Minton, Hollins. In 1869, Maw and Company tendered for this mosaic, and for that of Poulett-Thomson, for £38 the pair.[87]

9. *3rd Duke of Buckingham and Chandos,* Lord President of the Council, 1866–7. Barwell was asked to paint the Duke's portrait after a Board meeting held on 4 February 1868. At the same meeting it was agreed that Barwell should be paid £100 for 'heads', though the number was not specified.[88]

10. *1st Marquis of Ripon* [Earl de Grey] KG, Lord President of the Council, 1868–73.

11. *Henry Bruce* (later Lord Aberdare), Lord President of the Council, 1873–4. Barwell was not asked to paint the portraits of these last two Presidents until May 1875, when he agreed to do them for £20 each.[89] They were completed by February 1876, when the artist sent in his account.

Very many years later there was a plan to incorporate a frieze featuring portrait heads of more recent political chiefs in the major new building designed by Aston Webb. The plan is described in a letter dated 6 June 1904, from Thomas Armstrong, who had formerly been Director of the Art Division and Art Advisor to the Department of Science and Art, addressed to Sir Caspar Purdon Clarke, the Director of the Museum. Armstrong described how Mr Alexander Fisher, 'so well-known for his artistic work in enamel', had, while a National Scholar at the National Art Training School, designed a frieze to incorporate portraits of political chiefs. Suitable profile photographs had been obtained for reference, and Armstrong

82. PRO, Ed. 84/36, Board minute précis, 25 February 1869. Cartoon, V&A, Department of Paintings, 750–1870.

83. PRO, Ed. 84/36, Board minute précis. Cartoon, V&A, Department of Paintings, 751–1870. Neither painting, however, seems to have been accepted.

84. Cartoon, V&A, Department of Paintings, 8–1873.

85. Cartoon, V&A, Department of Paintings, 752–1870.

86. Cartoon, V&A, Department of Paintings, 232–1876.

87. PRO, Ed. 84/7, 5 November 1869. Cartoon, V&A, Department of Paintings, 753–1870.

88. PRO, Ed. 84/36, Board minute précis. Cartoon, V&A, Department of Paintings, 7–1873.

89. PRO, Ed. 84/67, 13 May 1875. Cartoon, V&A, Department of Paintings, 11–1873.

was anxious to proceed, because, 'As times goes on it will be more and more difficult to secure good portraits of the persons, and when I am dead nobody will care anything about the scheme'.

How right Armstrong was: by November the frieze by Fisher had been extracted from storage, and was hung in the new staff dining room. As a result of this display, one presumes that the Museum recoiled from suggesting that Aston Webb might incorporate it in his extension of the buildings.

So, once again, the portraits were banished to a store and only one came to light in 1972; it was identified as a result of finding Armstrong's letter in the Public Record Office.[90]

Opus Criminale

The floor of the west cloister (which must have been under the Sheepshanks Gallery, and was recently covered by linoleum) was laid down in black and white marble fish-scale pattern mosaic – a notably successful experiment which was later used elsewhere in the Museum.

On 13 April 1869, Captain (later Lieutenant-Colonel) E. Du Cane CB of the Royal Engineers called on Henry Cole. He wished to see the various mosaics that had been carried out by the mosaic class, Salviati, and other manufacturers, and he then put a proposal to Cole.[91] He suggested that convicts could so such work, and that perhaps Cole might agree to have some in the Museum. The meeting must have been cordial; Cole, as we know, was always ready to try something new, and Du Cane's proposal was a good social undertaking – what could be better than employing usefully a gang of hapless convicts? The two men parted with a promise by du Cane to put the proposition to the Home Secretary.

Official approval was given[92] and Moody's design for the pavement was sent to Woking prison, where it was handed over to 'Female Convicts'. Du Cane described how they set to work:[93]

This material is found to have many advantages over the ordinary tile pavement, and is being extensively used in the South Kensington Museum, where the name *Opus Criminale* has been applied to it. It is composed of fragments of refuse marble, such as is thrown aside in marble work. The mode of manufacture is as follows:—The Pattern which it is intended to produce, is traced on a board, or on

paper placed on a table, and enclosed within a frame. The fragments of marble are then chipped into pieces of suitable size and shape, and are laid close to one another on the pattern which has been prepared, the various colours of shades of the pattern being followed by marble of corresponding colour or shade. A layer of cement is then placed over the layer of marble, and of course penetrates the interstices between the fragments of marble; and this cement may, if necessary, be strengthened by a tile laid in the middle of its thickness. The mosaic tile, thus formed, is then taken to dry; and when this process is completed, it is returned to the workshop to be faced. Until this part of the process the tile has been laid on its face; but now it is laid on its back as it will appear when in position as a pavement, and the worker, with a piece of York stone, proceeds to rub it down, until the whole surface has been brought to a level and is sufficiently smooth; any inequalities which may have arisen from too great irregularity in the marble fragments are now corrected by removing the imperfect pieces and replacing them. It is found that, after a little instruction, a woman can perform each of these stages of the manufacture at the following rates:—

Setting	.99 ft. per diem
Cementing	9.44 ft. ,, ,,
Facing	1.80 ft. ,, ,,

The preparation of the patterns is of course the work of a foreman or instructor, and the designs may be furnished by an artist.

No doubt Henry Cole found the lady felons much cheaper than Minton or Powell. The Board had agreed that Cole could spend £40 6s 3d.

The Prince Consort Gallery

The gallery that runs down the centre of the South Court, from north to south, above the central arcaded corridor, is named the Prince Consort Gallery after a mosaic portrait of the Prince at the north end. Prince Albert had died in 1861, having seen the realization of at least the earliest parts of his cherished scheme of a complex of Museums at

65

90. PRO, Ed. 84/68, from the Abbot's House, Abbot's Langley, Hertfordshire.

91. Cole diary, 13 April 1869.

92. PRO, Ed. 84/36, Board minute précis, 27 October 1869, 'Inform Capt. Du Cane that it may be proceeded with, at a cost of £40.6s.3d. (Marquess of Ripon).'

93. London International Exhibition, 1871, Official Report on 'Miscellaneous Work done in Convict Prisons, Schools, and Reformatories'.

South Kensington. The portrait was designed by Sykes, and made in English ceramic mosaic by Minton, Hollins; the head itself is the work of Cole's daughter Letitia, and the spandrels are by William E. Alldridge. The design[94] was approved by Queen Victoria when she visited the South Kensington Museum in June 1863, for the first time since the Prince Consort's death. She took a great interest in the South Court and its decoration and asked if the Prince Consort had seen anything of it.[95] Five months later the Crown Princess Frederick paid a visit to the Museum; she told Cole that she was not popular with artists as they found her too critical, and added the sort of thing that Cole loved to hear, and took such pains to

XIV

65. *The Prince Consort's Gallery, c. 1876. Drawing by John Watkins*

record in his diary: 'My father used to say, "When we want Steam we must get Cole"'.[96] The mosaic was not finished until July 1865; nonetheless it was the first completed example of English ceramic (earthenware) mosaic,[97] since it predates all the mosaics in the 'Kensington Valhalla'.

After the enlargement of the South Court, a similar panel was considered for the south end of the Prince Consort's Gallery. Reuben Townroe produced a design for a portrait of Queen Victoria to be a companion piece to that of the Prince. In addition, the spandrels on either side were to contain portraits of the Princes and Princesses. Powell did some work on one of the spandrels, before lack of funds for payment called a halt to the project.[98] It was not subsequently resumed.

The overall decoration of the Prince Consort's Gallery was designed, and partially executed, by Godfrey Sykes, the remainder being painted by the firm of Thomas Kershaw. The area included the ceiling, which had sloping sides and a clerestory. The painted surface was divided into square coffers, 'which are effectively painted with a broad margin of red, and some ornament of a simple order'.[99]

The iron columns of the arcade below the gallery were painted brown, picked out with gold. The painted ceiling below the gallery was undoubtedly part of the general scheme by Godfrey Sykes. It was divided into seven bays corresponding with the form of the Southern Court, each bay forming a square ceiling panel, framed by a gilt moulding, and a broad band of blue with a guilloche. In the centre of each of these square compartments was a medallion in which was painted the royal arms, or the lions of England, or Scotland, or the Irish harp. Painted round this medallion was a representation of bronze scrollwork. The rest of each compartment was ornamented by diapering.[100]

Both floors of this central division are now

94. Cartoon, V&A, Department of Paintings, 47–1876.
95. Cole diary, 30 June 1863.
96. Ibid., 30 November 1863.
97. A report appears in the *Manchester Express*, 11 July 1865, which remarked that 'The work is placed in rather a dark situation.' The mosaic formed part of the collections of the Museum of Construction. See *13th Report . . . 1865* (1866), Appendix D, p. 228.
98. PRO, Ed. 84/67, Memorandum on the decorations to be completed, 1876.
99. *Builder*, 26 November 1864, p. 859.
100. Ibid.

66. *Godfrey Sykes's design for the gallery at the north end of the South Court*

blocked off, and the decoration obliterated. In fact none of the original decoration of the South Court has remained uncovered, except for the enormous semi-circular frescos at the north and south ends on the first floor, and one iron arch, recently exposed.

Lord Leighton's frescos

66 On the north wall of the South Court, above the gallery, are two large semi-circular recesses of 18 feet radius, and since the southward extension of the court in 1869 there have been two matching lunettes above the gallery at the south end. It was intended to decorate these four lunettes, but those at the north-west and south-west have remained blank. On the other hand, the great frescos of the *Industrial Arts as Applied to War* and the *Industrial Arts as Applied to Peace*, both by Lord Leighton, which decorate the north-east and south-east lunettes respectively, can still be seen.

A number of alternative decorative schemes had been explored during the course of several years, before these frescos were arrived at. In the autumn of 1863, before the two lunettes at the south end were made, G. F. Watts was invited to produce a design for a mosaic for one of the two lunettes at the north end. He 'proposed Scenes of Manufacture'.[101] The design took some time. In May 1865 Cole called on Watts, who promised to

have the design ready by 17 June.[102] He managed to complete the sketch before the end of the month, however, and showed it to Cole on 31 May.[103] It was intended that Watts should work on a full-size cartoon, and he asked for students to help him with the task at his house, but the subsequent fate of the cartoon is hazy. He was still asking Cole for student assistance early in 1866,[104] but after that silence falls.

In the meantime, however, in January 1865 the Department of Science and Art announced that a competition would be held for the design of the other space. The subject of the design was to be 'workmanship in any decorative art or manufacture'. The winner would receive £50, with a further £50 for supervising the enlargement of the design by students for execution in mosaic. The runner-up would receive £25.[105] It was to be an open competition, but the Department would also invite three chosen artists to submit designs for £50 each. Henry Stacey Marks was one of the invited artists,[106] and Ford Madox

101. Cole diary, 20 September 1863.
102. Ibid., 19 May 1865.
103. Ibid., 31 May 1865.
104. Ibid., 7 January 1866.
105. Board minute, 21 January 1865, in *12th Report ... 1864* (1865), p. 10.
106. PRO, Ed. 84/36, Board minute précis, 14 May 1865.

67. *Interior of the South Court, eastern portion, from the south,* c. 1876, *showing the copy by F. W. Moody of Raphael's* School of Athens, *proposed for the gallery. Drawing by John Watkins*

Brown was another.[107] The judges were to be Richard Redgrave, Godfrey Sykes, and H. A. Bowler (the Assistant Inspector for Art of the Science and Art Department).[108] Nothing further is known about the competition.

Also during 1865, Frank Moody offered, for £200, to make a copy of the *School of Athens* by Raphael for the lunette at the north-west of the South Court, to be carried out in mosaic.[109] Early in 1868 the resultant design was examined by John Everett Millais, C. W. Cope, and Solomon Hart, who advised against copying it in mosaic.[110]

By this time enthusiasm for mosaic was waning. Cole had met Minton, Hollins and Company the previous December, and they had estimated that Moody's design would cost £2,000 to execute in mosaic.[111] By July 1868 Cole was thinking in terms of frescos instead of mosaics. Watts was approached to design a fresco,[112] and agreed. He never completed it, however. When, as late as December 1873, Redgrave eventually wrote to enquire how the work was progressing, he was told that a design was in hand, 'but the matter has

not grown very far and I do not feel that I have any claims that need embarrass the new administration at South Kensington'.[113] Watts was asked to stop work.[114]

At the same time as the initial approach to Watts had been made in July 1868, Cole had also invited Frederic Leighton to paint a fresco. Like Watts, he had been offered £1,000, but unlike Watts, his work was ultimately to come to fruition. Leighton (1830–96) was a painter with an unusually wide training which had taken him all over Europe. He became known in England with his painting *Cimabue's Madonna Carried in Procession through the Streets of Florence,* which was exhibited in the Academy in 1855 and bought by the Queen. His

107. PRO, Ed. 84/36, Board minute précis, 16 February 1866.
108. Ibid., Board minute précis, 29 June 1865.
109. Ibid., Board minute precis, 30 November 1865.
110. Cole diary, 7 March 1868.
111. Ibid., 2 December 1867.
112. Ibid., 14 July 1868.
113. PRO, Ed. 84/67, Watts to Redgrave, 10 December 1873.
114. PRO, Ed. 84/36, Board minute précis, 29 January 1874.

paintings include many other scenes of cultural history, so he was obviously a good choice for South Kensington, especially as he had just completed a large fresco in Lyndhurst church. He was to become President of the Royal Academy in 1878 (receiving the usual knighthood) and was elevated to the peerage the day before he died.

In 1871, before it had been realized that Watts would never complete his work, an attempt had been made to commission decoration for a third lunette. F. R. Pickersgill RA was asked to produce a design for £1,000 and to superintend its enlargement by students for £4 a day.[115] Pickersgill VIII completed his design,[116] for *The Industrial Arts in Time of Peace*, for which he received £500,[117] and which was exhibited in the South Court. Shortage of money, however, caused the Board to defer any decision about translating the design into mosaic.[118] Presumably they subsequently decided against it.

Leighton, meanwhile, was believed to have been proceeding with his first fresco design since 1868. On 7 February 1870, however, Cole learned from the apologetic artist that nothing had been done. Leighton had been preoccupied with other urgent work, and had then suffered an attack of rheumatism. He now found that the work on the fresco, X *Industrial Arts as Applied to War*, 'will be nearly *double* what my first conjecture had been, and the design will call for some 30 or 40 figures – a lengthy undertaking as you see'.[119] Eight months later, in reply to an enquiry from Redgrave, the painter was even less optimistic. 'In that large court the lunette in question looks so moderate in its dimensions that I have measured it several times before I could believe how large it is ... [it] will require at least forty – more like fifty figures ...'[120] He eventually sent his design to Cole on 15 December.[121]

Leighton was against the use of student helpers. 'I cannot possibly entertain the idea, infinite as would be the saving of trouble, of painting my subject on a small scale to be enlarged by students',[122] he wrote on one occasion. Later he seemed to weaken to some extent: 'although my cartoon may be eventually enlarged and even roughly prepared by the students under my supervision, it shall in the end be painted by no hand but mine'.[123] This promise was later questioned.

After the approval of the design, Leighton embarked on the cartoon. The following July he

informed Cole that it was almost finished, but 'it would to my way of thinking be very advantageous for the work to be laid aside for some time that I may give the completing touches with a fresher eye and a rested mind'.[124] Could he leave the completion of the work until his return from his autumn trip to Italy? The cartoon would then be ready in the last week of November. Cole agreed, but it was not until January of 1872 that he was able to show the completed cartoon to the Committee of Council. In reply to an enquiry, Leighton estimated that the painting of the fresco would take him a year and that he would therefore charge £2,000.[125] During 1872 the cartoon was exhibited at the Vienna Exhibition.

Two months later Leighton was invited to produce a second design, which he agreed to do, firmly stating that it would take him a year.[126] This was to be the *Industrial Arts as Applied to Peace* XI which now occupies the south-eastern lunette of the South Court.[127] In fact it took him eighteen months. He sent two sketches of the second design to South Kensington in September 1873, after which he left for the Continent at once.[128]

Although the subject of painting the frescos was discussed during the Museum authorities' consideration of the 1874–5 estimates in November 1873, it must have been decided to shelve the proposals for a year, since the matter was not reopened until November 1875. After negotiation with the artist, it was agreed, 'F. Leighton to carry out, with the aid of students, his "War Cartoon" in three years, being paid £3,000 for the work.'[129] In May 1876, when Leighton

115. PRO, Ed. 84/36, Board minute précis, 23 June 1871.
116. Cartoon, V&A, Department of Paintings, 127 – 1885. See also *Decorations*, p. 9.
117. PRO, Works, 17/21/1, Correspondence November and December 1872.
118. PRO, Ed. 84/36, Board minute précis, 1 May 1875.
119. V&A, Leighton fresco file.
120. Cole correspondence, Leighton to Redgrave, 14 October 1870.
121. Cole diary. Sketch, V&A, Department of Paintings, 992 – 1873. See also Richard Ormond, *Leighton's Frescoes*, 1975, and Leonée and Richard Ormond, *Lord Leighton*, 1975.
122. Cole correspondence.
123. V&A, Leighton fresco file, May 1871.
124. Ibid., 27 July 1871.
125. Ibid., 29 January 1872.
126. Ibid., March 1872.
127. In the V&A, Department of Paintings, are the sketch, 993 – 1873, and the enlarged cartoon, 279 – 1907.
128. V&A, Leighton fresco file, 8 September 1873.
129. PRO, Ed. 84/36, Board minute précis, 22 November 1875.

returned from abroad, he learned that he had authority to proceed. It was intended that the art students should enlarge the cartoon, but they do not seem to have begun until after 31 October 1876, when Leighton was agitating for them to start work. There was then a further year's delay. The lunette was replastered and made ready for Leighton to paint in Parry's spirit fresco, but Gambier Parry himself, the inventor of the medium, advised the Museum authorities that 'a year should be allowed to elapse before attempts were made to paint on to the newly-applied plaster'.[130] In the summer of 1878 Leighton began work, and, on 5 February 1880, he triumphantly told Philip Cunliffe Owen, then the Director, 'I have this day finished my tasks on your walls. Mr. Ward will now take the border in hand after which the work will be ripe for public gaze.'[131]

James Ward, who subsequently painted a brown border with gold moulding round the picture, was a student who in future years was to play a considerable part in the history of both frescos. When his National Scholarship came to an end in 1876, Ward was engaged as an assistant by E. J. Poynter, at that time the Director for Art, and principal of the National Art Training Schools, who was then decorating the Museum's Lecture Theatre. During 1878 this work came to an end, and Ward was introduced by Poynter to Leighton, with whom he worked between that year and 1887. Although Leighton had said some years earlier that no hand but his own would touch the fresco, Ward was entrusted with a considerable amount of the work, except in the more significant areas of heads, hands, and feet. Ward describes Leighton's working method:

The finished designs . . . were made by Sir Frederick [sic] about a little less than one-third of the full size. They were painted in a brown monochrome tint and finished in a careful manner. Tracings of these designs were made in outline on tracing-cloth, on these tracings lines were ruled forming squares. A large canvas of full size was then prepared, and on this corresponding squares were drawn of a proportionate size larger than those on the smaller original designs. The design was then 'squared off' in outline on to a larger canvas. After the cartoon was enlarged on this canvas Sir Frederick painted over the principal figures in monochrome in light and shade, in order to secure an outline that would satisfy himself. The next thing to be done was the tracing off on tracing-cloth the whole of the en-

larged work; this accomplished, the traced design was pricked in holes with a needle point all along the outlines, and was transferred to the wall surface by means of striking the pricked tracing with a muslin bag filled with powdered charcoal. A transfer of the design was thus left on the wall, but owing to the nature of the wall surface . . . the charcoal outline could not be successfully fixed. All kinds of fixatives were tried, but without success, and the only effective proceeding was to go over the outlines with a black-chalk crayon.[132]

The day after he received Leighton's letter informing him that his work on the fresco was complete, Cunliffe Owen asked Sir Francis Sandford, Secretary of the Department of Science and Art, to send an official letter to the artist in which he would say that he had learned

. . . with much satisfaction that you have completed the fresco 'The Arts of War', to which you have given up so much of your valuable time. It is particularly satisfying that the decoration of the South Kensington Museum has been enriched in such a remarkable manner by this latest example of your Art, and I am glad to take this opportunity of expressing my thanks for the remarkable manner in which you have executed the important work upon which you have bestowed with such marked success, so much labour and talent.[133]

Cunliffe Owen hoped that Queen Victoria would visit the Museum to inspect this triumph of decoration, but as the border was incomplete, he preferred to wait until all the work was finished before he raised the subject of a royal visit with court officials. In April 1880 Leighton was willingly given permission for the cartoon of 'War' to be sent to the Melbourne Exhibition.

In general, the fresco was well received when it was first shown to the public. The *Builder*[134] considered that

. . . the variety of types of men, young and old, effeminate and brawny, of expressions ingenious and crafty, of attitudes hasty and leisurely, is a

130. V&A, Leighton fresco file, 9 January 1878, letter from H. B. Stanford to the Treasury.

131. Ibid.

132. James Ward, 'Lord Leighton, P.R.A., some reminiscences and an explanation of the method in which the South Kensington frescoes were painted', in *Magazine of Art*, xix (1896), pp. 373 ff.

133. V&A, Leighton fresco file, letter to Poynter, undated, but probably 19 April 1880.

134. *Builder*, 28 February 1880, p. 242.

source of pleasure without fatigue. The dignity of the composition is nowhere marred by rude movements, and a balance of light and shade is maintained with valuable effect ... The colouring is brilliant and voluptuous ... There can be little difference of opinion that the work is, perhaps, the most important hitherto executed by Sir F. Leighton.

The *Architect*[135] enthused over the 'very flower of Florentine youth', long and supple of limb, though these young men with 'poetic faces' and 'luxuriant hair' were thought to be more fitted to jousting than to war. J. Beavington Atkinson, writing in the *Art Journal*,[136] praised 'this eclectic and scholarly product. The picture is more than a studied compromise of careful compilation; it is a living creation', reverting, it was considered, to the style of the Cimabue procession painting twenty-five years earlier. *Building News*[137] criticized the architectural details and thought that Leighton should have called upon an architect experienced in Italian gothic for assistance.

The *Builder*[138] regretted that no place could be found from which to view the work 'as a whole'. This is perfectly true. At no time has anyone been able to look at this fresco from an adequate vantage point. The gallery in front of it is narrow, so that it is impossible to step back far enough from the painting to view it properly. When it was first completed it was possible to see it, albeit distantly, from the floor of the South Court, or even the opposite gallery. Today, however, following the reconstruction of the court in 1950, the fresco has been entirely boxed in, and all daylight excluded. So gloomy is the gallery that large numbers of visitors must walk by the painting without realizing what it is.

Upon the completion of the fresco at the north end of the court, the Department of Science and Art turned its collective eyes to the blank wall at the southern end. The design for *Industrial Arts as Applied to Peace* was already at South Kensington, and it was known that Leighton was prepared to paint it. After some preliminary skirmishing with the Treasury over financing the project, the south-eastern lunette was replastered, and, in due course, Leighton began to paint, receiving £3,000 as before. He did not finish until August 1886, when a private view was held for Members of Parliament and others.

This fresco attracted less critical appraisal than

68

68. *Detail of the fresco* The Industrial Arts as applied to Peace *by Frederic, Lord Leighton*

had its earlier companion piece, although before its completion the *Art Annual* published a lengthy description, underestimating by at least two years the time Leighton would take to finish his task. Like the war painting, the peace painting was very hard to see, even though the gallery was twice as wide as the one at the north end. In fact, explained the *Art Annual*, 'it is impossible for any but very short-sighted people to make use of them for purposes of inspection. To those with good eyes, the one fresco is best studied from the gallery of the other.'[139] This cannot now be done, until such time as the casing of the present restaurant is

135. *Architect*, 13 March 1880, pp. 179–180.
136. *Art Journal*, vol. xix (1880), pp. 179, 180.
137. *Building News*, 19 March 1880, p. 353.
138. *Builder*, 28 February 1880, p. 242.
139. *Art Annual*, 1884, p. 19.

69. *(above) Sketch for a painting panel of the ceiling of the northern gallery of the South Court, by Godfrey Sykes*

70. *(right) The ceiling of the northern gallery of the South Court*

removed. Cole had been alive to this problem, and, shortly after his retirement in 1873 he had raised the possibility of building a gallery across the centre of the court, from which both frescos could be viewed. This suggestion was not taken up, however.

Even though the frescos were hard to see, further efforts were made to beautify their setting. The soffits of the arches over the lunettes at the northern end of the court had been ornamented by Godfrey Sykes before his death in 1866. A number of years later Frank Moody and his assistants executed similar painted panels at the southern end. This undertaking was an indirect cause of Moody's eventual resignation from the Museum. By 7 January 1880 he had received £409 13s 1d out of a total vote of £665. He then presented an account for £109 8s 4d for three panels over the south-western lunette. This left four panels of the south-eastern lunette, which would take up the remaining £145 18s 7d. The Lord President approved continuation of the work, but the Office of Works stopped it. Early in 1882, Moody, in atrocious and at times illegible handwriting, sent a furious letter to Donnelly, Assistant Secretary to the Department, complaining of unfair treatment.[140]

An extract from this letter was sent to the

140. PRO, Ed. 84/62, 24 January 1882.

71. *(right) Painted decoration by F. W. Moody in the soffit of an arch at the southern end of the South Court (now Room 109)*

72. *(below) Painted decoration by W. E. F. Britten in the soffit of an arch at the southern end of the South Court (now Room 109)*

72

Treasury on 4 February 1882, with the comment that it seemed 'a hard case especially considering Mr. Moody's state of health'. Moody was by then suffering from pronounced mental illness. The Treasury remained unmoved, however, and at the end of 1882 the Museum administration decided to ask Moody to resign. The decoration was later completed by W. E. F. Britten, on the recommendation of Leighton.

The later history of Leighton's frescos is one of constant anxiety about their state of preservation. The medium used, Gambier Parry's spirit fresco, was experimental. Parry had evolved it in an attempt to recreate 'the classical "encaustic"'.[141] In 1883 he was challenged by a William Wallace, who wrote to the *Athenaeum*,[142] taking exception to the printed label in the Museum which claimed

that Gambier Parry had invented the medium used in Leighton's fresco. Wallace suggested that the process was identical with that of 'peinture encaustique' as described in Paillot de Montébert's *Traité Complet de la Peinture*, published in 1829. Parry energetically denied all knowledge of the book, and described his lengthy search for the 'secrets of the old encaustic', during which he had almost burned down his home, Highnam Court, Gloucestershire, 'through inadvertence of the inflammability of the materials'. Leighton had seen him using the medium for his own wall paintings in Highnam church, and pleased with the 'luminous effect', had subsequently used it

141. *Athenaeum*, 17 November 1883.
142. Ibid., 27 October 1883.

himself in Lyndhurst church, and later at South Kensington.[143]

The medium, however, was to prove unstable. The second fresco, *Industrial Arts as Applied to Peace*, gave the most trouble. Ten years after its completion (by which time Leighton had died) it seemed 'in places to be undergoing changes through the gum or resinous matter used – the medium having decayed so that the colour is loose and is disturbed by slight friction'.[144] In November 1896, James Ward, Leighton's former assistant, was called in. He repainted a small area, adding further wax to the medium. In August the following year he inspected the result with Professor Tilden, an expert, and found that 'the colours had stood perfectly'.[145] He then repainted further areas of the fresco, and afterwards pronounced both frescos 'in an excellent condition'. Meanwhile A. B. Skinner, who was at that time Keeper of the Art Collection, and who later rose to become Director, had been trying various methods of dusting the surface. He had experimented unsuccessfully with a 'blowing machine', but had managed to remove an amount of surface dust with a pair of ordinary bellows.[146]

In October 1901, however, it was pointed out to the Director that both paintings were excessively dirty, and that the surface of the Peace fresco became tacky when the atmosphere was warm and moist. Thomas Armstrong, the recently retired Art Adviser at the Department of Science and Art, inspected the frescos on 13 November, and reported that the War fresco should be cleaned, using a specially made blowing machine. The Peace fresco, however, was in a much less satisfactory condition. There were considerable portions where the colour had never quite dried, and there were others 'in which it is so much desiccated as to have no bond with the ground so that it can be removed by a light touch of the finger'.[147] Armstrong could make no positive suggestions for treatment. He concluded his report with a reference to a matter which he stated was outside his brief, namely the borders of the paintings, which for the sake of economy had been painted using Dutch metal instead of gold leaf, and which were now 'disgustingly sordid and quite unworthy of the Museum'.

Purdon Clarke, the Director, agreed that the shabby borders had 'repeatedly excited comment from visitors' and suggested that the Office of Works should do something to improve them.

The next person to examine the frescos was Professor Church, another expert. He reported on 16 September 1902, warning that they should on no account be touched by the staff with feather dusters, and in December he cleaned the War fresco, which took him nineteen days. The following May he spent eighteen days on the Peace fresco. The War fresco was cleaned first with bellows and a feather brush, and then with a very weak solvent, consisting of twenty drops of strong *liquor ammoniae* to a gallon of distilled water, which removed the sooty and tarry matter that was clinging to the surface.[148] Professor Church also noticed that some of the grains of sand on the surface of the plaster of the War fresco, which was much rougher than that of the Peace fresco, had fallen off, taking the paint with them. The surface thus appeared speckled with tiny spots of white, but these could easily be touched up.[149]

Predictably, Professor Church found the Peace fresco more problematical. There were two problems in addition to dirt.[150] In some places the paint surface was powdery, although 'a fine spray of diluted spirit medium will suffice to bind the pigment to the ground'. The second problem was 'glossy patches and streaks over a large part of the surface which should be uniformly *mat*'. When he came to work on the fresco on 4 May 1903, Church concluded that the glossy patches were caused by

> ... a singular change, only recently recognised, which linseed oil occasionally undergoes. Linseed oil is present in the Spirit-Fresco medium, being a constituent of the copal varnish which is its chief ingredient. By oxidation this linseed oil forms a solid insoluble compound which, under ordinary circumstances, does not suffer further change. Under conditions not yet ascertained this compound is transformed into an adhesive, acid compound actually soluble in water.[151]

143. Ibid., 17 November 1883.
144. V&A, Leighton fresco file, minute 23 June 1896.
145. Ibid., 11 August 1879.
146. Ibid., 13 August 1879.
147. Ibid.
148. Ibid., 24 January 1903.
149. Ibid., 16 September 1902.
150. Ibid.
151. Ibid., 17 June 1903.

Professor Church cleaned the painting, first with a Fletcher Foot-Blower, then with distilled water containing *liquor ammoniae* as before. This removed the surface gloss from the offending areas. He proposed to examine the fresco again in a few weeks, to see whether the shine reappeared. Meanwhile he suggested that James Ward should be invited to 'complete the restoration of this important work of art'. He concluded his report with an adverse comment about the 'deplorable and squalid condition' of the borders.

Purely by coincidence, James Ward himself, now headmaster of the Art School at Macclesfield, wrote to the Museum only two days after Professor Church had written his report, calling attention to the state of the fresco and offering to do what he could to restore it,

> . . . as I am the only person who knows exactly how and in what methods the frescoes at South Kensington were painted . . . I may be permitted to say here that Lord Leighton had the utmost confidence in me, and I know positively, if he were alive he would allow no one to touch the Frescoes but myself. I painted by far the greater part of these works, Lord Leighton finished off the principal figures, but trusted me with the underpainting, and with the whole of the painting of the Architectural parts, and other accessories. I also worked by the side of Lord Leighton, and saw every touch which he put on the walls.[152]

Ward began work on the restoration of the Peace fresco on 25 July 1904, and had finished by 24 August. He then felt that 'the whole fresco is at present in a firm and sound condition'.[153]

Ward then put forward, for the first time, a new theory as to why the Peace fresco was in less good condition than the War painting. It was, he suggested, because the Peace painting had been executed on an outside wall. By now the Cast Court had been built to the south of the South Court, but at a slight angle, so that there was a narrow space between them. Ward suggested that this space should be roofed in, to prevent the cold and damp on the outside of the wall causing condensation on the inside.

Nothing was done about roofing in the space

between the two walls, however, and in March 1910 Ward was back in the Museum, inspecting the surface of the Peace fresco, which showed shiny patches again. He suggested this time that the damage was being caused by heat from the sun on the outside of the wall.[154] He undertook more restoration work between 2 August and 19 August, when a further idea occurred to him. There was, he stated in his report,[155]

> . . . another, and I think more probable cause for the tendency of the 'Arts of Peace' to become dirty more rapidly than the other fresco, and that is on account of its particularly smooth surface, in comparison with the rough surface of the 'Arts of War' . . . This is the lesson of experience, which was not foreseen by Lord Leighton, as he had the wall of the 'Arts of Peace' fresco made smooth purposely, for he said that the wall of the 'Arts of War' was so rough that it was like 'painting on a gravel walk'.

It began to seem to the Museum authorities that the fresco would be for ever causing trouble – blistering, powdering, being scratched by the umbrellas of careless visitors, or even, it was thought, by 'deliberate mischief'; and in 1913 Basil Long suspected that it was once again being cleaned with feather dusters. When there was a likelihood of damage by bombing in 1918, the question of protecting both the frescos was raised. However, by the time a decision was reached – the Office of Works had no money for sandbags and suggested bags of sawdust instead, the ideal quality canvas for screens could not be found, and so on – war had ended.

The question of cleaning of the frescos was again raised in 1923, while James Ward was visiting a daughter in Southern Rhodesia. He wrote from there to say that he would help on his return to England, but he died in Africa at the beginning of 1924. Since then the paintings have been under the direct care of the Ministry of Works, later the Department of the Environment.

---

152. Ibid., 19 June 1903.
153. Ibid., 24 August 1904.
154. Ibid., 14 March 1910.
155. Ibid., 22 August 1910.

74. *Design by Richard Redgrave, RA, for the decoration of the National Competition Gallery. Watercolour*

CHAPTER VI

Other early work by Fowke, and further decoration

To the east of the South Court and facing the Sheepshanks Gallery on the west side was a double-storey building that formed the southern part of the eastern range of galleries. The ground floor, which opened into the South Court in the form of a cloister (now largely concealed in the kitchens of the Museum restaurant), was intended as courts to house the Indian, Chinese, and Japanese collections. The construction of these courts was finished by 1862. On the floor above the cloisters Fowke completed a long gallery with a glass roof, divided down its length by an arcade, which was intended for the reception and marking of the work of art students at the various schools throughout the country. On 15 August 1864, George Smith agreed to undertake the building for £8,105. The gallery was opened in 1865. At first it was reached only from the north, by way of the long gallery of the National Gallery, or from the west, by way of the narrow gallery between the North and South Courts.

When the South Court was extended after the removal of the iron building, the Oriental Courts and the gallery above them were also extended southwards, and access from the south was provided. This access was from the East Staircase, which was immediately to the south of it. Fowke had prepared designs for this staircase before 1864, when the specification was drawn up.[1] The work of which it formed part included the extension of the Oriental Courts and National Competition Gallery, and also a further new building to the south of the staircase – the plain, gaunt, Secretarial Wing, which is described later in this chapter.

A second staircase designed by Fowke that survives from this period is the even more splendid North Staircase. On 18 October 1864 Cole was informed that the final drawings for the staircase would soon be finished, so that quantities could

be estimated, and George Smith's firm undertook work to the value of £730 on the staircase at the end of 1864.[2]

Both staircases were elaborately decorated, as were the Oriental Galleries and the National Competition Gallery.

Decoration of the Indian, Chinese, and Japanese Courts

The general scheme of decoration of the Oriental Courts, which included painted walls and ceilings and tiled floors, was given, in 1863, to Owen Jones.[3] Jones (1809–76) was trained as an architect but became celebrated as a decorator; he provided the colour scheme for the interior of the Great Exhibition building, and designed architectural installations for the Crystal Palace when it was re-created at Sydenham. He was respected even more as a theoretician of ornament than as a practising decorator: his *Grammar of Ornament* (1856), illustrated with lush chromolithographs, became a standard work.

In September 1863 Jones was paid £179 7s for various designs,[4] presumably for the Indian Court, since he received £26 5s a year later[5] for supervising the decoration of that court. In May 1864 the Board agreed to pay him £150 for designs for both the Chinese and Japanese Courts.[6]

Various other sums are recorded – for instance the firm of Thomas Kershaw estimated £485 for painting Jones's design for the Japanese Court.[7]

XII

XIII

---

1. In the possession of Mr Ben Weinreb, March 1974.
2. PRO, Ed. 84/72, 18 October 1864; PRO, Ed. 84/4, 29 December 1864.
3. Jones was asked to suggest a design in April. PRO, Ed. 84/35, Board minute précis, 25 April 1863. See J. Physick and M. Darby, *Marble Halls*, 1973, p. 205.
4. PRO, Ed. 84/35, Board minute précis, 21 September 1863.
5. Ibid., 14 May 1864.
6. PRO, Ed. 84/36, Board minute précis, 31 May 1864.
7. PRO, Ed. 84/67, 12 May 1864; PRO, Ed. 84/4.

73. *(left) Cartoon by Reuben Townroe for the mosaic portrait of Owen Jones, for the Oriental Courts*

The *Builder* described the decorations of the Indian Court:

> The whole is treated on the non-naturalistic, non-imitative, or conventional principle; but, still, in one of the ceilings especially, there is a right and perfect bringing of 'realities to mind'. Mr. Jones has taken great pains with this work, having made a large number of full-size drawings. He is now preparing for the work of the court adjoining, which will be devoted to Chinese and Japanese art, and will be decorated in the Chinese manner.[8]

The *Art Journal*[9] gave further details:

> On entering the Court, the walls right and left present two large plain panels, flatted in Spanish Brown, over, probably, a plain paper pattern, which shows through the paint ... Above these spaces runs a broad florid border in gilt on a blue ground, above which is an upper panel of a buff colour, with a flower in a fleur-de-lis lozenge. The arches are arabesqued in gilt, also on a blue ground, and round them is a broad bordering arabesqued in vermilion on a green ground, the sides of the columns where spaces occur being buff and brown, corresponding with the panels, with a green figured border. The principal bordering which divides the panels is continued round the columns. The most elaborate and difficult part of the ornamentation has been the painting of the centre compartment of the ceiling, the white ground of which is entirely filled by a rose pattern, springing from a centre-piece, the whole encompassed by a design of flowers and leaves ...

The tile pavement was executed by Minton, Hollins. Besides the painting of Owen Jones, the windows to the cloister were filled with plaster tracery in a Moorish style, with stained glass, designed by the architect J. W. Wild. The glass itself was made by Powell and Sons, and the general intention of Wild's decoration was to simulate the windows of a mosque. He received £10 for the first window, and was asked to undertake the remainder for £11 in October 1866.[10]

For an unexplained reason, no payment for the

8. *Builder*, 26 November 1864, p. 857.
9. September, 1864, p. 283.
10. PRO, Ed. 84/54, Board minute copy; 23 March 1865, and 10 October 1866. Design, Print Room, E.3705–1938

work was made to Wild for eleven years. In July 1875, he wrote to the Museum stating that he would appreciate the payment of £11.[11] There appeared to be no funds available in the current works estimates, so it was decided, almost two years later, to make the payment out of Museum funds.[12]

73 After the death of Owen Jones, a body of admirers subscribed towards a memorial which, it was hoped, would be placed in the Museum. On 2 December 1874, the Duke of Richmond and Gordon accepted a mosaic portrait, designed by Reuben Townroe, which was placed on the south wall of the east cloister which Jones had decorated.[13] This was subsequently removed, and has now disappeared. None of the original decoration of the Oriental Galleries survives.

Decoration of the National Competition Gallery

74 Richard Redgrave RA was put in charge of the decoration of the National Competition Gallery.[14] The *Builder*[15] described the gallery and the proposed decoration:

> The entire area ... is divided into squares, by the piers which carry the roof and ceiling; and each square compartment has a large flat light in the ceiling. The pilasters, or projections from the piers ... carry impost-mouldings and semicircular arches, as well as cantilevers to the transverse beams which form the compartments of the ceilings; and the arches and piers are repeated to recesses along the walls. Space in the *plafond* between the cantilevers is arranged for ventilation. The tympana of the arches on the wall are to be divided into radiating panels, to contain subjects painted or produced in porcelain. A specimen treatment is now 'offered up'. The chromatic treatment is, in great part, of white and gold, but imitations of marbles are largely used for the piers and walls.

Further details can be learned from Thomas Kershaw's estimate, for £188, for painting part of the Competition Gallery.[16]

> The Whole of the Ceiling and Upper portions of walls prepare and paint in oil best flatted white. Small panels tinted and marbled. All the enrichments and other members to be gilded with best leaf gold.
> The Pilars & Pilasters to be coloured in distemper plain tints to match the General colour of the ones marbled.

> The Walls & Entrance Door framings to colour in distemper stone & deep green tint.
> Skirting coloured maroon tint the portions of the wall that are boarded to be papered with strong lining paper previous to being coloured.

Redgrave planned to commission artists to procure designs to decorate the various alcoves and lunettes, and Cole and Redgrave began the work of commissioning during 1865, after part of the gallery was opened. Members of the Royal Academy were not shy of visiting Cole and proffering their services. Cole records that during November 1867 W. F. Yeames called on him and offered to paint a lunette for 60 guineas, as he 'wished to connect himself with [our] decoration'.[17] The Duke of Marlborough, then Lord President, agreed to Yeames's suggestion, although the fee was only to be 50 guineas.[18] This did not deter Yeames, though, who, in less than three weeks was back in Cole's office with his preliminary sketch.[19]

The prompt action by Yeames must have given Cole an impetus to get things moving, because three days later, on 26 December, the Board resolved to ask for designs from H. Stacey Marks, A. E. Calderon, Frederic Leighton, Edward Poynter, G. F. Watts, Frank W. Moody, J. D. Watson, and A. Morgan, who was a former Art Student. Others eventually got drawn in, although some – Watts, for instance – backed out of the scheme. In March 1868 there was a meeting between Cole and some of the artists, among whom were Calderon, Eyre Crowe, Marks, G. D. Leslie, and Yeames, to settle the general theme which the paintings were to illustrate,[20] and in May they produced designs for Cole's inspection.[21]

---

11. Ibid., 2 July 1875.

12. PRO, Ed. 84/36, Board minute précis, 10 April 1877. Since 1870 the Office of Works had been responsible for building operations at South Kensington.

13. PRO, Ed. 84/36, Board minute précis, 2 December 1874. This followed the general form and size of the mosaics in the South Court, Cartoon, V&A, Department of Paintings, 14–1934.

14. 'Richard Redgrave to superintend experiment of National Art Students decorating the National Competition Rooms.' PRO, Ed. 84/35, Board minute précis, 24 March 1863.

15. *Builder*, 26 November 1864, p. 858.

16. PRO, Ed. 84/67, 20 January 1866; recommended on 17 January by E. R. Festing.

17. Cole diary, 25 November 1867.

18. PRO, Ed. 84/36, Board minute précis, 5 November 1867.

19. Cole diary, 23 December 1863.

20. Ibid., 12 March 1868.

21. Ibid., 12 May 1868.

75. *(above left)* Landscape Painting, *a lunette formerly in the National Competition Gallery, by G. D. Leslie*

76. *(above right)* Modelling from Life, *a lunette formerly in the National Competition Gallery, by Eyre Crowe; The model is Sapper Nellis*

77. *(left)* Model Drawing, *a design for the decoration of a lunette in the National Competition Gallery, by Godfrey Sykes*

The finished project illustrated drawing, painting, and modelling, with various decorative panels of children. In all, there were eighteen canvases, several of which were in position during 1869:[22]

1. *Drawing from Still Life*. Designed and painted by D. W. Wynfield.

2. *Composition of Children*. Designed and painted by A. Morgan.

75 3. *Landscape Painting*. Designed and painted by G. D. Leslie.

4. *Composition of Children*. Designed and painted by Frank W. Moody, assisted by W. Wise, a former Art Student employed in Moody's studio in the Museum.

5. *Skeleton Drawing*. Designed and painted by H. Stacey Marks.

6. *Composition of Children*. Designed and painted by an Art Student, Beattie.

7. *Flower Painting*. Designed and painted by F. B. Barwell.

8. *Composition of Children*. Designed and painted by W. Morrison.

9. *Modelling from Life*. Designed and painted by   76
Eyre Crowe. Sapper Nellis, one of the Royal Engineer detachment, acted as model.

10. *Drawing from Life*. Designed and painted by W. F. Yeames.

11. *Composition of Children*. Designed and painted by Frank W. Moody.

22. *17th Report . . . 1869* (1870).
23. Cole diary, 22 February 1869, 4 July 1872.

84

12. *Sketching from Nature.* Designed and painted by A. Morgan.

13. *Composition of Children.* Designed by Richard Redgrave and painted by R. C. Puckett.

77 14. *Model Drawing.* Designed by Godfrey Sykes, and painted by J. Emms.

78 15. *Composition of Children.* Designed and painted by A. Morgan.

16. *Freehand Drawing* – Giotto's Round O. Designed by Richard Redgrave (not completed by 1874).

17. *Composition of Children.* Designed by Frank W. Moody and painted by him assisted by W. Wise and O. Gibbons.

18. *Study of Anatomy.* Designed and painted by Frank W. Moody.

After the gallery was extended southwards in 1869, following the removal of the Boilers, large, elongated painted canvases were positioned at this end. Val Prinsep called on Cole and offered to decorate one of these panels (Henry Cole later *79* sat for one of the figures),[23] and F. R. Pickersgill *80*

78. Agriculture, *a design for the decoration of a lunette in the National Competition Gallery, by Alfred Morgan*

79. *(below)* Distribution of Art Prizes, *a painting formerly in the National Competition Gallery, by F. R. Pickersgill*

80. *(bottom)* Distribution of Art Prizes, *a painting formerly in the National Competition Gallery, by Val Prinsep. On the left, the soldier is Sapper Nellis; in the centre is Lord Leighton with Richard Burchett, Headmaster of the Art Schools on his left; Henry Cole is the third figure from the right.*

81. Distribution of Art Prizes *(detail of ill. 80)*

82. *The National Competition Gallery, from the north, c. 1876. Drawing by John Watkins*

81 was commissioned to paint the other; for this they were each to be paid 100 guineas.[24]

The southern extension of the gallery necessitated a certain amount of redecoration, which *82* was undertaken by Kershaw in 1869 for £87.[25]

The completion of the ornamentation dragged on into the mid-1870s, being carried out by Frank Moody and his assistants, H. W. Forster (who received a commission in December 1870 to paint twenty-five roundels for £50)[26] and a National Scholar named Archer (who painted eleven spandrels, for which the Board approved a fee).[27] In 1875 Moody was approached to paint two still undecorated spandrels for £100,[28] which was approved on 12 September 1875.[29] Work was still incomplete in 1876, when Moody produced an estimate for finishing it:

	£
A lunette for which Mr. Redgrave made a design enlarged by Mr. Wise, and never put up, say	50
4 spandrels at North End	210
Canvasses and fixing	10
Mr. Moody has made a design for two of these which has been approved	
36 amorini in the roundels of the spandrels of central arches at £3 each	108
Modelling, moulding and casting rosettes accidentally forgotten	4
	£382

Note: *Mr. Redgrave's design, and Mr. Moody's are in the Library.*[30]

Later development in the National Competition Gallery

In 1909 the wood and glass roof of the gallery, which by then housed the Ionides Collection, the Jones Collection, and the Watercolours, was found to be in need of complete renewal. The work was undertaken in the financial year 1909–10.[31] Also in 1910 the spaces between the central piers of the arcade were filled in to provide more wall space for exhibition purposes,[32] the construction work being finished by April 1911.

The eighteen paintings from the sides of the gallery and those by Prinsep and Pickersgill from the south end had been removed during the re-roofing and reconstruction work. One cannot help but wonder if there had been any liaison between the Museum and the Office of Works,

because when Basil Long of the Department of Paintings came to replace the two large pictures he found that they did not fit. Alterations had made the spaces for them too large, and an entirely different shape. A cornice had been constructed, which, when the eighteen other pictures were replaced, would mask a portion of them.[33]

A. P. Oppé, then the Deputy Director of the Museum, held the opinion that the Office of Works ought to alter the cornice.[34] It was not until the following July that steps were taken by the Office of Works, who supplied board cut to size to be inserted in front of the lunettes, in line with the edges of the pilasters, in order to bring the pictures forward into view again. This hid all the mouldings and flutings which had originally surrounded the paintings,[35] but nevertheless, after discussion with the Director, Oppé gave orders that, with slight modification, this procedure should be adopted.[36] The paintings were then cleaned before being replaced. Meanwhile a question was asked in the House of Commons by James Grant MP as to what had become of the series of paintings. He was assured that steps were being taken to replace them.

One further problem was to arise. It was found that the canvas of Val Prinsep's large picture had contracted and become distorted. Various solutions were proposed, but in the end two narrow strips, from the top and centre bottom, were cut out of the picture to flatten it, with 'apparently satisfactory results'.[37]

The picture by Prinsep and its companion by Pickersgill were replaced on the walls of the gallery during November 1913, but were removed, with the lunettes, just before the Second World War. They are now in store.

24. PRO, Ed. 84/36, Board minute précis, 18 March 1869.

25. PRO, Ed. 84/7, 9 April 1869 estimate agreed.

26. Ibid., 22 December 1870.

27. Ibid., Board minute précis, 9 December 1870.

28. Ibid., 1 May 1875.

29. PRO, Ed. 84/67.

30. PRO, Ed. 84/67, Memorandum upon the Decorations to be completed, 1876.

31. Letter from Sir Schomberg McDonnell to Sir Robert Morant, Permanent Secretary to the Board of Education, 11 February 1909.

32. Request from Basil Long, V&A, Department of Paintings, 27 May 1910.

33. PRO, Ed. 84/69, Basil Long, 4 September 1911.

34. Ibid., 15 September 1911.

35. Ibid., Ed. 84/69, diagram 24 July 1912.

36. Ibid., 2 September 1912.

37. Basil Long, 19 September 1913.

PLATE X (*opposite above*) Industrial Arts as Applied to War, *a design by Frederic, Lord Leighton, for a lunette fresco in the South Court (now Room 102). Oil*

PLATE XI (*opposite below*) Industrial Arts as Applied to Peace, *a design by Frederic, Lord Leighton, for a lunette fresco in the South Court (now Room 109). Oil*

PLATE XII (*overleaf left*) *Design by Owen Jones for the decoration of the Oriental Courts. Watercolour*

PLATE XIII (*overleaf right*) *Design by Owen Jones for the decoration of the ceiling of the Oriental Courts. Watercolour*

83. (*left*) *The North Staircase, c. 1876. Drawing by John Watkins*

84. (*below*) *Design for the ceiling of the North Staircase, by Godfrey Sykes, together with other decorative details*

Decoration of the North Staircase

The two most notable features of Fowke's impressive North Staircase are the ceiling, designed by Reuben Townroe, following a sketch left by Godfrey Sykes, and the one huge window that Henry Cole had insisted on, which contained stained glass also designed by Reuben Townroe. Both these features were undertaken in the late 1860s, at the same time as the general decoration:

At the top of the staircase, opposite the great window, arches led into the painting galleries towards the south and east. Fowke had originally intended that these should have columns of Portland stone, but it was then decided to change to marble, which was supplied by George Smith and Company, the builders, for £58.[38] The colour scheme of the walls was maroon, with a chocolate dado. The mouldings of the window architraves and of the arches, the mouldings on the pilaster capitals, and the carved marble capitals, were all gilded, as were the other enrichments. The sides of the arches facing the picture galleries were painted green with gilding. The decorating firm of Thomas Kershaw and Sons was commissioned to undertake all this work in April 1868 for a cost of £126.[39] Minton, Hollins undertook the tile pavement in the area for £67.[40]

In August 1870 *Building News*[41] reported on the recently completed ceiling.

83

XV

38. PRO, Ed. 84/36, Board minute précis, 20 January 1865.
39. PRO, Ed. 84/6, 23 April 1868, ordered on 27 April.
40. PRO, Ed. 84/36, Board minute précis, 23 March 1865.
41. 19 August 1870, pp. 127, 128.

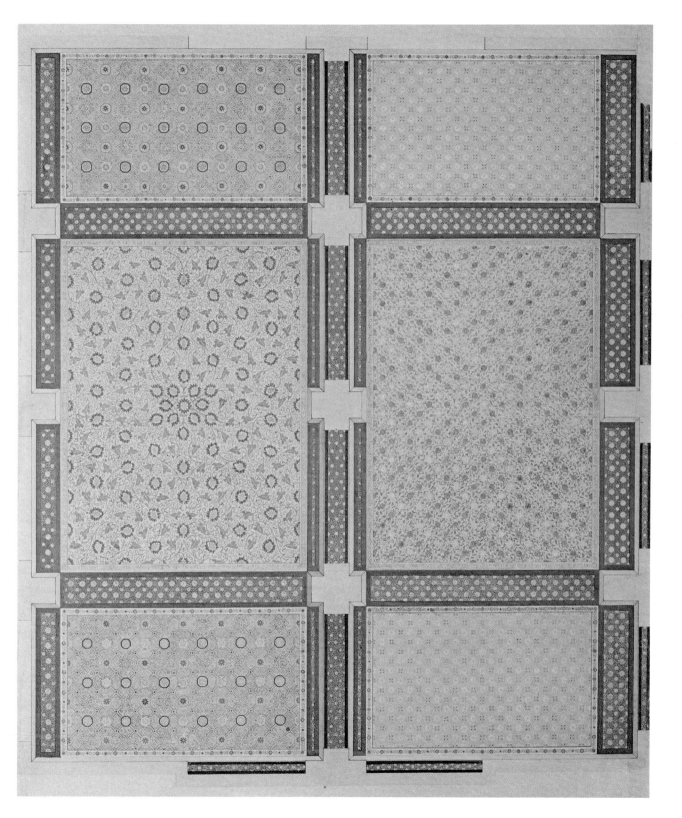

PLATE XIV *(opposite) Design by Godfrey Sykes for a mosaic, including a medallion portrait of Prince Albert, in the tympanum of an arch in the Prince Consort's Gallery above the South Court. Watercolour*

85. *(right) The stained-glass window of the North Staircase, designed by Reuben Townroe and made by Lavers and Barraud (destroyed)*

86. *(below) Cartoon by Reuben Townroe for a panel of the North Staircase window*

84 The wooden construction is properly revealed and decorated, each rafter being bracketed down to the corbels of the cornice. A raking portion is carried round the walls, and an oblong space in the centre is level, and divided into panels, the central one square, and a narrow oblong one at either end. A delicate octagonal gilt metal grille occupies the main portion of the space of the central square panel. This being over the gaselier [*sic*] provides good means of ventilation. Carved pendants mark the point of intersection of the main beams of the ceiling.

But the decoration did not find favour with *Building News*. In general, the effect was good and the treatment rich and delicate – gold and white and grey, with the ground of the panels dark. Closer inspection, however, was disappointing:

> Thus, then we find that in a most costly work all that has been spared has been thought and invention on the part of the designer: that one monotonous pattern fills the whole of the numerous panels: and that the commonest Greek fret is the invariable border around them all.

During the summer of 1864 consideration had been given to the provision of stained glass in the large window, some 19 feet by 11 feet, on the first landing. It was decided[42] that the artist would be chosen by competition from those 'of all nations'. Scale designs were asked for, with a full-size cartoon of a portion and a specimen of glass. The winner would receive a prize of £40, and the runner-up £20. The judges were Earl Somers, Lord Elcho, Beresford Hope, Gambier Parry, D. Seymour, Captain Fowke, L. Stirling MP, Sir Matthew Digby Wyatt, Layard, and Redgrave. So far as we know, the expected flood of entries from all over the world did not materialize,

85 and the prize went to the resident designer Reuben

42. PRO, Ed. 84/36, Board minute, 12 July 1864; *12th Report . . . 1864* (1865).

89

Townroe. Matthew Eldon received second prize, and special consolation awards of £10 were given to Townroe's partner, James Gamble, and to one Alfred Hassam. The subject to be illustrated – descriptive of trades – had been chosen from Ecclesiasticus, Chapter 38, verses 24 to the end. The glass was made by Lavers and Barraud, who were prepared to undertake the work for 26 shillings a square foot, adding that 'we take it for granted that as an artist, Mr. Townroe will enlarge his sketch himself, and supply us with the cartoons, with colours arranged upon them – if he does not do so, it will hardly be his window, and the cost will be increased by 10/- per foot'.[43] Approval for the estimate was given on 9 June 1866.[44] When complete, the window was exhibited in the Paris Exhibition in 1867. *Building News*[45] had nothing good to say for it. The details were of the 'stupidest nonsense ornament'; the 'sham projections and perspectives are palpable absurdities, and the general effect is spotty and unsatisfactory in the extreme'.

At the foot of the staircase there was, at that time, a smaller window with glass by Powell and Sons designed by Frank Moody. The design was divided horizontally: above was the Scheme of Philosophy; and below Architecture, the Fictile Art, and the Art of Working in Metal. When the North Staircase was cleaned and repaired in 1913, it was suggested that an additional window should be inserted in the east wall,[46] but there is no evidence to suggest that this was carried out.

The great north window glass was a victim of the Second World War. There is today no trace of the lower window. This may have been removed during the alterations made necessary by the construction of the conservation workshops in the 1920s. Sykes's and Townroe's ceiling can still be seen, and was restored in 1975.

The decoration of the East Staircase

Nothing is now known of the original wall colouring of the East Staircase, but the ceiling was designed by Godfrey Sykes, and was painted by Thomas Kershaw and Sons in February 1866 for £126.[47] All the carvings and mouldings and the iron centrepiece were gilded. The cast-iron railings were also designed by Sykes and made by George Smith and Company.[48]

The staircase affords an illustration of the care that the Museum authorities devoted to even the

86

87

88

87. *The stained-glass window, designed by F. W. Moody and made by Powell & Sons, formerly at the foot of the North Staircase (destroyed)*

smallest detail of the building. Not long after completion it was found – somewhere about 1873 – that the stone steps had become badly worn by the continual tramping of visitors. The question of repair was taken up by General Scott, who had been appointed to Fowke's post after the death of the latter, and E. R. Festing, a Royal Engineer officer, who had been Deputy-General-Superintendent at South Kensington since 1864.

43. PRO, Ed. 84/5, 27 April 1866.
44. PRO, Ed. 84/36, Board minute précis.
45. *Building News, loc. cit.*
46. PRO, Ed. 84/71, 29 July 1913.
47. PRO, Ed. 84/67, 15 January 1866, ordered by Festing on 30 January.
48. Sykes's balustrade was of the same pattern as that used on the North Staircase, and the Lecture Theatre Staircase. When the Library staircase was built, the same design was also used.

At first they considered the possibility of covering the stone with strips of lead, but came to the conclusion that this would not last very long and would need annual repair; they were also influenced by the 'meanness' of its appearance. Lead had already been laid on the office stairs, and it had to be renewed twice in one year, although it was thought not to have had one-twentieth of the traffic of the East Stairs.

As the East Staircase was one of the principal internal architectural features of the Museum, Scott and Festing considered that it should be well decorated and 'possess a dignified character. This being a museum of decorative arts it has been the practice to make experiments in decoration and, as the opportunities have arisen, new methods and new materials have been frequently tried *in situ*, it was therefore considered specially appropriate to try some method of repairing the stairs which should be serviceable and decorative.'

As a result, one step was experimentally laid with glass mosaic, with a gunmetal edging; a little later six others were similarly covered. Eventually the Office of Works approved the whole of the staircase being treated in this way. Festing noted that the First Commissioner had himself inspected the experiments and personally sanctioned the completion of the scheme.

Frank Moody designed the mosaics on the   89

88. *(above) The ceiling of the East Staircase*

89. *(right) The East Staircase: mosaic floor decoration by F. W. Moody*

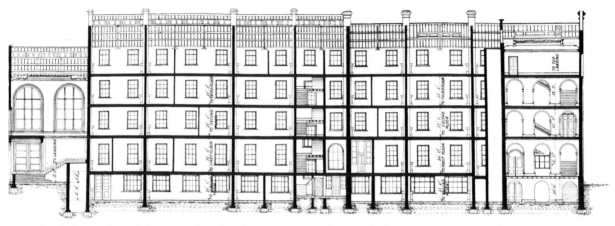

90. (above) Section through the Secretariat wing, from the west

91. (opposite) Ceramic chimneypiece in the Board Room, designed and modelled by James Gamble, and made by Minton, Hollins & Co.

treads and landings, and these were executed by Jesse Rust and Powell and Sons. The tile pavement at ground level was designed and made by Minton, Hollins. It was not until 1875 that Festing reported that everything was finished.[49]

When the North Stairs became worn in 1876, Festing approached A. B. Mitford of the Office of Works for permission to begin similar decoration. Festing was told that it would be an unwise extravagance, and 'that we were "cutting our throats" in asking for such a thing'.

One important piece of furniture, no longer in position, but fortunately preserved, is a case for a hot-water coil. Though its designer was not known when it was removed during the 1950s, it proved to be the work of Alfred Stevens, one of the few artifacts he provided for South Kensington. The case, of white-painted iron, relieved by ormolu moulding, was made by Henry Hoole and Company of Sheffield who, in August 1866, were asked to make sure that it was finished in time for the Exhibition to be held in Paris during the following year. They charged £105 10s.[50]

In March of the same year, Henry Cole had been asked by Earl Granville, Lord President of the Council, to find out on what terms Daniel Maclise would undertake a fresco for the walls of the staircase.[51] Whether Maclise was too busy, or his charges too high, is not recorded, but nothing came of the proposal. In view of the fact that Maclise later unsuccessfully offered South Kensington his cartoon for the mural in the Houses of Parliament of Wellington and Blücher for £1,000,[52] it may be that Cole could not find the money for either painting.

The Secretariat Wing

There was one other building that Fowke planned as part of his first phase of building operations at South Kensington. It was a building with no elaborate scheme of decoration, simply because it was not open to the public. This was the Secretariat Wing, an extremely plain building to the south of the eastern galleries and the East Staircase, between the Boilers and Brompton Oratory. George Smith tendered in 1862 to build this block; Richard Redgrave and Cole met to discuss the plans in July.[53] The building was ready during the summer of 1865, when Cole noted the 'removal of my Office to East of building'.[54] This allowed certain of the old buildings near Exhibition Road to be demolished, George Smith offering £50 for the material.[55]

The new office building soon proved to be too small, and almost immediately plans were drawn up to extend it and to build a proper Board Room. Work on the enlargement was put in hand more than a year after Fowke's death, during the autumn of 1867, at a cost of £6,357.[56] The Museum authorities ordered three elaborate chimneypieces, designed by James Gamble, from Minton, Hollins; they were sanctioned by the Lord President, the Duke of Richmond, for £325. One

49. 22nd Report . . . 1874 (1875), p. 392.
50. PRO, Ed. 84/5, 24 August 1866.
51. PRO, Ed. 84/36, Board minute précis, 17 March 1866.
52. Cole diary, 2 April 1868.
53. PRO, Ed. 84/3, 29 March 1862; Cole diary, 4 July 1862.
54. Cole diary, 13 September 1865.
55. PRO, Ed. 84/4, 11 July 1865.
56. PRO, Ed. 84/6, 18 May 1867, sanctioned on 15 October.

of these was intended for the Board Room, another was to be exhibited in the Museum galleries, and the third would be installed in the Edinburgh Museum.[57] The Treasury auditors soon queried the expenditure, and asked why such an elaborate chimneypiece was needed for the Board Room. To placate them, the Board agreed to take it down, and place it in the Department of Circulation so that it could be sent round the country as a specimen of modern majolica.[58] They never did this, however, despite a follow-up enquiry from the Treasury.[59] It remains in the Board Room. George Smith supplied the bookcases for the Board Room in 1870 for £187.[60]

After 1872, when the elephantine Cast Courts were built next to the Secretariat Wing, conditions in the offices deteriorated. The trouble was caused by smoke from the fireplaces. Among the numerous complaints, was one received by Norman MacLeod, the Assistant Secretary, from John Donnelly, a Royal Engineer who was at that time Inspector for Science (it must be remembered that the secretariat of the whole of the Department of Science and Art, not just of the South Kensington Museum, was housed in this building). Donnelly wrote:

> Last year my throat was seriously affected by attempting to sit and work in my office during East winds, and I was warned by two medical men not to do so again.
>
> It is not a question of mere inconvenience of a smoky chimney from which a few puffs come into the room every now and then. When there is a high North East wind the down rush of air is so great that the fire flares into the room for minutes together as the Vice-President saw. – At the present moment it is impossible to distinguish a face at the other side of the room, though the windows have been constantly open . . .
>
> I trust something may be done *at once*, as it is impossible for me to work in the room.[61]

Nothing was done at once, however. John Taylor of the Office of Works, which was by now responsible for all structural alterations at South Kensington, was no friend to the Department of Science and Art. He continued to block all requests for several years. At first the Department asked for the chimneys to be raised above the height of the Cast Courts.[62] Then Captain Festing had the idea of raising the level of the whole building by an additional floor, thus relieving overcrowding in

the offices at the same time. A breakthrough seemed to have been achieved in 1877 when the Department circumvented Taylor and the Office of Works and went direct to the Treasury, who allowed a sum of £2,500 in the 1878–9 estimates for the extra storey to be built.[63] The Department was doomed to disappointment, however. Taylor told the First Commissioner of Works that work should not be started until the following May. The Department objected, as May was the period of their 'greatest pressure of business', and suggested August 1878 instead. Taylor agreed, provided work could start at the beginning of that month, as it would take at least four months to complete.

The Science and Art Department bore the winter of 1877 with hope and made their plans for a disruption of the offices in the autumn. 'With surprise, yet trust that there may have been some misunderstanding, which can be obviated' the Department heard in July 1878 from the First Commissioner that the Treasury had deleted the money for building from the Estimates.[64] The First Commissioner had been instructed to reduce the spending on Public Buildings by £30,000.

While South Kensington protested to the Treasury, Taylor thought the time was ripe to experiment with a stove newly arrived from New York, and costing between £100 and £150. The Treasury, with a sigh of relief, sanctioned the stoves, but refused the extra storey.[65] The stoves were a failure, however, and in June 1880 Norman MacLeod wrote direct to the Treasury, asking them to reconsider the provision of an extra storey.

This the Treasury did, requesting the First Commissioner to draw up plans and to prepare a supplementary estimate for the work. Gleefully Taylor reported that there was simply not time –

57. PRO, Ed. 84/36, Board minute précis, 22 December 1871. It arrived in Edinburgh by 5 February 1872, but cannot now be traced.

58. Ibid., 20 November 1872.

59. Ibid., 13 December 1872.

60. PRO, Ed. 84/36, Board minute précis, 20 June 1870.

61. PRO, Works, 17/24/9.

62. Ibid., sections and plans. Taylor considered that the trouble was caused arranging for construction 'from time to time without regard to the general design or to the effect of one building upon another', 23 June 1877.

63. Ibid., 28 July 1877.

64. Ibid., 8 July 1878.

65. Ibid., 26 December 1879.

it was then July – to prepare drawings and specifications, to obtain tenders and so on, and then be able to complete the work before the winter. South Kensington, determined not to lose the advantage, asked the Treasury to 'allow' the First Commissioner to proceed with the work at once. William Law, on behalf of the Lords of the Treasury, therefore instructed the First Commissioner to 'carry out the work with as little delay as possible'. A minute marked 'Immediate' was transmitted to Taylor urging him to 'proceed', and he replied that 'steps shall be taken at once in this matter'.[66] So they were, but it had taken over seven years of smarting eyes in the Department of Science and Art to get the work done.

The Raphael cartoons

One further notable undertaking of Fowke's, which must be regarded as an engineering feat rather than a building activity, was the transportation from Hampton Court to South Kensington of the Raphael cartoons.

Before the death of the Prince Consort in 1861, Henry Cole had been trying to obtain Queen Victoria's permission for the removal of the Raphael cartoons from Hampton Court to South Kensington, a plan proposed by Prince Albert himself. Although the requests from the Department of Science and Art were received sympathetically, events did not move quickly. The Board, under Earl Granville, decided on 15 March 1865 formally to ask the Lord Chamberlain if the cartoons might be borrowed. Probably because of the special regard the Queen had for the Museum as a result of the Prince's intense interest in its establishment, she gave her permission.[67] This was reported in the press during April, bringing the not unexpected storm of protest. But within days a committee consisting of the President of the Royal Academy, the President of the Institute of Civil Engineers, Tite, Redgrave, and Fowke, had been formed to decide how best to transport the cartoons.[68]

J. C. Robinson did not support the move; he felt that the conditions at South Kensington would be less favourable than those at Hampton Court, where the cartoons had survived for the last two hundred years. On the other hand Richard Redgrave, in his dual role as Inspector-General of the Department of Science and Art, and Surveyor of the Queen's Pictures, was firmly of the opinion

that the paintings would be placed under far greater protection at Kensington; the risk of damage from fire would be less, and more important, the pictures would be more readily accessible to a far greater public.[69]

Both Dr Hofman FRS and Dr Frankland FRS agreed with Redgrave, and moreover, took the view that the lighting of the gallery by gas would not have any harmful effects.

A further protest came from R. N. Wornum and Sir Charles Eastlake at the National Gallery, for Cole proposed to put the Raphael cartoons in Room 94, which then held National Gallery pictures. Needless to say, Wornum and Eastlake felt that the Raphael cartoons would more properly be placed in the National Gallery itself.

Eastlake and Wornum were no match, however, for the formidable combination of Queen Victoria, Henry Cole, and his close friend Richard Redgrave, who had been appointed Surveyor on Cole's recommendation to Prince Albert. The cartoons were moved at the end of April,

... under the direction and superintendence of Captain Fowke. The first operation in moving the cartoons was taking them out of their frames, which occupied two days. A large van carrying, by rubber slings, a case of sufficient size to hold all the cartoons was specially made from the designs of Captain Fowke; it was brought down by night to the Palace, and soon after daylight the following morning we commenced the work of lowering the cartoons from a window of the room in which they were, and packing them in the van. Captian Fowke superintended the latter part of the operation, having stationed me [Captain Festing] on the scaffolding outside the window to see that they were carefully taken down. We both accompanied the van on its journey by road to London, which was performed without the slightest accident, and by four o'clock in the afternoon the cartoons were all safely lodged in their new gallery without having sustained the slightest injury, the whole of the work having been done under the direct supervision of Captain Fowke and myself, and every precaution taken that the faces of the cartoons should not be

---

66. Ibid., 9 July 1880.
67. Cole correspondence, letters from Phipps to Cole, 5 March 1865, and Spencer Ponsonby to Cole, 17 March 1865.
68. PRO, Ed. 84/36, Board minute précis, 6 April 1865. 29 April 1865, Report of the Commission on heating and ventilation of the South Kensington Museum, 1869, p. 81.
69. Ibid., pp. 82–3.

arrived at the Museum.[72] Before the cartoons were put on display to the public they were inspected by Sir Charles Eastlake, Lord Elcho, Austen Layard, and others, to examine their condition. They remained in Room 94 until 1939, when they were placed under the Lecture Theatre and bricked up for the duration of the war. They have since been exhibited in Room 48.

In 1893 a major piece of work was carried out in the gallery which then housed them. Fowke's original roof was taken off and replaced. Later, at the suggestion of Festing, the staircase at the east end of the gallery, which had been put there thirty years earlier to provide a separate entrance at the insistence of the National Gallery, was removed. In this way an extra room, 30 × 20 feet, was provided. This led into a set of rooms in which the Sheepshanks Collection was now displayed. These paintings had been removed from the original Sheepshanks Gallery in about 1875, when Reuben Townroe and James Gamble were asked to decorate the rooms, for £150. This plan of decoration, however, was never carried out, and they were papered with Morris wallpaper.[73]

92

touched. The extent of this work may be judged from the fact that the case for the cartoons measured 18 feet by 12 by 4, and the van was 20 feet long by 8 wide, and 18 feet high to the top of the framing, and was drawn by eight horses. About 40 workmen were employed in the work. The cost of the service was about £250.

93

A room had been specially prepared for the cartoons, the hot-water pipes having been removed from along the walls, and placed down the middle of the room in trenches made in the thickness of the floor. This alteration has been attended with very good results, and the warming and ventilation of the room are very satisfactory.[70] A blind is fixed over the sky-light to keep out the light of the sun, and there are green blinds under it, which are drawn when the room is not open to the public, or when there is too much light.[71]

The van, and the team of horses which transported the cartoons, were photographed as they

70. Room 94 had been redecorated by Kershaw the previous July, PRO, Ed. 84/36, Board minute précis, 12 July 1864, and George Smith's estimate for the heating, Ibid., 14 July 1865, was £252. H. G. Wells, *Love and Mr. Lewisham*, Ch. 17, '. . . in the spacious solitude of the Museum gallery devoted to the Raphael Cartoons sat Lewisham . . .'

71. Captain E. R. Festing, R.E., 8 May 1865, in *Report* of the Commission on the heating, lighting and ventilation of the South Kensington Museum, 1869, p. 86.

72. J. Physick, *Photography and the South Kensington Museum*, 1975, Pl. 13.

73. When this had to be renewed in 1893, T. Armstrong asked Jeffrey & Co. to copy the Morris paper, and said that Morris's permission should be sought. However, Jeffrey & Co did not wait, feeling that there would be 'no objection on Messrs. Morris's part to let you have the Marigold in the altered colour'. They supplied 100 rolls at 5/6d per roll. PRO, Ed. 84/68, 9, 10 November 1893.

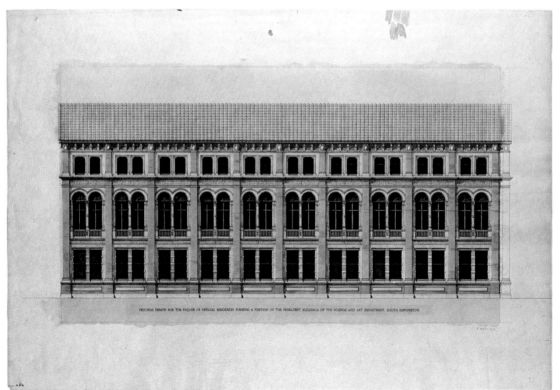

ORIGINAL DESIGN FOR THE FAÇADE OF OFFICIAL RESIDENCES FORMING A PORTION OF THE PERMANENT BUILDINGS OF THE SCIENCE AND ART DEPARTMENT, SOUTH KENSINGTON.

CHAPTER VII

Fowke's second stage

Although the early building operations at South Kensington were remarkably swift, they were easily outpaced by the speed of Francis Fowke's own forward planning. Before the North and South Courts were even roofed in, Fowke had planned out in detail an ambitious development of the whole Brompton Park House site, of which the permanent buildings so far described in this book formed only a small section on the eastern side. The earliest version of the plan was in existence in 1860, and Fowke continued to modify and adjust it until the time of his premature and comparatively sudden death in December 1865.

The parts of the overall scheme that were eventually realized were the Residences for the Museum superintendents, which were begun in 1863, thus predating the conclusion of the work based on Fowke's earlier phase of planning, described in the preceeding chapters; the new Art Schools; and the large range of buildings towards the north of the site which incorporates the Lecture Theatre and the Refreshment Rooms, and which was incomplete when Fowke died.

Fowke presented the earliest version of his plan to the Parliamentary Select Committee of 1860. It included all the permanent buildings then existing, which comprised the Sheepshanks and other painting galleries, and the soon to be completed North and South Courts. Everything else was to be swept away, including the Boilers. Although the plan was never wholly realized, it does contain the nucleus of quite a large part of the Museum as it is today, and several features are clearly recognizable. These include the Lecture Theatre range, and the open space in front of it, which was then intended to be an extensive, splayed garden, 240 feet in depth, on the site of the present quadrangle, but more than twice as large. Closing this garden to the south was to be an open arcade for the exhibition of sculpture, 150 feet from the southern boundary. It can be seen from Fowke's elevation that he meant the Lecture Theatre block to be visible from Cromwell Road.

To the west, Fowke intended that the building would extend right up to Exhibition Road, with an Art Museum in a block on the corner with Cromwell Road. To the north of this, and slightly set back from Exhibition Road, were Residences for officials of the Museum, with galleries as well. Northwards still, Fowke planned art schools, which reached right to the northern boundary, occupying the present site of the Henry Cole Building. Flanking the west side of the central

PLATE XVI *(opposite above) Detail of the centre part of a design (not executed) by Francis Fowke for the completion of the South Kensington Museum buildings, 1865. Watercolour*

PLATE XVII *(opposite below) Design by Francis Fowke for the Residences, on the west side of the present quadrangle. Watercolour*

94. (below) Elevation of Fowke's proposed building, 1860. Lithograph by Vincent Brooks

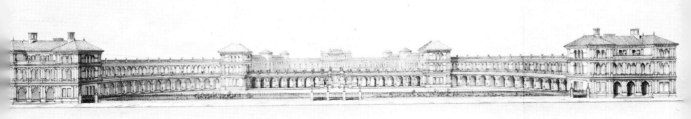

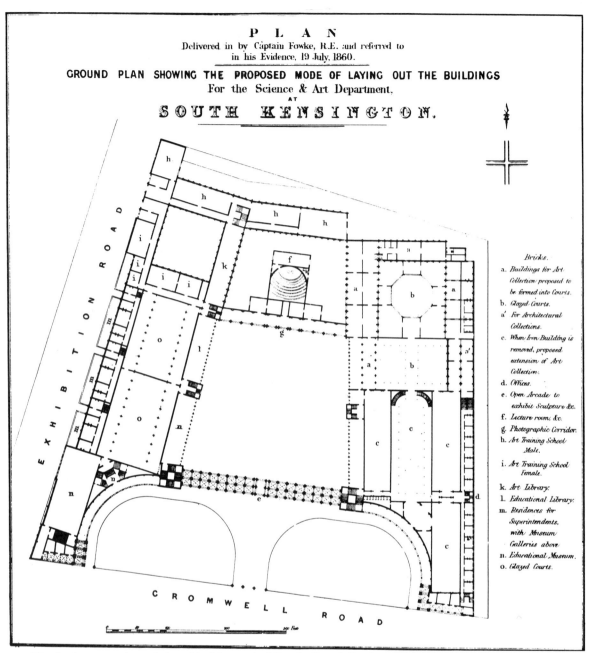

PLAN
Delivered in by Captain Fowke, R.E. and referred to
in his Evidence, 19 July, 1860.

GROUND PLAN SHOWING THE PROPOSED MODE OF LAYING OUT THE BUILDINGS
For the Science & Art Department.
AT
SOUTH KENSINGTON.

Bricks.
a. *Buildings for Art*
   Collection, proposed to
   be formed into Courts.
b. *Glazed Courts.*
a' *For Architectural*
   Collections.
c. *When Iron Building is*
   removed, proposed
   extension of Art
   Collection.
d. *Offices.*
e. *Open Arcade to*
   exhibit Sculpture &c.
f. *Lecture room, &c.*
g. *Photographic Corridor.*
h. *Art Training School*
   Male.
i. *Art Training School*
   Female.
k. *Art Library.*
l. *Educational Library.*
m. *Residences for*
   Superintendents,
   with Museum
   Galleries above.
n. *Educational Museum.*
o. *Glazed Courts.*

95. *Plan for the proposed completion of the Museum buildings by Francis Fowke, 1860*

garden, punctuated by an ornamental staircase feature, were a portion of the Educational Museum, and the Art Library, which were separated from the Residences by two large glazed courts. To the east side of the garden was the Sheepshanks Gallery, another staircase, and courts for the art collections on the site of the Boilers. The Lecture Theatre range of buildings met the existing eastern range at the junction of the Sheepshanks Gallery and the Turner and Vernon Galleries. Thus, although the Sheepshanks Gallery was visible from the main Cromwell Road approach, the Vernon and Turner Galleries were concealed from it by the Lecture Theatre range. This accounts for the presence of external ornament on the Sheepshanks Gallery, and its absence on the Turner and Vernon Galleries.

The site is not a regular rectangle, because

98

Exhibition Road meets Cromwell Road at an acute angle rather than a right angle. This caused Fowke considerable problems, and he admitted to the Committee that he had found it 'extremely difficult'[1] to design a building which would fully occupy the site. At the end of the century the architects who entered the competition to design further new buildings – the competition won by Aston Webb – found similar difficulties. Fowke turned the drawback to his own advantage. He splayed out the two wings which stretched south-wards on either side of the Lecture Theatre so as to create a heightened perspective effect of reces-sion to the spectator approaching from the south. He masked the awkward angles at junctions by linking the terminal buildings at the extreme south-east and south-west corners to the central arcade across the front by two quadrant arcades, which, sweeping round a carriage drive and garden, would have formed the principal entrance to the Museum. Fowke clearly became dis-satisfied with the details of this solution, because the various modified versions of the plan which he produced in later years show constant alterations to the alignment of the terminal buildings, and some attempts to make at least parts of the two wings parallel to one another.

The greater part of the Museum would have been of two storeys, with the Lecture Theatre and the terminal blocks emphasized by an additional storey. The staircase blocks were also of a tower-like construction. Flying in the face of the then current fashion for Gothic, Fowke proposed to continue to use the north Italian Renaissance style already adumbrated on the Sheepshanks Gallery.[2] In the main, the buildings were to be of red brick and stone, with any decoration confined to the southern and western façades, as anything to the east and north would have been 'thrown away'.[3] One advantage of his plan, explained Fowke to the Committee, was that, if approved, it could easily be erected section by section, although a certain regard to method would be necessary to build the schools first, 'because part of the ground which it is proposed to occupy by the residences is occupied by the present schools. To get rid of those schools you must build new schools; the residences could then be built, and by these means the whole of the old houses and the wooden schools could be dispensed with.'[4] The Committee wondered whether the building could be put up

piecemeal over a ten-year period, thus spreading the costs. Fowke was prepared to accept this. 'You must spread the execution of any building over a certain number of years; the difference is very great between beginning at the bottom and building upwards, and beginning at the end and building onwards.'

The question of costs had been considered by Fowke. He estimated that the erection of the Residences and the schools would cost £27,000. The total cost of his planned development would be £214,000, which he had computed from estimates for various portions at 3s, 4d, and 6d a cubic foot, with ornamented parts at 1s. His precedents had been those portions of the Museum that were already built; the Sheepshanks Gallery, with two ornamental fronts (east and west) had cost 6d a cubic foot, whereas the Female Training School on the ground floor of the extreme northern building had worked out at only $3\frac{1}{2}$ per cubic foot. He stressed, however, that these calculations could only provide an approximate estimate.

Fowke admitted at this hearing that although he was the architect to the Science and Art Depart-ment, he had not been articled; he had, as an officer of Engineers, always made a special study of architecture, and had been employed as an architect by the War Department for many years.

He quoted, in his defence, the horrible recent example of the National Gallery in Dublin. The Office of Works had called in a 'very eminent architect' who had produced designs for a beauti-ful but (presumably in the eyes of the Science and Art Department) entirely unsuitable building. He, Fowke, had then been called in, and drawn up plans for a much more convenient gallery. Modestly, the Captain revealed that he had only mentioned this to the Committee to show them that the Department of Science and Art knew that it was doing better than 'a person who has merely the ordinary knowledge of a general architect.' There had been a similar set of circum-stances at Edinburgh where a new museum was being put up.

---

1. Select Committee, 1860, para. 2391.
2. In his evidence (*loc. cit.*, No. 1750), Sir Francis Scott, Bart., was firmly convinced that all buildings ought to be of 'pointed Gothic', because they better fulfilled the 'desiderata of economy, common sense, and simplicity in their construction'.
3. *Loc. cit.*, No. 2396.
4. *Loc. cit.*, No. 2398.

... The requirements of the department were stated by the professors, and they were sent to the Office of Works. Through a misunderstanding, a design was prepared at the same time by the Office of Works, and by the Department of Science and Art. The design by the Office of Works was a very beautiful and clever design, but totally unsuitable... and ... very uneconomical. The building designed by the Office of Works gave a floor space on all floors of about 58,000 feet, while the plans prepared by the Department of Science and Art gave 77,000 ... The plan by the Department of Science and Art was finally approved ...[5]

Questioned whether the Office of Works should consult Departments and then superintend the subsequent building works, Fowke disagreed most strongly; 'Certainly not in the case of the Science and Art Department. I believe that the most economical and the most fit course would be for the Department to carry out the works itself.'[6] (The Department in fact continued to be responsible for its own construction work at South Kensington until 1870, when this responsibility was taken over by the Office of Works; a change very much for the worse, ushering in an era of bureaucratic frustration and delay.)

The Office of Works, not unnaturally, felt that it was coming out of the 1860 Select Committee hearings rather badly, and asked that its Secretary, Alfred Austin, might be allowed to attend to give the other side of the story.[7] Austin stated that, as far as the Edinburgh Museum was concerned, Fowke was quite wrong, as his design had not been sanctioned by the Office of Works, nor had the First Commissioner seen anything of his proposals for South Kensington.

The Select Committee, after sifting the mass of evidence presented to them, concluded their report to Parliament by recommending that the wooden buildings and the old houses on the South Kensington site should be removed as soon as possible, both to reduce the risk of fire and for reasons of economy. The iron building and the temporary brick building of Pennethorne, on the other hand, should remain for the time being. The Committee also recommended that any new buildings to be erected should be capable of being worked into a general plan for the whole site. Such a plan, continued the Committee, had been shown to the members by Captain Fowke. The Committee exhorted Parliament to sanction the

urgent works, costing a total of £44,000: £17,000 for the roofing of the North and South Courts, which had not yet been undertaken, and £27,000 for the building of new Art Schools and residences for the Museum superintendents. The Treasury gave its permission for the erection of the new schools and Residences in 1862. It will be clear from this that the earliest building work based on Fowke's ambitious second stage was undertaken before the completion of the work associated with the earlier phases of development.

Fowke now decided to revise his 1860 plan, moving the Residences from their original location bordering Exhibition Road to a site 100 feet further east, along the western side of the central gardens. This position had originally been earmarked for the Art and Educational Libraries. The Art Schools now occupied an L-shaped site running northwards from the residences, then turning east along the northern boundary, to the north of the Lecture Theatre. By adding an extra storey to the Art Schools, Fowke was able to economize on ground space, leaving vacant the land on the extreme north-east, over which the Art Schools had also been originally planned to extend. This vacant land was later occupied by the Science Schools, now the Henry Cole Building.

Surviving records of this phase of the Museum's building operations are sparse, while the detailed plans seem to be non-existent. The plans of the official Residences and the Art Schools were submitted to the Board on 6 July 1861, and three weeks later it was decided to ask for tenders from respectable builders. The Board approved the tender from George Smith for £2,000 for the Schools on 26 April 1862.[8]

Blanchard agreed to provide the terracotta pilasters, columns and lintels (for ten openings) for the east wall of the ground floor of the Residences. His estimate for two friezes in red, and string mouldings in buff, terracotta was £77, and this was approved by the Board on 24 February 1863. In October, Blanchard was paid a further £743. Smith's tender for completing the building of the

5. *Loc. cit.*, No. 2471.
6. *Loc. cit.*, No. 2474.
7. *Loc. cit.*, Nos. 2545–2599.
8. Specification for the carcass of the range, dated March 1862, is in PRO, Ed. 84/15; 6 July 1861, Board Minute précis, PRO, Ed. 84/35; 16 October 1862, PRO, Ed. 84/3.

96. *Design for the Residences: section from the south, drawn by Henry Saxon Snell, 1862*

Residences for £4,845, received the Board's sanction on 5 September 1863. Cole noted in his diary that by 24 March 1862 the 'Official residences brickwork begun' and that by 30 May it was 'up to the ceiling of Museum'.

While this work was in progress Fowke drew up a report[9] in which he explained that the eastern front was to be 'of a much more ornamental character' than the western, since the eastern front 'forms a part of the façade of the interior quadrangle', whereas the western front would eventually be hidden by a further range of buildings to the west of it. The ornament was to be 'of terracotta, which has been modelled by Mr. G. Sykes and his assistants'. Only the top two floors were to be occupied by the Residences. The ground floor would be part of the Museum. 'This arrangement was made to provide an uninterrupted connexion between the parts of the museum on each side of the houses.' The entrance to the Residences was to be on the western side. Fowke used the residences at the British Museum as a 'standard of comparison as to size and amount of accommodation', but whereas the British Museum houses were of four different sizes,

The residences of this department are of only two classes or sizes, and according to the above standard measure as follows:—

South Kensington Museum

1st class house . . . . 4,197 superficial feet
2nd class house . . . . 2,995 ,, ,,

In the interior the houses have been constructed with every attention to ventilation and sanitary arrangements, but at the same time with strict regard to economy as to the absence of all decoration and expensive finishings.

In February 1863, the Residences were allotted to the General Superintendent, the Engineer, the Deputy Superintendent and the officer of the Sappers. Rooms were also reserved for the Keeper of Art or his assistant. By May 1863 the residence building was complete, and required only the finishing touches of interior paint and wallpaper.[10] Thackeray visited Henry Cole on the 13th of the month in order to see the new marvels, over which he was proudly taken.[11]

At the end of June, Cole was able to start moving in his furniture from his house, then in Onslow Square, and on 7 July the great day came, when after an inspection of the premises by Lord Grosvenor, Cole was able to record that he had slept in the Residence for the first time.

In August there was a slight hint of criticism due to 'reports of incipient dry-rot ... for want of ventilation in 3rd floor', but this did not stop Cole from displaying his latest addition to South Kensington to G. F. Watts, who called on him during September and 'greatly admired the terracotta building'.[12]

Since the completion of the Museum building by Aston Webb in the early twentieth century, the Residences, reconstructed inside, have been used as Museum galleries and offices.

---

9. *10th Report . . . 1862* (1863), pp. 130, 131.

10. PRO, Ed. 84/35, Board Minute précis, 24 February 1863. Smith's tender of £745 for painting and papering has been postponed (*loc. cit.*, 5 September 1862). The 1871 Census returns show that Residence No. 1 was then occupied by Captain Festing and a cousin, Arthur Mammott, an Oxford undergraduate. Henry Cole lived next door in No. 2; his household numbered eleven, including his wife, three daughters, two sons, a parlourmaid, needlewoman, housemaid and cook. In No. 3 was Richard Thompson, together with three sisters, two nephews, two nieces, a visitor, and a cook and a housemaid. Squeezed into No. 4 were Philip Cunliffe Owen, his wife, five daughters and an 8-month-old son, a governess, housemaid, children's maid and a cook.

11. Cole, diary, 13 May 1863.

12. Ibid., 29 June, 23 August, 29 September 1863.

97. *(right) Terracotta decoration of the ground-floor windows of the Residences (west side of the quadrangle), designed by Godfrey Sykes and made by Blanchard & Co.*

98. *(far right) West side of the Residences, seen through the eastern arch of Fowke's 1862 Exhibition building, as it was blown up by the Sappers in 1864*

99. *(centre left) The garden adjacent to the Residences (now the Exhibition Road entrance)*

100. *(bottom) Section through the Art Schools from the north*

Fowke also reported on the Art Training Schools:

The building to contain the male and female art *100* schools being situated in the rear of other proposed buildings, has been kept of a perfectly plain exterior. It is three stories in height, and as the lower floor is most valuable for museum space, while a large amount of top lighted space is necessary for the art schools, it was manifestly an economy in erecting the school building to raise it up and leave a space under it which could eventually be employed as a museum, at a considerable saving of both space and cost.

The building has been constructed throughout *101* with fireproof floors, the girders supporting which have been made hollow, and thereby employed to carry the hot-water pipes for heating the several stories. These troughs are carried through external

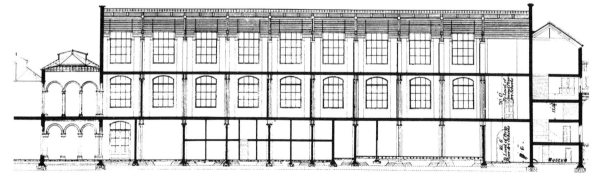

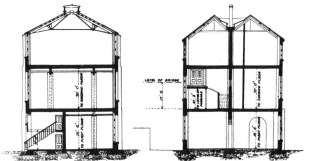

101. (left) The Art Schools, photographed in 1904

102. (below) Sections through the Art Schools

103. (centre right) The joiners' shop, 1869

102

walls, and terminate in iron grated boxes through which a constant supply of fresh air is obtained. The windows are made very large, and with wide intervals between them to suit the requirements of lighting for the school, and with a like object to the upper floor the windows are continued a considerable way into the roof as skylights, an arrangement by which a command of light is obtained at any required angle of elevation. The exit or upper ventilation is provided for on this floor by a lantern along the entire length of the roof, and in the lower by a swing sash in the upper part of the window. The building is constructed without interior walls, so as to allow the interior to be divided by screens at pleasure, and thus give the greatest freedom to the changing wants of the School.[13]

Under the northern range of the Art School, which was positioned in the north-west corner of the site, George Smith, the builder, was asked to adapt the ground floors into two-storey quarters for Sappers.[14] This he did for £987. Since that time one large room has always been called the 'Picquet Room'. The decision to build the Sappers' barracks and also the 'workshops for carpenters' was taken by the Board on 19 December 1862.[15] The joiners' shop is still in use and a photograph of 1869 could well have been taken recently, except for the top hat being worn. The rooms built to accommodate the Sappers, and the Art School, are now partly used by the Museum,

103

13. *10th Report . . . 1862* (1863), p. 131.

14. PRO, Ed. 84/4, 3 January 1865.

15. PRO, Ed. 84/35, Board minute précis. According to the 1871 Census return, apart from the four official residences accommodating thirty-seven people, there were eleven Sappers from 38 Company, Royal Engineers, in the barracks, Sergeant Benjamin L. Spackman (then aged 37), his 18-year-old second wife, two sons and one daughter, and a general servant. In the Foremen's residences were the foreman of works, and the foreman of gas and their wives; the occupants of 'Officers' Quarters' were a cook and a footman. The total number of people living in the Museum was sixty.

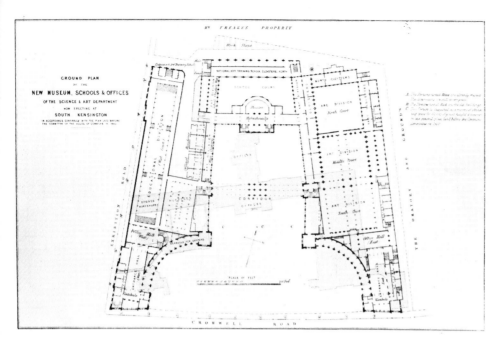

on the ground floor, but the upper storeys are still used by the Royal College of Art.

The amount of money which was estimated would be spent on the various building works during 1862 was:

Residences	£8,775. 6s. 6d.
Schools	£4,832. 2s. 2d.
Staircase building	£ 819. 15s. 0d.
Connecting building	£ 842. 16s. 0d.
Stairs	£ 296. 0s. 0d.
Terra Cotta work, Tiles for Roofing, about	£ 500. 0s. 0d.
Excavations	£ 116. 0s. 0d.
Artificers, draftsmen etc.	£ 800. 0s. 0d.

Fowke's overall plan continued to undergo changes. The plan of 1863, drawn by John Hackett of the Royal Engineers, which first shows the revised siting of the Residences and the Art Schools, also manifests other changes in Fowke's thinking. The Lecture Theatre is of a somewhat different form, and for the first time the Refreshment Rooms are also located in the same area. The Lecture Theatre block has been moved back northwards from the junction of the Sheepshanks and painting galleries, which was its earlier position. The open colonnade across the front has also been moved northwards, bringing it some 120 feet nearer to the Lecture Theatre. It now links the two staircase towers. The arcaded quadrants on the south side are retained but are now flanked by

104

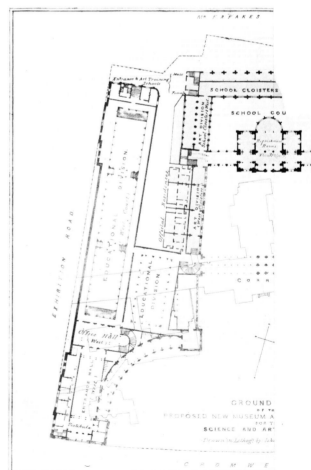

106. *(right) Plan showing proposed buildings for the Museum, revised to November 1865, with further revision at the south-west corner, c. 1866*

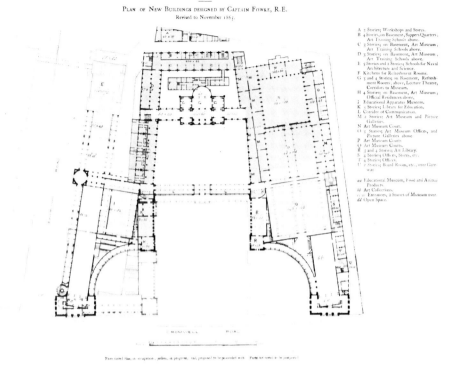

PLAN OF NEW BUILDINGS DESIGNED BY CAPTAIN FOWKE, R.E.
Revised to November 1865.

A 2 Stories; Workshops and Stores.
B 4 Stories; on Basement, Sappers Quarters; Art Training Schools above.
C 3 Stories; on Basement, Art Museum, Art Training Schools above.
D 3 Stories; on Basement, Art Museum; Art Training Schools above.
E 5 Stories and 2 Stories; Schools for Naval Architecture and Science.
F Kitchens for Refreshment Rooms.
G 3 and 4 Stories; on Basement, Refreshment Rooms; above, Lecture Theatre, Corridor to Museum.
H 4 Stories; on Basement, Art Museum, Official Residences above.
I Educational Apparatus Museum.
K 3 Stories; Library for Education.
L Corridor of Communication.
M 2 Stories; Art Museum and Picture Galleries.
N Art Museum Court.
O 3 Stories; Art Museum Offices, and Picture Galleries above.
P Art Museum Courts.
Q 3 Stories; Art Museum Courts.
R 3 and 4 Stories; Art Library.
S 4 Stories; Offices, Stores, etc.
T 4 Stories; Offices.
U 2 Stories; Board Room, etc., over Gateway.

aa Educational Museum, Food and Animal Products.
bb Art Collections.
cc Entrances, 2 Stories of Museum over.
dd Open Space.

107. *(below) Perspective of Fowke's proposed Museum. Watercolour*

large entrance halls, with their southern faces re-aligned to take account of the curved frontage of Cromwell Road. Three large galleries were to be built along Exhibition Road on the former site of the Residences, and, as a major change on the east side, Fowke now planned another large court to the south of his South Courts, which were to be renamed the Middle Courts. A fragmentary plan, probably dated about 1864, shows Fowke's revision of the Lecture Theatre which has assumed the arrangement that it still retains today. Both these plans are interesting in that they are superimposed on an outline of the Pennethorne building and the old house on the site.

The construction of the Lecture Theatre range of buildings, which linked the painting galleries on the east of the site to the new art schools and Residences on the west, was the next major building operation at South Kensington. The essentials of this new portion of the Museum were the Lecture Theatre building itself, a three-storey pavilion; with a two-storey building of three bays to the west, and a similar building to the east, where there was only room for two bays and a linking corridor, on account of the irregularities of the buildings then existing. It is clear from a plan of November 1865, however, that Fowke intended to adjust the irregularity in the shape of the quadrangle by knocking down the west wall of the Sheepshanks Gallery and realigning it at a more

105

106

directly northerly angle. This operation was carried out as part of Aston Webb's completion of the Museum at the turn of the century.

XIX
XX
107
The Lecture Theatre building was the focal centre of Fowke's entire design. Its façade was very ornate. It was in three bays, the central bay being twice as wide as the two side bays, and surmounted by a pediment, the supporting pilasters of which formed the division between the bays. Three arched recesses formed a balcony at first floor level. In the centre of the ground floor was a large doorway, which was intended to be the principal entrance to the Museum. The doorway led directly into a suite of three refreshment rooms which occupied the ground floor of the pavilion. The front of the first floor, immediately behind the façade, was to be occupied by a gallery for the display of ceramics, running the whole length of the range of buildings, including the two flanking sections. The Lecture Theatre itself, which was raked, with the highest portion towards the south, was to be above the ceramic gallery. The central section of the back of the Lecture Theatre building is apsidal, with the Central Refreshment Room and the Lecture Theatre above it extending into the apse. The whole of the north side of the building is hidden from the public view by the art schools. At the west end of the range of buildings, between the residences and the Art School, is the West Staircase, now usually known as the Ceramic Staircase, for the building of the carcass of which George Smith estimated £1,217.[16]

108
109
It is not easy now from the surviving records to establish the precise date when the building work on the Lecture Theatre range began, but a minute of the Board, on 19 March 1864, recorded the decision that George Smith's firm was to be invited to put in an estimate for the cost of the basement storey of the Lecture Theatre. The carcass of the northern range progressed rapidly. The Board decided in July 1864 that the builders who had tendered for the construction of the Foreign Office (H. B. Little; Piper & Wheeler; Holland & Hannen; Cubitt & Co.; Kirk & Parry; Lucas Brothers; and Smith & Taylor) should be invited to submit tenders for South Kensington, and presumably the choice fell on Smith. During the summer of 1865 Fowke had raised the question of a suitable choice of a good quality brick, and in
110
September of that year, Earl Granville sanctioned the purchase of 200,000 Fareham bricks for the

cost of about £1,200.[17] On 10 August 1865 Festing prepared a progress report:

> The whole of the Stock Brickwork is up to the Eaves of the Residences, and that at the back of the centre building is 8 or 9 feet higher.
>
> The red brickwork is up to the level of the cornicions of the Residences which is as far as it can go at present.
>
> The terra cotta cornicions of the side buildings had all been delivered and that of the western side is nearly all fixed.
>
> The trusses and purlins of the roof of the side buildings are ready and those of the western side will be fixed as soon as Blanchard has finished his work there.
>
> The ironwork of the roof of the centre building is reported to be in an advanced state and will be ready by the time it is ready.[18]

During the autumn the temporary lecture theatre designed by Pennethorne was dismantled, as it was beginning to be in the way of the workmen.[19]

In 1865 Cole began to be concerned about Fowke, not only on the grounds of health, but also because of the manner in which he was running his office. Details are sparse, but we know that the Director spoke to Fowke in May concerning the expenses of his drawing office,[20] the chief draughtsman in which was John Liddell.[21] Fowke told Cole that he did not think it would be easy to produce an estimate for the cost of his working drawings,[22] and only five days later Cole recorded that he talked 'very seriously to Fowke about his neglect of his office: which he took very well',[23] and Henry Scott urged his brother Engineer to look for an additional draughtsman.[24] Fowke then produced a report in which he gave his view

---

16. PRO, Ed. 84/4, 25 July 1865.
17. PRO, Ed. 84/36, Board Minute précis, 20 September 1865.
18. PRO, Ed. 84/54. There is a progress report by Festing on preparatory drawings in PRO, Ed. 84/72, dated 18 October 1864. These included 'General Elevation of front of Theatre (this has been put aside for the present for more urgent work)', details of centre arches, roofs, flooring and staircase.
19. Smith was willing to demolish it and keep the material, for which he offered £70; he was prepared to pay £100 if he were given permission to re-use the bricks on the interior work. PRO, Ed. 84/4, 8 July 1865. On 10 October 1865, Cole noted in his diary that the roof of the old lecture theatre had been removed.
20. Cole, diary, 1 May 1865.
21. Appointed 22 December 1864 at £5 a week. PRO, Ed. 84/36, Board minute précis.
22. Cole, diary, 3 May 1865.
23. *Loc. cit.*, 8 May 1865.
24. *Loc. cit.*, 9 May 1865.

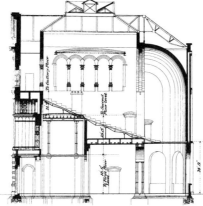

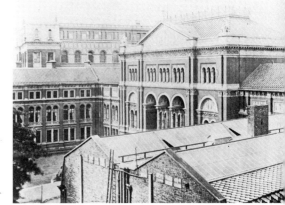

108. *(above) Section through the Lecture Theatre building, from the south*

109. *(right) Section through the Lecture Theatre and Refreshment Rooms, from the east*

110. *(far right) The Quadrangle in 1872*

that it would cost at least £2,520 to complete the working drawings for the new buildings by the end of the current financial year;[25] shortly after this he discussed with Cole the possibility of leaving the Department of Science and Art, presumably with the intention of resuming his career in the army.[26] Almost immediately afterwards, C. Rowe Dillon was appointed a manager of the drawing office, at a salary of £6 a week.[27] Liddell complained that he was being made a 'scapegoat'.[28]

In August, Fowke fell ill, and was found by Cole lying on a sofa in his house.[29] His illness was not a total surprise to Cole, who had learned as early as 1862 that Fowke's heart was not strong.[30] A month later Fowke's doctor, Haden, visited Cole to repudiate Mrs Fowke's hope that Fowke was not in danger, at which Cole himself went down to Eastbourne where Fowke was resting, and found him very weak.[31] At the beginning of October Fowke had a visit from Philip Cunliffe Owen, who thought that he was 'feeble'. On 2 December Fowke at length returned to Kensing-

ton from Eastbourne, but died two days later. Cole recorded in his diary, 'Heard that Fowke had died about 4.30'.[32] He was 42 years of age.

Fowke's death was a great blow to South Kensington. Queen Victoria wrote: 'The Queen is *truly, deeply* grieved at this. It is again one of her beloved, adored Husband's fellow workers in all that was great & good who has been taken away! He is a great, great loss. Pray say so to Mr. Cole.'[33]

Cole himself paid tribute to Fowke as 'a man of

25. PRO, Ed. 84/36, Board minute précis, 11 May 1865.
26. Cole, diary, 12 June 1865.
27. PRO, Ed. 84/36, Board minute précis, 22 June 1865. Dillon's salary was raised to £7 a week on 8 January 1869.
28. Cole, diary, 25 July 1865. 'As it was necessary to have a Scape Goat in the Drawing Office, he was made so. He was reduced to a Machine, but submitted as he was a poor man.'
29. *Loc. cit.,* 19 August 1865.
30. *Loc. cit.,* 2 March 1862.
31. *Loc. cit.,* 19 September 1865.
32. *Loc. cit.,* 4 December 1865.
33. Facsimile in Cole's *Miscellanies,* vol. xii, before f. 327 (V&A, Library).

science, possessing a fertility of invention that amounted to genius'. He said:

> At this period, when Art is so transitional, and Science is making so many discoveries, and men's minds are seething with inventions; when the use of new materials is being constantly manifested, and the new adaptation of old materials is being constantly entered upon, England has lost a man who felt the spirit of his age, and was daring enough to venture beyond the beaten path of conventionalism. Captain Fowke, to my mind, was solving the problem of the decorative use of iron, and by appreciating the spirit both of the gothic and Renaissance architects, was on the threshold of introducing a novel style of architecture.[34]

The Board expressed the wish that a commemorative bust of Fowke should be placed in the Museum, and Thomas Woolner was asked to execute this in either marble or terracotta for not more than 100 guineas.[35] On 27 December 1866, Cole, Scott, and Donnelly went to Woolner's studio to see the result, which seemed 'a good likeness'.[36] It was sent to the Paris 1867 Exhibition and is now in the Museum Library.

After Fowke's death,[37] his post was taken over by Henry Scott,[38] and because the Lecture Theatre as it is today differs so considerably from Fowke's original ground plan of 1860, it is often assumed that Scott was responsible for all the changes. On the evidence of the revised plans of 1863, 1864, and 1865, however, it must surely be clear that the building, even though it was not completed until 1868, is the work of Francis Fowke.

The Lecture Theatre buildings were finished in 1869. The surviving estimates from George Smith the builder are as follows:

Other work in the building which had been given to different contractors included the roof of Sicilian tiles by Robert Brown of Surbiton Hill, at one shilling per foot run; blinds by James Williams of Jubilee Place, Chelsea for £121 2s 8d; tiles for the lavatories, designed by James Gamble with lions, unicorns, and the cipher 'VA', by Minton, Hollins, for £56 6s, and £414. George Jennings of Palace Road Wharf, Lambeth, provided the fittings for the lavatories for £504 6s, C. Jeakes did out the kitchens for £885, while Minton, Hollins tiled the walls with plain tiles for £268. Hart & Son provided at least one lamp, with four ground-glass globes for the lavatories for £8.

The complex schemes of decoration of the

---

34. *Journal of the Royal Society of Arts*, xiv (1865–6), 59–60.
35. PRO, Ed. 84/36, Board minute précis, 12 January 1866.
36. Cole, diary.
37. Liddell used the occasion of Fowke's funeral to create some unpleasantness, complaining to Cole (diary, 12 December) that his name had deliberately been left out of the official list of those who had attended. Although Liddell was asked in February 1866 to prepare designs for the proposed new library, which he agreed to do for £20 (PRO, Ed. 84/5; these are now in the Print Room), he had exasperated Cole to such a degree that when asked by Liddell to support an application for the post of Clerk of the Works at Windsor, Cole refused. Cole later recorded in his diary, 4 June 1866, 'Mr. Liddell called – disgusted that I wd not see him. I told Scott that he must write, & see him if he wanted to see anyone. He sd he had a claim on Fowkes exrs for £50 for the [Albert] Hall drawings.'
38. Captain E. R. Festing had been appointed Fowke's Deputy in November 1864 (Cole, diary, 3 November), at £3 a week (PRO, Ed. 84/36, Board minute précis, 22 December). Cole had staff trouble and was told by Redgrave that there was dissatisfaction at 'my partiality & promotion of the Engineer Officers. That Poole was disgusted at Festings receiving pay for architectural work – Simkins at his low pay & so on' (diary, 27 December 1864). Major-General Festing, CB, FRS, became Director of the Science Museum.
39. Specification, PRO, Ed. 84/15.

---

29 September 1865	Building the kitchens[39]	£1879
18 January 1866	To provide and fix windows of the ground floor with plate glass, the main corridor and the apse with the best 26oz. sheet glass	£590
28 February 1866	Finishing ground floor corridor	£1336
27 March 1866	To cover roof of lecture theatre with milled lead	£1833
18 April 1866	To cover cornice with milled lead	£116
4 July 1866	To build lavatories	£953
	To extend kitchens	£403
18 December 1867	To furnish lecture theatre	£1087
1 December 1868	To build two air shafts in angles of buttresses of apse, from level of ceiling of refreshment room to top of parapet	£45. 15s.
3 March 1870	Mahogany doors to lecture theatre	£52. 10s.

Lecture Theatre façade and also the interiors of the Refreshment Rooms, the Ceramic Staircase and Gallery, and other parts of the range of buildings are described in the following chapter.

On 13 May 1869, the *Daily News* carried an article on

... the new Lecture Theatre, [which] is now completed, with the exception of decorations. It is a lofty and handsome building, capable of accommodating 500 persons, and there are rooms resembling private boxes at the end and sides that will seat another hundred. The Lords of the Committee of Council on Education have requested Sir Charles Wheatstone, Sir Michael Costa, Professor Tyndall, Mr. Bowley (of the Crystal Palace), Lieutenant-Colonel Scott, and Captain Donnelly, R.E., to report upon the acoustic properties of the building. It was accordingly opened for the first time last night to commence the experiments. There was a numerous attendance of ladies and gentlemen, including several noblemen, members of Parliament, and others interested in the success of the Science and Art Department. The business of the evening, according to a notice on the admission tickets, was to obtain 'audible and visible demonstrations of the varieties of musical pitch.' These were given in the shape of a lecture by Professor Guthrie ... Mr. Cole introduced the lecturer, stating that the theatre was the inheritance of Captain Fowke's; his successors were endeavouring to carry out his ideas and to make the building perfect in its hearing capabilities. When the proceedings commenced it was at once apparent that acoustic perfection was very closely reached, for at the extreme end of the spacious building the voice was heard with the utmost distinctness, and various experiments with bells and wires left no doubt that there was but little room for improvement.

The Lord President and the Vice President were among those who sat in the private gallery at the back of the theatre. This gallery did not survive for long, and, by bricking up the arches at the sides and rear, additional rooms were formed.

Other trials carried out to probe the qualities of the hall were by Mr Ella, with musical instruments, and Arthur Sullivan, with voices. To these trials the public were admitted for one shilling, with reserved seats for twice that sum.

The Refreshment Rooms, which took the place of the earlier temporary rooms beside the Brompton Oratory, were opened during 1868. They comprised three rooms, the central room, which has a semi-circular northern side, following the plan of the Lecture Theatre above it; and a smaller, square room on either side, the Grill Room (east) and the Green Dining Room (west).

In the small, enclosed, courtyard to the north of the Refreshment Rooms, various meagre outbuildings were put up in 1867 and 1868; these included such necessities as kitchens and an ice house, built for £154 from Scott's design. The contractor for this work was George Smith. The stained glass in the windows of the Refreshment Rooms served to block out the view of these buildings from the diners. The kitchens, disused since the Refreshment Rooms closed at the outbreak of the Second World War, survived, although derelict, until 1970. In that year they were either demolished, or converted into work rooms and a studio for photography.

As early as April 1866 the Department was considering the fitting of the new kitchens behind the Lecture Theatre building and Jeakes, of 51 Great Russell Street, sent a specification: among the items listed were a roasting range; a 'long apparatus consisting of a double fire Hotplate with soufflé oven on the top in the corner, heated by the spent heat of the left hotplate and between the two fires, a large oven under heated by the second fire.' There were also to be a 'stockpot plate heated by gas, with a set of 16 blocks of gas burners in 4 sections on the combustion principle ...' and a double jacketed steam pan for cooking 'large quantities of Hams'.

A new catering contractor, Fred Hill of the Oval, submitted his tender on 26 December 1867.[40] His figures were based on a rental of 1d for every 15 visitors. He offered, as suggested by P. C. Owen, a reduction on charges for the Museum staff and students. They would be expected to use the second-class room, which was the Grill Room. There was also to be a third-class service, in 'some place set apart for the mechanics and all workmen etc. employed at the Museum buildings and even of the humble working class visitors.' Hill also sent specimen tariffs for the first- and second-class rooms, and a shortened menu for staff and students. The first-class menu had 32 items, including:

40. PRO, Ed. 84/222. The Board decided on 12 August 1867 that the glass, crockery, and knives, forks etc., were to be supplied by the Department of Science and Art (PRO, Ed. 84/35, Board minute précis).

Steak Pudding	1/-
Sausages and mashed potatoes	1/-
Veal cutlets and bacon	1/3d.
Jugged Hare	1/6d.
Cold chicken and ham	2/-
Tarts in season	6d.
Ices or jellies	6d.
Stilton, Cheshire, Pickles, Celery, Salad	3d. ad libitum

The second-class menu listed 44 items, including:

Minced beef	8d.
Veal cutlets	10d.
Stewed rabbit	10d.
Poached egg and spinach	1/-
Steak pudding (large)	9d.
Steak pudding (small)	6d.
Buns and sponge cakes	1d.
Bread, butter, cheese	1d.

These prices were not cheap but they remained more or less constant at least till the end of the century.[41] The Refreshment Rooms themselves remained in use until the Second World War; after the War the present restaurant in the South Court replaced them. The decoration of the three Refreshment Rooms, which is described in the following chapter, is of particular interest, especially as it has survived to this day more or less intact.

The plan of November 1865 for the whole of the South Kensington site shows that Fowke's ideas were still developing fast at the time of his death. The terminal buildings adjoining Cromwell Road have been brought parallel to the Lecture Theatre. Behind the eastern entrance is a large gallery for the art collections, and on the western side is a gallery about 250 feet in length, in which it was intended to place the Educational Museum, and the Food and Animal Product collections. Immediately to the east of this was a court 136 feet by 94 feet, for the Educational Apparatus Museum. Entirely new was the provision of a large building to the north-west intended for the Schools of Naval Architecture and Sciences, which was eventually to be built by Henry Scott. Fowke's arcaded quadrants are still retained on this plan, but copies of it exist on which Scott's proposed modifications, replacing the quadrants by rectangular buildings occupying more of the open space at the south, have been superimposed.

All Fowke's alterations to his plans between 1860 and 1865 show progressive increases in the amounts of land to be covered by buildings, which gradually encroach upon the areas originally planned for gardens. The plan of November 1865 is for a building of 13,072,476 cubic feet, as against the 6,500,000 cubic feet proposed in 1860. Obviously such a building could not fail to be more expensive than the first version, and at a Board meeting on 19 November 1865 it was decided that the Treasury should be asked to make an application to Parliament to sanction the increased expenditure that was anticipated.

The revised plan was sent to the Treasury, accompanied by a letter dated 5 December,[42] one day after Fowke's death! The letter quoted Fowke's remark to the 1860 Committee (2431) that he would rather not be bound by these estimates, which he had made in a very few minutes, cubing out the building.

In fact, however, the buildings which had since been erected, representing 3,292,936 cubic feet, had cost less than Fowke had originally estimated per cubic foot, because he had in some places built an extra storey instead of occupying further ground space. The total expenditure to date had been £92,987, out of the original total estimate of £214,000. The new estimate was £481,072; nonetheless, 'considering the highly ornate character of portions, this museum, if completed according to the present plan, will probably be the cheapest public building of architectural pretension ever erected in this country.'

The letter concluded by suggesting that since the total sum required was very large, the Lords Commissioners might prefer to sanction only part of the expenditure at first, omitting some of the most ornate and thus most expensive parts. This modified expenditure would be £220,000. Enclosed with the letter were statements of the cost of the buildings so far erected, and of the estimated cost of completion.

---

41. Since the earliest refreshment rooms there had been, as there still are, complaints about service or food. In 1884, Alan Cole, Sir Henry's son, thought 1s 9d for his lunch too high (PRO, Ed. 84/222, 11 September), while in 1897, the contractors showed a 'want of care and consideration' in serving meals, and a member of the museum's staff, H. A. Belshaw, had found that at Harrod's everything was 'so well done', and that there was 'such a large choice of dainty dishes' that he walked to the store for lunch each day (PRO, Ed. 84/222, 12 July).

42. PRO, Ed. 84/54.

Statement of the cost of the Permanent Buildings erected at South Kensington

BUILDING	CUBIC CONTENT	TOTAL COST			COST PER CUBIC FOOT
Official Residences	465,456	£19,216	1.	11d.	10d.
New Schools & connecting building	869,106	£21,349	17.	4d.	6d.
North Court	547,349	£11,727	6.	9d.	$5\frac{1}{4}d.$
South Court	483,810	£13,420	13.	1d.	$6\frac{3}{4}d.$
Galleries east of North Court	346,600	£7,626	5.	8d.	$5\frac{1}{4}d.$
Galleries east of South Court	166,387	£6,604	5.	2d.	10d.
Stores and Office Building & continuance of Galleries east of South Court	277,770	£8,776	14.	9d.	$7\frac{1}{2}d.$
Workshops	92,336	£2,387			$5\frac{1}{4}d.$
Vernon & Turner Galleries	362,264	£8,198			$5\frac{1}{4}d.$
Long Gallery, & Female Training School	187,935	£4,000			5d.
Sheepshanks Gallery	151,200	£3,500			$5\frac{1}{2}d.$
Kitchen Building adjoining Theatre	44,133	£1,879			$10\frac{1}{4}d.$
	3,994,335	£108,685	4.	8d.	$6\frac{1}{2}d.$

**Statement showing the probable cost for completing the Permanent Buildings
14 October 1865**

BUILDING	CUBIC CONTENT	PROBABLE COST PER CU. FOOT	PROBABLE TOTAL COST	
Theatre Building now in progress	777,581	1/-	£38,879	
East and West Library buildings	972,315	1/-	£48,615	15s.
New South Court extension	1,464,120	7d.	£42,703	10s.
Continuation of store buildings	214,720	8d.	£7,157	6s.
Police and Housekeeper's apartments	123,480	8d.	£4,116	
Buildings over roadway near East Entrance	19,239	8d.	£641	6s.
South Eastern Entrance Court	399,355	7d.	£11,647	17s.
South Eastern Entrance building				
South Western Entrance building	811,440	1/3	£50,715	
East and West Quadrant arcade	159,300	1/-	£7,965	
Octagon, screen walls, urinals &c.	161,122	7d.	£4,699	7s.
Slip between Library & Court	9,600	7d.	£280	
Circular external staircase building	101,400	1/6d.	£7,605	
Laboratory & Science Schools	788,436	10d.	£32,851	10s.
Loggia or arcade	197,120	1/-	£9,856	
Tower	349,920	1/-	£17,496	
Court	937,500	7d.	£27,343	15s.
Arcade at back of Tower	75,140	1/-	£3,757	
Theatre near Science Schools	118,496	9d.	£4,459	
Arcade ,, ,, ,,	76,140	1/-	£3,807	
Narrow arcade near ,, ,,	18,900	1/-	£945	
Court	728,640	7d.	£21,252	
Centre Screen Arcade	142,272	1/-	£7,113	12s.
Alteration to Sheepshanks Gallery and junction with Theatre Building	244,798	9d.	£9,179	18s.
Bridge across Exhibition Road, iron trellis construction	119,925	10 9/11d.	£5,000	
	9,001,959	9 13/16d.	£368,085	16s.

After some months' hesitation, and an exchange of further letters, the Treasury agreed to sanction the expenditure of £195,000 over a period of six years.[43] South Kensington thus had a go-ahead for the building of a large block for the Schools of Naval Architecture and Science (E on plan); an Educational apparatus Museum (I on plan); a three-storeyed block for an Educational Library (K on plan); a block of three or four storeys for the Art Library (R on plan); a large museum court (Q on plan); office extensions, and a board room. Only the Schools of Naval Archi-tecture and Science, and the offices and board room, were eventually built exactly in accordance with this plan. A block for the Art Library was eventually built so as to close the southern side of the garden; from each end of this two courts (Rooms 41, 45) extended southward, that on the west (Room 41) being occupied by the Education and the Science Library.

---

43. Cole noted in his diary, 8 January 1867, that Whitehall had told him that although the Treasury was well disposed towards South Kensington, it was 'afraid' of the House of Commons.

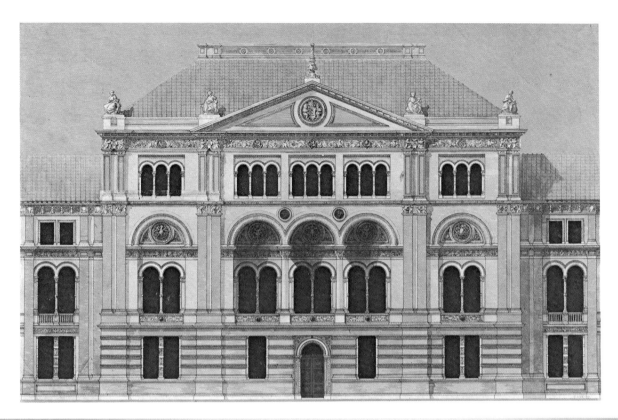

CHAPTER VIII

Decoration of the Lecture Theatre

Following hard upon the loss of Francis Fowke was a further death which the South Kensington administration could ill afford. As early as March 1862 Cole had learned that Godfrey Sykes's left lung was infected. Late in 1865 his condition deteriorated, and he went to rest in Hastings. He returned to South Kensington, apparently somewhat recovered, on the very day of Fowke's death. Early in 1866 Cole was horrified to receive a letter from Sykes, at Hastings, which he wrote on 10 January, having consulted a doctor:

His report of me is most gloomy. He gives me no hope. He says the malady from which I am suffering the most is a disease of the kidneys – called I think 'Bright's disease' and incurable. This terrible sentence I have hesitated for some days to communicate to you as I did not wish to bother you with my troubles – but tonight I have thought it right I should do so & say I will try a few more days here & then if I am not a little better I must come home. One little ray of hope I have – 'Can Mr. Haden suggest anything'. I will write a line by this post and ask him.

I certainly breathe better here & today my pulse the Dr. reports to be a little stronger but I am so fearful of being laid up here. I am anxious without some good change taking place to be at home . . .[1]

Shortly after sending this letter, Sykes returned to London, and Cole visited him at the end of February, finding him very low. 'He complained he was dying an unmanly death. . . . thought his money very ill-earned & wept a little.'[2] Four days later Sykes died, 'aged 41 years. For weeks he had scarcely eaten anything.'[3]

In his obituary of Sykes,[4] printed in the *Journal of the Society of Arts*, Cole reveals that Sykes wanted to see the decorations for the Guards' Ball in the 1862 Exhibition building shortly before it

was demolished, he was too weak to walk up the stairs, so Fowke, 'as he had a great affection for him', picked him up and carried him in his arms.

After the death of Sykes, the Board sent a message of sympathy to his widow, but an application in March by the Lord President for the granting of a pension to her was put off for a whole year until the new financial estimates were dealt with.[5] This seems somewhat unsympathetic, and it is to be presumed that Mrs Sykes did not view the promise of an early exhibition of her husband's work as an adequate substitute. It did not take the South Kensington Museum long to organize a large exhibition of Sykes's drawings. The reception of this was so mixed, that it might have been better to have left his terracotta and other decoration in the Museum to speak for him instead.

At the time of his death, Sykes was working on the decorations for the Lecture Theatre building. As in the case of Fowke, his work was continued after his death. Sykes had left copious drawings and sketches, some very slight, which were drawn upon for inspiration by his two successors, James Gamble and Reuben Townroe.

. . . in consequence of Mr. Sykes's death, his pupils, Mr. Gamble and Mr. Townroe, will take joint charge of the studio for preparing the Decorative designs of the Museum, and each will act in the absence of the other. It is their Lordships' wish that each of the artists should form under his direction a class of four pupils, selecting promising young students, who will receive an allowance for their services as soon as they are reported to be valuable. Mr. Gamble and Mr. Townroe will receive in future each six pounds a week for their services.[6]

---

1. V&A Museum Library, Cole correspondence.
2. Cole, diary, 24 February 1866.
3. 28 February 1866. He was, like Fowke, buried in Brompton cemetery.
4. March 1866, pp. 296, 297.
5. PRO, Ed. 84/36, Board minute précis, 17 March 1866.
6. *Loc. cit.*, 10 March 1866.

PLATE XXII *(opposite) Ceiling of the first flight and dome of the first landing of the Ceramic Staircase, designed by F. W. Moody*

113. *Fowke's design for the southern façade of the Lecture Theatre building*

The Lecture Theatre façade

113 The first part of the embellishment of the new building to be completed was the exterior of the south side, which was begun in 1864, while Fowke and Sykes were still alive. It was faced with red brick and much terracotta and mosaic. The terra-cotta dressings and other ornamental details were designed by Godfrey Sykes, and in general matched those that were already in position on the eastern face of the Residence. The modelling was the work of James Gamble and Reuben Townroe, and the decorations were all manufactured by Blanchard & Co. They also produced the frieze of masks and cupids from designs by James Gamble.

The main feature of the façade was three enormous recessed arches, the height of the first floor. It had been Fowke's original intention that the six columns required would be of red granite. Six columns of Mull granite were duly ordered in 1864 from James Wright of the Polished Granite Works, Aberdeen, for £189.[7] They arrived the following year, but in June 1865 Fowke had changed his mind about using them as planned, and persuaded the Board to approve his suggestion that the granite columns 'prepared for outside the

Lecture Theatre be used inside the Museum, and terra-cotta columns substituted'.[8] If these granite columns were eventually used in the Museum, they are in all probability those that Henry Scott later placed at the ends of the corridor between the two large cast courts.

The terracotta columns which Fowke had decided to use in the Lecture Theatre front were designed and modelled by Sykes.[9] Each consists of

> ... six drums, three of which are fluted, and have a *114* bough, modelled from nature, laid free over the *115* flutings. The alternate three are modelled with *116* figure subjects, and typify three divisions of man's life: Childhood, Manhood, and Old Age. Childhood – 1. The Baby. 2. Playfellows. 3. Playing at Soldiers. Manhood – 1. The Bridegroom. 2. The Warrior. 3. The Cup of Temptation. Old Age – 1. The Dignity of Age. 2. The weariness of Age. 3. The Degradation of Age.[10]

7. Ibid., 31 August 1864.

8. Ibid., 17 June 1865.

9. The memorial to Sykes in Sheffield consists of a copy of one of these columns, surmounted by a gilt urn. *Art Journal*, 1875, p. 29.

10. *Decoration of the South Kensington Museum 1862 to 1874*, 1875 (unpublished), p. 14.

114. *Terracotta columns for the Lecture Theatre façade, designed by Godfrey Sykes and made by Blanchard & Co., c. 1865*

115. *(below left) Terracotta decoration of the Lecture Theatre façade, designed by Godfrey Sykes and made by Blanchard & Co.*

116. *(below right) Detail of Sykes's Lecture Theatre columns, 1865*

117. *(top) Godfrey Sykes's first design for the pediment of the Lecture Theatre, representing the Great Exhibition of 1851*

118. *(above) The mosaic decoration of the Lecture Theatre pediment, made by Minton, Hollins & Co., from the design by Reuben Townroe*

Blanchard agreed to make these for £228 within eight weeks of the receipt of the order from South Kensington.[11] Cole was rather hurt when he escorted Lord Overstone over the buildings on 8 February 1866, for though the latter 'admired the outsides [he] took no notice of the columns'.[12] The 15-foot high terracotta columns were among Sykes's last works for the Museum, and we do not know whether he ever saw them executed and standing in the grounds before being placed in position. Several examples of Sykes's decorations were erected in the Champ de Mars, Paris, at the 1867 International Exhibition.[13]

11. PRO, Ed. 84/4, 23 October 1865.

12. Cole, diary. In a letter to Cole, 20 March 1866, G. E. Street wrote that he was afraid that he would never be converted to 'the branches of foliage round the shafts'.

13. 'Blanchard and Co., Lambeth . . . Two large columns, designed by Godfrey Sykes, late of the Kensington Museum, of tinted terracotta, not well finished, supporting arch, specimens of façade of new buildings for the Kensington Museum; pilasters with divisional panels, with enrichments in them, wanting in sharpness and good finish, no parts of ornament undercut, twisted columns &c., all of good colour and well fired; wing walls, in connection with this piece of work, built in red brick; a very good example of brickwork by Messrs. Smith & Taylor, Brompton', in 'Terra-cotta' by M. A. Pulham, in *Reports of Artisans* on the 1867 Paris Exhibition, London, Society of Arts, 1867, pp. 175, 176.

119. *(above) Design by Godfrey Sykes for the terracotta frieze on the Lecture Theatre façade*

120. *(far right) Design by Godfrey Sykes for details of the terracotta decoration on the Lecture Theatre façade*

121. *(right) Philosophy, mosaic designed by James Gamble and Reuben Townroe, on the Lecture Theatre façade*

117
118

Godfrey Sykes's first design for the Lecture Theatre façade was not liked by Cole, and in December 1864 Sykes agreed to work on a mosaic for the pediment on the subject of the Great Exhibition of 1851. Following Sykes's death, the mosaic was designed by Reuben Townroe, after Sykes's sketches.[14] It was made by the South Kensington Museum mosaic class in English earthenware mosaic, superintended by Minton, Hollins, for £500.[15] The work was undertaken during 1868.

Among Sykes's sketches were three for roundels for coloured mosaics beneath the recessed arcade. These were expanded by Gamble and Townroe into more finished designs, and represent Poetry, History and Philosophy. The first mosaic was

executed by Salviati in Venetian glass mosaic for £50; the second in English glass mosaic by Jesse Rust for £60, and the third in English ceramic mosaic was by W. B. Simpson, who charged £60 also.[16] The majolica spandrels to these roundels were designed by Gamble and Townroe, again based on slight sketches by Godfrey Sykes. They were executed by Minton, Hollins. Henry Cole noted that the mosaic made by Rust was delivered to Gamble on 1 June 1868.[17] There were several

121

14. In November 1867, Richard Redgrave 'strongly advised' that the subject in the pediment should be in 'allegory', Cole, diary.

15. PRO, Ed. 84/6, 12, 23 December 1867.

16. PRO. Ed. 84/36, Board minute précis, 18 December 1867. According to PRO, Ed. 84/6, two circular mosaics cost £145.

17. Cole, diary.

areas for which Sykes had left no designs. Among these were the majolica tiles in the soffits of the arches in front of the Lecture Theatre, which were designed and modelled by Gamble, and made by Minton, Hollins, who charged £182 10s.[18]

During the spring of 1868 the Board considered the use of large-scale terracotta sculptures as part of the decoration of the new building, probably to be placed on the skyline.

A suggestion for obtaining terracotta copies of some existing contemporary sculptures had been made as early as 1863, but nothing had come of it.

122. Instruction, *terracotta group designed by Percival Ball and made by Doulton & Co. for the Lecture Theatre façade, c. 1870*

The artists and the works suggested were: J. H. Foley, *Boy at stream*; W. Calder Marshall, *Ophelia*; Patrick MacDowell, *Day Dream*; Henry Weekes, *A Mother's Kiss*; John Lawler, *Bather*; and C. B. Birch, *Love Test*.[19] When the idea was resurrected in 1868, (Sir) J. E. Boehm was first approached, but although he agreed to sculpt a figure or group, the outcome of the undertaking is not known.[20] Percival Ball was then asked to execute two statuary groups for £250.[21] Terracotta copies were made in 1870 by Doulton of Lambeth in the company's 'best imperishable material' for £80, and the results, two groups representing 'Instruction' are placed on either side of the Lecture Theatre pediment.[22]

122

Surmounting the pediment is a terracotta base for a flagpole, in the form of two putti grasping the staff. This was designed by James Gamble, and made by Blanchard & Co.

On the apex of the rectangular roof of the Lecture Theatre itself is an iron railing designed by Godfrey Sykes, and indeed signed by him.

The firm of Joseph Hart & Son, of Wych Street, submitted a tender for making this in February 1866:

> Cast iron cresting, consisting of 58 circular standards, 6 square standards, at external angles fitted with dragons. To be completed in 11 weeks. £385. Cresting made of iron and copper, to be completed in 14 weeks. £870.[23]

There remains one important group of decoration: mosaic panels and lunettes. These, brown and buff in colouring, were designed, probably after Sykes, by Reuben Townroe, and made by the South Kensington Museum mosaic class, superintended by William E. Alldridge, for

---

18. PRO, Ed. 84/5, 26 April 1866, PRO, Ed. 84/36, Board minute précis, 5 May 1866.

19. PRO, Ed. 84/36, Board Minute précis, 30 May 1863.

20. PRO, Ed. 84/6, 15 May 1868. Boehm stated that his fee would be 26 guineas for a quarter-size model, 18 inches high, or £150 for a 6-foot figure.

21. PRO, Ed. 84/36, Board minute précis, 30 May 1868, Ed. 84/6, 26 May, 1868.

22. When Doulton's saw Ball's groups in August 1870, they added an additional 14 guineas to their estimate as a fee to Ball in order to touch up the terracotta when it was delivered from the mould.

23. PRO, Ed. 84/5, 28 February 1866. Scott was unable to persuade Hart to lower his price, and was forced to order the cheaper, cast-iron version. Lettered 'Built In The 29th Year Of The Reign Of Queen Victoria By Francis Fowke Capt RE And Godfrey Sykes Artist An Dom MDCCCXVI.'

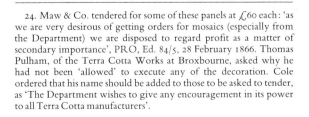

123. *(top) The Lords President and Vice-Presidents of the Committee of Council on Education. Mosaic panel, designed by Reuben Townroe and made by Minton, Hollins & Co., for the Lecture Theatre façade*

124. *(above) Design by Godfrey Sykes for a mosaic panel depicting South Kensington officials and designers*

125. *(right) Lithograph reproducing the mosaic panels on the Lecture Theatre building*

123
124

Minton, Hollins.[24] Round the lunettes are inscribed 'Wisdom exalteth her children and layeth hold of them that seek her,' and 'All wisdom cometh from the Lord, and is with him for ever.'

There are, in addition, five panels by Townroe, each being about 4 feet 6 inches high. Three of

24. Maw & Co. tendered for some of these panels at £60 each: 'as we are very desirous of getting orders for mosaics (especially from the Department) we are disposed to regard profit as a matter of secondary importance', PRO, Ed. 84/5, 28 February 1866. Thomas Pulham, of the Terra Cotta Works at Broxbourne, asked why he had not been 'allowed' to execute any of the decoration. Cole ordered that his name should be added to those to be asked to tender, as 'The Department wishes to give any encouragement in its power to all Terra Cotta manufacturers'.

THE BUILDING NEWS. MAR 3. 1876.

SCIENCE AND ART DEPARTMENT

MOSAIC·DECORATIONS·FROM·THE·EXTERIOR·OF·THE·NEW·BUILDINGS·

MAJOR GENERAL SCOTT K.C.B · R.E· ARCHITECT

SOUTH · KENSINGTON · MUSEUM

125 these are on the western side; in the centre is a group emblematic of the Department of Science and Art. On the panel to the left of this, a female figure leads a group of peers and members of the House of Commons connected with the Department. The peers are in coronation robes. They are, reading from the left, the Earl of Derby, Viscount Palmerston, the Duke of Marlborough, the Duke of Buckingham and Chandos, Earl Russell, Benjamin Disraeli, W. E. Gladstone, Sir Stafford Northcote, Lord Sydenham, F. Cory, and T. Milner Gibson. The panel to the right depicts members of the Department of Science and Art, connected with the Museum. They are Richard Redgrave, RA, Sir Henry Cole, Godfrey Sykes, Captain Fowke, J. Lockwood Kipling, Gilbert Redgrave, James Gamble, Matthew Eldon, J. D. Wakefield, and Reuben Townroe. The reason for the inclusion of Lockwood Kipling (the father of Rudyard Kipling) is something of a mystery. He does not seem to figure among the records of the Museum, but as he had been a student at the School of Art in the Potteries, as well as at South Kensington, it is presumed that he was connected with the terracotta and mosaic work.

On the eastern side of the lecture theatre is another representation of Science and Art, and to the left of this a panel depicting J. W. Henley, Lord Taunton, Earl Granville, the Marquis of Salisbury, W. Cowper Temple, Lord Stanley of Alderley, C. B. Adderley, Lord Aberdare, and Robert Lowe.[25] On the right side is another panel. This does not, however, date from the same period, for the easternmost bay was not constructed until 1901 by Sir Aston Webb, when he realigned the eastern wall of the quadrangle. He put in a mosaic panel to match the others: it is described on p. 215.

The surviving estimates from Blanchard for all three years are as follows:[26]

126. Enamel plaque commemorating Sir Henry Cole's dog Jim, in the south wall of the Quadrangle

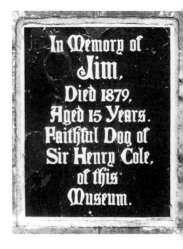

As might be expected, the doorway at ground   *127* level, intended at that time to be the Museum's main entrance, was designed and fashioned with care and splendour. The two pupils of Sykes used sketches left by their master, and the door seems to have been quite closely based on the one Alfred Stevens had designed for the Jermyn Street   *128* museum. The bronze doors themselves were electrotyped by G. Franchi and Son. In fairly high relief, the six panels show Chemistry (Davy); Astronomy (Newton); Mechanics (Watt); Architecture (Bramante); Sculpture (Michelangelo); and Painting (Titian); these were also exhibited in Paris, 1867. Above is the inscription 'Better is it to get wisdom than gold' from Proverbs 16:16. Over the doors are majolica figures of 'Science'

25. According to a 'Statement of Cost' of the decoration of the Museum, received from Sir John Donnelly in March 1899, the cost of the figures and mosaics for the Lecture Theatre building was £1,286, PRO, Ed. 84/57.
26. PRO, Ed. 84/4, 5 & 6.

4 August 1864	11 double abaci for the coupled columns of 1st floor ... the pair	£1 12s.
22 September 1864	The whole of the terra-cotta work from the top of the cornice to ground storey, centre building	£774
	3 bays on either side	£353
16 February 1865	Archivolts, mouldings etc. for large arches	£314
23 October 1865	Parapet and pediment (in ten weeks)	£393
11 January 1866	Two chimney-caps for lecture theatre	£57 10s.
15 March 1866	Three lunettes for back arches over the large centre columns	£86
7 December 1867	Spandrels	£58

127. *Design for the principal doorway of the Lecture Theatre building by Godfrey Sykes*

128. *(below left) The doorway and doors of the Lecture Theatre building, designed by James Gamble and Reuben Townroe*

129. *(below right) Detail of the terracotta decoration of the doorway of the Lecture Theatre building*

and 'Art', and spandrels, all made by Minton, Hollins & Co., based on designs by Sykes. The terracotta surround, decorated with lizards and snakes basking in the sun, was the work of Blanchard, and cost £98 10s. Minton, Hollins charged £160 for the two figure panels and the spandrels, which were ordered in April 1868.[27]

The electrotyping of the doors themselves cost £180,[28] and to make them even more splendid,

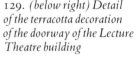

129

27. PRO, Ed. 84/4 & 36, Board minute précis, 24 April 1868.
28. PRO, Ed. 84/6, estimate, 3 January 1867.

the Department wanted them to be gilded. Franchi, having made the electrotypes, estimated that to electro-gild the doors would cost another £500. It was impossible to get a lower estimate, and enthusiasm at South Kensington for the project cooled rapidly. Although the Board still agreed that the doors should be gilded, it was stipulated that the final cost must not exceed £100.[29] Obviously, at this figure nothing worthwhile was going to be achieved, and eventually the man who had been seeing to the painting of the museum rooms, Kershaw, received the commission as a very fifth-rate best, as he charged only £57. For this sum, he agreed to slap on a coating of Dutch metal, two coats of best gold leaf, and two coats of varnish.[30] How long this gilding stood up to the weather is not known. It was still there in 1899, but none of the photographs shows it, so one must presume that, as on the figure of the Prince Consort on the Albert Memorial, it disappeared relatively swiftly.

Cole was immensely proud of his buildings, especially as in the main, the critics were impressed. Douglas Galton, of the Office of Works, even told him after an inspection that the Department of Science and Art should make the 'architectural design for the War Office'.[31] When Cole went to Dulwich to see Barry's new College he found it 'interesting but far less stylish than our own red brick and Terra Cotta'. Cole was told by Layard on 19 July 1868 that 'Triqueti had told him the finest buildings in London are now ours', and a year or two later the French architect Eugène Viollet-le-Duc asked, and was given, permission to publish drawings of the Museum buildings.[32]

The Lecture Theatre interior

The ceiling of the Lecture Theatre was painted sky-blue, and lighting was provided at night by an enormous burner 27 feet square, suspended 15 feet below the glass and iron ceiling, with a grating to allow for ventilation. This device, supplied with some 700 fish-tail burners, was by George Forrest & Son, and cost £38.[33] Several people present at the acoustic trials in 1869 commented upon the mellow and delightful soft glow produced by the gaslight.

It was natural, considering the lavish scale of decoration being undertaken throughout the Museum, that a room affording such scope for embellishment as the Lecture Theatre would not remain for long unadorned. During 1868 Edward Poynter, whose work features largely in the Grill Room, part of the Refreshment Rooms suite on the ground floor of the building, was approached to prepare a design for the apse of the Lecture Theatre. Although Poynter, who later became President of the Royal Academy, worked for several years on this project, it did not come to fruition. A model of the apse, however, with Poynter's design painted on it, has been preserved to this day. The design and model were complete by March 1870, and Poynter was given the Department's permission to display them at the Royal Academy exhibition.[34]

Poynter described the design to Henry Cole in a letter:

xxix

> In the centre at the top, & in the unfinished band below it, will be a conventionalised representation of the general scheme of Creation – the Sun, Moon, Day & Night, the Stars, &c, beasts rocks, rivers, plants, birds, rain, snow, &c all done in the simplest decorative manner.
>
> Below, the picture will be divided into two parts; that to the left will treat of matters connected with Art and Poetry, that to the right with Science & Philosophy.
> On the left.
> Beauty unveils herself to the world of Art & Poetry; youth respectfully kisses the hem of her robe. To the right of Beauty is a figure representing the Imaginative faculty: she gives a pen to a youthful poet. Further to the right (to the left of the spectator) is a group of figures listening to the inspired song of the Poetess. Above them is a picture of Dante & Virgil crossing the Styx (from Dante's Inferno) suggestive of the vivid power of the imagination.
> On the right.
> Truth sits enthroned & trims the Lamp of Know-

---

29. PRO, Ed.84/67, 1 February 1868; Ed. 84/36, Board minute précis, 23 March 1868.
30. PRO, Ed. 84/6, 10 April 1868; ordered 20 April 1868.
31. Cole, diary, 2 May 1870.
32. Ibid., 20 March 1870, 19 July 1868; PRO, Ed. 84/12, 20 October 1871.
33. PRO, Ed. 84/36, Board minute précis, 4 May 1868.
34. Department of Sculpture, A.12-1973. Poynter agreed to make the model and decorate it for 300 guineas. Included in this sum was 'the cost of a journey to Italy for studying the system of mosaic and mural decoration in the churches & palaces there'. PRO, Ed. 84/6, 30 July 1868; Ed. 84/67, 18 March 1870. The model was subsequently illustrated in the *Architectural Review*, 11, 1897, p. 124. It was No. 145 in the exhibition 'Marble Halls', at the Victoria and Albert Museum, 1973. See J. Physick and M. Darby, *Marble Halls*, 1973, p. 206.

130. *Designs by Godfrey Sykes for an ornamental screen at the northern end of the Prince Consort's Gallery; used instead at the head of the Lecture Theatre staircases*

ledge held up by a youth to illuminate the world of Science. On her left a group of female figures & two children represent Instruction. On her left again (& to the right of the picture) a group of figures represents Humanity awakening to the knowledge of Truth. One slothful figure is angry at being disturbed, another remains asleep &c. – Above is a picture of the Death of Socrates, suggesting the strength of Philosophy.

Below are two ranges of figures which were partly completed when I took the design from you in April last. Representative men sit beneath & above them are abstract figures of the Arts & Sciences, which they represent. Some alteration will have to be made in the positions of these figures, so as to make them correspond with the principal scheme of placing all the Arts on one side & the Sciences on the other. Galileo & the figure of Astronomy above him will be moved, for instance, to the seat next beyond Archimedes; & Homer will be placed next to Ictinus on his left (or to some other position on the left of the picture) . . .[35]

It was decided to reproduce the design by Minton Campbell's mosaic process, and in July 1872 Poynter chose the figure of Michelangelo to be executed full size as a trial. The experiment was a failure, and nothing more is on record until four years later, when Poynter, not at all discouraged, wrote to suggest that the unfinished schemes for decoration in the Museum should be completed, as it was 'unquestionably most important' that they should be used as 'a means of *Education* for the students in the Training Schools & National Scholars'.[36] He took pains to point out that the £200 for the decoration of the soffit of the Lecture Theatre arch included payment for his design and assistance. This arch divides the main hall of the Lecture Theatre from the apse. The decoration on its underside was put in hand, and is still to be seen.

Encouraged by this success, Poynter came forward again another year later with an extremely lavish proposal, which was that the coved ceiling of the theatre should be covered by glass mosaics to his own designs, as well as the large areas of wall.[37] Various estimates were obtained, and it was found that the work would cost at least £6,100.[38] Once again, no more is heard of the suggestion, and as the mosaics were certainly never executed, it is not difficult to imagine the reaction of the First Commissioner to the proposal.

The staircases leading to the Lecture Theatre from the first floor have iron rails designed by Godfrey Sykes, and screens of iron on the top landing, designed by Sykes, modelled by James Gamble, and made by Smith. The latter also cast

130

35. PRO, Ed. 84/67, 2 January 1871.
36. *Loc. cit.,* 16 December 1876.
37. Ibid., 11 November 1877, Poynter to MacLeod.
38. PRO, Ed. 84/36, Board minute précis, 20 November 1877; Ed. 84/67, 30 November 1877.

iron ornaments in the spandrels of the screens from wax models by Gamble for £45.[39] Sykes's designs, used here, had originally been made for a screen intended to stand at the northern end of the Prince Consort's Gallery, but never erected. The ceilings on the landings, painted in grisaille by W. Wise and O. Gibbons, were designed by F. W. Moody. William Bell Scott designed a mural for one of the staircases, and although it was never executed, the sketch is preserved.[40]

As soon as Roy Strong became Director in 1974, he asked the Department of the Environment to make a complete survey of the Museum's roofs, many of which were letting in rainwater at an alarming rate. The first roof to be rebuilt was that of the Lecture Theatre, a necessity made urgent by an unfortunate accident. A student of the Royal College of Art had penetrated the roof-space, walked across the inner glass ceiling and fallen

through onto the audience of a lecture. Fortunately he survived although badly injured. The Lecture Theatre had to be closed until 1977 as the ceiling could only be repaired by completely filling the room with scaffolding.

The inner ceiling was made solid and the opportunity was also taken to rebuild the outer roof, and instal air-conditioning.

The West Staircase

Of all the decorations within the Museum sanctioned by the Board, the most controversial has always been the highly ornamented West Staircase (or Ceramic Staircase), which later was the

XXI

XX

131
132
133
134

---

39. PRO, Ed. 84/6, 27 January 1868. The staircase rails are similar in design to those of the North, East and Board Room staircases.

40. V&A Museum Print Room, No. 7356.I.

135. *The Ceramic (West) Staircase, designed by F. W. Moody*

Robbia ware and mosaic. The third flight, leading up to the Art Schools (now the Royal College of Art), remains incomplete.

The 'Della Robbia' panels and friezes were   *135* modelled by Moody assisted by R. Lunn, Albert Gibbons and E. Wormleighton, and executed by Minton. The ceilings, domes, panels and spandrels were in Colin Minton Campbell's new and experimental process of vitrified ceramic painting (the tesserae are hexagonal).[42] The subjects of the paintings on the ceilings and spandrels were painted by Moody, and three spandrels by W. Wise, Owen Gibbons, and executed by Minton. Cole's diary records (29 May 1868) that he was suggesting experiments for the colour of Moody's staircase to show the majolica to advantage. In May 1870, Scott sent the Office of Works, a list of 'Artists employed on Decorative Work'. Besides Moody, Townroe and Gamble, 'Artists', who were paid £6 a week, these were Beattie, Lunn and Wise at 1s 6d an hour – they were 'Modellers'. In addition, Alldridge as 'Moaicist' received 1s 6d an hour and Foster, a National Scholar, 1s.[43]

The four side panels of the first flight represent   XXII Literature, Music and Art. The coved ceiling has a painting showing the Pursuit of Art by Man. At either side, in the centre, were once medallion portraits of Queen Victoria and Prince Albert.

There are two domes on the landing, one of them with Ceres, Mercury and Vulcan, representing respectively Agriculture, Commerce and Manufactures, grouped round a terrestrial globe; in the spandrels are figures representing Surveying, Painting, Sculpture, and Architecture. The other dome shows Apollo and Minerva and Poetry, Music and Art, grouped round a celestial globe. The figures in the spandrels are of Spectrum Analysis, Geometry, Chemistry and Astronomy.

The coved ceiling of the second flight contains an allegorical group of Wisdom seated on a throne, with Ignorance, Superstition, and Apathy, overthrown by Science and Truth.

target for destruction by Sir Cecil Smith, in the years immediately before the First World War. It was saved only by a determined effort (described in Chapter XIV) by a small group of dedicated men, led by Sir Henry Cole's son, Alan, who was determined that every move by the Director should be made as public as possible.

The carcass of the staircase was built by George Smith for £1,217, during 1865. But for Sykes's death early the following year, undoubtedly the decoration of the staircase would have been designed and supervised by him, but for better or worse, the Lord President asked Frank Moody to prepare a scheme.[41] Moody seized the bait enthusiastically, and as a result the staircase of two flights was entirely encased in so-called Della

41. PRO, Ed. 84/4, tender dated 25 July 1865. It was first proposed to use Portland stone for the steps, but this was changed to Cadeby stone (PRO, Ed. 84/4, George Smith, 12 October 1865, for £181). (In about 1966, the Ministry of Public Building and Works laid lino tiles, and metal edging to the treads.) PRO, Ed. 84/36, Board minute précis, 12 March 1866.

42. 'On a new method of producing durable mural paintings by fictile vitrification' by A. S. Cole, *Journal of the Society of Arts*, 19, 1870, pp. 65–72.

43. PRO, Works 17/24/1.

The third flight is undecorated, but the two domes have paintings of Cupids with the garland of Fame, and the heads of Phidias, Michelangelo, Raphael and Titian in one, and Archimedes, Galileo, Bacon and Newton in the other.

To complete this rather overpowering ensemble, Moody produced two stained-glass windows for the first landing. That on the left was of 'Art' with figures of Rubens, Rembrandt, Titian, Michelangelo, Raphael, Palissy, Palladio and Benvenuto Cellini. This was drawn from Moody's design by W. Wise on to muslin and painted, and then transferred to glass, which was fired and completed by Powell & Sons. The window on the right was, of course, emblematic of 'Science', and included portrayals of Newton, Leibniz, Copernicus, Galileo, Euclid, Archimedes, Priestley, Wollaston and Watt. The design was also drawn on to muslin by W. Wise, assisted in the transfer to glass by Owen Gibbons, E. Wormleighton and H. W. Foster, and the glass was finished by Powell & Sons. Although the paintings and ceramic decoration can still be seen, the stained glass has now been replaced.

Moody designed the mosaic pavement on the landing, which was made by Minton, Hollins.[44] This and the floor tiles, on sixty-eight risers, cost £226.[45] For designing the stained-glass windows, Moody asked for a fee of £55, and this request received the approval of the Board in October 1865.[46] Powell's estimate for their part in the work was £110.[47] G. Franchi provided eight gilt electrotype reproductions for use in the mouldings for £20 in 1867.[48]

Of all the newspapers taking an interest in the growth of the Museum's building, the *Standard* was pre-eminent, although it was not always too accurate in some of the descriptions. A lengthy review appeared on 5 February 1869, under the heading 'Metropolitan Improvements'. The report was generally favourable, but expressed one reservation:

Everybody has heard of the Royal heart, on which was engraved the name of ... Calais; and assuredly should a *post-mortem* examination be ever held of the remains of any official of South Kensington, the operator might well expect to find the right and left ventricles stamped respectively in highly-illuminated and gorgeously-inexplicable letters with the never-failing local legend of 'Science and Art'.

The ultimate bathos had been reached, continued the *Standard* by filling all the odd corners and spaces with the monogram 'SA'. Little did the paper realize that, far from dying out, the habit received a fresh impetus thirty years later when there was a change to 'VA'.

Not everyone was completely in agreement with the *Standard*'s somewhat heady praise of the decoration. A correspondent (signing himself Scrutator) to the *Architect*[49] was much more critical, considering the painted ceilings 'entirely inappropriate' and asserting that 'there is about the whole of the staircase, and indeed about many of the new decorations, an apparent laxity in the use of the human figure, which is not a very hopeful sign. In the dado there are unfortunate creatures crammed into sloping panels in the most painful and acrobatic fashion.' Another correspondent, writing to the *Builder*,[50] though quite liking the staircase, observed that the masks in the sloping panels were lopsided, with one eye higher than the other, 'a decoration which I cannot but consider a fearful violation of good taste and common sense.' Lord Leighton was not enthusiastic either, and told Henry Cole that he had thought 'Moody's majolica staircase bad in modelling'.[51]

Despite these adverse comments, work on the staircase progressed steadily, and it was completed in 1871. Among the costs were £128 to Kershaw for painting the walls greyish-green and gilding all mouldings,[52] £174 8s 4d to Powell & Son for painting, firing, leading and fixing the two windows on the landing,[53] and £1,400 to Minton, Hollins for panelling the staircase.[54]

Late in 1876, the Director, Philip Cunliffe Owen, told the Board that due to the spreading

44. *Decorations of the South Kensington Museum 1862 to 1874*, 1875 (unpublished), p. 13.

45. PRO, Ed. 84/6, 4 February 1868; Ed. 84/36, Board minute précis, 12 February 1868.

46. PRO, Ed. 84/36, Board minute précis, 12 October 1865.

47. PRO, Ed. 84/61, 19 May 1866, '... P.S. Specimen we made from Mr. Moody's drawing is not paid for; we have sent the account ... There is no hurry about it but thought better to tell you to prevent confusion afterwards.'

48. PRO, Ed. 84/6, tender dated 16 April, ordered 11 May 1867.

49. 13 February 1869.

50. 24 April 1869.

51. Cole, diary, 8 June 1868.

52. PRO, Ed. 84/7, April 1869.

53. Ibid., 12 July 1870; PRO, Ed. 84/36, Board minute précis, 21 July 1870.

54. PRO, Ed. 84/7, 23 April 1869, Ed. 84/36, Board minute précis, 23 June 1871.

In 1878 the staircase received an unexpected bonus in the form of a memorial to Sir Henry 136 Cole. After Cole's retirement as Director in 1873, a group of admirers started a fund for a suitable testimonial to commemorate his contribution to the foundation and development of the South Kensington Museum. Frank Moody designed a majolica panel with a mosaic portrait of Cole in the centre, executed by Florence Cole. Characteristically Cole took an active interest in the preparation of his memorial. He was understandably offended when, in February 1875, the Board pronounced that it had decided not to allow in the Museum any portrait of a living person.

> ... such is the representative official view of my services & personal services to those in the Museum. Owen owes his whole position to me: MacLeod whom I shielded for his neglect & incapacity in the accounts. Sandford who wd not have opened the Exhibition of 1862 without my help. I had got so hardened to the blows and ingratitude that I can truly say I am now indifferent.[55]

The Duke of Westminster asked the Board to reconsider, and eventually permission was granted. Work then progressed, and in July 1877 Cole saw 'Moody and Florry completing the Portrait for the Tablet which looked well.'[56] Poynter, who was asked to pronounce on its artistic merits, told MacLeod that he did not care for the mosaic portrait, 'but it must be remembered that [Cole] took a great interest in the revival of this material as a means of decoration; and therefore its use here is appropriate.'[57]

Other ornamentation for the staircase included large sculpted figures of Plato and Aristotle, which were not approved; and mosaic portraits of the Queen, Prince Albert, and the Prince and Princess

fame of the Ceramic Staircase, other museums were applying for specimens of the majolica decoration. He submitted the suggestion that Minton might be given the authority to reproduce 'specimens' for sale. As Norman MacLeod had no objection, a suggested price list for various items was drawn up:

	£	s.	d.
Coloured fruit border 3' 5½ inches wide		2	5	0
Upright panel, 12 inches wide, in two colours		2	10	0
Dado, 2' 7", height about 4 feet	20	0	0
Panel, orange ground, 7 feet long	5	0	0
Large panel with names of artists	20	0	0
Piece of leaf moulding, white and yellow, 18 inches by 3¾ inches			2	0

and various other small pieces for 2/- or 2/6d.

55. Cole, diary, 27 February 1875.
56. Ibid., 4 July 1877.
57. PRO, Ed. 84/67, 9 August 1878.

PLATE XXV *(opposite) Painted panels by Sir Edward Burne-Jones in the Green Dining Room*

137. *(right) The ceiling of the Ceramic Gallery, showing the friezes incorporating names of ceramic-making regions, gas fittings, and an electric-light fitting, 1910. Detail of ill. 138*

of Wales, which were made by the ladies of the mosaic class,[58] and two of which can be seen in a view of the staircase by Watkins, but which have subsequently disappeared.

According to a 'Statement of Costs' of the decoration of the Museum, received from Sir John Donnelly in March 1899, the West Staircase cost £3,760.[59]

The Ceramic Gallery

137
138
Moody played quite a major role in the decoration of the first-floor gallery, known as the Ceramic Gallery. He designed the ceilings, which, together with those of the Lecture Theatre staircases, were painted under his superintendence by W. Wise, for which his estimate was £250.[60] Godfrey Sykes, shortly before his death, designed a painted frieze of the names of places where pottery had been manufactured, to run round the gallery. This frieze was painted by E. F. Brewtnall, Hubert Herkomer, and E. J. Gregory, all former students of the School of Art. Minton, Hollins & Co., who submitted an estimate of £414,[61] designed and made the tiles for the floor. James Gamble decided to make use of majolica-decorated columns, similar to those planned by Godfrey Sykes for the Centre Refreshment Room. The majolica for ten columns was made and fixed by Minton for £620.[62] The colour scheme for them was in grey and white. Round the drums were the names of Pousa, Vitalis, Luca della Robbia, Maestro Giorgio of Gubbio, Francesco Xanto, Veit Hirschvögel, François Charpentier, Johann Böttcher and Josiah Wedgwood in letters of the pictorial alphabet designed by Godfrey Sykes, and which still decorates the Centre Refreshment Room. The columns were removed early in the present century, amid a storm of protest, and replaced by plain plaster columns, which themselves were later removed.

The colour scheme was generally light in tone, with soft white paint between the cornice and ceiling, and the pilaster capitals gilded.[63]

The most interesting feature of the decoration of the Ceramic Gallery, however, was the stained glass, designed by William Bell Scott. Along the whole length of the gallery on the north side were fourteen windows (now bricked up, but still visible from the outside). Scott first met Henry Cole about the decorations in January 1867.[64] He was then commissioned, first to design glass for

139
140

58. PRO, Ed. 84/67, Memorandum upon the Decorations to be completed, 1876.

59. PRO, Ed. 84/57.

60. The westernmost portion of the ceiling was repainted in 1898 by Philip Conard, a former student of the Schools, for £20, PRO, Ed. 84/68.

61. PRO, Ed. 84/67.

62. PRO, Ed. 84/6, 17 March 1868.

63. PRO, Ed. 84/7, Kershaw's estimate for the western portion was £127, 20 July 1869. According to Sir John Donnelly's 'Statement of Costs', PRO, Ed. 84/57, the Ceramic Gallery cost £1,205.

64. Cole, diary, 28 January 1867.

138. *(above) The Ceramic Gallery in 1910*

139. *(left) Designs by William Bell Scott for the windows of the Lecture Theatre staircases*

two windows at £50 each,[65] and later to prepare a whole series.

So as not to darken the interior by using traditional strongly coloured glass, Scott employed a new method, in which the pictures are designed

> by the point of a brush on sheets of milled glass, producing an effect like that of large, transparent pen-and-ink drawings or etchings, ... and the only colour added, the yellow stain, is the colour least obstructive, and the least demoralizing to the eye.[66]

Initial difficulties in the firing of such large panes (between 3 and 4 feet high) were overcome, and the artist's only disappointment was that the firing

65. PRO, Ed. 84/36, Board minute précis, 16 October 1867. Morris & Co. submitted a design for a four-light window in the gallery, together with an estimate of £209, and a request for £3 10s for the drawing.

66. *Decorations of the South Kensington Museum 1862 to 1874*, 1875 (unpublished), pp. 20, 21.

140. *Design by William Bell Scott for a window in the Ceramic Gallery*

made the pictures fainter. The method had a great advantage in that the artist himself was able to prepare the final product.

The overall scheme of the subjects, which was suggested by Henry Cole, was to illustrate successive periods of ceramic manufacture, to correspond with the chronological arrangement of the ceramic objects displayed in the gallery. The subjects were: 1. Chinese; 2. Japanese; 3. Egyptian; 4. Greek; 5. Hispano-Moresque; 6. Majolica; 7 and 8. Dutch, Flemish, and Dresden ware; 9 and 10. French (Palissy, Sèvres); 11. Luca della Robbia; 12. English (mechanical processes); 13. English (skilled workmanship); 14. incidents in the history of English pottery.

The windows on the Lecture Theatre staircases were also filled with stained glass designed by Scott, illustrating the arts and crafts of civilized life. The windows of the West Staircase represented classical subjects: Pygmalion, Vulcan forgiving the bolts of love, watched by Venus and Cupid, Ceres teaching Triptolamus the use of the plough, and Orpheus.

The windows of the East Staircase depicted incidents in the lives of Giotto and Raphael: Cimabue discovering the young Giotto as a shepherd drawing on a stone, Giotto painting in the Arena Chapel in Padua, watched by Dante; Raphael working on a picture of St Michael in Perugino's studio, and painting the portrait of Pope Julius.[67]

During 1869, Festing experimented in lighting one end of the ceramic gallery by gas lights placed outside the windows. On the whole, he reported, the experiment was successful, though on squally nights gusts of wind interfered with the light.[68] Later, gas lighting was installed inside.

William Bell Scott's glass was removed during the early years of this century and was rediscovered in store in a fragmentary state in 1974.

The Green Dining Room

The decorations of the Green Dining Room, the westernmost room of the suite of three Refreshment Rooms on the ground floor of the Lecture Theatre building, are some of the most interesting in the Museum. Late in 1865, Cole, Redgrave and Fowke took the venturesome step of asking the new firm of Morris, Marshall & Faulkner to prepare designs and estimates for the western room. £100 was allowed for preliminary sketches.[69]

The moving spirit behind the firm of Morris, Marshall and Faulkner, which was founded in April 1861, was William Morris (1834–96), poet, designer and socialist. Associated with the firm were his friends the painters Edward Burne-Jones, Dante Gabriel Rossetti and Ford Madox Brown, and the architect Philip Webb. Faulkner was business manager; and Marshall was a surveyor friend of Brown's. In its early days, when its

67. See an account in *The Architect*, 27 February 1869.
68. *17th Report ... 1869* (1870), p. 361. Such a method had previously been used at the new Houses of Parliament. See M. H. Port, *The Houses of Parliament*, 1976, p. 230.
69. PRO, Ed. 84/36, Board minute précis, 30 November 1865.

131

premises were in Red Lion Square, the firm received mainly ecclesiastical commissions, especially from the architect G. F. Bodley. Stained glass was predominant in its output: Morris's great textile and wallpaper designs were yet to come. In 1865, the firm moved to Queen Square. Marshall and Faulkner had dropped out, and Morris was fully in charge, although his financial position was becoming difficult.

It was something of a turning point in the firm's fortunes when, in 1865–7, it received commissions to decorate rooms in two prominent secular buildings: these were the Armoury and Tapestry Rooms in St James's Palace, and the Dining Room at South Kensington. Although the former were somewhat altered later, the latter remains as the classic example of Morris's early domestic decorative style.

Later, white paint and blue and white china were to figure in his interiors, but here a certain shadowy gloom shows that he was still under the influence of the Gothic Revival.

141
142 The decorations of the Green Dining Room were described by the *Standard* on 26 December 1868, when they were almost complete:

> [The decorations] are in the Elizabethan style, the lower portion of the walls being panelled, while the upper part is decorated in low relief in coloured plaster.

The panelling was painted bluish green, which the *Standard* did not find entirely satisfactory.

> Above this plain panel, which reaches to the height of about four feet six inches, is a second range two feet six inches in height, each panel containing, on a gilt ground, alternately groups of foliage and painted figures. Of these there will be in all 68 ...

XXIII > The wall above the panelling is decorated in a manner, as we believe, almost entirely new. It is of plaster, on which the pattern is moulded in low relief. The ground is pale green, and on it is traced in a darker green a series of conventional willow branches, with flowers and fruit.

Although this ornamentation was, at first glance, 'exceedingly effective', closer inspection revealed that it was composed of blocks about three feet square, and, although every effort had been made to conceal the joins, the recurring nature of the pattern drew the observers' attention to them.

> Above the plaster work we come next to a frieze, about three feet in height, and of a very quaint design, consisting of a series of small blue panels, containing alternately a dog, a hare, and an exceedingly conventional 'tree'. Above and below is an indented border with a red ground, the lower border presenting in the larger spaces between the panels a series of conventional flowers, and the upper a series of setting suns. Above this again is a shallow egg and tongue cornice on a red ground, the eggs and tongues being gilt and the mantles blue.

> ... The floor is of red tiles, octagon and square, *XXIV* and the furniture of massive oak in the style of the period. Perhaps the best thing in the room is the window glass ... [The windows] are filled with small round panes of a light green-coloured glass, embellished with deliciously quaint little representations – semi-conventional, semi-naturalistic – of various birds, beasts, and fishes ... There are also in the three windows six oblong painted panels of a considerably larger size, each containing a female figure. These windows are decidedly the best part of the room, and may receive almost unqualified praise.

> Very different are the doorways, which are not only weak, but absolutely contemptible. They can hardly, indeed, be called doorways at all, being little more than mere holes in the wall lined with woodwork painted in the same bilious blue-green as the rest of the panelling.

Documentary records of Morris's tenders and designs are scanty. However, the firm estimated £272 for the three stained-glass windows, exclusive of packing and fixing.[70] The three windows each contain two panels, depicting a girl picking flowers, except in one where she plays a musical instrument. The next year Morris asked for £277 14s 0d for colouring and gilding the plaster ceiling, and painting the panelled dado. A further £291 6s 0d would be required for designing the seventy panels with figures and 'patterns' with gold, above the dado.

Philip Webb was responsible for much of the decoration of the West Room. W. R. Lethaby, a later commentator, notes that the Webb accounts record, between 1 July 1866 and 20 November 1867:[71]

---

70. 'The character to be explained by our Mr. Morris in private interview with you'. PRO, Ed. 84/5, 13 September 1866. 'Recommended', 20 September.

71. *The Builder*, 6 March 1925, p. 383.

141. (above) Designs by
Sir Edward Burne-Jones
for painted panels in the
Green Dining Room

142. (right) Stained-glass
windows, designed by Sir
Edward Burne-Jones and
Philip Webb, in the Green
Dining Room

133

Kensington Designs £12.
Wall pattern in plaster for S. Kensington Museum
  £7.
To Kensington Museum about modelling animals
  and boughs.
Six quarries, beasts etc.
Patterns to flat of ceiling.
Design and working drawings panelling.
Window border.
To S. Kensington to arrange about painting.
Cornice pattern.
Pattern for bearers.

Lethaby's description of the Green Dining Room supplements that of the *Spectator*:

The ceiling was designed in relation to four ventilating 'sun-burners', but this has unhappily been altered in our usual haphazard way. It was divided into panels, having sharp-leaved decoration painted on them in yellow. Webb's beautifully drawn full-sized cartoons of these still exist. They were pricked through (I think) into the wet plaster, so that the drawing remains if the colouring has to be re-done. *143* The frieze has dogs running after hares: the idea of this, Webb told me, was borrowed from a font in Newcastle Cathedral, and I find a drawing in his sketch-book of 1864 of the 'shield of Rob: Rhodes', with a running dog. The wall is covered with plaster-cast slabs, each having a branch of olive in relief. The panelling of oak, stained green, was prepared for a series of painted panels of the months by Burne-Jones, alternating with vegetation like herbal drawings. Burne-Jones seems to have had assistance with the figure panels, but they are his in the main.

xxv The figures painted on the panels represent the twelve months of the year, or the twelve signs of the Zodiac; with two extra depicting the sun and the moon. Aymer Vallance in his *William Morris his Art his Writings and his Public Life*, 1897, stated:

It is characteristic of Mr. Morris's scrupulous thoroughness that, after the panels were finished, he came to the conclusion that the work, having been carried out by different painters, was not uniform enough in style to make a consecutive or harmonious scheme of decoration. Accordingly he insisted on having them all repainted almost afresh by the hand of Mr. Fairfax Murray.

There can be no doubt that the original designs of the figure panels are those of Burne-Jones.

The plaster panels of foliage and flowers were

143. *Detail of the font in Newcastle Cathedral, showing the hound motif used in the panels in the Green Dining Room*

designed by Morris & Co. and modelled by a former art student, W. Wright.[72] The firm of George Smith & Co. were the actual makers. Lethaby considered that the modelling of the olive branch repeating-pattern panels was probably by Webb, as well as the animals in the frieze above.

The contract for the tile pavement in the Green Dining Room was awarded to Messrs Boote, for £45 5s 0d.[73]

The Department of Science and Art had bought from H. Stacey Marks his watercolour entitled *May Day in the Olden Time*,[74] and Marks had given Cole authority to use it in any way he wished as part of the Museum's scheme of decoration. It was enlarged and transformed on to

---

72. According to the unpublished *Decorations of the South Kensington Museum 1862 to 1874* (1875), p. 18. However, L. M. Wade in 'Rowland Morris', *R.C.A. Students' Magazine*, I, No. 4, 1912, p. 89, says that the diaper and frieze were designed by R. Morris.

73. PRO, Ed. 84/67, 22 December 1866. (Maw, £40 10s; Whetstone, £35; Minton, £59 10s). According to the statement on the costs of the Museum decoration received from Sir John Donnelly in March 1899, the west refreshment room cost £1,127. PRO, Ed. 84/57.

74. Cole, diary, 'Told Mr. Marks I would recommend Board to buy his picture of May Day for decoration of Museum', 1 February 1868.

porcelain by Amy E. Black of the porcelain class. This ceramic painting was then incorporated into a buffet, made in walnut by Gillow & Co., with an inscription 'May-Day, May-Day, the Blithe May-Day, the Merrie Merrie Month of May'. It was installed in the Green Dining Room, having previously been exhibited at the London International Exhibition of 1871.[75] The report of this exhibition by J. Hungerford Pollen states that the buffet was designed by Moody, but it is elsewhere ascribed to Gilbert Redgrave, Richard Redgrave's son.[76]

Renovation to the decorations of the Green Dining Room were carried out in the mid-1920s at the instigation of Lethaby, who, in February 1925, wrote to Sir Eric Maclagan, then the Director, to the effect that he considered the Morris Room had been 'terribly disfigured in our slovenly way in bringing in the electric light.'[77] As Philip Webb's 'trusted assistant' George Jack was still living, Lethaby hoped that he might be allowed to repair the disfigurement, and also to superintend the repainting of the ceiling, which had become badly discoloured. The matter was urgent, as Jack was getting on in years, '. . . he represents Webb and is the Morris tradition in existence. This can never be again.'[78]

Work began during December 1925, the ceiling being repainted and re-stencilled. The room was re-wired 'in such a way that the pipes are almost invisible'.[79] Jack designed some new light fittings, which were made by the firm of Osler and Faraday.[80]

Only two of Burne-Jones's painted panels needed treatment, one for cracking, and the other where the panel had contracted, forcing the 'hard varnish-laden paint into ridges which had in some cases broken and exposed the wood'.[81] It was not until a further ten years had passed that Basil Long was informed that the painted panels were beginning to flake[82] and it was decided that all the panels should undergo conservation. May Morris agreed that the panels looked 'dim and tired'[83] and felt that although the restorer might be 'tempted to do the work almost too well', the watchful eye of Sir Eric Maclagan would be a safeguard. All the panels were taken to the restorers of the Ancient Monument section of the Office of Works on 22 April 1936, and the work was completed by February 1938 when the last of them was replaced in the Green Dining Room.

144. *The Centre Refreshment Room designed by James Gamble, after recent restoration, looking north*

They are still to be seen, as are the other original decorations of thise room. During 1978, under the supervision of the Department of Furniture and Woodwork, assisted by Jo Darrah of the Department of Conservation, the room was redecorated by Messrs. Campbell Smith, during which the panelling was returned to its former colour.

The Centre Refreshment Room

The Centre Refreshment Room has an entirely different character from the Morris room, more in keeping with the rest of the Museum decoration. This is hardly surprising, as the design was begun by Godfrey Sykes shortly before his death, and

144
145

75. Cole, diary, 10 May 1870, 'Marks & Yeames came. Marks approved of making his May Day into a sideboard.' See also *Official Reports*, London International Exhibition, 1871, I, p. 78.

76. On 31 October 1870, Cole noted in his diary that he had 'agreed with RR that Gilbert should only look after Architecture.' Redgrave was later appointed Chief Draughtsman in 1878 (PRO, Ed. 84/37, Board minute précis, 25 October 1878).

77. V&A Museum, Morris Room file.

78. *Loc. cit.,* Lethaby to Maclagan, 3 June 1926.

79. Ibid., letter, George Jack.

80. Ibid., letter, Office of Works, 7 May 1926.

81. Ibid., Office of Works report, 7 May 1926.

82. Ibid., 28 September 1935.

83. Ibid., 14 February 1936.

PLATE XXVI (opposite) The Centre Refreshment Room, decorated to designs by James Gamble

PLATE XXVII (overleaf left) January, a tile panel in the Grill Room, designed by Sir Edward Poynter

PLATE XXVIII (overleaf right) Summer, a tile panel in the Grill Room, designed by Sir Edward Poynter

145. (left) Design by James Gamble for the doors leading into the Centre Refreshment Room

146. (centre left) The coat of arms of Sir Henry Cole, forming part of the decoration in the Centre Refreshment Room

to the royal dairy at Frogmore created by John Thomas for Prince Albert, which is similarly decorated in ceramic tiles. The design and colour scheme of the room is the work of James Gamble. It was described by the *Standard* on 26 December 1868, while incomplete:

XXVI

> The skirting for about four feet in height, is to be faced with dark red, or rather perhaps chocolate tiles, the same colour being carried to the same height in the case of the pillars, and in this case ornamented with a raised trellis-work pattern. Above this comes a narrow strip of white in similar material; above that again, another narrow strip of yellow; then a considerable space of white; and finally, above all a yellow cornice.

146

The *Building News* amplified this in 1870:[85]

> The walls, columns and pillars have white plinths, and bases, and a chocolate-coloured dado above, which in the columns is enriched by yellow lines and white rosettes. This dado is surmounted by a band about a foot high, of white amorini upon a yellow ground.

The room showed 'scholarly adaptation of recognized precedents', but, although sumptuous, bright, and cheerful, lacked 'harmony and repose'.

The most controversial part of the ceramic decoration was the facing with majolica tiles of the four large free-standing columns across the mouth of the apse part of the room. This was the idea of Godfrey Sykes, who informed Cole a few days before his death that he was planning majolica columns for the refreshment room below the Lecture Theatre.[86] The columns were designed

147

his work was carried on by his two successors, James Gamble and Reuben Townroe, augmented with their own ideas. Although the room was opened for use in 1868, the decorations were not completed until some years later because of the amount of decorative work being carried out elsewhere in the Museum at the same time. The *Standard* described it as 'a dining-room which, year by year, never seems to approach completion.'[84]

A restriction placed on the selection of decorative materials was that they must be washable. This led to the choice of an overall veneer of ceramic tiles. Perhaps this idea was originally suggested to Cole by a visit at the end of July 1863

---

84. 27 March 1869.
85. 20 July 1870, p. 55.
86. Cole, diary, 30 January 1866.

SVMMER

PLATE XXIX *(opposite above) The Grill Room, with the grill designed by Sir Edward Poynter, and made by Hart & Son*

PLATE XXX *(opposite below) Design (not executed) by Sir Edward Poynter, for a painted ceiling in the Lecture Theatre apse*

147. *(right) Columns in the Centre Refreshment Room, designed by James Gamble*

148. *(right) Design by Godfrey Sykes, for a decorative initial letter, made in modelled ceramic and used in the Centre Refreshment Room*

149. *(far right) Letter from an alphabet designed by Godfrey Sykes and made by Minton, Hollins & Co. for the decoration of the Centre Refreshment Room*

and modelled by James Gamble, and made by Minton, Hollins & Co. for £257.[87] The *Standard* found the effect 'decidedly incongruous', and the *Building News* stigmatized the columns as 'sham columns in a casing of crockery built up round a brick core'.

The *Standard* reported that the arches between the columns were to be filled in with terracotta panelling, the open portions of which were occupied by blue tiles with painted figures.

Large looking glasses by Gibbs & Canning were another feature of the room, with majolica surrounds designed by James Gamble, who also included the arms of Sir Henry Cole in majolica over the eastern doorway. Godfrey Sykes designed the frieze which runs all round the room at the level of the cornice. It takes the form of a quotation from Ecclesiasticus 2:24, in white letters on a yellow ground, using Sykes's own decorative

87. PRO, Ed. 84/6, 27 April 1867, ordered 11 May.

150, 151. *(below left and right) Ceramic decoration by James Gamble and made by Maw & Co., over the entrance doorways (now blocked) into the Centre Refreshment Room*

152. *(bottom) Stained-glass window in the Centre Refreshment Room, designed by James Gamble and made by Powell & Sons*

alphabet: 'There is nothing better for a man than that he should eat and drink, and make his soul enjoy good in his labour —— XYZ.'

    148
    149

The chimneypiece now in the room, which came originally from Dorchester House in Park Lane, was designed by Alfred Stevens himself, from whom Sykes inherited the tradition which he passed on to Gamble and Townroe.

Alfred Stevens also designed the tables (only one survives) in the Refreshment Room, which, according to the *Standard* were

> ... of somewhat peculiar construction, the frames being of ornamental iron work, and the tops grey marble slabs, enclosed also in an ornamental iron frame. They have a good effect, but are almost miraculously small; four people, apparently, being expected to dine on a tiny slab scarcely bigger, it would seem, than the seats of any one of the two pairs of chairs placed round it.[88]

The windows, as in the case of those in the Green Dining Room, received the applause of the

    152

---

88. PRO, Ed. 84/6, 17 March 1868, 'We will make you 6 tables in fine finished white iron, with the edge strengthened, prepared for marble slabs, at 90/- each', Henry Hoole & Co. Twelve other tables were supplied by George Smith for £34, PRO, *loc cit.*, 12 June 1868.

Standard. They were of lightly stained glass designed by James Gamble.

> The painting consists simply of an arabesque pattern, traced on an almost clear ground, and interspersed with one of the oddest assemblages of mottoes drawn apparently at random from the most quaintly incongruous sources we have ever yet had the luck to encounter.

The mottoes included biblical quotations, extracts from the *Ingoldsby Legends*, and a host of sayings such as 'Hunger is the best sauce', 'A feast is made for laughter, and wine maketh merry', 'A good cup makes all young', and 'Welcome's the best dish in the kitchen'.

The windows were made by Powell at the Whitefriars Glass Company. The first of them was ordered on 1st December, 1869. Powell tendered for the four, at 16s 11d per square foot.[89] It was not until 1871 that the remaining three were ordered. Gamble then agreed to finish them and see to the payment of Powell for a total of £807 4s 9d.[90] The tile pavement, large red octagons and small black squares, was undertaken by Maw & Co. for £130.[91] The wall tiles were by Minton, who tendered £983[92] for them in 1867, and a further of £465 two years later.[93] In the financial year 1873–4 Minton received £295 more for wall tiles for the centre Refreshment Room;[94] from which one can judge the protracted nature of the operations. The decoration work was still incomplete in 1875. In May, Gamble was asked to produce an estimate for completing the cornice, and the soffit of the arches in the Refreshment Room. He agreed to undertake the work for £150, his designs to become the property of the Museum. This figure was increased when included in the estimates for 1877–8 to £400, as it included other work together with painting and gilding.[95]

The ceiling of the Centre Refreshment Room is of enamelled iron, as part of the policy of using washable materials. It was reported in the *Building News*[96] that Henry Cole had been impressed by the enamelled iron railway advertisements, and the ease with which (it seems) designs could be produced. Various people offered to produce paintings on enamel, including Sir Coutts Lindsey, Louisa, Marchioness of Watertord, the Duchess of Cleveland and John Leslie.[97] Nothing came of these suggestions, however, and the ceilings as they are today were designed and painted by

James Gamble. The large iron plates were fired at Messrs Willing's works in Birmingham after painting, and on their return were screwed to the wood fillets which supported the earlier plaster ceiling.

The decoration of the Centre Refreshment Rooms cost £2,506 in all, it was later stated.[98]

The Grill Room

The East Refreshment Room, also called the XXIX Dutch Kitchen or the Grill Room, because of the large iron grill which stood in it, was designed by Edward Poynter, later Sir Edward Poynter, PRA.

This room was, according to the *Standard*

> ... the most successful in point of decoration, of the entire group. There is a comfortable, home look about it which, even apart from any considerations of art, would suffice to give it the first place ... The style adopted is that of the old fashioned blue Dutch tile, set in panelling ... The panels are in plain dark XXVII walnut, the tiles being the work of pupils in the art XXVIII schools of the museum, and very carefully and spiritedly executed ... first, just above the floor, a course of alternate fruits and flowers; then one of land or sea scapes; then fruits and flowers again; then one of groups and figures, chiefly mythical; and finally a third course of fruits and flowers along the top.

The lower rows of smallish tiles reached about 6 feet above the floor. The mythological subjects represented Andromeda, Venus, Proserpine, Rhodopis, Atalanta, Sappho, Eurydice, Medea, Ænone, Helen and Europa, repeated several times. These, the seascapes and the simpler tiles

89. PRO, Ed. 84/7, June 1869.

90. Henry Scott was not satisfied, as the figure appeared to conceal Powell's payment as well as Gamble's fee. Powell's figure later arrived as £300 for three windows. The Lord President recommended that the Office of Works accepted Gamble's figure, to include his fee for designing and painting the glass. PRO, Ed. 84/7, 5 June, 27 June 1871; Ed. 84/36, Board minute précis, 23 June 1871. Powell received £200 in 1871, PRO, Works 17/24/1.

91. PRO, Ed. 84/67, 22 December 1866. (Minton, £206, or £187; Whetstone, £130; Boote, £138 10s.) Additional estimates are in Ed. 84/5 & 6.

92. PRO, Ed. 84/6, 3 September 1867.

93. 4 March 1869, PRO, Ed. 84/7. Gamble was sent to Italy in 1869 to study terracotta.

94. PRO, Works 17/24/1.

95. PRO, Ed. 84/36, Board minute précis, 16 December 1876.

96. 2 April 1875, p. 365.

97. PRO, Ed. 84/36, Board minute précis, 7 April 1870, Cole, diary, 6 March, 18 March 1870.

98. PRO, Ed. 84/57, 'Statement of Cost' of the decoration of the Museum, received from Sir John Donnelly in March 1899.

153 were painted by ladies from the Art School. Poynter's estimate was:

	£
44 circular panels of figures and „ „ „ landscapes at	
£1. 0. 0. each	88
2 Designs of pattern-work	5
	£93

Above these rows of tiles were much larger tile panels, showing young women in more-or-less contemporary dress, representing the Seasons and Months. Poynter's estimate for this was:[100]

	£
16 spaces and two smaller over grill –	
2 designs over grill at £15 each	30
1 design for month of March with border	25
11 designs for other months at £20	220
2 designs for largest spaces rep. Autumn and Summer each with 4 figs. at £45	90
2 designs rep. Spring and Winter with 2 figs at £25	50
	£415

In 1870 the *Graphic* published a short report concerning the ceramic decorations, which were the work of 'a class of female students, who occupy a room by themselves, and work under the immediate superintendence of an art-master. The class was commenced about eighteen months ago; and the progress that has been made during that time reflects credit alike on pupils and instructors.' The *Graphic* congratulated South Kensington for having found a new and interesting occupation for young women. Henry Scott, at this time, compiled a list of the ladies he was employing as porcelain painters. They were Miss Black, Miss Walker, Miss Judd, Miss Earle, Miss Hall, Miss Cambridge, who were all paid at the rate of *6d* an hour, except for Miss Black who received *9d*.[101]

In 1886 an ex-student of the Art School, Alexander Fisher (later to become well-known for his metalwork), of Hogarth Studios, Fitzroy Square, was commissioned to make full-size copies of the sixteen panels representing the Months and Seasons. These copies were for the Department of Circulation, and Fisher was paid £12 for each of the seasons and £10 for each of the months, making a total of £168.[102]

153. Ladies painting tiles for use in the decoration of the Grill Room

All the plaster work that Poynter designed for the ceiling and frieze, for a total of £150 (including a row of white peacocks round the cornice, which was regarded with scorn by the *Standard*), was modelled by W. Wright, and made by George Smith & Co., both of whom had done similar work in Morris's room. The tile floor was executed by W. Whetstone for £35.[103] The stained-glass *154* windows were made by Crace and Sons, probably in 1874. During that financial year the firm was paid for £102 10*s* for two windows.[104]

The grill itself, which gives its name to the *155* room, was made by Hart, Son and Peard for *156* £165.[105] It is signed and dated 'E.J.P. 1866'. The *Standard* reported on the grill with enthusiasm:

A noteworthy feature in this room is the huge fireplace, from which it takes its name. This occupies a large proportion of one side of the apartment, and is very 'high art' indeed. In the centre is a good-sized fireplace, covered by a large gridiron for the broiling of chops and steaks, for the supply of which this room, as its name indicates, is especially set apart. On either side of the fireplace and

99. PRO, Ed. 84/67, 22 May 1867. Poynter also was to charge 3 guineas per day for superintendence at the Schools.

100. 27 July 1869, PRO, Ed. 84/7.

101. PRO, Works 17/24/1, 26 February 1870.

102. PRO, Ed. 84/68, October 1886.

103. PRO, Ed. 84/67, 22 December 1866.

104. Tender passed to the Office of Works, 23 May 1873, PRO, Ed. 84/36. Cole, diary, 23 May 1873, 'Mr Crace called Abt Poynters room windows', and PRO, Works 17/24/1.

105. PRO, Ed. 84/6, March 1867. (Benham & Sons, £168; M. Feetham & Co., £248.)

154. *(right) Stained-glass window designed by Sir Edward Poynter for the Grill Room, and made by Crace & Co.*

155. *(far right, above) The grill in the Grill Room, designed in 1866 by Sir Edward Poynter and made by Hart, Son & Peard.*

156. *(far right, below) A hinge, in the form of an eagle, on one of the doors of the grill*

beneath it are a series of highly elaborate 'hot chambers', for the warming of plates and other kindred purposes; the doors and other portions of these chambers being richly decorated with Tudor roses and other ornaments in iron and polished brass.

The total cost of the decorations of the East Refreshment Room, excluding the grill, was £1,345.

The Refreshment Rooms Corridor

Redgrave and Cole determined to have three sculptured bas-reliefs in the Refreshment Rooms Corridor, inside Godfrey Sykes's golden doors leading from what is now the quadrangle. At that time this was intended to be the main entrance to the Museum. These sculptures were entrusted to Felix M. Miller. After a preliminary consideration of various media such as majolica, terracotta, Sicilian marble, and alabaster, it was decided that these bas-reliefs should be in plaster.

Miller described the three works:

The Relief over the central door represents Science and Art proper: the former is advising a youth who holds a chemical apparatus to inquire into the nature of the Elements; the latter is in the act of rewarding or crowning an art student. In the centre are two infantine figures or genii, the one in the act of lighting his torch at the lamp of learning, the other having lighted his, is endeavouring to keep the flame alive. The Relief on the East side represents Industrial Science and Industrial Art; the former is placing the distaff and hammer (the emblem of commercial handicraftsmanship) in the hands of a youth, with instructions; the latter, a youth, is submitting a vase, and Industrial Art is presenting him with the appliances for painting and decorating it. In the small centre panel the first is personated by

Arkwright inventing his loom, and the other by Palissy viewing examples of his Pottery after taking them from the furnace. The Relief on the West side represents Mechanical Science and Mechanical Art; the former is directing the attention of a youth to a winged wheel as suggestive of speed and power; the latter is giving directions for first proportions, beauty and utility. The first is personated in the centre panel by Stephenson contemplating steam as a motive power in combination with the five mechanical powers, and the second by Telford projecting the Menai Straits Bridge. By the introduction of the figures of youth with the emblematic figures, it was intended to express the educational character and nature of the Department of Science and Art.[106]

Miller was asked early in 1870 to execute the reliefs, and his estimate to model the two side spandrels for £50 each was accepted on 5 November.[107] These reliefs do not seem to have survived later re-ordering of the gallery.

The ceiling of this corridor, which is below the Ceramic Gallery, was decorated by H. H. Stannus, an architect and instructor at the Art School, in the mid-1880s. His decorations were painted over in 1910–11 (see p. 257).

The elaborate decorative schemes for the Museum led, time and time again, to trouble with the Treasury. Projects cost more than was estimated, or took so long to achieve that, as time went on, the original vote of money was forgotten. Those who suffered were usually the members of the Museum's own team of decorators. In the 1884–5 estimates, £200 was set aside for painting the Refreshment Rooms Corridor ceiling. Owing to a bureaucratic slip-up the work was not commenced until February 1885, and the Treasury insisted that the £200 would only be forthcoming for the work if it was completed by the end of March. Not unnaturally this condition was not kept, and Stannus also discovered that he had exceeded his estimate by £23 0s 1d. The Office of Works declined to pay the extra, and continued to do so despite repeated appeals from South Kensington. Stannus wrote angrily to the Museum, 'I find that deducting the *money I paid out of pocket* . . . I have made *fifteenpence* an hour ! ! ! "[108] That seems to be all he did make, because on

13 April, Sir R. Welby wrote from the Treasury that although the matter would not come before the Public Accounts Committee, no excess was to be allowed, and presumably no payment made to Stannus.

Stannus's sufferings were small, however, compared with the injustices that had in earlier years been meted out to Frank Moody. He, with his student helpers, had been occupied in many different areas of the Museum, the West Staircase, ceilings in the galleries, designs for mosaics, and it is an unfortunate fact that at times he was kept for years awaiting payment. Admittedly he was inclined to underestimate the amount of work and cost which would be involved in certain undertakings, but there were occasions when he even found himself obliged to pay the students' wages out of his own pocket. In his earlier days Moody gives an impression of a generous and enthusiastically willing temperament, but he became increasingly embittered. Numerous letters of his are preserved, long, involved, and violently indignant.[109] It is noticeable that his handwriting becomes more and more difficult to read, for his health suffered, as is hardly surprising. Ultimately this breakdown resulted in the decision of the Board in 1882 that he should be asked to resign. Whether or not this ruling was conveyed to Moody, he sent in his resignation as Instructor in Decorative Art, and as Decorative Artist to the Museum, in February 1883.[110]

He died in September 1886.

106. *Decorations of the South Kensington Museum 1862 to 1874*, 1875 (unpublished), pp. 18, 19.
107. PRO, Ed. 84/7.
108. PRO, Ed. 84/68, 29 March 1886.
109. PRO, Ed. 84/67.
110. The Board had decided in December 1882 that Moody should resign 'owing to ill-health', PRO, Ed. 84/38. See also, 'An Art Teacher: the late F. W. Moody', by Owen Gibbons in *Magazine of Art*, XVI, 1892–3, pp. 404–8; 'Some Recollections of the National Art Training School and the Old Museum', by Richard Lunn, in *The R.C.A. Students' Magazine*, I, No. 3, pp. 61–63, 84–87; 'Recollections of the Old School', by George Clausen, *loc. cit.*, I, No. 7, 1912, pp. 155–61. Moody was the son of Canon H. R. Moody, Rector of Chartham, Kent, for fifty years. In 1874, he designed a mural monument to his father in 'Debased' or 'Pagan' style, which led to an argument with the rector, a consistory court, and the rejection of the monument; see *The Story of a Monument. A tale of clerical intolerance*, by F. W. Moody, 1874.

CHAPTER IX

Three new projects

During the later 1860s, three large building projects were begun under Henry Cole's supervision. They were to be the last works that he carried through before his retirement in 1873. The dismantling of part of the 'Boilers' made possible the re-erection of the superfluous parts as a museum at Bethnal Green; on the space that they had occupied at South Kensington two new courts were set up.

On another part of the site a new building for the Science Schools was constructed. In the later stages of these projects some influence was exercised by the Office of Works, which, in 1870, began to assume control over the Department of Science and Art's works office. This development is described in the next chapter, but some of the effects are seen in this one.

The Bethnal Green Museum

When the demolition of the 'Brompton Boilers' began at their northern end, during December 1864,[1] the authorities of the Department of Science and Art decided to suggest to the Treasury that the iron building might be divided into three

157
158
159
160

---

1. Cole, diary, 30 December 1864.

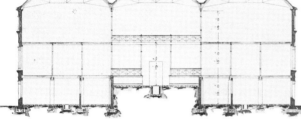

157. *(above) Design by J. W. Wild and General Scott for the Bethnal Green Museum*

158. *(right) Interior of the Bethnal Green Museum, c. 1876. Drawing by John Watkins*

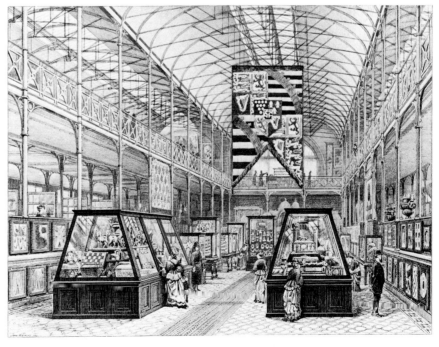

portions which could then be offered to 'authorities in north, east and south districts of the Metropolis'.[2] Captain Fowke was, shortly afterwards, requested to prepare designs to show how best the iron building could be adapted for the use of local museums.[3] It was estimated that to take down seven bays of the building and to erect it somewhere, 'supposed about five miles from Kensington', would cost something in the order of £10,300.[4]

That the suggestion was made, was a consequence of various proposals, discussed over the years, for the establishment of museums on what were the outskirts of London, particularly in the northern and eastern suburbs. It was the Great Exhibition that sparked off the proposals. In 1851, the Commissioners of the Exhibition were sent a

memorial by merchants and bankers of the City of London proposing the formation of a collection illustrative of the produce of various countries. This, it was suggested, could form the nucleus of a trade museum for the East End.

This proposal came to nothing, and the idea lapsed until the Marquis of Westminster presided at a meeting in 1860 at which was read a letter from William Cowper, the First Commissioner of Works, in which he promised government aid for any scheme that afforded recreational and intellectual improvement for the area. Lord Ebury proposed that energetic efforts should be made to

2. Board minute précis, 20 March 1865, PRO, Ed. 84/36.
3. Ibid., 15 March 1865.
4. 14 November 1865, PRO, Ed. 84/4.

159. *(left) Interior of the Bethnal Green Museum, 1971*

160. *(below) Model of the south side of the Bethnal Green Museum*

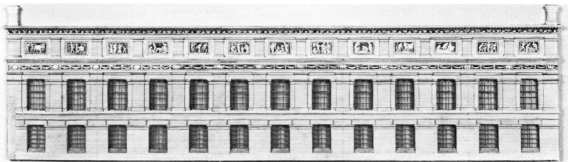

establish a public library and museum. Once again nothing happened.

Another attempt to provoke action of some sort was made in 1862, when (Sir) Antonio Brady, Alderman Rose and others petitioned the 1862 Exhibition Commissioners to found a museum, and one more try was made in 1864 by the Earl of Shaftesbury, Lord Ebury, Sir Charles Eastlake and others. It was not until 6 May 1865, though, that the position began to look rather more hopeful. On that day, the Lord President of the Council, Earl Granville, chaired a meeting at South Kensington, in order to consider the creation of museums of art and science, and also to see if the Iron Building could be useful for that purpose. The meeting was attended by Lord Ebury, William Cowper, H. A. Bruce and A. S. Ayrton, as well as a large number of Members of Parliament and of the clergy. They were encouraged by a letter from the Bishop of London, giving his approval for the scheme, and the meeting was unanimous in giving its own blessing. During an adjournment of six months for investigations to be made, various propositions were considered, and Gladstone provided additional impetus by suggesting that a pilot scheme should be initiated somewhere in East London, and offering to lend items from his own collection.

Thus inspired afresh, Antonio Brady, the Rev. Septimus Hansard (rector of Bethnal Green), and Dr Millar, negotiated at the end of the year with the trustees of the Poor Lands in the parish of Bethnal Green for the purchase of ground for the erection of a museum. The land had been valued at £300 an acre, but it was eventually agreed that £2,000 should be paid to the trustees for about 4½ enclosed acres, which were rented to butchers, and from which the public had been excluded.

Among the principal subscribers towards the purchase of the land were Messrs Truman, Hanbury, Buxton & Co. (£200), the Corporation of the City of London (£157 10s), the Society of Arts (£100), Baroness Burdett-Coutts (£100), Henry Hoare (£100), Thomas Twining (£100), the Grocers' Company (£100), the Fishmongers' Company (£52 10s), and Messrs Charrington (£50).[5] The site was offered free to the Department of Science and Art, and gratefully accepted.[6]

Estimates were requested from contractors for taking down parts of the 'Boilers' and re-erecting them at Bethnal Green; and for replacing them at South Kensington with a permanent building. The most expensive of the estimates (received during the first week of October 1867) was from Piper & Wheeler for £13,970; the lowest was that of S. Perry & Co. for £11,874 and this company was awarded the contract.[7] The redundant parts of the 'Boilers' were removed by Christmas of 1867,[8] and at Bethnal Green progress was swift; when Cole visited the site on 24 March 1868 he found that the building was already 'up to Museum ground floor'. A disappointment was in store for the builders who discovered that the original iron columns removed from South Kensington were defective; new ones were made.[9]

Although the iron framework of the 'Boilers' was partially re-used, the new building was given an outer clothing of brick, not of sheet like the old building at South Kensington. The new brick façades were designed by J. W. Wild, in General Scott's office. Plans, elevations and sections were also prepared (some being signed by Scott and dated 1867 and 1868) for a Keeper's House, a Refreshment Room and a Lecture Theatre, but these were not realized. Wild's watercolour perspective shows a tower and curator's house which were never achieved, but excavations during 1980 in the approximate position of the tower revealed foundations.

On the building, the principal decorative feature was a series of twenty-six mosaic panels running down each side of the exterior, at the top of the walls. Subjects from Agriculture were represented on one side, and from Art and Science on the other. Those on the north side are Ploughing, Sowing and Hoeing, Training Trees, Mowing, Haymaking, Shearing Sheep, May Flowers, Wheat Harvest, Hopping, Picking Apples, Fishing, Buying Beasts, The Dairy. On the south side, Pottery, Painting, Architecture and Building, Sculpture, Music, Poetry, Science and Art, Astronomy, Plane Geometry, Chemistry, Spectral Analysis (using coloured stones) Mechanics, and Botany.[10]

xxxi

161

5. Select Committee Report, 1898, p. 531. App. 25.
6. Cole, diary, 7 December 1865; and PRO, Ed. 84/36; Board minute précis.
7. PRO, Ed. 84/6, 7 October 1867.
8. 15th Report . . . 1867 (1868), p. 204.
9. PRO, Ed. 84/7, 8 April 1869.
10. Designs are in the Department of Prints and Drawings, nos. E. 1059 to 1087–1927.

The designs for these mosaics were by Frank Moody, full-size drawings being prepared by W. Wise. The female students of the South Kensington Museum Mosaic Class made the mosaics under the superintendence of S. Cooper of Minton, Hollins & Co. Minton's quotation of £420 for twenty panels was accepted in January 1870.[11] Inside the building a mosaic floor was laid by E. F. du Cane's female prisoners, to the fish-scale design used beneath the Sheepshanks Gallery at South Kensington, for £286 6s 0d.[12]

The Board decided on 8 July 1870 that, as soon as the building was sufficiently completed, the Animal Products and Food Collections were to be transferred to Bethnal Green. When Scott and Cole went out to East London in August, they found the Museum nearly finished,[13] and as a result the Board felt that the opening could be planned for May 1871.[14] Considerable delays ensued, however, and the building was still unfinished, and deteriorating through lack of heating, in December 1871.[15] A Royal opening was eventually arranged for June 1872, and for this Cole was allowed £4,500 to cover all the costs. He asked for an additional £500 but this was refused by the Treasury, and Cole was told that he had to do the best he could with the money he had been allocated; local authorities, it was suggested, could pay for any seats constructed outside the building. South Kensington's administration had hoped to have the boys of the Chapels Royal in attendance, but this proved not to be possible; instead Sir Charles Stainer and a choir were engaged,[16] as well as the Band of the Honourable Artillery Company, who came along for ten guineas.[17]

After the opening, probably about Christmas 1872, a mishap befell a family named Horne, for part of the ceiling descended on Mrs Horne and her children. The Lord President approved a payment of £15 to them as compensation.

The Department of Science and Art wanted Festing to be the first Director of the Bethnal Green Museum, but he elected to remain at South Kensington as Assistant Director.[18] The library and the school of art which had been promised by the Board[19] in 1870, did not materialize; for many years afterwards there was a local feeling that the Museum did not fulfil its anticipated purpose and it was described as a 'white elephant'. The then Bishop of Stepney, Cosmo Lang (later

161. *Reproduction of a design by F. W. Moody for a mosaic panel for the exterior of the Bethnal Green Museum*

Archbishop of Canterbury) regarded the Museum as a 'lost opportunity'.[20]

Most of the railings that surround the building came from Hyde Park, where they had been torn down in 1866 during a demonstration.

The Science Schools

While the transformed Boilers were rising again at Bethnal Green, a considerably more elaborate building was in course of erection at South Kensington. This was to accommodate laboratories and teaching rooms for a School of Naval Architecture. Such a school had not been part of Fowke's original proposals for the building complex, for the idea had not matured until a conversation between Lord Clarence Paget and Henry Cole at the Admiralty on 7 January 1864. Cole then learned that the government had decided to establish a School of Naval Architecture, which, it was hoped, would be entirely at South Kensington and directly under the control of the Department of Science and Art and not, as Cole was able smugly to record in his diary, under the Admiralty, 'wh: was incompetent'.[21]

162

11. Recommended on 7 January 1870 and revised on 27 January. PRO, Ed. 84/7.

12. PRO, Ed. 84/7, 10 October 1870. Quotation from E. F. Du Cane, Office of Directors of Convict Prisons, 44 Parliament Street.

13. Cole, diary, 2 August 1870.

14. Board minute précis, 5 August 1870, PRO, Ed. 84/36.

15. Board minute précis, 30 December 1871, *loc. cit.*

16. Board minute, précis, 13 June, 15 June 1872. PRO, Ed. 84/36.

17. Ibid., 28 June 1872.

18. Board minute précis, 25, 27 June 1872, PRO, Ed. 84/36.

19. See Minutes of Evidence taken before the Select Committee on Museums of the Science and Art Department, 13 May 1898, No. 2329 (Mr. John Lobb).

20. *Loc cit.*, No. 2711 (17 May 1898).

21. Cole, diary, 7 January 1864.

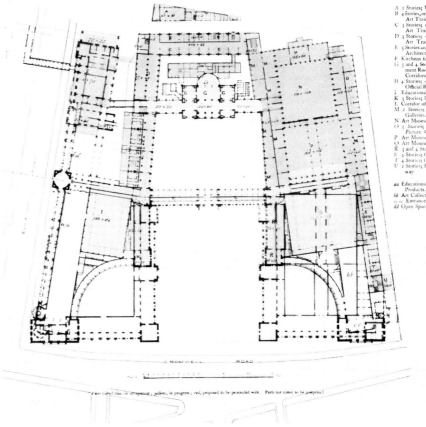

PLAN OF NEW BUILDINGS DESIGNED BY CAPTAIN FOWKE, R.E.
Revised to November 1865.

162. *Plan showing proposed buildings for the Museum, revised to November 1865, with further revision at the south, c. 1868, and showing the Science Schools to the north-west*

A 2 Stories; Workshops and Stores.
B 4 Stories; on Basement, Sappers Quarters; Art Training Schools above.
C 3 Stories; on Basement, Art Museum; Art Training Schools above.
D 3 Stories; on Basement, Art Museum; Art Training Schools above.
E 5 Stories and 2 Stories; Schools for Naval Architecture and Science.
F Kitchens for Refreshment Rooms.
G 3 and 4 Stories; on Basement, Refreshment Rooms; above, Lecture Theatre, Corridors to Museum.
H 4 Stories; on Basement, Art Museum; Official Residences above.
I Educational Apparatus Museum.
K 3 Stories; Library for Education.
L Corridor of Communication.
M 2 Stories; Art Museum and Picture Galleries.
N Art Museum Court.
O 3 Stories; Art Museum Offices, and Picture Galleries above.
Q Art Museum Courts.
R 3 and 4 Stories; Art Library.
S 4 Stories; Offices, Stores, etc.
T 4 Stories; Offices.
U 2 Stories; Board Room, etc., over Gateway.

aa Educational Museum, Food and Animal Products.
bb Art Collections.
cc Entrances, 2 Stories of Museum over.
dd Open Space.

Francis Fowke died before plans had become more than tentative, and it was Henry Scott who drew up the first designs for the new building – though not, of course, without much active assistance from Cole. The latter records during July and August 1866 that he had spent time making the ground plan and designing the west front of what he variously called the School of Naval Architecture or Science Schools.[22] It was not until 28 May 1867 that the contract for the carcass of the building was awarded to the firm of George Smith, whose tender had been the lowest at £24,971. No doubt it had been Smith's long experience in working for the Department that had enabled him to undercut most of his competitors, who included Cubitt (£25,972), Holland and Hannen (£26,115), Lucas Brothers (£25,718) and Mansfield Price (£25,800).[23]

Unlike the new South East Courts (or Architectural Courts) which were designed to be buried entirely within the Museum's extension, and as a result would not have any need for exterior ornament, the new Schools were to be on an extremely conspicuous site flanking Exhibition Road. The building had, therefore, to be a showpiece illustrating the red brick and terracotta style evolved by Cole, Fowke and Sykes. Consequently, an elaborate decorative scheme was drawn up, based on Sykes's ornamentation of the Museum's Lecture Theatre building. The same manufacturer, Blanchard, was commissioned for much of the terracotta, and Fareham red brick was used for the outer walls.

Henry Scott's Schools building was an open rectangle, the lower part of which, through the basement and ground floors, was filled in as a lecture theatre with a glass roof. This thus filled an inner courtyard of about 54 feet by 41 feet. The building itself is some 160 feet in length by 70 feet wide. To Exhibition Road, the Schools display an elevation of seven bays, four storeys high

163

---

22. Ibid., 2 July, 8 July, 4 August 1866.
23. PRO, Ed. 84/6, 18 May 1867.

(though internally the levels and the number of storeys vary disconcertingly), with a one-bay projection at either end, capped by a pediment. On the north is an archway leading through to the Museum and Royal College of Art, of two storeys and a mezzanine. Internally, the building is absolutely utilitarian, with large, high rooms, intended for libraries, examination halls, masters' rooms, and so on, and the main feature is the huge staircase which rises through the entire height of the building round an open well lit by a skylight. The flights of stairs of Cadeby stone are about 7 feet wide, and within open arcades. The staircase was the subject of discussions between Cole and the architect J. W. Wild,[24] who designed the terracotta balustrade, which was made by Doulton & Co.[25] The newels and the massive handrails are of Portland stone. Wild is said to have been responsible for all the interior planning and structural arrangements,[26] and hoped for further work on the decoration. In this he was largely disappointed. He seems to have planned no corridors, and internal communication on the upper floors above the level of the lecture theatre

164

163. (top left) The Science Schools (now the Henry Cole Building) from the north-west

164. (top right) The staircase of the Science Schools, c. 1872

165. (above) Interior well of the Science Schools, showing the external corridors, c. 1872

24. Cole, diary, 4 December 1867.
25. Doulton tendered £195 against Blanchard's £235. PRO, Works 17/22/4, 6 July 1871.
26. Richard Lunn, 'Some Recollections of the National Art Training School and the Old Museum', *R.C.A. Students' Magazine*, (1912), 87.

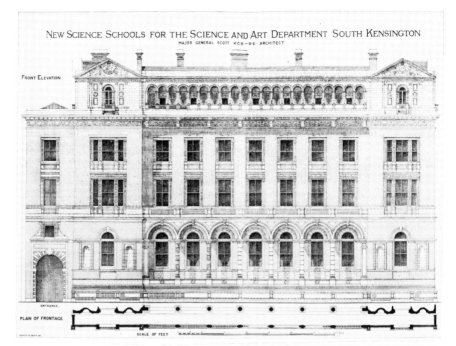

166. (right) Elevation of the western façade of the Science Schools

167. (below right) Elevation of the southern façade of the Science Schools

165 was effected by three covered galleries which were somewhat precariously bracketed out from the walls, but on different levels from the main floors. This added to the confusion of the very oddly planned interior. In fact, one has the distinct impression after a ramble round that the designers of the elevations, staircase, and floor levels at no time consulted with one another. The floors of the Schools were of mosaic, laid out by Colonel du Cane's women convicts at Woking, at a cost of £300.[27] Most of the interior of the building, with the exception of the staircase, was recast by the Department of the Environment for Museum use during the late 1970s and early 1980s.

166   It was on the exterior that most effort was
167 lavished by Cole and his colleagues. On the Exhibition Road façade, the principal features, apart from much terracotta ornament, are the open round-headed colonnade on the ground floors, and at the top, an open arcaded balcony. At the beginning of 1868, Cole recorded that the capitals of five of the ground-floor terracotta columns were in position, and that the Schools were up to that height generally.[28] These columns are identical to those on the Lecture Theatre front of the Museum, designed by Godfrey Sykes and

27. Permission given by the Office of Works on 3 April 1872, PRO, Works 17/22/3.
28. Cole, diary, 23 January 1868.

149

modelled by James Gamble. The Science Schools suffered from Treasury economies and during 1869 work came to a halt when funds ran out. Much of the terracotta, which had already been delivered, was left lying on the site of the 1862 Exhibition, on the opposite side of Exhibition Road.[29] After a delay of about a year, work was resumed; by the end of 1870 the building was up to its full height, and was being roofed.[30]

168
169
The top-floor gallery is bracketed 5 feet 5 inches forward from the main walls, supported on iron girders clothed in terracotta. It is composed of twenty-one round-headed arches. The floor of this balcony is also of terracotta, being made up of slabs each about 2 feet 3 inches by 1 foot 6 inches, and 6 inches thick. Much of the terracotta of the upper portion of the building was designed by James Gamble, who pleased Cole by calling the upper columns the 'Cole columns', an act which met also with the approval of Henry Scott.[31]

They were made by A. Wilson and Sons,[32] and included Cole's motto.

The decoration of the ground floor windows, designed by Gamble using Sykes's sketches, was executed by J. Pulham, while that of the basement, the remainder of the ground floor, first and second floors, the principal entablature and the pediments were the work of Blanchard.[33] The mosaics in the pediments, depicting the Queen,

29. Letter from the Office of Works, PRO, Ed. 84/54, 2 July 1869.
30. *18th Report . . . 1870* (1871), p. 379.
31. Cole, diary, 11 May 1868. The columns are illustrated in *Survey*, Pl. 59b.
32. They put in the lowest tender, for £806 15s, on 7 October 1868, PRO, Ed. 84/6. Blanchard's estimate was £1,543, Blashfield's, £1,443 8s 3d, and Pulham's £1,285.
33. Blanchard asked for £537 for additional terracotta for the walls of the roadway through the building, and the two entrance arches. The firm tendered £337 for the terracotta of the entablature, pediments and parapets. PRO, Works 17/22/4, 17th Contract, 11 August 1870.

168. *Design by Godfrey Sykes for terracotta columns used on the upper loggia of the Science Schools, west side*

169. *The upper loggia of the Science Schools, c. 1872*

170. (below) The tiled ceiling of the entry from Exhibition Road beneath the Science Schools, designed by James Gamble and made by Gibbs & Canning

171. (right) The bridge connecting the Science and Art Schools

Prince Albert, and their heraldry, were designed by Frank Moody.

Full-sized working drawings were prepared by W. Wise, and these were used by the South Kensington Museum Mosaic Class, superintended by Samuel Cooper, for Minton, Hollins & Co., and cost £284 6s.[34] One of Moody's assistants, Richard Lunn, later recorded that Gamble really wanted these pediments to be filled with sculptured groups.[35]

170

James Gamble also designed and modelled the ceramic decoration of the entrance archway ceiling, which was manufactured by Gibbs & Canning, but Minton made the tiles for the bridge that links the building with the Royal College of Art,[36] as they did also for the blue, white and yellow tiles in the soffits of the ground-floor arcade, which were also Gamble's work. Doulton's produced the terracotta chimneys from Gamble's drawings.[37]

171

Flanking his Schools, along Exhibition Road, Scott had designed a terracotta wall which was made by Doulton's for £202 18s, but the firm ran into trouble over the capping for it. On 15 March 1873, Scott wrote to Douglas Galton of the Office of Works explaining that Doulton's were not able to 'make the capping straight enough for a portion just on the level of the eye of those who walk past the building'. In place of terracotta, therefore, Smith was asked to quote for

marble (£301), or red Aberdeen granite (£979). The marble was ordered on 9 April 1873.[38]

The most elaborate scheme for the decoration of the Schools is that on the east side, and on both sides of the bridge; invisible to the general public, it is an almost unknown work, and cannot be seen to advantage as it is nowadays extremely filthy. Frank Moody was commissioned to design a complete wall of sgraffito work in plaster, and this was executed under his direction by W. Wise, Owen Gibbons, E. Wormleighton and H. W. Foster.[39] By October 1871 they had achieved this up to the windowsills of the second floor.[40]

Moody was justifiably proud of this experimental decoration, which has survived a century

34. PRO, Ed. 84/57. Scott asked Maw & Co., and Gibbs & Canning to quote a figure for glazed plaques, each 2 ft × 1 ft 9 in for the entrance ceiling. Maw wanted £1 10s 4d each, but as Gibbs & Canning quoted only 6s 4d, they were awarded the contract on 20 November 1871, PRO, Works 17/22/4.

35. R. Lunn, *loc. cit.*, p. 87.

36. Tender for £147, 20 December 1871, PRO, Ed. 84/7.

37. The 18th Contract (*loc. cit.*) was for the terracotta chimney caps. Doulton's quoted £50 and was awarded the contract; the other firms who tendered were Blanchard, £75 10s; J. Cliffson, £90; Gibbs & Canning, £122 15s; J. Blashfield, £150. Scott thought that Doulton's figure was too low (29 November 1870).

38. PRO, Works 17/22/3, 15 August 1873.

39. *Decorations*, pp. 26–28. A slightly later building, with similar decoration is F. C. Penrose's St Paul's Choir School in Carter Lane.

40. PRO, Ed. 84/54, 17 October 1871. According to a 'Statement of Cost' received from Sir John Donnelly, 3 July 1899, this work cost £1,191 11s 8d, PRO, Ed. 84/57.

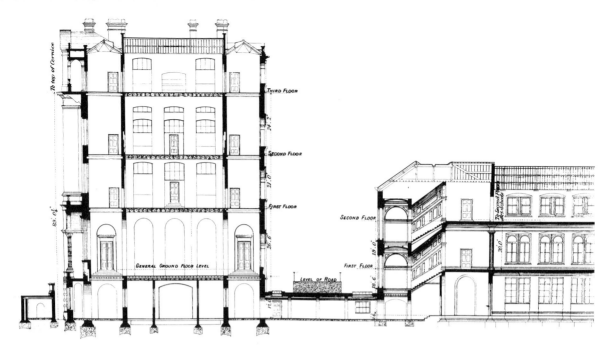

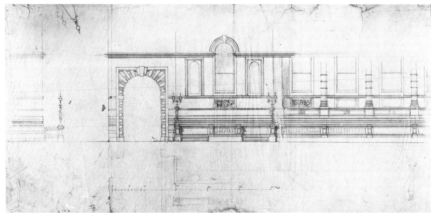

172. *(above) Section through the Science Schools, from the south*

173. *(left) Design by James Gamble for the entry to the Science Schools from Exhibition Road*

174
175
176

in good condition, except for the dirt. Not only did Moody sign it at eye level at the north end – 'The Experiments In Plaster Designed By F. W. Moody Were Executed By The Art Students A.D. MDCCCLXII' – but he left a detailed and lengthy account of his methods.[41]

The sgraffito technique had already been tried, on a small scale, on the western wall of the Sheepshanks Gallery (see Chapter III). It was necessary to cover the area of wall to be decorated with two layers of plaster, a dark under layer, and a light layer on top. A full-sized drawing of the proposed decoration was prepared, and was

> transferred to the wall by tracing the lines through the paper on to the wet and yielding plaster, or if the drawing is executed in charcoal, it may be

> printed on the wall by turning its face towards the plaster and rubbing firmly at the back; then with an ordinary desk penknife, which was found to be the best tool, the artist firmly incises the outline, cutting through the upper layer into but not through the black layer below; he then scrapes away the upper layer and exposes the black wherever the black is wanted, leaving the upper layer wherever white is wanted, and in this way any design in two tints can be executed with rapidity and effect ... Although designs are very generally executed in black and white, any colours which are permanent when mixed with plaster can of course be used.

41. Quoted in Alan S. Cole, 'On the art of "Sgraffito" decoration', *Papers read at the Royal Institute of British Architects*, 1872–3, pp. 127–140. The quotations below are on pp. 129, 130.

174. *Engraved plaster decoration on the east side of the Science Schools, designed by F. W. Moody and executed by students of the Art Schools*

175. *(top right)*, 176. *(centre right) Reproductions of details of F. W. Moody's designs for engraved plaster decoration on the east side of the Science Schools*

Various experiments were made with the composition and colouring of the plaster. As well as the two coats in which the design was cut, it was necessary to apply an undercoat straight to the wall. At first this was made of one part ground selenetic lime to four parts of rough sand and a little plaster of Paris. In places, however, it was found that this layer did not adhere properly to the wall, and a new recipe was tried: one part selenetic, two parts Barra clay and five parts coarse sand. This was not wholly successful, however, and in 1973, during a gale, one panel of decoration fell off the wall and was smashed.

The black layer was made of one part lime, one and a half of black oxide of manganese and two of Barra shale or clay. The white coat was composed of silver sand, lime and whitening. The three coats of plaster invariably stuck together firmly. The undercoat was applied at a thickness of $\frac{3}{4}$ inch. The black layer was at first $\frac{3}{8}$ inch thick, but it was found that it tended to expand and bow out, so therefore it was kept to a minimum thickness of less than $\frac{1}{4}$ inch. The top coat was hardly more than $\frac{1}{16}$ inch thick.

The ornamental designs were of necessity linear. It was possible, however, to introduce hatched shading, provided that the hatched lines were not so close together as to cause the resulting white ridges to break off. Painted shadows could also be applied, and some parts of the decoration were executed entirely by painting rather than by sgraffito. On some of the ground-floor panels, shadows were introduced by elaborating the sgraffito process: the design was cut in three, instead of two, layers.

> ... first, the ordinary black layer, then a grey layer, and last, the ordinary finishing coat. To obtain the shadow we cut through the upper coat only; but when we want to come to the background we cut through both that and the shadow coat. In this way we have produced the appearance of a drawing with tinted shadows, and in this way no doubt still greater variety and refinement could without much difficulty be produced in *sgraffito*.

This decoration was applied to an expanse of wall more than three storeys in height on the building which was, at that time, the tallest in South Kensington; each storey was pierced by a row of round-headed windows, so the remaining flat areas were rather awkward in shape. They were brought to order by dividing features in low relief, rather different on each storey: on the top, panelling; in the middle storey, pilasters; and on the ground floor, medallions and panels. The sgraffito decoration was composed of Moody's characteristic version of Renaissance grotesque ornament.

The building was ready for occupation by the students and their teachers at the end of 1872, but it was not until 18 August 1874[42] that General Scott told the First Commissioner of Works that the building was finished. There then followed an argument concerning the sum of £5,657 9s 3d, which, it was said, had been overspent. The Treasury finally gave its sanction for the money to be paid to the contractor on 19 February 1875.

The finishing touch to the building was eventually added in 1886, when iron gates were installed in the archway leading under the Science Schools from Exhibition Road. These gates were much involved with the fortunes of James Gamble, one of Scott's design team. As the Science Schools approached completion, Scott proposed that the arch on Exhibition Road should be closed by decorative wrought-iron gates, and Gamble indicated that he was prepared to design these, and some lamps, for a fee of £100.[43] However, when

money became short in 1874, these were not considered by Scott to be as important as some other schemes of decoration within the Museum. So Gamble agreed with the Office of Works to postpone work on them. In any case, Gamble was now under notice, for during September 1874 Scott told him that, since work on the South Kensington decoration was now running out, he would not be able to keep Gamble on after 31 December. 'Be pleased to consider this note, therefore, as an official notice that the Office of Works will not require your services after that date'.[44] Gamble asked Scott what right he had to dismiss him, as he was employed by the Department of Science and Art, and referred the matter to Sir Francis Sandford. The latter was abroad, and it was not until the end of November that Gamble was reminded that from 1870, when the Office of Works had assumed control of building at South Kensington, both Gamble and Townroe had not been paid by the Department of Science and Art, but by the Office of Works. Therefore, General Scott had acted quite properly.

Whatever the coolness between Scott and Gamble, it did not prevent Scott from writing to the *Building News* to state that much of the decorative work on the Science Schools was 'Mr. Gamble's own, and he assisted materially in making the general design what it is'.[45] And in 1877 Gamble was back again; in that year, certain works, unfinished during the preceding lean years, received authorization for their completion. Gamble asked Scott if he 'would allow him to enquire' if he knew what he was to be re-employed upon. Scott very frostily replied[46] that he had received no instructions regarding Gamble, but upon enquiry 'I have been informed that the Department of Science and Art have been authorized to complete the Refreshment Rooms ... It appears to be therefore, that your re-employment now rests with that Department ... and as you apparently have not received any communication from that Department, you had better properly address yourself to them.' Gamble was still in residence in his studio years after

---

42. PRO, Works 17/22/2.
43. PRO, Ed. 84/7, 30 June 1871.
44. PRO, Ed. 84/67, 26 September 1874.
45. *Building News*, 3 March 1876, p. 233.
46. PRO, Ed. 84/67, 10 May 1877.

Scott's own summary dismissal by the First Commissioner of Works.

He did not, however, succeed in carrying through his designs for the wrought-iron gates, despite a fierce wrangle with Sir John Taylor, architect to the Office of Works. His estimate for the gates and bronze lamps had been £1,370.[47] Nothing further was ever heard of the lamps, but in the Estimates for 1884–5 provision was made at last for the gates. As soon as he heard of this, Gamble wrote to the Office of Works to remind the First Commissioner that he had a design 'already prepared, and which was approved by my master, Mr. Alfred Stevens, Sir Henry Cole, Mr. Poynter, Mr. Redgrave'. The design was, so far as Gamble knew, with Colonel Donnelly, and was 'in agreement with the architecture and ornament of the Building, of which I originated a considerable portion'.[48]

John Taylor's reaction to Gamble's letter was only to tell his Secretary that he saw 'no reason why Mr. Gamble should be employed on this service'.[49] He proffered no reason for this decision, nor was he asked for one; Gamble was simply told that the Board did not desire to avail themselves of his offer. Piqued by his brusque rejection, Gamble wrote to Donnelly. When working on the Science Schools, he said, he had received a verbal order from the Museum's Director to carry out a scheme for gates, lamps, iron railings and statuary for the niches of the Exhibition Road façade, although subsequently the railings had been abandoned in favour of a terracotta balustrade. His designs, and plaster models of the lamp and part of the gates, had been handed over to the Clerk of Works.

Donnelly sent a copy of Gamble's letter to the First Commissioner, reminding him that as the designs had been made at public expense, the Board of the Science and Art Department was 'not aware of any reason why this design should not be carried out'.[50] Nevertheless, if Gamble's designs were not wanted, Donnelly suggested that new designs might be obtained through a competition among the students of the Art Schools.

Taylor, to whom Donnelly's letter was referred, turned down Gamble again, but approved a competition, on condition that the design should cost nothing, and the cost of the gates should not exceed £300.[51] By now it was midsummer and

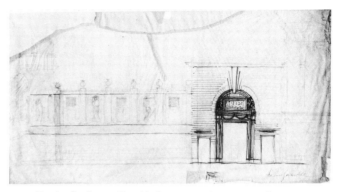

177. *Design by James Gamble for a screen (not executed) linking the Science Schools to the Museum*

the students were on vacation. Gamble advanced his claims again, but to no avail.[52]

When the Art Schools reassembled in the autumn, the matter was taken up once more, but now the Committee of Council on Education declined to put up the money to support a competition, and urged the Office of Works to use the designs it had already paid for from Gamble.[53] Taylor ordered a search for Gamble's design and models, which had been in the care of the Office of Works for about eight years. The Clerk of Works at first denied all knowledge, but finally admitted to a few fragments of a lamp, and spandrels, found in the room 'occupied by Genl. Scott's modellers'. Taylor reported, predictably, that these were 'of no use to anyone'.

By this time, as it was well into November, the wrangle had been going on for far too long, and the First Commissioner resolved 'to proceed with the gates on our own account';[54] so early in January 1885, Taylor himself produced a design which was sent to South Kensington for approval. Approval was given, subject to some modifications, and in April 1885 Taylor asked for estimates from three firms of metalworkers, Starkie Gardner & Co., Turner & Co., and Hart, Son & Peard. Starkie Gardner thereupon submitted a design of his own, based on Taylor's, and estimated to cost

(margin note left: 177)
(margin note right: 178, 179)

47. PRO, Ed. 84/67, 27 November 1874.
48. PRO, Works 17/8/1, 21 April 1884.
49. Ibid., 30 June 1884.
50. Ibid., 1 July 1884.
51. Ibid., 19 July 1884.
52. Ibid., 26 August 1884.
53. Ibid., 28 October 1884.
54. Ibid., 14 November 1884.

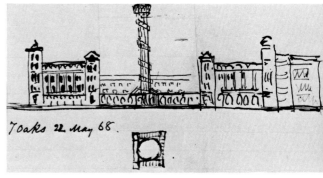

7oaks 22 May 68.

178. *(left) Design by Starkie Gardner for the iron gates to the Science Schools, 1885*

179. *(below left) The gates of the entry from Exhibition Road beneath the Science Schools*

180. *(above) Sketch illustrating a proposal by Henry Cole to duplicate the Science Schools building as an extension to the Museum, 1868*

£288. Surprisingly, Taylor recommended it, and Starkie Gardner was instructed to carry out the work.[55] The gates remain in place today, though somewhat battered by lorries.

The Science Schools, it will have become clear, are a less than completely coherent building, showing signs of hasty planning as well as of experimental decoration. Nonetheless, they have received high praise. H. S. Goodhart-Rendel recalled that in his youth, in the early years of the present century, he was told, 'and I unquestioningly believed' that the façades of the building 'were a work of the highest excellence. That I should have been so told, I confess, surprises me. Buildings between 30 and 40 years of age, as this building then was, generally have few friends, but my belief has never faltered. It still seems to me a work of art that was a classic from the moment of its birth.'[56]

The Architectural Courts

Cole noted in his diary on 5 January 1867 that he had started designing a new court for the Museum. This was to occupy part of the site of the Boilers, and would be an extension of the permanent buildings southwards from the Sheepshanks Gallery. The building that eventually arose, the

55. Ibid., minute by Taylor, 30 September 1885.
56. H. S. Goodhart-Rendel, 'Brompton, London's Art Quarter', *R.I.B.A. Journal*, January 1956.

181. *Drawing made by the Museum Design Office illustrating Henry Cole's proposal sketched in ill. 180*

Architectural Courts, consisted of two huge halls, running from north to south and separated by a narrow three-storey gallery, each storey opening into the adjacent halls. The purpose of these courts was to contain the Museum's collection of plaster casts of large-scale architectural sculpture; the most prominent feature was the cast of Trajan's Column.

182   General Scott was the architect of the Architectural Courts, again assisted by J. W. Wild. The specification for the completion of the carcass was drawn up by 21 July 1870,[57] and during the year following the building received its roof.[58] The proportions of the Courts are enormous: each is 135 feet long by 60 feet wide, with a height to the centre of the curved glass roof of 83 feet. A narrow gallery runs round each of them 50 feet from the ground, to which were once fixed hundreds of gas jets. The passage between the Courts, with two galleries above, is 17 feet wide. Each court originally had a ceiling of 286 squares of ground glass each 3 feet 6 inches square, placed directly on to the iron framework (made by the Horsley Iron Works)[59] without any putty, to allow for the

expansion and contraction of the metalwork. Even before the Courts opened, this roof let in the snow, as Cole noted in his diary on 3 February 1873: 'Fall of snow which entered the roofs of the new courts and flooded [them] – the louvres being fixed – ceiling came down.'

The opening of the western court to the public took place during July 1873, with a private view. The construction of Trajan's Column was nowhere near finished, though Captain Festing, one of the three Museum Superintendents, hoped that it would be at some time during 1874.[60] The exterior of the new courts – two huge blank gable walls of red and yellow bricks, towering over the remnant of the Boilers – aroused considerable speculation as to what might be inside, but the South Kensington officials 'preserved a strict silence on the subject, while the approaches to the new court have been carefully railed off from

57. PRO, Ed. 84/15, Works 17/22/1.
58. *19th Report . . . 1871* (1872), p. 388.
59. PRO, Works 17/22/1.
60. *21st Report . . . 1873* (1874), p. 381.

public intrusion'.[61] So when the new courts did open (the opening of the eastern court followed later in the year), press coverage was wide, and, on the whole, favourable.[62]

XXXIII The high walls of the court were distempered. In his diary on 4 January 1872 Cole recorded that experiments in colouring had been made. Crimson and orange had been tried but Redgrave had objected to the crimson as being too 'cutting'. In the end the courts were painted in shades described as 'olive-green and purple red'.[63] In the western courts the lower walls were red, and the upper (above the balcony) green; with the contrary arrangement in the other court. Ornamentation was concentrated upon the high-level balcony. Its supporting brackets, the mouldings of the arcades above, and other mouldings, were picked out with stencilled patterns. Furthermore, the 'spaces between the brackets ... are done in panels, in which are inserted the names of cities celebrated in the history of art, alphabetically arranged from Ahmedabad to Zurich. Lower down appear the names of distinguished masters of all countries, with the date of their birth and death.'[64] These decorations were designed and executed by Reuben Townroe.[65]

The central passage was also decorated. At each end of it are a pair of granite columns, which are probably those ordered in August 1864 by Francis Fowke for the arches in front of the

Lecture Theatre and abandoned when it was decided to use terracotta instead. In May 1872 the artist John Millais visited the new courts with a friend, and wrote to tell Cole that they had both been struck

> with the beauty of the simple stonework pillars, & balcony, which are so quiet after the *over* decoration of the apartments, that I cannot but send you a warning against some distinctive experiments of coloured ornamentation which I see under the balcony ... I am sure the decoration as proposed will spoil the effect. Leave it as it is & I am sure you will never regret it. Show rooms shd be made not to assert themselves ...[66]

Millais's advice was not taken. Not only was the decoration under the balcony carried through, the central passage was also decorated. Its columns were painted in 'white and chocolate colours, and gilt capitals' and its ceiling was composed of 'thin strips of wood, about 2 in. wide, coloured white, and laid on a series of iron girders painted in blue

61. *Building News,* 4 April 1873, p. 384.
62. *Art Journal,* 1873, p. 276 (see also vol. for 1871, p. 231) *Builder,* 4 October 1873, p. 789 (illus. p. 787); *Building News,* 25 April 1873, p. 469; 31 October 1873, pp. 473–5. *The Architect,* 19 April 1873, p. 208; 26 April 1873, p. 220; 10 May 1873, p. 249; 24 May 1873, p. 273.
63. *Building News,* 25 April 1873, p. 469.
64. Ibid.
65. *Decorations,* p. 25.
66. Cole correspondence, Millais to Cole, 21 May 1872.

182. *Section through the Cast Courts, with Room 45 on the left and the Secretariat wing on the right*

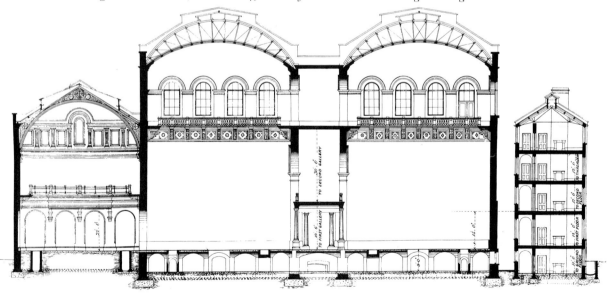

183. *(above left) Design by F. W. Moody for a window blind for the Cast Courts*

184. *(above right) Part of the mosaic floor of the corridor between the Cast Courts, designed by F. W. Moody and and executed by women convicts at Woking Prison*

and white'.[67] The western court and the passage have recently been restored, so this decoration can once again be seen.

183 Certain decorative features have disappeared, however. For instance, Frank Moody designed a series of painted and transparent blinds for the windows; he hoped that, if they were liked, they could be used as cartoons for stained glass. He painted them himself, with assistance from O. Gibbons and W. Wise.[68] They no longer survive.

Below the new courts is a basement, and three plate glass panels, 10 feet square, were set into the floors of each court to let light into the vaults below.[69] These panels were also made a decorative feature, for they were covered with transparent glass mosaic:

Upon the ordinary solid glass slab has been laid a geometrical and somewhat serpentine pattern of coloured glass, chiefly in low tints of green and purple, wholly transparent, with the exception of a central figure, which has been worked in opaque white tesserae. This, catching the eye, gives importance to the whole design, which is, in fact, a transparent mosaic in which, though the divisions between the pieces are clearly visible, they are far smaller (and of course, far cheaper) than the leading

needed for a stained glass window. The effect, as seen from above, is decidedly satisfactory; while below, though of course a certain amount of light is obstructed by the opaque and even by the transparent parts of the upper surface, sufficient is still transmitted for all needful purposes. These lights are manufactured by Messrs. Powell, of Whitefriars.[70]

The mosaics were designed by Moody, and full-sized drawings were prepared by W. Wise, O. Gibbons, E. Wormleighton and H. W. Foster.[71] They cannot now be seen either from above (since the floors of the courts are covered with linoleum), or below.

The floor of the corridor was of mosaic, made 184 by the female convicts of Woking Prison, under the direction of Lt. Col. Du Cane. The designs were by Moody, and the full-size drawings by his four assistants just named.[72] This stretch of floor is one of the few pieces of *opus criminale* that has

67. *Building News*, 25 April 1873, p. 469.
68. *Decorations*, p. 25
69. *Building News*, 25 April 1873, p. 469.
70. *The Architect*, 24 May 1873, p. 273.
71. *Decorations*, p. 25.
72. Ibid.

185. *The eastern Cast Court, north end, 1872, as the decorative work was nearing completion*

structural advantages of the invention, it will prove of considerable value in a sanitary point of view replacing as it does, the spongy and porous substance with which the walls of our houses and public buildings are at present coated and substituting for the same a hard impervious material, having a glassy surface, capable of being washed without injury. These qualities, while they render it incapable of absorbing and retaining the germs and seeds of disease, will also I believe prove of great importance from an artistic point of view.' Not only, continued Scott, was the plaster suitable for fresco, but it would be admirable for sgraffito decoration. Scott reported that the War Office was using his invention, and that the Office of Works had given permission for its use in the new architectural courts. Scott was very careful to emphasize to the Department that, although the process had been patented, he wished for no financial gain and had declined any sort of royalty arising from its use in the Museum, or on any public building of which he was superintending the building works.[76] Whether the new plaster actually was used in the Architectural Courts is not known.

The Architectural Courts must have been (as perhaps they still are) the most immediately impressive and evocative rooms in the Museum, and it seems entirely fitting that they should have been celebrated in literature. In Chapter x of *Love and Mr Lewisham* (1900), H. G. Wells wrote:

As one goes into the South Kensington Art Museum from the Brompton Road, the Gallery of Old Iron is overhead to the right. But the way thither is exceedingly devious and not to be revealed to everybody, since the young people who pursue science and art thereabouts set a peculiar value on its seclusion. The gallery is long and narrow and dark ... and over the balustrade one may lean and talk of one's finer feelings and regard Michael Angelo's horned Moses, or Trajan's Column (in plaster) rising gigantic out of the hall below and far above the level of the gallery.

escaped covering over by later generations and remains visible.

185   The eastern court contained a number of casts of Indian architecture. Most prominent among them was a cast of Akbar the Great's Hall of Private Audience from his palace at Fathpur Sikri near Agra. This was contained in a 'cube-like erection of uncouth proportions', which dominated the eastern court, as Trajan's Column did the western. One end of this structure was decorated with sgraffito work.[73] This was presumably that by Frank Moody which he was authorized to begin in 1872,[74] and which, a year later, was the subject of recriminations between him and Captain Festing because the materials had cost more than they should, and the plaster had not adhered to the walls (a problem that had cropped up in the sgraffito work on the Science Schools).[75]

As it happened, General Scott had invented a new kind of plaster, which he had commended in a letter to the Department of Science and Art on 11 January 1871. He said that 'In addition to the

---

73. *Art Journal,* 1873, p. 276.
74. PRO, Ed. 84/37, Board minute, précis, 25 June 1872.
75. PRO, Ed. 84/67, 16 April, 21 April 1873.
76. V&A Museum, General Scott file.

CHAPTER X

The end of the South Kensington building programme

Henry Cole said of himself that 'if he had always waited for orders he would never have got anything done', and it was said of him that 'if he had always waited for people to get out of the way he would never had made any progress'.[1] It is not surprising, therefore, that he aroused resentment among his official colleagues and superiors. Nor is it surprising that they began to fight back. It was in the late 1860s and early '70s, while the three building projects just described were in progress, that South Kensington was gradually brought to heel. Cole's retirement in 1873 was the most important factor in the power struggle. So far as the building activities were concerned, the enlargement of the authority of the Office of Works, under Acton Smee Ayrton in Gladstone's first administration (1868–74), worked against South Kensington; and the works office could not survive the dismissal of General Scott in 1883.

Revised plans for the future

Until the end of the 1860s, the Department of Science and Art hoped to implement Captain Fowke's plans for the completion of the Museum. It was on the basis of these plans that government money had been requested, and granted by the Treasury, for the projects dealt with in the previous chapter. On 23 October 1869, the Treasury, preparing its estimates for expenditure in 1870–1, wrote to South Kensington to find out what progress had been made.[2] They had before them a plan dated January 1869, embodying the Fowke proposals as revised at that time. It seems that their suspicions had been aroused by the word 'laboratories', for the Science Schools were labelled 'School of Naval Architecture and Laboratories'.

Cole and Scott reported on the progress of the building works that had been sanctioned in 1866. The Science Schools (marked E on the plan) were built to the level of the second floor, but were now at a standstill for want of funds, while ironwork and terracotta, already purchased, were deteriorating on the site. (Cole and Scott reassured the Treasury that laboratories might appropriately be installed in a place of scientific instruction). The new Architectural Courts (Q on the plan) were also half erected. A court to house the Educational Apparatus (I), matching the Architectural Courts in the western wing of Fowke's design, had not been begun, but Cole and Scott claimed, 'the equivalent of its space, applicable to like purpose, is provided' in the Science Schools. Although Cole goes on to say that the Schools 'include the exhibition space, or more than the exhibition space, which was to have been provided in I', this seems like special pleading, for there was no room for the Educational Museum in the Schools and it was never housed there. Ranges for the Art Library (K) and the Educational Library (R), intended to face each other across Fowke's forecourt, had not been begun (and were never built). The office block (T) and the Board Room (U), on the eastern edge, were complete.

As Cole and Scott reminded the Treasury, an expenditure of £195,000 had been sanctioned in 1866, 'to be spread over a period of six years, of which we are about to enter the fifth' (i.e. 1870–1). In a later minute[3] Cole stated:

Original Estimate for the Service	£195,000
Gross amount of Votes and Re-Votes up to 31 March 1870	£89,000
Total amount of Expenditure up to 31 March 1870	£89,000
Vote required for 1870–71	£60,000
Further amount required for completing the work	£46,000

---

1. *The Architect*, 12 June 1873, p. 13.
2. PRO, Ed. 84/67.
3. Ibid., December 1869.

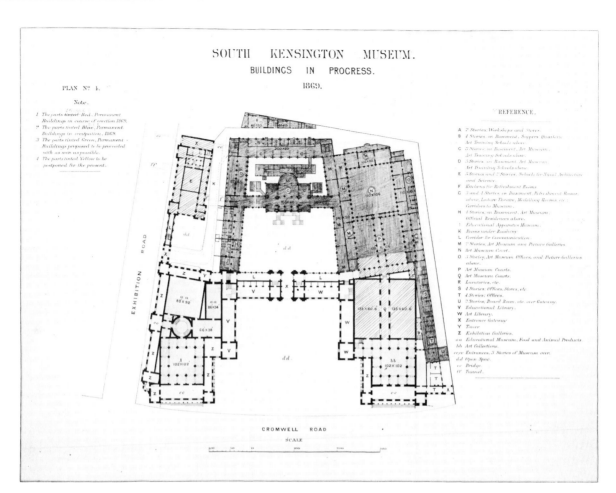

162

Owing to various circumstances, Cole did not in the end get any money for 1870–1. One development which must have confused the issue was a further revision of the South Kensington plans which he announced to the Treasury in the minute already quoted. Although the vote of £195,000 had been sanctioned on the basis of Fowke's plans, these had now been adapted by Henry Scott. 'These alterations', it was claimed, 'will cause no excess on the sum of £195,000...'. Whereas in Fowke's plan the southern frontage of the Museum, towards Cromwell Road, had from the very beginning been dominated by two curving wings, now, in Scott's plan, the frontage was rectangular. It still followed roughly the same form: two wings coming forward to enclose a central open space.

At the request of the Treasury, Scott and his staff prepared a model of the proposed building. This was finished by mid-January 1870, when the architects James Fergusson and Sydney Smirke were asked to comment on it. Although no record of their views has been traced, it can be assumed that they were favourable.[4] The Chancellor of the Exchequer asked for the model to be sent to the Treasury Board Room for examination,[5] and Cole and Scott composed a long argument in support of it.[6] After pointing out reasons why the Museum needed more space (this

part of the argument was to be reiterated with increasing desperation for many years), they made some neat points intended to show how economical the South Kensington building operation could be. Fowke's plan, approved in 1866 had afforded

13,072,476 cubic feet of space, and was estimated to cost £481,072 (and such portions of it as have been executed) had cost about 9d per cubic foot. The present revised plan will afford 17,200,000 cubic feet and, not withstanding the increased value of labour during the last five years, it may, it is estimated, be executed for a total expenditure of £685,000, or less than $9\frac{1}{4}d$ per cubic foot. The estimate includes all external decorations, and a fair amount of internal decoration ...

This, they suggested, compared very well with other public buildings.

The expenditure on the British Museum ... has exceeded £1,100,000 on a smaller area than that which will be occupied by the South Kensington Museum, and it affords a less amount of space. Its cost per cubic foot has been, in fact, 1s 6d., or nearly double that of the South Kensington Museum.

The costs per cubic foot of the South Kensington buildings had ranged from '6d to 1s. per cubic foot, according to the amount of decoration bestowed on them (the average being under $9\frac{1}{4}d$.)', whereas 'the cost of the India Office has been at least 1s. 2d. per cubic foot, of the Foreign Office 1s. 4d. per cubic foot, whilst that of the Houses of

186. (opposite above) Plan for the proposed completion of the Museum buildings, by Henry Scott, 1869

187. (opposite below) Model of the proposed Museum buildings, completed according to the plans of Henry Scott, 1869: bird's-eye view from Cromwell Road

188. (below) Model of the proposed Museum buildings (see ill. 187): view from Exhibition Road

4. There can be no certainty about this, although it was later implied by the Department. Cole recorded in his diary, somewhat ambiguously, on 17 January 1869, that Fergusson had called and 'criticized' earlier plans for the new buildings.
5. PRO, Ed 83/72, 29 January 1870.
6. PRO, Ed. 84/54, 31 January 1870.

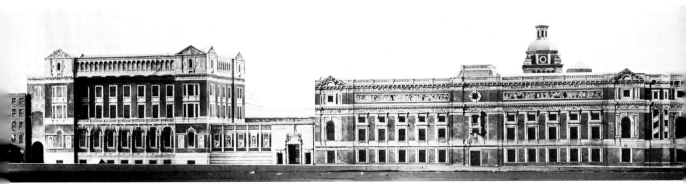

Parliament has risen as high as 2s. and 3s. per cubic foot.' The minute went on to suggest that it was a great advantage for South Kensington to have its own team of artists on the premises.

> Whereas, Sir Charles Barry for the decorative carving of the stonework of the Houses of Parliament, was obliged to form a school of decorative artists receiving a high rate of remuneration, the construction of the South Kensington Museum is carried on with the assistance of decorative artists trained in the art schools, by whom such a valuable opportunity of commencing their career is eagerly sought.

And the opportunity was not lost to put in a good word for terracotta:

> By the adoption of terra-cotta for the decorative portions of the structure, not only has the heavy expenditure entailed by ornaments carved in stone been avoided, but a material much cheaper than stone, which is the same time better able to resist the London atmosphere, been made use of.

Whether the Treasury was impressed by the model and the explanation of it is not known, because before long South Kensington's entreaties for money were turned into pleas for survival. It was during March 1870 that the South Kensington authorities learned that the Treasury, in an attempt to gain greater control over the erection and maintenance of public buildings, had decided that all such buildings should henceforward come under the charge of the Office of Works. This followed upon the appointment on 11 November 1869 to the post of First Commissioner of Works (in succession to Austen Layard, who had become Ambassador to Spain) of Acton Smee Ayrton, formerly a Parliamentary Secretary to the Treasury. This was a controversial appointment. Layard was the distinguished archaeologist who had excavated Nineveh, and might therefore have been assumed to be fitted by knowledge and experience to look after Britain's national architecture. Ayrton, on the other hand, prided himself on knowing nothing about art. An abrasive character and sarcastic speaker, he liked to present himself as the friend of the working classes: his constituency was Tower Hamlets, in the poor East End of London. On 8 November 1869 he spoke at Stepney about the new responsibilities he was about to take up. 'There were people very fond of what is called art', he said, 'and some of them were very artful people, too.' He saw it as his duty to get the better of them:

> He was appointed to represent the Crown and the public, who had to pay the expenses of the Crown, as the employer of architects and other professional men ... It was his duty to look after those professional persons – not to be one of them. What he had to do was to see that people in office did not make too many demands upon the public purse for public works and buildings; above all, to take care that people who had fancies did not indulge them at the public expense ...

Just to make clear exactly where he stood, he remarked:

> There was a certain sort of people in this country who had been educated in our public schools and universities, and who, instead of looking at matters as they stood at the present day, began by looking back to see what was done two or three thousand years ago in Greece or Rome. These people might be said to live in a world of their own.[7]

In Ayrton's world, what mattered was (as *The Times* leader commented) a 'well trained habit of refusing to sanction public expenditure'.

Ayrton lived up to his pronouncements, and soon had the architectural profession in an uproar. He threatened to set the Treasury Solicitor on to the lethargic Alfred Stevens, who was making very slow progress with the Wellington Monument intended for St Paul's Cathedral. He dismissed E. M. Barry from his appointment as architect to the Houses of Parliament, a post which Barry had attained after the death of his father, Sir Charles Barry, who designed the new Palace of Westminster. And, of course, he assumed control of the building works at South Kensington. He authorized the completion of the Science Schools and the Architectural Courts, which were already begun, but nothing more.

The Department of Science and Art, which had done what it pleased with its buildings for sixteen years, fought back. W. E. Forster, vice-president of the Committee of Council on Education, had a couple of unsuccessful skirmishes with the Treasury. Then an attempt was made to convince the Treasury of the necessity of South Kensington's

---

7. *The Times*, 9 November 1869.

independence by detailed argument. Cole and his colleague, Captain Festing, produced memoranda on the buildings and their maintenance, designed to prove that a resident workforce under the control of the Department was indispensable.[8] These memoranda failed in their purpose, but it is worth quoting extensively from them, since they present an interesting picture of the everyday working of a mid-Victorian museum.

Cole began in characteristically hyperbolical style:

> The public at present have facilities by day and night for using the South Kensington Museum, which are not afforded by any other Public Gallery or Museum. Unlike other places the Museum is never closed to visitors for alteration, repairs, cleaning, or re-arrangement of its objects, and throughout the whole administration the interests of the public as students or visitors are made the first object.

With an admirable solicitude for the convenience of the public, he went on to claim that

> The daily works of cleaning, heating, ventilation, lighting, removal and arrangement of objects especially necessitated by loans ... are carried out with promptitude and without inflicting inconvenience on the visitors. The works, when necessary, are performed in the very early morning, or are carried on through the night, so as not to interfere with the use of the Museum. Any accidental defects in lighting or breakage or leakage are immediately remedied. Daily attention is requisite for nearly 40,000 superficial feet of top lighting, for 13,000 gas jets (as many as light the streets of the City), for eight miles of heating pipes supplied from 16 boilers, for the fire-mains and water-pipes, lavatories, water-closets etc. All these works are connected with the Buildings and their maintenance, and the repairs, if not done immediately, would fall into arrear and would disorganise the whole establishment.

His staff of 60 labourers and artisans were, he claimed, absolutely necessary to the daily running of the Museum, and would be no less necessary even if the Office of Works assumed responsibility for maintaining the building. Cole's indispensable men could maintain the building in between their other work, why not let them go on doing so?

> For instance, one or more painters are constantly employed in painting and stopping leaks in the sky-lights etc., and it is far more economical and effective to have a system permanently and quietly

in action at such works than to have a number of contractors' heedless journeyman painters at one time on the roof, pretty liable to drop their tools on glass cases containing, for instance, crystals and jewellery so generously lent by Mr. Beresford Hope. ... It would be difficult, if not impossible, to divide the work between the two authorities. Men are employed at one time of day at work on the structure and another on the work of the Museum. A smith for instance may repair a lock out of order at one time of day, and at another time may be repairing or cleaning a valuable specimen of iron-work. The attempt to divide the work would cause a wasteful duplication of the staff and lead to great difficulties, and if the same men were employed and partly paid for one work and partly for another, the labour in keeping and auditing the accounts would be enormous. Above all, the responsibility for the safety of the Museum would be seriously impaired, and a system of dual administration introduced.

Festing followed up with a schedule of the works staff.

> The staff consists of the following:
> A. One resident Foreman of Works who exercises a general superintendence over all workmen in the occupied portion of the Buildings and premises, whether employed in repairs, cleaning, shifting cases or objects, or in any other work; he is responsible that the work is done with a due regard not only to its efficiency, but also to the safety of the objects in the Museum. He is always summoned by the Police, the first, when anything goes wrong, either by night or day.
> B. One second Foreman of Works not resident on the premises, whose work is more particularly confined to superintending the workshops and the manufacture of cases, fittings etc. He also superintends the ventilating arrangements.
> C. One Deputy Foreman who particularly superintends the labourers in cleaning the Museum etc. He does not reside on the premises.
> D. One Gas Foreman (Resident) whose duty is to light and extinguish the gas throughout the Museums and Schools, assisted by a chief gas attendant and six other attendants selected in turn from those labourers who are fit for the work ...
> E. Twelve to fourteen carpenters whose work consists of doing the jobbing repairs about the Museum, making cases, fittings etc., and fitting up objects for exhibition. These men are often employed on

---

8. PRO, Ed. 84/55, 7 April 1870.

different works at different times of the day; for instance, before the Museum is open, the polisher may be renovating the polish of the swing doors, where they have been scratched; afterwards he will be at work in the shop, polishing cases etc. . . .

G. Two painters, who beside the work which would come under the head of 'Furniture and Fittings', are constantly employed in painting and stopping the roofs . . .

H. Forty-five to fifty labourers whose work consists of cleaning the floors, windows etc., of the Museum, and the outsides of the cases, in shifting cases and large objects, and in helping to erect scaffolding or temporary partitions. The stokers who attend to the heating apparatus and the men who attend to the ventilation are included in the number. It will be readily understood that these men are also necessarily employed in different sorts of work at different times. Before breakfast on certain mornings the greater part are employed in washing floors, a work which from its great extent and the small time available for its execution, requires a considerable number of men, and this to a great extent governs the number of men necessary for the Staff of the Museum. At other times of the day the same men would be employed in cleaning windows, or erecting scaffolding, or shifting cases or objects, or any other work.

There is also a detachment of Royal Engineers quartered on the premises, consisting of 1 Sergeant and 13 rank and file, whose primary duty is to act as Fire Picquet and keep in order the fire engines, hoses, hydrants etc.; but they are also employed as photographers, as clerks in offices, or Art Library, and as artisans, each according to his particular ability.[9]

It would appear that Ayrton was not softened by these attempts to reason with him. He conceded that students of the Art Schools could continue to undertake the external and internal decoration of the Museum, from designs by, or initiated by, members of the Department. Otherwise the Office of Works would deal with all building operations.

The Department of Science and Art, having lost control of its local workforce (who for the time being remained at South Kensington, but were paid by and answerable to the Office of Works), now returned to its pleas for more space in new buildings. No new buildings had been authorized for 1870–1, but a meeting of the Board on 16 December 1870 decided to urge the First Commissioner of Works to relax his prohibition in 1871–2. Henry Cole sent to the Commissioner on

7 January 1871 a detailed estimate of the space at that time occupied by the various parts of the Museum, and the extra space that was required.[10] His tables provide an interesting picture of the Museum, and are reproduced as Appendix 2. In brief, Cole estimated that a further 531,857 square feet of space were urgently required: 193,414 for the Art Division; 65,010 for the libraries and the Educational Division, 61,904 for the Science Collections, and 211,529 for administrative premises. It will be observed that the section of the Museum that is least well provided for is the Science Collection. Complaints had been raised from time to time that science had fared badly in comparison with art. As early as 15 April 1863, a correspondent had complained to the *Daily News* that 'scarcely any money at all had gone towards science'. 'In fact, I know', wrote 'S.F.R.', 'that sums have been over and over again voted for science objects which have been spent for other purposes' and deplored the fact that Lyon Playfair was no longer on the Board of the Science and Art Department. Now, in 1871, Cole made the suggestion that the science collections might be moved to a building of their own in the South Kensington neighbourhood. It seems that this was the first time that this solution (eventually adopted, some thirty years later) was officially put forward.

Cole asked the First Commissioner of Works to apply to the Treasury 'for a general sanction to the execution of the plan and model sent . . . in 1869, and estimated to cost £463,000, in addition to what had been authorized in 1866'. But his arguments once again achieved nothing, and no new building was authorized in 1871–2.

Early in 1873 came a turning point in the Museum' fortunes. Cole retired during April. Not unnaturally, when his retirement was announced, there was speculation as to who would be his successor. Henry Scott heard that it was likely to be Philip Cunliffe Owen, one of the three Museum Superintendents.[11] While at the Bethnal Green

189

---

9. The establishment of Sappers was reduced in 1880. A letter was sent by the Department to the Deputy Adjutant-General, Royal Engineers, deprecating this action, and the Lord President decided to speak to the Secretary of State for War. Board minute précis, PRO, Ed. 84/37, 12 August 1880.

10. PRO, Ed. 84/15, 7 January 1871.

11. Cole, diary, 28 April 1873.

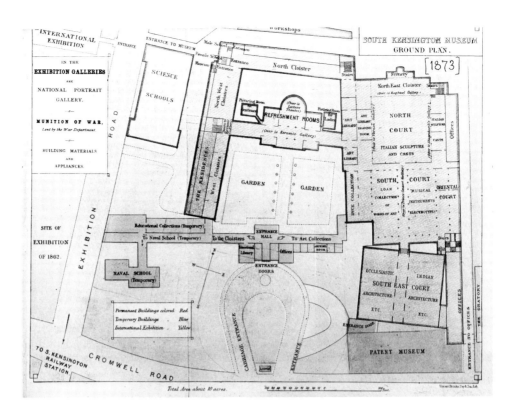

189. *Plan of the Museum in 1873*

Museum on 2 May 1873 with the King of the Belgians, Cole discussed his retirement. The King remarked that 'we are all public servants & ought to resign in time'. Later that day Cole attended a Board meeting at South Kensington and proposed to Lord Ripon, President of the Council, that Major Donnelly, the Inspector for Science, should be appointed Director. The Lord President agreed that the suggestion was 'worth considering'.[12]

In the event, an interregnum of almost a year followed, during which the Government considered a plan to remove the South Kensington Museum from the control of the Department of Science and Art and to place it under the Trustees of the British Museum. This suggestion was cautiously received by Bloomsbury, but viewed entirely without enthusiasm by South Kensington. Nevertheless, a committee was set up, containing representatives from both sides, to consider the practical consequences of the proposed arrangement. The British Museum was represented by Sir Augustus Wollaston Franks, the Director, Charles Newton, Keeper of Greek and Roman Antiquities, and John Winter Jones, the Principal Librarian. South Kensington was represented by Norman MacLeod, Assistant Secretary of the

Department of Science and Art, John Donnelly Inspector for Science, and Sir Francis Sandford, Secretary of the Education Department. C. W. Merrifield acted as Secretary.

By August 1873, the committee had agreed in principle[13] that the art collections of South Kensington should go to the British Museum, so far as legally possible. Some gifts and bequests, such as the paintings of John Sheepshanks, could not be moved owing to the conditions laid down by the donors. Future purchases for the collections would be the responsibility of the British Museum. The art and educational libraries were to stay at South Kensington, under the control of the Department of Science and Art, and the Department's own offices would remain there. It became apparent that a somewhat confusing allocation of buildings would have to be made at South Kensington. Some would belong to the Department; others, housing museum collections that could not be removed from the site, would be administered by the British Museum.

C. W. Merrifield realized that this would not work, and set about lobbying Sandford in an

---

12. Cole, diary, 2 May 1873.
13. Private memorandum from Winter Jones, P.R.O., Ed. 84/233.

incisive memorandum.[14] He conceded that the South Kensington authorities had 'given a great deal of trouble both to the Treasury and to the Cabinet, and Ministers personally, by contriving to make Cabinet questions of departmental matters', and that their expenditure had been excessive and insufficiently controlled. Some reform might therefore be needed. He went on,

> It is very clear to me, both from my own knowledge, and from what has transpired at our Committee, that we shall never get the British Museum to take away from South Kensington so much as will enable the Committee of Council on Education to dispense with a regular museum staff. The collections interlock at every point, local and administrative, like the fingers of clasped hands. If we import the Trustees, we shall have double staff and divided authority. I have never seen such an arrangement work either cheaply or satisfactorily. Moreover, the *officers* of the British Museum seem inclined to take over only the pick of the S. K. collections, and to avoid responsibility to an extent which will prevent their giving us any relief, while it will give them an embargo on the free use by the public of our collections.

Merrifield then ventured some critical remarks which he later deleted from his memorandum.

> I don't think that the Trustees ... can have any idea how very useless the present administration of the [British] Museum has rendered its collections to the public, except to that small portion of it which enjoys a learned leisure, or influential introductions. Their whole practice is in the direction of history and archaeology, & religious conservation of what is rare and curious, not without some exclusiveness as regards the public. From this view, it is quite opposed to the purposes of instruction and of free sacrifice to instruction, which hold at South Kensington.

Having thus dealt with the British Museum, Merrifield did not spare South Kensington. 'You are very well aware', he wrote, 'that I do not approve of the existing state of things at South Kensington.' He considered that South Kensington's methods had developed from the work of staging Educational exhibitions, and

> it is no wonder that the personnel still clings to its original raison d'être. It is very desirable that there should now be a little repose, if not repression – and at any rate a little more exclusive adherence to strict Museum duties ... One defect at South Ken-

sington has been want of high culture, and even of power to appreciate it. The staff is deplorably *indoctum*, except so far as regards its self-education in the Museum. I hope this will not be forgotten in any new appointments or promotions.

Merrifield suggested that this could be remedied 'by appointing a safe man to the Directorship ... and subordinating him to the Secretary at Whitehall (at the moment, yourself) ... If you or your successors controlled his Estimates, and if he could only address ministers or the Treasury through you, that would be effectual...'.

The committee reported in December 1873.[15] It suggested dividing up the buildings but emphasized the difficulties, and the Treasury, realizing that the proposal to hand South Kensington to the British Museum was impracticable, quietly allowed it to drop. Since Cole's retirement his responsibilities had been assumed by Norman MacLeod, Assistant Secretary of the Department of Science and Art. In February 1874, Philip Cunliffe Owen was appointed Director. He did not, however, take up Cole's position as Secretary of the Department. This was assumed by Sir Francis Sandford, who joined it with his responsibilities as Secretary of the Education Department. MacLeod continued as Assistant Secretary, acting as controlling officer at South Kensington. Thus the policy advocated by Merrifield was carried through.

Now that South Kensington's future seemed more settled, it was possible to return to the building plans. In March 1874 MacLeod reopened negotiations on the basis

1. That the time has arrived when buildings must be provided for the Art and Educational Libraries.
2. That in fulfilment of a promise to the Executors of the Revd. Alexr. Dyce a Gallery must be built for his very valuable collection.
3. That the erection of a Building in which to exhibit Educational Models and apparatus is very urgent.
4. That Examination Rooms are greatly wanted.
5. That in considering these immediate requirements it is most important to regard them as part of a general plan.
6. That the original plan must be modified in consequence of the alteration in height of the Buildings E. and Q.

---

14. PRO, Ed. 84/233.
15. Ibid.

190. *(right) Block plan showing new buildings proposed for the Museum by Henry Scott, 1874*

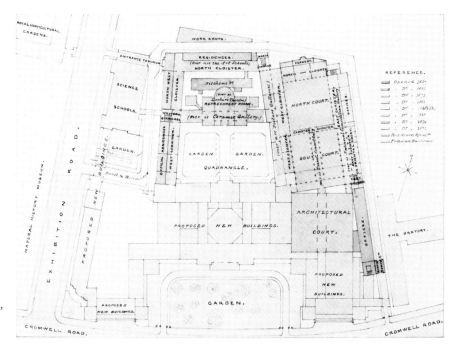

191. *(below) Model of the proposed Museum buildings, completed according to the plans of Henry Scott, 1874*

On Friday, 10 July 1874, the Duke of Richmond, Lord President, and the Vice-President, Viscount Sandon, met the Chancellor of the Exchequer, Sir Stafford Northcote, the First Commissioner of Works, Lord Henry Gordon Lennox, and W. H. Smith, Secretary to the Treasury, at Kensington to inspect further plans and models by Scott. Judging by entries in Cole's diary for 2 and 3 July, Scott had become disillusioned and disinclined to fight for his plans, but Cole was working behind the scenes to stiffen his resolution. In the event, one of the plans received general approval, apart from certain alterations which Scott was asked to make.[16]

Scott and his draughtsmen therefore set to work preparing the drawings for the completion of the entire complex. By the following January a model had been completed, but Scott estimated that he would need another year to produce all the drawings, so no money was requested for the year 1875–6.[17] In August 1875, Scott was authorized to proceed with working drawings for the south-east wing, but the Treasury reminded the Department of Science and Art that no final

190
191
192
193

16. PRO, Ed. 84/72, Memorandum by Norman MacLeod.
17. PRO, Ed. 84/75, Memorandum by Sir Francis Sandford, 1 January 1875.

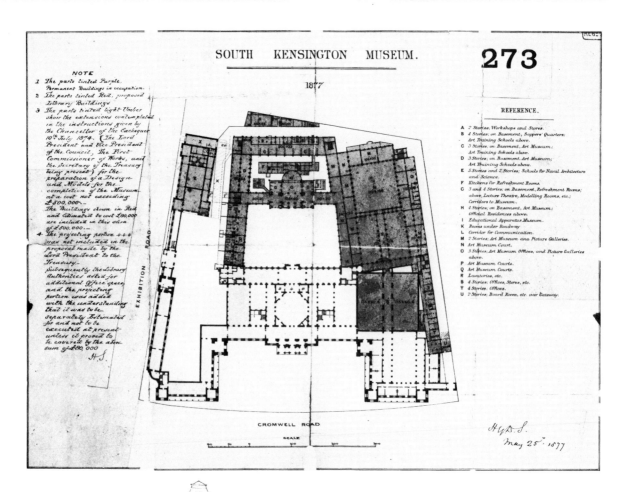

1877

NOTE

REFERENCE.

CROMWELL ROAD

SCALE

192. *(above) Plan, 1877,
by Henry Scott, showing
new buildings for the
Museum in accordance
with his proposals of 1874*

193. *(right) Perspective of
the façade of the South
Kensington Museum,
drawn from the model
embodying Henry Scott's
proposals of 1874 (see
ill. 191)*

194. *(below right) Section
through the eastern portion
(south of the Cast Courts)
of the new buildings
proposed for the Museum
in 1874 by Henry Scott*

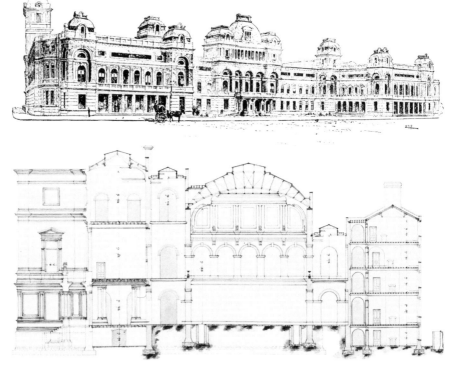

sanction to carry out the whole plan had yet been given.[18]

The main change in the new plan was the filling in of the central space south of the range of buildings already intended as (and eventually realized as) the library block. This series of new courts, laid out side by side on a level with the Architectural Courts, replaced the courts that had been planned for the south-western extension of the Museum. In the new plan, narrow ranges of galleries ran round the south-western edges of the site, leaving an irregular empty space within.

194
195
196
197

While the new drawings and models were in preparation, Scott's position was growing weaker. From February 1875 the Office of Works took responsibility for paying his salary and that of his

---

18. Ibid., 13 August, 23 August 1875. A set of plans, sections and elevations is in the PRO, Works 33/1662-1685.

195. *(right) Ground plan of the south-western portion, at the junction of Cromwell Road and Exhibition Road, of the new buildings proposed for the Museum by Henry Scott in 1874*

196. *(below) Elevation of the Exhibition Road façade of the new buildings proposed for the Museum by Henry Scott in 1874*

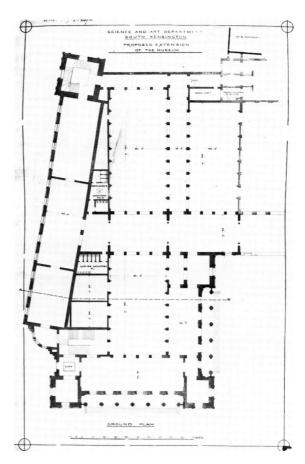

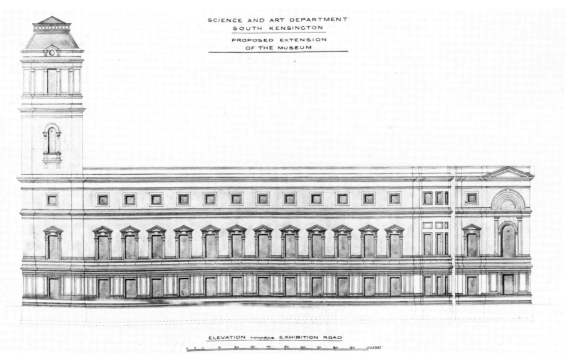

198
200 men, and for several months there was wrangling with the Treasury about how much and how often Scott should be paid. Eventually, it was agreed that he should continue at his previous rate of £60 per month. He had six men working for him (Messrs Dillon, Townroe, Down, Bridgman, Chapman and Castle) at rates ranging between £2 6s 3d and £6.[19] In May 1876 two of these men, Down and Chapman, were dismissed. Scott

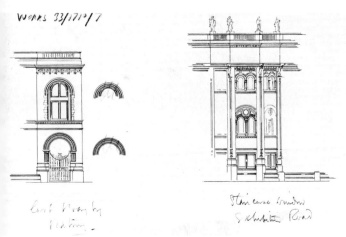

SIDE ELEVATION

volunteered to forgo his own salary in order that they might be paid, but then heard that £34 would be sent to him as final payment for his own services.[20] Shortly afterwards, however, his fortunes revived. Unexpectedly, on 2 June, the First Commissioner of Works was given authority to proceed with the building of the new Art Library, and so Scott was re-engaged.[21] It was not long before the Treasury was haggling over his pension rights.[22] At least, however, he was once again superintending a fresh building project.

The Art Library range

The range of rooms forming the Art Library *199* block links the eastern and western wings of the *200* museum, and forms the southern side of the *201* Quadrangle. It replaced the 'junction' building, *202* the single-storey brick range, which had been erected almost at the beginning of the South Kensington operations to connect the Boilers with the old houses in the western part of the site, in which the schools had at first been accommodated and which, by 1874, contained the Educational Collections.

The Treasury authorized the building not only of the two-storey cross range (which contained a long exhibition gallery on the ground floor, and, above, three connecting rooms for the Library), but also of two courts to the south of the range, one at each end. The central space between the two courts where further courts were intended (according to Scott's plans) to abut on the southern side of the Library range, was left empty. Curiously, *203* the Treasury agreed to the building of a façade on *204* this southern side, but this, uncalled for in the *205* master plan, was never built, and the new building presented a plain unfinished brick wall to the passer-by in Thurloe Place, until Aston Webb's new building of 1899–1909 concealed it. The total budget for the project was £80,000, to be spread over three or four years, £5,000 being voted for the current year.[23]

197. *(top) Elevation of the western façade of the new building proposed for the south-east corner of the Museum site by Henry Scott in 1874*

198. *(above) Designs for the entrance to the Museum beside the Brompton Oratory, and for a staircase window in Exhibition Road, prepared by Henry Scott in accordance with his proposals of 1874*

19. PRO, Works 17/24/8, 18 February, 8, 16 April, 4 May, 29 July 1875. In each of the years from 1874 to 1880 Scott received £720, except in 1875, when it was £786 16s 1d. His office wages varied between £1,075 9s 8d, and £1,665 6s 11d during the same period. PRO, 17/24/8, 12 December 1881.
20. Ibid., 19 May 1876.
21. Ibid., 13, 26 June 1876.
22. Ibid., 6 June, 11 July 1878.
23. PRO, Ed. 84/15, 1 June 1876; Ed. 84/54.

Scott informed the First Commissioner on 3 January 1877 that the contract drawings and specifications for the new library and adjacent courts (now Rooms 41 and 45) were complete. They were sent to the Treasury and did not re-appear until November 1877. It was only in January 1878 that advertisements appeared in the daily papers and architectural weeklies soliciting tenders.[24] Thirteen firms tendered: the lowest tender was from Newman & Nabb for £43,619 and the highest from William Downs & Co. for 54,600, but the firm selected was Perry & Co., who tendered for £45,000.[25] Doulton's made the terracotta decoration;[26] and for the façade facing

24. PRO, Works 17/22/5, 10 January, 28 May, 14 June, 1877.
25. PRO, Works 17/22/4.
26. Ibid.

199. *(above) The ground-floor gallery beneath the Art Library (now Rooms 22/24)*

200. *(right) The interior of the Art Library*

201. *(below left) Section through the Art Library, from the west*

202. *(below right) Section through Room 45 and the Library staircase, from the west*

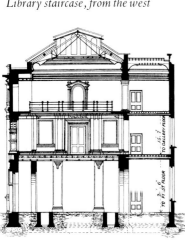

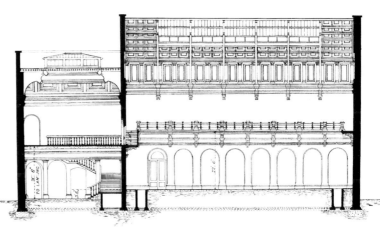

203. *(left) The great plane tree on the site of the present Room 43, south of the Art Library. Etching by George Wallis, Superintendent of the Art Museum, given to General Donnelly, Christmas 1887*

204. *(centre left) Exterior of the south side of the Art Library, c. 1890, showing the great plane tree*

205. *(below left) Plan of the Museum, 1882, after the completion of the Art Library and Rooms 41 and 45*

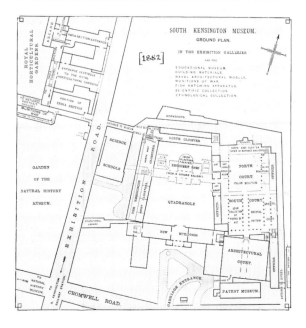

into the quadrangle Scott chose to use unrubbed bricks 'which are harder and more durable', rather than the rubbed bricks which he had used on the Lecture Theatre and the Science Schools.[27]

The three-storey façade of the Library consists of seventeen bays, with a central projection of three bays. The decoration in terracotta is the same as on the earlier buildings by Fowke and Scott. Above the round-headed first floor windows is a series of fifteen mosaic panels designed by Reuben Townroe. One of Moody's assistants, Richard Lunn acted as a model for some of the figures, which he found 'very tiring work'.[28] These panels illustrate Engineering, Mining, Building, Fine Arts, Drawing, Astronomy, Steel Smelting and similar subjects, and appear to have been designed for the eastern façade of the quadrangle, which in Fowke's and Scott's various proposals was to be refaced to match the western and northern sides.[29]

Townroe also designed some of the interior decoration of the Library, notably the plaster overdoors, which are signed and dated by him. The cases and bookshelves were designed by John Taylor, the architect of the Office of Works, who submitted his designs to the Secretary of the Office of Works for approval in February 1883. The firms of Higgs & Hill, George Smith, Holland & Hannen, and George Trollope & Sons were invited to tender. The last-named firm submitted the lowest tender, £2,085 for the Library level, and £3,378 for the gallery level, and was awarded the contract in June 1883.[30]

When Cole looked round the unfinished Library in September 1881, he commented disparagingly: 'Terra Cotta poor. No open ventilation

27. PRO, Ed. 84/55, 8 & 9 March 1882.
28. Lunn, *loc. cit.*, p. 62.
29. *Building News*, 30 June 1876, p. 685.
30. Elevations and other designs in PRO, Works 17/22/7.

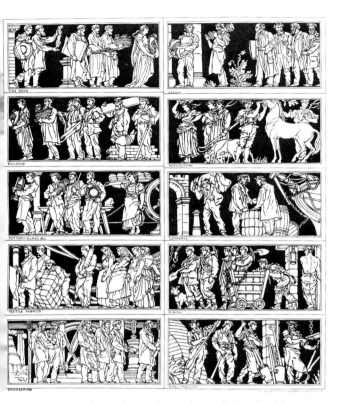

206. Lithograph reproducing designs by Reuben Townroe for mosaic panels for the decoration of the Quadrangle, some of which were used on the northern façade of the Library

in WCs. Evidence throughout of meanness.'[31] The meanness seems to have extended to the structure itself, for in April 1882 John Taylor wrote a letter of complaint to the Secretary of the Treasury in which he reported that, when looking over the Library, he had 'observed that the roof... had deflected considerably in some places. I have now made a closer inspection, & find that the principals are much too weak and that owing to their being an unusual distance apart, the purlins and the pole plates of the lantern lights have sagged considerably, the effect being that the vertical lights in many places do not fit to the cills so as to keep out the weather. The walls have also been thrust out where there are no cross walls to support them. The supports of the ceiling of the Library are also too weak.' Therefore, continued Taylor spitefully, in his opinion the roof was so defective that it ought to be strengthened at once and he recommended that 'although the ceiling may not be actually dangerous', as a matter of prudence, it should be strengthened also, and

asked the Treasury for approval to do the necessary work for about £300.[32] An attempt was made to blame the Department of Science and Art for this failure, but the Department was able to point out that since General Scott was no longer a member of their staff, they could not be held responsible. The Treasury gave Taylor permission to undertake running repairs on 20 June 1882.

The Library was the first of the Museum's buildings to have electric light installed as part of its fittings, though it was not the first where the new form of lighting had been tried out. Taking his cue from his predecessor, Francis Fowke, Robert Festing had, as soon as it became apparent that electricity would be suitable for use in the Museum, become an enthusiast. He and Captain Abney were given permission, during May 1877, to visit Paris, and, as the Board's decision is recorded, 'make enquiries as to the applicability Monsieur Jablouchkoff's electric light, to the lighting of the Museum'.[33]

The Department, while eager to encourage experiment at South Kensington, evidently realized that the time had not yet arrived for electric light, and in November 1878, Festing was allowed to go to Paris again to visit the works of Sautter, Lemmonier & Co., to make further enquiries.[34]

The increasingly heavy costs of lighting the Museum by gas during 1876-7 had led Festing to consider alternative means, which, while equally convenient and safe, 'may be more effective and yet not more expensive'.[35] He looked into the use of mineral oils, but dirt and safety caused him to reject this medium and turn to electricity. There had already been attempts to light buildings by electricity, 'but its extreme intensity and the difficulty of sufficiently diffusing it have hitherto prevented its use'. 'I understand', continued Festing, 'that it has been used in Paris for lighting some large shops, where also the difficulty as to the intensity of the light has been overcome by an arrangement for dividing the electric current so as to have several lamps in the circuit of one machine.' Festing had not been able to obtain much information about these trials.

31. Cole, diary, 8 September 1881.
32. PRO, Ed. 84/33, 3 June 1882.
33. PRO, Ed. 84/37, Board minute précis, 11 May 1877.
34. Ibid., 8 November 1878.
35. E. R. Festing in *24th Report... 1876* (1877), p. 491.

During 1878, however, he held his own experiments in one of the galleries on the western side of Exhibition Road, using 'two medium sized Siemens' machines, and two of that maker's lamps, one of which was fitted with a holophotal lens, and the other with a silvered parabolic reflector'. The apparatus was made available by the War Office, for whom it was being tested by Captain Abney. Festing had to hire an engine, which proved unsuitable, however, as it did not run sufficiently well to provide a steady light.

The room in which the experiments were conducted was 130 feet long by 30 feet wide, and the two lights were diffused by white calico stretched across the ceiling. Sufficient light was produced to see a small painting from a short distance away, but not enough to enable the viewer to stand well back in order to look at large paintings. 'Moreover, in consequence of the unsteadiness of the engine the electric current was irregular, therefore the lamps required constant attention and the lights flickered.' In spite of this setback, Festing was sufficiently encouraged to buy an 8 hp engine, so that he could continue with experiments.[36]

Thus, during 1879, further study of the problems was undertaken. Arrangements were made with the British Electric Lighting Company for testing a Wilde's machine and lights in the Raphael Cartoon Gallery, and in one of the Sheepshanks rooms, but the lamps buzzed so irritatingly that the trial was soon stopped. The company told Festing that the problem could be overcome, but apparently they were too optimistic, for shortly afterwards they went out of business. The light produced had, however, been judged quite satisfactory, and more experiments were undertaken with lamps lent by Mr Werdermann, in the old rooms of the Art Library, where seven lamps were installed, with good results, about five feet above the readers' tables.[37]

The first permanent electric lights were placed in the South Court during 1880. Lord Leighton had complained to the Museum authorities that he thought that the gas lighting in the Court might damage his recently completed fresco, *The Industrial Arts as applied to War*, so, as the 'Brush system, lately introduced into this country from America', appeared in so many respects to be the best suited for the purpose, 'a dynamo-electric machine and eight lamps on this system were therefore purchased to light up the eastern half of the court'. The result was so magnificent that eight more lamps were acquired to illuminate the western portion of the court, and during June the lighting of the entire room was begun. The costs over the next six-month period worked out at only £69, whereas Festing computed that gas would have cost £287. The generator was placed in a shed between the office building and the remnants of the Brompton Boilers, and the capital outlay was £400 for the generator itself, £384 for the lamps and their fixing, and an additional £420 for a steam engine. The financial saving was so enticing that very soon lights were placed in the Raphael Cartoon Gallery and the Sheepshanks Galleries, making in all a total of 32 lamps.[38] They were also installed in the library, and it was decided that, as there was no more space available in the grounds for the engines, no further lights were to be introduced until the current could be supplied commercially.

The collapse of the South Kensington development plan

The Art Library range was the last building to be achieved at South Kensington in accordance with the Fowke/Scott plans. During the 1880s and the early 1890s, all attempt to revive the South Kensington programme were frustrated by the Treasury and the Office of Works. But the Department of Science and Art was itself by no means in decline. When Norman MacLeod retired in December 1881, John Donnelly, previously Inspector for Science, became chief executive at South Kensington, and when Sir Francis Sandford retired in 1884 from his position as joint Secretary of the Education Department and the Department of Science and Art, Donnelly became Secretary of the latter Department, which once more enjoyed independence. Donnelly now had his chance to foster his own speciality, and presided over a great expansion in scientific education in the last two decades of the century. The Museum, however, was in a less flourishing state. The Director, Philip Cunliffe Owen, had become recognized as an organizer of international exhibitions, and was granted frequent and protracted leave of absence from the Museum to pursue this avocation.

36. *26th Report ... 1878* (1879), p. 562.
37. *27th Report ... 1879* (1880), pp. 530, 531.
38. *29th Report ... 1881* (1882), p. 487.

Meanwhile the Director for Art in the Department, the painter Thomas Armstrong (who in 1881 succeeded Edward Poynter, himself the successor of Richard Redgrave) took an increasing interest in the curatorial activity of the Museum. Thus there were divergent interests at South Kensington and the building programme perhaps suffered from lack of strong advocacy.

In August 1880, Cunliffe Owen asked the Vice-President of the Committee of Council on Education for permission for Scott to prepare plans for a south-western pavilion to house the Asiatic Collections, and the request was forwarded through Sandford to the Office of Works.[39] The Treasury turned the proposal down, and was not won over when a sketch plan and a memorandum by Scott were sent on 30 November 1880.[40] This new plan for the south-west corner of the site contained not only galleries running round the edge of the site, as envisaged in Scott's plan of 1877, but also courts filling what had been an inner empty space in that plan. The Treasury insisted that no further buildings would be erected at South Kensington until a careful enquiry had established their necessity.

A year later, in December 1881, the building estimates for the Department of Science and Art in 1882–3 came before George Shaw Lefevre, the First Commissioner of Works (in the second Gladstone administration), and he saw the opportunity for economizing. The sum of £1,800 had been requested as salaries for Scott and his staff, but Shaw Lefevre realized that they were not likely to get any work to do, and were therefore an expensive luxury. He pointed out to the Treasury:[41]

> The Art Library was commenced in 1877–78 and for three years before that very little new work was undertaken, but the staff of Architect, Clerk of the Works, &c., was maintained at a cost of about £2,000 per annum upon the understanding, I believe, that they were engaged upon plans for the further extension of the buildings.
>
> The total expenditure on new buildings since the year 1874–75 including an estimate to the close of the current year, has amounted to no more than £48,925, while the charge for the Architect and his Staff has been £15,825, or at a rate of 33 per cent on the work executed. If the first three years be excluded and the account be taken from the date of the commencement of the Art Library, the charge for the Architect's staff is £9,773 for works executed to the value of £46,669, or about 21 per cent. An

ordinary Architect's charge would not have exceeded £5 per cent on the work in addition to the salary of the Clerk of the Works.

> It appears improbable that any further additions will be made to the buildings of the Science and Art Department during the next three or four years.

So Shaw Lefevre suggested that it was time for Scott and his staff to go, and, for the Treasury, Lord Frederick Cavendish agreed with him. He told South Kensington that no provision for their salaries would be made in the estimates for 1882–3, and that they should be dismissed as soon as possible. Scott was employed on a monthly contract and his men by the day, so their departure was to be abrupt. Moreover, Scott was to be instructed 'to surrender to the First Commissioner all the plans and models which he has prepared of existing or future buildings connected with the South Kensington Museum, and of their decoration, fittings and furniture'.[42]

The Treasury's edict was received with consternation at South Kensington. Not unnaturally, nobody wanted to break the news to General Scott. Sandford side-stepped the issue by deciding that 'we can say nothing as to General Scott – personally – as he is an affair of the Bd. of Works, & *not* of this Department', and it was through the Office of Works that Scott learned the bad news, subsequently discovering that his old employers on the Committee of Council for Education had acquiesced in his dismissal.[43]

South Kensington attempted to fight back. Donnelly, its chief executive, drafted a letter for his political master A. J. Mundella, Vice-President of the Council, and Cunliffe Owen prepared an accompanying memorandum on shortage of space in the Museum. The letter went to the Treasury on 11 January 1882.[44] Donnelly claimed that the exterior and surroundings of the Museum had been left 'in an indescribable state'. The offices were 'so confined, crowded and insufficient, as to be absolutely dangerous to the health of the staff'. The entrances to the Museum, through which over a million visitors passed each year,

39. PRO, Ed. 84/54, 18 August, 6 September 1880.
40. PRO, Ed. 84/72, 29 September 1880; Ed. 84/54, 30 November, 18 December 1880.
41. PRO, Ed. 84/54, 17 December 1881.
42. PRO; Ed. 84/55, 3 January 1882.
43. Ibid., 6, 11 January 1882.
44. Ibid., 9 January, sent 11 January 1882.

207. *The entrance to the Museum, from Exhibition Road, adjacent to the Royal College of Art, in the 1890s*

were only temporary, and quite unworthy. One of them, that from Exhibition Road, 'would scarcely be considered fit for a wine vault of any pretensions', crossly wrote Donnelly. 'Pithy & true, but?', wrote Mundella on the draft, and substituted the word 'dangerous' for the lively phrase. The minute went on to argue that it was cheaper to employ Scott than an outside architect.

The Treasury passed the letter to Shaw Lefevre, who proceeded to demonstrate to his own satisfaction that the contrary was true. He calculated that the expense of maintaining General Scott's office since 1 April 1874 had been £15,125 (having allowed certain deductions from the previously mentioned sum of £15,825). If an outside architect had been employed – not only to design the works actually carried out, but also to prepare plans for the completion of the Museum, as Scott had done – his commission would have amounted only to £6,584. Mundella had urged that Scott, if dismissed, should be entitled to compensation, but Shaw Lefevre would not allow this. His report,[45] with a supporting letter from the Treasury,[46] went on to South Kensington, where it was covered with agonized annotations by General Scott. By now Scott was in enforced retirement at home in Sydenham, growing very anxious over the future prospects of his family of fifteen children. He must have felt trapped in an arithmetical nightmare. As we have seen, the chief point used against him was that if the cost of his office (£15,825) was set against the work actually done (£48,925), it appeared that architect's costs were running at the very high level of about 33% of building costs; an outside architect, however, could only have charged at the ratio of 5%. Scott pointed out that the ratio of architect's costs to building costs was so unfavourable because little building had been done since 1874: that was because little money had been made available, and he could hardly be blamed for that. Shaw Lefevre had written that if the completion of the Museum (estimated to cost £500,000) was 'proceeded with at no greater speed than during the last three years vizt. at an expenditure of £15,000 per annum, thirty-seven years would expire before the work would be completed, and the charge for superintendence at the present annual rate added to the present charge, would amount to £66,000 which would be nearly three times the amount of the usual architect's commission.' Despairingly, Scott noted: '... By extending the time for the completion of the works, this amount may be correspondingly *increased*!' He was caught. If building at South Kensington proceeded slowly or stopped, the maintenance of the works office could not possibly be justified.

So Scott prepared some figures to try to show that at least during the period 1 April 1874 and 31 March 1882 his efforts had saved the Department money,[47] and Mundella launched another appeal to the Treasury, insisting that the Department of Science and Art premises were too small, uncomfortable and insanitary, and asking for the restoration of the Department's own works office, independent of the Office of Works.[48] His letter went off two days after the death of Sir Henry Cole, which he could hardly have considered a good omen.

Nothing was achieved, for the Treasury simply sent on the letter to the Office of Works, and transmitted Shaw Lefevre's dismissive comments back to South Kensington.[49] It becomes quite obvious from these documents that the Office of Works was trying to denigrate Scott. Shaw Lefevre had already suggested, in his report of

45. Ibid., 1 February 1882.
46. Ibid., 8 February 1882.
47. Ibid., 6 March 1882. PRO, Ed. 84/38, Board minute précis, 28 March 1882, 'Under circumstances explained by General Scott, sketches and models by Captain Fowke should not be handed over to Office of Works'.
48. Ibid., 20 April 1882.
49. Ibid., 12 June 1882.

1 February 1882, that Scott's designs were not original, merely adaptations of Fowke's. He now pronounced that Scott's design for the south-west corner of the site 'does not seem to be in harmony with what has already been completed, especially with that portion in Exhibition Road, which is of great beauty', hence the proposed new frontage would appear 'incongruous and unsatisfactory'. It was Scott who had designed the façade of the Science Schools in Exhibition Road to which Shaw Lefevre (or, more probably, John Taylor) refers, so this observation was a howler and brought consolation to South Kensington.

Along with Shaw Lefevre's letter came a report prepared for him by his architect, John Taylor, in which personal animus emerges more clearly. In a passage later deleted by the Secretary of the Office of Works, Taylor wrote:

> So far as I am personally concerned in this matter nothing would give me greater pleasure than to be relieved of the duties at South Kensington Museum, as the Science and Art Department is the only one with which I have come in contact in my official capacity where I have found it exceedingly difficult to carry out my duties satisfactorily because of the desire which has always been shown to set aside the control which this office is supposed to have in regard to works, alterations, &c., and in fact to undertake whenever they possibly can, the exercise of such services by their own workmen and out of funds which are not provided by this Department.

The rest of Taylor's report was devoted to a more reasoned attempt to refute the Museum's claims that more accommodation was needed. It seems that he had himself caused an inquiry to be made as to overcrowding in the offices, but the Museum contested his optimistic statistics.

Influenced by these reports the Treasury once again took a generally negative line, but they did concede that in the estimates for 1883–4 the comparatively small sum of £15,000 might be allowed for works at South Kensington. Mundella snatched at this, and wrote to the Treasury welcoming the concession and again pleading the merits of General Scott's design. A meeting was arranged between Mundella and Leonard Courtney of the Treasury in December 1882, but by then the Treasury had decided that no more than £5,000 would be allocated.[51]

A fresh obstacle had cropped up. Finishing off the Museum according to the plan would require the demolition of the remaining portion of the Boilers at the south-east corner of the site. This contained the Patent Museum, and the Treasury had been advised by the Patent Commissioners that the building could not be demolished without previous legislative sanction. This once again raised the question of the future of the Science Collections, of which the Patent Museum formed a significant part. Early in 1883, Mundella forwarded to the Treasury statements by Donnelly and Earl Spencer, President of the Council, strongly urging the establishment of a separate Science Museum,[52] and in June the Treasury set up a Committee to report on the Scientific and Technical Collections. This eventually produced its report in 1886. No action was taken on this, and another Treasury Committee was set up in 1889. Gradually, however the scientific lobby made itself heard.

On 16 April 1883 General Scott, who had become demoralized and ill as a result of his treatment by officialdom, died, worn out by his troubles, and no further progress was made in South Kensington's building campaign for eighteen months. Then, in November 1884, the new President of the Council, Lord Carlingford (who had succeeded Earl Spencer in March 1883) took up the cudgels again with the Treasury. He reiterated South Kensington's discomforts, recalled the shabby treatment it had received in the preceding few years, and tried to use the recently published report of the Royal Commission on Technical Instruction (the Samuelson Report) as a lever with which to budge the Treasury. Sir Reginald Welby, for the Treasury, accepted that something must be done. He considered that the disposition of the scientific collections was the only question that ought to delay matters; but since it was a matter of settled policy, in his view, that these collections should be moved into new premises on the western side of Exhibition Road, while the art collections should remain on the eastern side, there was 'no reason why the two questions should not be dealt with separately'.[53] As to General Scott's plans, however, he felt it would be unwise

---

50. Ibid., 14 August 1882.
51. Ibid., 16 December 1882.
52. Ibid., 28 February 1883. See also Sir D. Follett *The Rise of the Science Museum*, 1978.
53. Ibid., 28 November 1884.

to proceed any further with them, since they had met with so much opposition.[54]

The matter was referred to the Office of Works, just in time to receive a crushing rebuff from Shaw Lefevre, who was on his way out to become Post-master General. Yet again he contested South Kensington's assessment of its own needs. He pointed out that some space was to become available when the Pitt Rivers collection, which had been on exhibition for six years, was removed, and suggested that more could be found by weeding the collections. His view of the future was:

> There can be no doubt that the buildings of the Museum at South Kensington cannot long remain in their present incomplete state, and that an addition must be commenced before long in a style adequate to and in harmony with the existing structure: this new extension, the ultimate cost of which will be great, may be built by degrees as the requirements of the Museum increase: but in my view there is no immediate necessity for the extension which cannot be met by provisional arrangements; a postponement for one or two years longer will give time for the removal of the contents of the Patent Museum.

When the time came for completing the Museum, however, General Scott's designs should not be used, for they 'are, in my opinion, most unsatisfactory, and I should not be prepared to recommend to Your Lordships to submit them to Parliament for approval'. He claimed that he had tried hard to spare Scott's feelings, 'but since the death of that Officer, there can be no longer any object in further entertaining a plan open to so many objections'. He went on to reveal that 'sketch designs for an alternative façade have been prepared in this office, but the plans have not been submitted to the Science and Art Department, and may not therefore accurately meet the requirements of the Museum: this is, however, a detail which could doubtless be readily arranged.'[55]

The Department of Science and Art was outraged to discover that the Office of Works had been drawing up plans behind its back. A ludicrous wrangle ensued, as the Department demanded to see the plans, and the Office refused to surrender them on the grounds that there was only one copy, and they were of a 'rudimentary ... character'.[56] The Department eventually saw them in November 1886. They had been prepared by the old enemy, John Taylor, so they met with little favour

at South Kensington. It seemed that Taylor had gone to considerable trouble to save the large plane tree standing just south of the new Library range, by designing a courtyard to contain it, and this was thought to be wasted labour. Yet another plea was made for Scott's designs.[57] It appears that Scott's model (which has not survived to the present day) was kept on display in the Museum, perhaps as a defiant gesture by South Kensington. The model was mentioned and illustrated by the *Magazine of Art* early in 1887, which was very critical of the depressing appearance of the Museum, especially of its two temporary entrances, one a 'base, ugly, unfinished brick structure with a lean-to like a cart-shed', and the other, adjacent to the Art Schools, which was 'an excrescent structure of wood stuck on to the wall some feet above the level of the Museum, which is reached by a flight of wooden stairs such as might be expected to lead to a beer-cellar or coal-hole'.[58]

Still surviving on the site were the various old houses, which had been in a tumbledown state when the Museum moved in in 1857. A Royal Engineers officer lived in one, but in March 1889, Festing reduced his accommodation, proposing to give the extra room thus obtained to the Circulation Department. In addition, James Gamble was to be turned out of his studio, being given about two weeks' notice. He protested to Festing, and appealed to Donnelly and Cunliffe Owen. They thought it right that Gamble should go, but felt that he should be treated in a 'considerate manner', suggesting that he should be allowed to stay until the end of June, which would give him time to find another studio. Several other rooms in this house were then being used as the Museum's photographic studio.[59] The Residences were also still in occupation by Museum officials, but the suggestion had already been made by the Treasury that they should be used as office accommodation

54. PRO, Works 17/25/2, 17 December 1884.
55. PRO, Ed. 84/55, 26 January 1885.
56. PRO, Ed. 84/72, 21 March 1885. 'I made plans for the completion of the South Kensington Museum in 1883, a complete set of plans ... I had no great central towers; I had a central feature, suitably finished with terminal towers, but they were of no great height.' Sir John Taylor replying to Lord Balcarres, at the Select Committee on Museums of the Science and Art Department, 1897. *Report*, 1897, p. 368, nos. 7318, 7319.
57. Ibid., 19 November 1886.
58. *Magazine of Art*, x (1887), 7–8.
59. PRO, Ed. 84/67 and plan.

if the Museum were short of space.[60] The suggestion was endorsed, in what proved to be the final round in South Kensington's battle for buildings.

The second Gladstone administration was defeated in June 1885 and was succeeded by a Conservative government under Lord Salisbury, which was dislodged the following year for a four-month period by the third Gladstone administration. Then Salisbury returned until 1892. It was in December 1886 that the Office of Works in his government once more turned to the South Kensington question. One official, R. Bailey, went down to inspect the office accommodation and reported in South Kensington's favour:

The rank and file of the staff are distinctly overcrowded, and the worst feature of the situation is that some 16 clerks are compelled, for want of room space, to sit about in the corridors. This is a state of things which, in my experience, is without a parallel in a Government office.

The Offices themselves are well adapted for their purpose, but the Department has outgrown them. The accommodation merely requires to be supplemented, & it appears to me that it would be a waste of money to abandon the present Offices to build entirely new ones.

He suggested that two of the residences should be converted to offices, and that this would satisfy present needs.[61]

This suggestion was taken up by Sir H. W. Primrose, Secretary to the Office of Works,[62] who also recommended that space should be gained by shifting the collection of naval models to Greenwich. Primrose's assessment of the position was shrewd and sensible. He realized that there were two agencies with differing interests at South Kensington: the Department of Science and Art, which needed offices and examination rooms to support its educational work throughout the country; and the Museum, which, though technically a branch of the Department, was 'so powerful & conspicuous that it sometimes almost assumes the attitude of an independent department'. Primrose observed 'a certain competition' between 'the parent department & its strenuous offspring' for space, and suggested that the Office of Works should distinguish clearly from which branch at South Kensington each demand issued.

The Department was still pressing for the completion of the buildings. Primrose concluded:

So much of the site available for these buildings has been already occupied that any future expansion must bring them forward to their ultimate frontage and involves therefore a previous settlement of the elevation which that frontage is to present, and of the general design & disposition of the buildings which are hereafter to occupy the still vacant land adjacent to the existing structure.

He felt that neither Scott's design, nor John Taylor's version, could any longer be regarded as satisfactory, and recommended that

for a building intended as a temple of art, & therefore peculiarly exposed to artistic criticism, occupying moreover so conspicuous a position, it wd. be wiser to employ an architect of acknowledged standing, rather than proceed on designs prepared by men who, however capable, are not professed architects, & whose work wd. have to be discussed and settled, & then the sanction of the Treasury & of Parliament wd. have to be obtained.

Here at last was a sensible way ahead.

But when South Kensington received a letter[63] from the First Commissioner of Works embodying Primrose's suggestions, this met with the usual displeasure. In an exceptionally lengthy letter to the Treasury, W. Hart Dyke expended some thousands of words on minutely detailed objections. Tempers boiled over at the Office of Works. 'Any amicable arrangemt. with such an ever grasping Dept. is impossible. They reject as impracticable *all* the suggestions made by the F[irst] C[ommissioner] . . . and renew their eternal plaint about want of accommdn.', wrote R. Bailey. Lapsing into the language of war, he threatened: 'I see nothing for it but to starve [the] S[cience] & A[rt] Dept. into submission.'[64]

---

60. PRO, Works 17/25/2, 28 September 1886.
61. Ibid., 2 December 1886.
62. Ibid., 9 December 1886.
63. Ibid., 5 January 1887.
64. Ibid., 20 April 1887.

CHAPTER XI

The Competition

The Treasury and the Office of Works, having remained for years unmoved by the pleas of the South Kensington Museum for new buildings, suddenly relented in 1890. Their change of heart was later said to have been due to a Cabinet decision.[1] All existing designs and plans for extension were now abandoned, and arrangements were made to obtain a design for a new building through a limited competition. This was a method the Office of Works had grown accustomed to using when new public buildings were required, since it was easier to administer than an open competition.[2]

The task that faced the competitors was to fill up an irregular site, half of which was already covered by buildings of various kinds. An observer, standing on the corner of Cromwell Road and Exhibition Road and looking across to the site, would have seen in the foreground the empty land which the new building was to occupy. Beyond that, on his extreme right, in the shadow of the new Brompton Oratory church now more or less complete, a range of office buildings presented an unfinished blank end wall to the street. Westwards of this was the rump of the iron building, and, set further back and towering over it, the huge blank end walls of the Cast Courts. In the middle of the site the elaborate buildings round the Quadrangle were now concealed behind General Scott's new Art Library block, with two large courts (Rooms 41 and 45) projecting towards the street: these had all been left with

---

1. W. J. Downer, 21 October 1895, PRO, Works 17/25/8.
2. Select Committee, 1897, p. 30, nos. 477–479.

213. *(opposite) Sir Aston Webb's new Museum designs: preliminary sketch for the elevation of the Main Entrance, in a neo-Romanesque style*

208. *(above right),* 209. *(right) The remains of the Brompton Boilers, south of the Cast Courts, in October, 1897*

unfinished brick walls, awaiting further additions. In the north-western corner of the site could be seen the group of old houses used by the schools, growing daily more decrepit. And beyond them was the one really large and architecturally coherent building on the site, externally, at least – the Science Schools. It is not surprising that many of the competitors felt obliged to take their tone from this building. It now appears altogether subordinate to the great bulk of the new Museum building, but in 1890 it must have seemed a dominating feature, to which new buildings must accommodate themselves.

To fill up the site satisfactorily must have seemed an awkward problem to the competitors. The new building, however, offered them a compensating opportunity for display: along Cromwell Road and Exhibition Road they would have to design façades, which, for ever afterwards, would be the public face of the Museum. Our observer, standing at the corner of the two roads would be able to see, in his mind's eye, both façades, which would meet at the corner opposite him. In the competition, a view of the new buildings from this point was required of the competitors, and the judges attached importance to it.

Once the competition was approved, the Department of Science and Art was requested to produce a statement of its requirements. This document[3] seems extraordinarily perfunctory. More than a quarter of it deals with an electricity generating station for lighting the Museum. Another provision on which some emphasis is placed is accommodation for the examination of students – not only examination rooms, but 'a top-lighted court about $160' \times 60''$ for the exhibition of students' work, and adjacent rooms 'for the unpacking, stamping, sorting etc. of the works'. As we have seen, the National Competition of students' work was an important feature of the Department's work, but it seems here to have preoccupied the authorities almost to the exclusion of the Museum.

Of the Museum's needs the statement spoke briefly. 'The Eastern portion should ... contain the accommodation for the Administration of the Department of Science and Art; the centre, the increase to the Libraries and to the space for the European Collections; and the Western portion the Oriental Collections.' For the European collections '45,000 superficial feet of floor space, part in top-lighted courts, part in side-lighted rooms' was requested; for the libraries (i.e. for both the Science and Art Libraries) space for 60,000 volumes, and – an astonishingly economical requirement – 'two working rooms about $20' \times 15'$ each'; and for the Oriental collections '60,000 to 65,000 superficial feet of floor space – of which about one fourth in top-lighted courts'.

The main entrance was to be in the centre of the South front, with another public entrance at the North-West corner, and 'service entrances at the East and West wings'. This is how the building is arranged today, but the requirement that 'the entrance to the Art Library should be as direct as possible from the central main entrance' was eventually not complied with.

Apart from requesting a police lodge and staff refreshment rooms, the Departmental brief said no more. It was supplemented by the 'Instructions and Conditions' sent to competitors by the Office of Works during January 1891. Among other things, they were told that their designs, 'which should pay regard so far as may be necessary to the style of the existing buildings', should be drawn to a scale of 16 feet to the inch, and should include a plan of each floor; an elevation of each of the principal fronts and courts, the one to Exhibition Road showing a portion of the Science Schools; at least two complete longitudinal sections, and two transverse ones; and a plan, elevation, and section of 'a compartment or bay of a fairly representative portion of the external architecture drawn to a scale of an inch to a foot'. They were to supply 'a perspective view from the south-west angle, showing the fronts to Cromwell Road and Exhibition Road ... and also a view showing the interior of the principal courts and galleries'; and additional views if they wished. The drawings were to be in ink only, without shading or colour. It was suggested that the external façades should be designed for execution in 'red brickwork with stone dressings, red brickwork with terracotta dressings, or stone only'. The designs were to be submitted by 1 July 1891.

Eight architects were selected to compete. The Government nominated T. E. Collcutt (1840–1924), whose Imperial Institute was nearing completion across the road; Aston Webb (1849–1930),

---

3. PRO, Ed. 84/215, July 1890.

who had recently, with his partner Ingress Bell, won the competition for the Birmingham Law Courts, and now stood on the threshold of a brilliant career; J. Macvicar Anderson (1835–1915), then Vice-President of the Royal Institute of British Architects; and Sir T. N. Deane (1828–1915), the Irish architect best known for his Science and Art Museum and National Library in Dublin, which had just earned him his knighthood.[4] Alfred Waterhouse, President of the RIBA, was invited to nominate a further four architects, and suggested T. G. Jackson (1835–1924), best known for his Elizabethan revival or 'English Renaissance' buildings in Oxford; R. Norman Shaw (1831–1912), the most eminent of late Victorian domestic architects, whose New Scotland Yard building was just complete; William Emerson (1843–1924), most of whose major buildings were in India; and John Belcher (1841–1913), then engaged upon the Institute of Chartered Accountants in the City of London, which was to blaze the trail for flamboyant Edwardian baroque that he handled with uncommon virtuosity.

Anderson declined the invitation,[5] and was replaced by Mervyn Macartney (1853–1932), whose main work was in neo-Georgian domestic building.[6] Macartney's master, Norman Shaw, also dropped out,[7] owing to pressure of work. The ecclesiastical architects Bodley and Garner were suggested in his place, but they too declined,[8] and William Young (1843–1900), was selected. A Scot, he had previously been suggested by the Office of Works 'as there is no Scotchman now on the list'.[9] The final line-up was Collcutt, Webb, Macartney, Deane, Jackson, Young, Emerson and Belcher.

The competition was to be judged by the Lord President of the Council, the First Lord of the Treasury, the Chancellor of the Exchequer, the First Commissioner of Works, and a single 'Professional Assessor'. Alfred Waterhouse, having just selected half the competitors, was now invited to be Assessor. He was assured that 'the choice of design will probably proceed on somewhat broad considerations and it is not anticipated that the duties of the Assessor will entail any very minute or laborious examination of the plans. In these circumstances, it is proposed to fix the Fee . . . at four hundred guineas'.[10] The fee first suggested had been 500 guineas, but this had been considered 'somewhat high' by the Treasury, and had

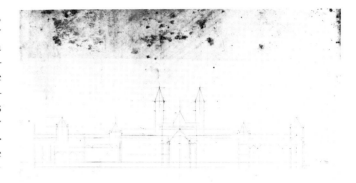

210. *Sir Aston Webb's new Museum designs: a preliminary outline elevation to Cromwell Road*

been reduced.[11] In the event, the panel of judges was joined by the Vice-President of the Council and A. J. Mundella, MP; the Chancellor of the Exchequer escaped owing to 'exceptional pressure of work'.[12]

Six months was none too long for the competitors to prepare their drawings. Protests were sent to the First Commissioner and to Waterhouse, and it was agreed that the competitors need not submit so many drawings as had been required at first. The drawings were submitted anonymously, each competitor adopting a monogram, and supplying an envelope so marked, containing his visiting card. These are still on the file in the Public Record Office, although the drawings themselves are not, having presumably been returned to the competitors.

The judges had done their work by 30 July 1891. 'At a meeting this day at the Foreign Office, the Committee of Selection decided in favour of . . . the design . . . with the Monogram S.K.M. The envelopes . . . were subsequently opened . . . when it was found that the accepted design was that of Mr. Aston Webb'.[13]

---

4. The government would have liked to nominate Alfred Waterhouse but, as the First Commissioner of Works wrote, 'You have already privately intimated to me that you would prefer to stand outside.' PRO, Works 17/23/9(7) 14 November 1890.

5. PRO, Works 17/23/9(25), 23 November 1890.

6. PRO, Works 17/23/9, 13 January 1891.

7. PRO, Works 17/23/9 (41), 17 January 1891.

8. PRO, Works 17/23/9 (81), 17 February 1891.

9. PRO, Works 17/23/9, 1 January 1891.

10. PRO, Works 17/23/9 (43), 24 January 1891.

11. PRO, Works 17/23/9 (47), 26 January 1891.

12. PRO, Works 17/23/9 (119), 29 June 1891.

13. PRO, Works 17/23/9 (133), 30 July 1891.

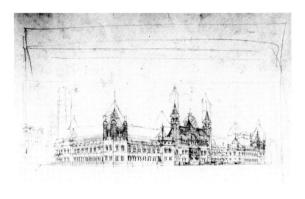

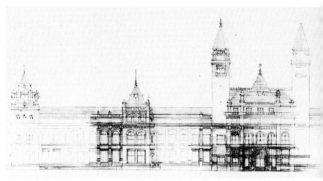

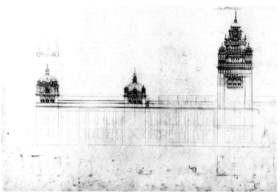

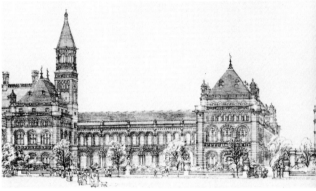

211. *(top left) Sir Aston Webb's new Museum designs: preliminary perspective sketch*

212. *(top right) Sir Aston Webb's new Museum designs: preliminary elevation to Cromwell Road*

214. *(centre left) Sir Aston Webb's new Museum designs: preliminary elevation to Cromwell Road*
215. *(centre right) Sir Aston Webb and Ingress Bell: competition design for the Imperial Institute, 1887, in a neo-Romanesque style*

216. *(left) The Main Entrance of the Natural History Museum, designed by Sir Alfred Waterhouse, in a neo-Romanesque style*

217. *(opposite above) Sir Aston Webb's new Museum designs: elevations to Cromwell Road and Exhibition Road, submitted in the competition, 1891*

218. *(opposite below) Sir Aston Webb's new Museum designs: sections through (top) the Main Hall from the west, (bottom left) the Cromwell Road frontage from the east, (right) the Exhibition Road block from the east, submitted in the competition, 1891*

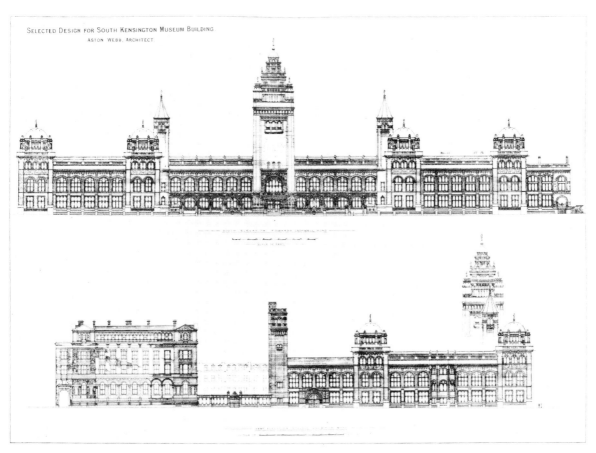

SELECTED DESIGN FOR SOUTH KENSINGTON MUSEUM BUILDING
ASTON WEBB, ARCHITECT.

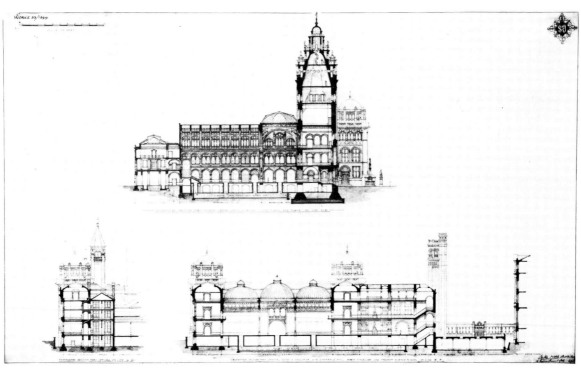

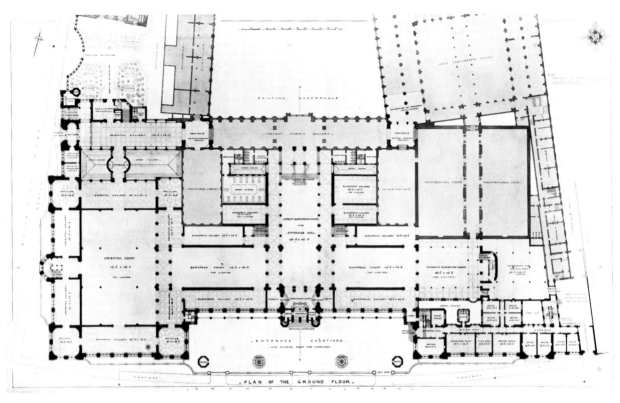

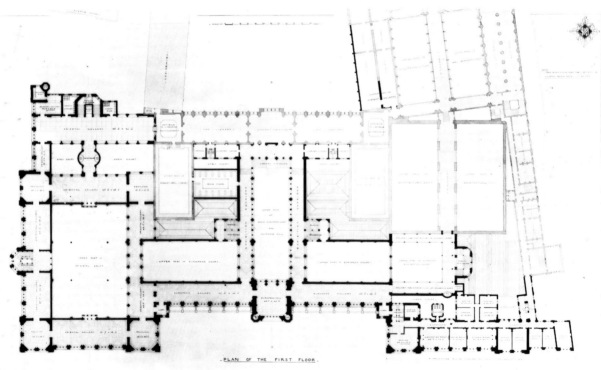

219. *(top) Sir Aston Webb's new Museum designs:*
ground plan submitted in the competition, 1891

220. *(above) Sir Aston Webb's new Museum designs:*
first-floor plan submitted in the competition, 1891

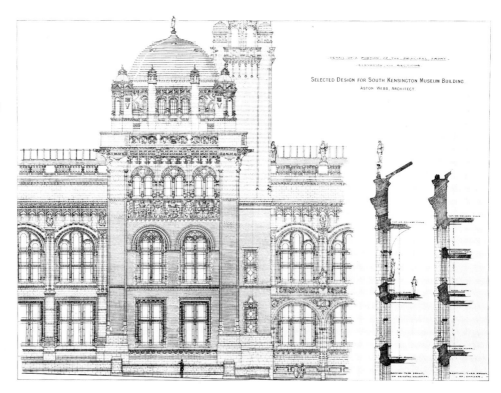

221. *(right) Sir Aston Webb's new Museum designs: elevation of a domed pavilion and lift shaft on the Cromwell Road frontage, submitted in the competition, 1891*

222. *(below) Sir Aston Webb's new Museum designs: perspective view from the south-west, submitted in the competition, 1891*

218
219
220
221
222
223
224

Webb's design was eventually much modified in the light of practical necessity. It will be interesting here to consider it, and the other designs, on their abstract merits. The architects, having received a rather imprecise brief, must have approached the competition to some extent as if it were an ideal project; as if they were being asked to provide their own notion of what a museum should be. The conditions of the competition had hinted that the style of the new building should bear some resemblance to the brick and terracotta style of Fowke and Scott; but within this limitation the architects were free to adopt whatever style they preferred, and this they did, most of them using a more or less eclectic style, classical rather than Gothic, such as they would have used just as readily on any public building, whether it was a museum, a bank or a swimming bath.

What mattered was their handling of their preferred style. Alfred Waterhouse, the Assessor, in defining his principles of judgement,[14] stated that in the internal and external elevations he would look for 'general symmetry, dignity and rhythm ... beauty of ... outline, and the general balance of parts.' In addition he attached great

---

14. PRO, Works 17/23/9 (148).

223. *Sir Aston Webb's new Museum designs: preliminary sketch for a pavilion dome and lift tower*

224. *A dome and lift tower as built to Sir Aston Webb's Museum designs*

importance to the 'artistic treatment of details'. He intended to award marks in respect of each aspect of the designs, and the different maximum markings that he specified indicate the comparative importance in his eyes of the various features of the designs. He marked the elevations, and the details, out of 80. Various practical matters earned lower marks. 'Light' (i.e. 'the treatment and position of windows or ceiling-lights') he marked out of 70; wall space out of 40; extra accommodation, beyond what was specified in the requirements, out of 50; harmonious relation to the existing buildings out of 40; and cost ('giving the highest number to what I conceive to be the least expensive design') out of 50.

'Excellence of Plan', however, he marked out of 100, so that a good plan counted for more than any other feature. Here he was looking for 'simplicity, symmetry of plan and directness of communication ... position and arrangement of staircases, both for beauty and convenience.' Since

the existing buildings rambled all over the place, it was impossible to make the whole Museum coherent, however finely planned the new addition might be. Furthermore, splendours of planning are soon obscured when a building is filled with exhibits. Nonetheless, Waterhouse and, presumably, the competitors, felt that planning was the thing.

If, in devising their ideal museum, the competitors had looked for precedents, they might have considered first (and no doubt did) Waterhouse's Natural History Museum (1871–81) a few yards down Cromwell Road from the South Kensington Museum. From abroad, they might have recalled the Kunsthistorisches Hofmuseum in Vienna, recently completed to the designs of Gottfried Semper and Carl von Hasenauer. Both these museums, comparable in their huge scale to the new South Kensington Museum, were symmetrical buildings, with elaborate grids of galleries, walls and corridors spreading out from a central staircase (the single part of a museum interior where an architect could let himself go, knowing that no exhibits would interfere with his effects), and enclosing here and there quadrangles and courtyards. This kind of grandiose planning was a product of academic neo-classicism, especially in France. It could be applied to museums more easily than to most public buildings, since museums had no function, and endless enfilades of ceremonial rooms were quite in order there, although they would have been inconvenient for government ministries, prisons or hospitals. In the late eighteenth century, the moment at which the modern public museum was born, architects in France, from Boullée and Durand down to the students at the Academy of architecture, revelled in museum planning, and their imaginary projects remained as a body of precedent, especially those of Durand published in his *Précis des leçons* (1802–9).[15] Most neo-classical museums however, such as the Altes Museum at Berlin (1823–30 by Schinkel), the Glyptothek at Munich (1815–30 by Klenze) and the Dulwich Gallery (1811–14 by Soane) were comparatively small in relation to the monumental imaginary projects, and had quite simple plans. It was not until later in the century that enormous museums gave opportunities for monumental planning. Such an opportunity was offered by the South Kensington competition, and, although by that time neo-classicism was no longer an ideological force but only one style among many, we may be sure that the architects were influenced by the tradition of neo-classical planning.

Alfred Waterhouse gave Aston Webb full marks for planning. 'The Central Hall, European Courts, Oriental Court at one end and Students' Court at the other would make the most splendid suite of apartments for Exhibition purposes I know of anywhere. The plan makes them practically one room architecturally, though diversified in an ingenious and most artistic manner.'[16] He gave Webb full marks also for details (80), and 70 out of 80 for his elevations. The other marks were: light 60/70, wall space 40/40, harmony 30/40, cost 45/50 and accommodation 45/50. With a total of 470 out of 510, Webb was comfortably ahead of all the other candidates save one.

The principal attraction of his plan was the free flow of space from one huge court into another. Something of this survives even in the much altered design that was eventually built, though it must be said that it is very largely wasted space. In the notes that Webb supplied on his design, he emphasized the symmetry of his plan, but otherwise said little of its architectural qualities, contenting himself with calling attention to the commodious office and packing areas he had provided, with staff refreshment rooms beneath; the fireproof floors; the match-boarded walls ('for easy fastening of exhibits thereto'); the provision anywhere of direct lighting either from the top or the side; and 'the domed pavilions on the second floor, which on the Oriental side, would be finished as Arab halls, with domed ceilings, forming an appropriate setting for the exhibits'.

The style of Webb's building was described by the *Builder* as 'a rich variety of Romanesque', and by the *Building News* as combining 'many of the beauties and artistic capabilities of the Romanesque, with the grace and playfulness of Spanish Renaissance'.[17] Alfred Waterhouse, who had just built the Romanesque Natural History Museum, must have observed this choice of style with approval. He would also have read with interest some of Webb's comments on his design:

With a façade of so great a length and a recessed centre ... it becomes imperative to strongly mark the central entrance by a feature which shall dominate and give unity to the whole, and bearing in mind the coupled towers of the Natural History Museum, and the lofty single tower of the Imperial Institute, I have elected to mark the centre of my design also with a tower which would hold its own with its neighbours and by its varied design would I believe, group well with them, and assist to form a crown of towers almost unique in Europe ...

Care has been taken in designing the general outline of the building to consider its effect in conjunction with the Natural History Museum and a diagram has been prepared showing their relative outlines. The towers are practically of the same height, and the main ridge and pavilions are also

15. See H. Seling, 'The Genesis of the Museum', *Architectural Review*, cxli (1967) pp. 103–114.

16. PRO, Works 17/23/9 (150–152), 18 July 1891. The reports on the other candidates quoted in this chapter, follow on this file.

17. The competition drawings were exhibited in August and reviewed by the principal architectural journals: *The Builder*, 8 August 1891, pp. 97 ff.; *The Building News*, 7 August 1891, pp. 171 ff.; *The British Architect*, 21 August 1891, pp. 131 ff. Subsequent quotations in this chapter are from these reviews unless otherwise specified.

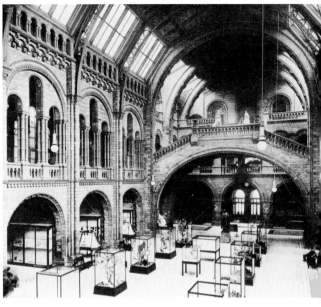

225. *(above left) The Main Hall (Room 43) in 1962*

226. *(above right) The Main Hall of the Natural History Museum, designed by Sir Alfred Waterhouse*

227. *(left) Sir Aston Webb's new Museum designs: perspective of the interior of the Main Hall from the north, submitted in the competition, 1891*

very similar, thus neither building would dwarf or interfere with the other, while the change of outline from the steep roofs of the Natural History Museum to the domes and lantern of my design would afford the necessary variety for the effective grouping of the two buildings.

A comparison of Webb's projected central hall with Waterhouse's central hall in the Natural *226* History Museum seems to show a strong affinity *227* between the two architects. Webb was noted for his rapid assimilation and skilful handling of many styles, and the subsequent history of his design was to demonstrate his adaptability and resource.

Runner-up to Webb was John Belcher. To him *228* also Waterhouse awarded full marks for planning; *229* and with full marks (80) for elevations and 70/80 *230* for details, Belcher was running neck and neck *231* with Webb so far as the architectural qualities *232* of his design were concerned. Practical matters *233* pulled him down. With 50/70 for light, 35/40 for *234* wall space, 25/40 for harmony, 30/50 for cost and

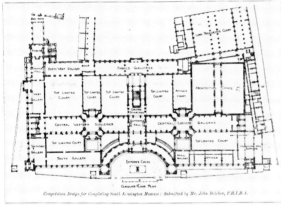

228. *(above) John Belcher's competition designs: perspective view from the south-west, drawn by W. B. McGuinness*

229. *(left) John Belcher's competition designs: ground plan*

36/50 for accommodation, he mustered only 426 marks, as against Webb's 470.

Waterhouse was full of praise for this entry: 'a magnificent design, the most original of the 8.' Its attractions were increased by the two impressive perspective drawings that Belcher sent in; these depend for their effect on the use of wash, which had in fact been forbidden by the conditions of the competition. The exterior perspective, in the opinion of the *Building News*, seemed 'to conjure up in the mind the ruins of some stately edifice in the Venetian Lagoons: the dark and massive features appear to rise out of a wet shiny pavement or lake.' The main mass of the building is somewhat to the rear, behind lower wings which project forward. This makes for a monu-

mental effect in the perspective, but Waterhouse pointed out that the passer-by in Cromwell Road would hardly be able to see the higher rear part of the building, since it would be masked by the lower parts. Belcher proposed to use brick and Portland stone, so his exterior would have a more variegated effect than appears in the perspective. The interior perspective of the staircase makes a tremendous impression, but, as the *Builder* shrewdly noted, 'the scale and distance of the interior effect seem very much exaggerated'. The interior plan, however, has an immediately comprehensible quality. On arriving in the entrance hall the visitor finds long central galleries opening out to right and left of him. These act as a spine for the building, providing access to most of the courts to the North and South, and ending in staircases, which lead to an upper spine gallery. This feature, somewhat reduced in scale, turned up eventually in Aston Webb's final, revised, designs; there, however, it is functionally superfluous since most of Aston Webb's other galleries and courts have an east-west axis, and lead into each other. Belcher's central galleries, and the

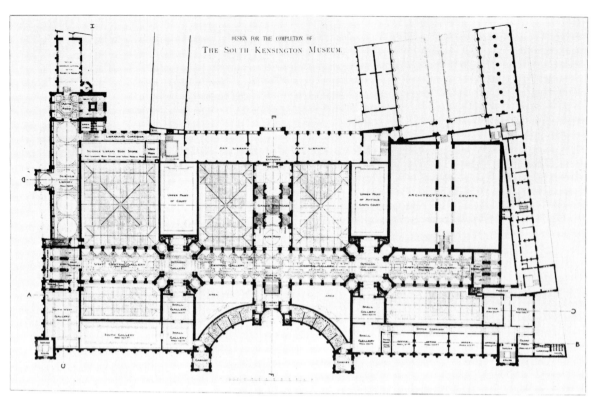

DESIGN FOR THE COMPLETION OF
THE SOUTH KENSINGTON MUSEUM.

194

230. (opposite above) John Belcher's competition designs:
first-floor plan

231. (opposite centre left) John Belcher's competition
designs: elevations to Cromwell Road

232. (opposite below left) John Belcher's competition
designs: elevation to Exhibition Road

233. (opposite below right) John Belcher's competition
designs: perspective views of the Entrance Hall and main
staircase

234. (below) John Belcher's competition designs: elevation
of the western dome in the Cromwell Road frontage

these columns, described as 'lanky' by the *Builder*
and 'weak, attenuated' by the *Building News*,
were terracotta bas-reliefs of female figures supporting
escutcheons with the names of great artists (Gottfried Semper was one of these). The *Building News*
considered the reliefs to be out of scale, and
pointed out that they had no structural base. From
an academic point of view this criticism is correct,
but Belcher delighted in such apparent solecisms,
which give his architecture a special excitement.
The interplay of solids and whimsically applied
classical features in his huge tower is typical of his
massively playful approach; Waterhouse generously praised it as 'exciting one's admiration by
the beautiful fancies its design embodies'.

William Emerson's plan was criticized by
Waterhouse as 'confused and cut up', and earned
only 40 marks. He gave the elevations 60/80,
noting that the exterior 'presents attractive details';
but the interior details he considered 'lacking in
refinement and elegance' and worth only 45/80.
He awarded 25/40 for wall space and 34/50 for
cost. But he gave Emerson full marks for harmony
(40) and accommodation (50); and for light (70),
which he considered the 'strong point about the
design'. Emerson's total marks were 364.

Emerson, Young, Deane and Jackson proposed
to build along the line of Exhibition Road: the
main frontages of their buildings would meet
consequently at an acute angle, thus causing difficulties in planning. All three adopted the same
solution. They conceived their plans in terms of
large inner halls and courts on the square, enclosed
by a range of smaller galleries hugging the perimeter of the site. Odd triangular spaces were left
over as light wells. Aston Webb's first plan was
entirely on the square but eventually he adopted a
layout similar to those of Emerson, Young, Deane
and Jackson. All four of these competitors set
back their main entrances from Cromwell Road,
disguising the curved line of the street: Webb
eventually adopted a curved frontage.

As well as a central dome, visible on the exterior, above his central octagon, Emerson proposed domed roofs over his large courts. He
provided a perspective of the west court: its roof,
as the *Building News* described it, rested 'on four
semi-domes; the latter spring from beams thrown
across the angles of the court, but the arrangement
has too much the *tour de force* effect to be pleasing,
and the angles in soffit of ceiling filled with

235

octagonal halls interposed in them were, in
Waterhouse's view, inadequately lit, though he
praised Belcher for studying top lighting. Like
Webb's, Belcher's plan is on the square and does
not follow the irregular street frontage.

It is only to be expected that Belcher's handling
of the classical style should be criticized. An order
of columns ran all round the ground floor: here,
as Waterhouse observed, 'the rules of the Italian
masters as to proportion have been freely de-
parted from ... the principal columns are $11\frac{1}{2}$ and
$12\frac{1}{2}$ diameters in height instead of 10.' Between

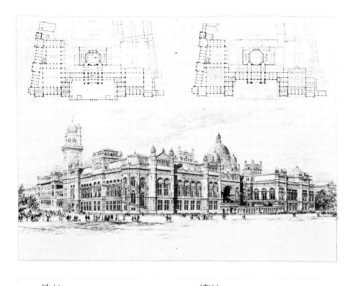

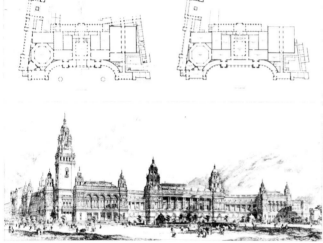

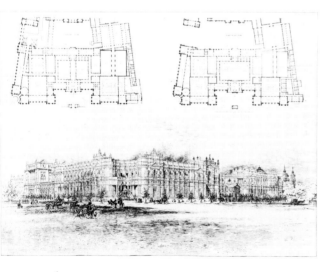

235. *(left) William Emerson's competition designs: plans and perspective view from the south-west*

236. *(centre left) William Young's competition designs: plans and perspective view from the south-west*

237. *(below left) Sir Thomas Deane's competition designs: plans and perspective view from the south-west*

circular panels are awkward.' Emerson's perimeter galleries are divided into bays, 13 feet 6 inches to 17 feet wide: this was generally thought to be disagreeably constricting, though it might be better received today, when cathedral-like exhibition halls are out of fashion.

Emerson's exterior, in red brick and terracotta, is in a highly eclectic Renaissance style with much decoration, including a continuous frieze all round the building beneath the cornice. Perhaps the most noticeable features are three spiral staircases on corners, in the manner of the Château de Blois.

William Young obtained 362 marks, only two less than Emerson. Waterhouse gave him full marks for elevations, remarking that 'the depth of the window recesses and the columniation pervading the façades, would give them a very rich expression, though the two heights of columns to the first storey, South front, are to be regretted.' He observed that 'this is a very ambitious design; it has one tower at an angle, 220 feet high, two on either side of the entrances 155 feet, and eight others along the two façades 115 feet, besides a smoke shaft (Venice Campanile) 135 feet high.' He gave Young 60/100 for plan, 60/80 for details, 35/40 for harmony, 39/50 for cost and 33/50 for accommodation. These reasonably good marks were offset, however, by 35/70 for light and 20/40 for wall space; he commented that the top lighting was inadequate and that most of the walls could not take large objects. He also pointed out that there were no lavatories for visitors.

Young's style was a fairly disciplined kind of classicism, relying on repetition rather than variety: all his eleven towers have the same profile. The Cromwell Road façade reads as three blocks, linked by quadrants, but this hardly relates to the plan of the galleries behind. The architectural reviews found little to say of this design, beyond praising its dignity.

The design of Sir Thomas Deane and Sons was quite different from Young's, for, as Waterhouse noted, 'the author says, he trusts to monotony for

236

237

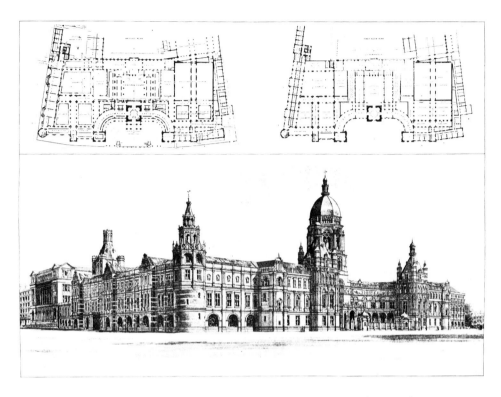

238. (right) Sir Thomas Graham Jackson's competition designs: plans and perspective view from the south-west

his general effect. He indulges in no towers, not even a visible chimney.' His plan included two open cloister courts, two smaller light-wells, and a service corridor: all this Waterhouse felt was a waste of space. Accordingly he awarded 50/100 for plan; and only 15/40 for wall space, and 20/50 for accommodation. The open courts, however, helped with the lighting which earned 60/70. Elevations and details were given 50/80 and 37/80 respectively. But Deane (whose total was 320) obtained full marks for cost (50) and harmony (40).

The style of his decoration, which Waterhouse evidently thought would fit in with that of Fowke and his associates, was a very fancy North Italian Renaissance, based on the Certosa of Pavia.[18] It was to be executed in terracotta and brick, to match the South Kensington style; and Deane carries all round his building the line of the string-course above the ground-floor arcade of the Science Schools. Whether his terracotta decorations, copies from the Certosa of Pavia, would have harmonized with those of Godfrey Sykes is difficult to tell without the detailed drawings.

The happiest feature of Deane's design is the treatment of the corner of Exhibition Road and Cromwell Road. In front of a semi-circular colonnaded recess is a circular fountain: from the colonnade access is gained to a circular entrance hall behind, flanked by square pavilions. This is very neat on the plan, and might have been a pleasing group of rooms to visit, but it leads nowhere in particular.

Sir Thomas Graham Jackson's design, though it earned full marks for accommodation (50) and high marks for cost (47/50), was deficient in plan (30/100) in Waterhouse's view. 'There are no long drawn out architectural vistas, or fairly proportioned Courts. The galleries are much cut up.' Furthermore, 'there is very little wall space in the Courts' – 15/40 for wall space. The courts 'are glazed at a sensible height' but 'the curved galleries can hardly be said to be lighted for exhibition purposes': light was awarded 40/70. With moderate marks for elevations (50/80), details (55/80) and harmony (30/40), Jackson achieved 317.

The main feature of his design was 'an enormous tower 57 feet square, surmounted by a cupola 240 feet high'. Despite this, his building was felt by the *Builder* to be 'rather nondescript and deficient in marked character'. In an attempt, presumably, to remain in keeping with the South Kensington style, Jackson modified his usual Elizabethan manner. There are his favourite

238
239

18. Deane described his design in *The Builder*, 19 September 1891, p. 227.

239. *Sir Thomas Graham Jackson's competition designs: perspective view of the interior of the Central Court*

240. *Thomas Collcutt's competition designs: perspective view of the interior of the Central Hall*

shaped gables; the main porch has strapwork cresting; and the entrance lodges have ogee cupolas. But intermingled with these 'Anglo-Jackson' elements are unfamiliar features. There is a sort of Abbot's Kitchen roof over the North-West staircase; the principal dome seems to belong to the early Italian Renaissance while the pyramidal roofs of the pavilions that flank it derive from French Renaissance architecture; and the corner turret combines both French and Italian elements. Jackson was, perhaps, less devoted to symmetry than the other competitors: he admitted irregularly shaped courts into his plan, and on his elevation frankly revealed the office block at the eastern extremity.

The perspective of his Great Central Court shows it to be an example of cast-iron architecture not unlike the existing South Court, except that its walls are more or less in Romanesque style. 'The effect is certainly not refined or architectonic,' remarked the *Builder*. At least, however, Jackson drew some exhibits in this court.

240
241 In Thomas Collcutt's Central Hall, also, a few plaster casts stand around, utterly dwarfed by
242 a towering dome. Collcutt's design aroused only a

lukewarm response. Waterhouse gave it good marks for cost (44/50) and accommodation (50/50); but in other respects it earned only middling marks (40/100 for plan, 50/80 for elevations, 40/80 for details, 35/70 for light, 20/40 for wall space, 20/40 for harmony). Its style was a rather nondescript Renaissance, with oriental features, according to the *Building News*: 'indeed, the towers at the South-East and North-West extremities have what might be called Chinese hats, while all over the skyline are little pepper-pot cupolas of a vaguely Indian flavour, and the flat dome has a Byzantine appearance. The plan is emphatically on the square, and it is set well back on the site, 'so as to shut it off from those approaching from the East,' as Waterhouse observed, 'while its western front, not being continuous with that of the Science Schools would prevent its being much seen in the approach from the north.'

Mervyn Macartney's design was the odd man *243* out. It was in a severely classical style, with hardly *244* any windows: 'a new Newgate', the *British Architect* called it. It was to be entirely built of Portland stone. It did not attempt to fit in with the existing buildings. Furthermore, Macartney

241. (right) Thomas Collcutt's competition designs: elevation of the Main Entrance

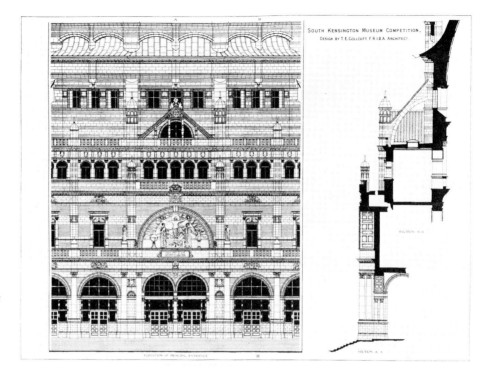

242. (below) Thomas Collcutt's competition designs: plans and perspective view from the south-west

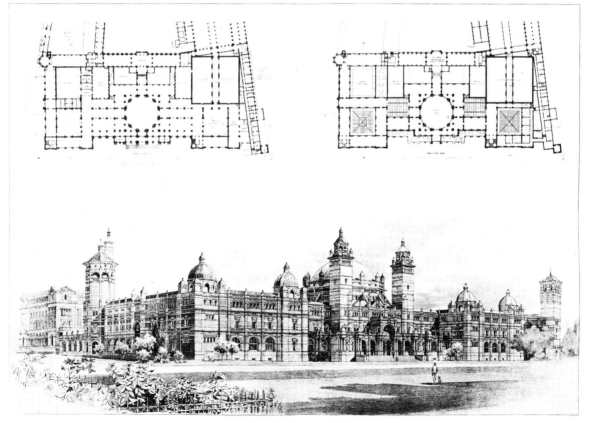

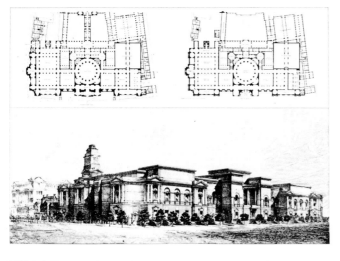

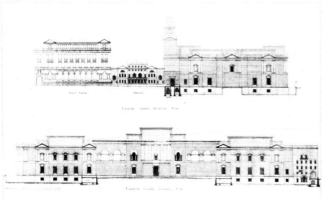

243. *(top) Sir Mervyn Macartney's competition designs: plans and perspective view from the south-west*

244. *(above) Sir Mervyn Macartney's competition designs: elevations* (above) *to Exhibition Road and* (below) *to Cromwell Road*

proposed to pull down the existing residences and erect new ones beside the Science Schools, fronting on to Exhibition Road, presumably to disguise the discord between his building and the Schools. Waterhouse consequently awarded him nil for harmony. However, given the classical style of this design, Waterhouse could see some virtues in it, and gave him 50/80 for elevations, and 30/80 for details. In this almost entirely top-lit building, 'very few absolutely dark corners can be detected

when the plans are carefully studied, though I cannot think', said Waterhouse, 'that the light would be in all respects sufficient for the purpose': he awarded 45/70 for light. Macartney's design was reasonably economical (cost, 40/50), but deficient in space (15/40 for wall space, 22/50 for accommodation). It did, however, have an unusually clear plan, to which Waterhouse gave 75/100. The principal feature was a central court, circular and domed, which Macartney called the 'Index Court'. This was, as nearly as could be managed, the heart of the building: three long, equidistant corridors led away from it, to the east, north and west, giving access to the various courts and galleries. From the Index Court, staircases led upwards to the north-east and north-west. This plan imposed order on the confusion of South Kensington more successfully than any of the others. Macartney's style of building was not appropriate to South Kensington; the *British Architect* considered that 'the general effect is severe and uncompromising to a degree which few Britishers would ever tolerate.'

The most interesting of the designs was, perhaps, that by John Belcher, although, as H. S. Goodhart-Rendal remarked in a lecture at the RIBA many years later, rumour denied him the true parentage of it. Nonetheless, it 'was greatly admired by young architects and students, and in anticipating Edwardian baroque, it certainly showed the shape of things to come.'

'Although an unexecuted design,' said Goodhart-Rendal, 'it showed strikingly the direction in which fashion was moving when Webb transformed the elevations with which he had won the competition into those that he eventually executed and which remains to us now.'[19] For it was to be almost twenty years before the new building was complete, and it was to be almost ten years before work on it started. Webb, constantly revising his designs to accommodate conflicting demands from the Department of Science and Art, had ample opportunity to reconsider the finer points of the architecture.

19. 'Brompton, London's Art Quarter', *R.I.B.A. Journal*, January 1956.

CHAPTER XII

Doldrums

The aftermath of the competition

Concluding its review of the designs for the new building, the *Builder* remarked: 'It is to be hoped that no time will now be lost in carrying out the building to its completion. Its existing state has long been a national discredit.'[1] Unfortunately many delays were to occur, owing to bureaucratic faint-heartedness, and to the growing administrative disorder at South Kensington, which was to be exposed by a Select Committee of Parliament in 1897. Aston Webb's design was to be pushed and pulled about from all directions.

Alfred Waterhouse was the first to try to touch it up. Already on 30 July 1890 he told D. R. Plunkett, First Commissioner of Works, that 'it seems to me that the pavilions [on the main façade] attract too much attention, and the wall spaces between them not enough'.[2] He suggested that the height of the walls might be increased. He also suggested that the parapet on the Exhibition Road frontage might be altered slightly 'to prevent the Science Schools appearing to crush the new buildings'.

As we have already noticed, Webb's plan was strictly rectangular with the southern side roughly following the line of Cromwell Road. Consequently the western frontage did not follow the line of Exhibition Road (since the junction between the two roads is not a right angle), and Waterhouse suggested that it should be altered so as to do so, since 'it would be much better seen as approached from the north'.

As soon as the initial formalities were over, Aston Webb got down to work preparing more detailed drawings, in consultation with the Museum authorities and the Office of Works, but it rapidly became apparent to all of them that it was not going to be plain sailing. The architect submitted to Donnelly some revised sketch plans of the ground and first floors in October and November.[3] In Donnelly's opinion, these showed a 'great improvement', but there were still some

points which he thought not 'quite satisfactory'. His first concern was that the office space had been reduced, and he suggested that Webb's original plan might be reverted to. After a few minor suggestions concerning fireplaces, Donnelly went on to more important things: 'The ends of the European Courts have been made apsidal in order no doubt to hide the obliquity of the Western European Court to the Oriental Court. These apsidal ends will be most inconvenient as Exhibition space …' So far as the plans relate, albeit distantly, to the present plan of the Museum, the apses to which Donnelly objected are in the approximate position of the present Raphael Cartoon Gallery; and perhaps, though not necessarily at such an early stage in development, Webb was also considering a symmetrical arrangement with an apse at the eastern end of the Sculpture Gallery, now Room 50. At any rate, he stuck to his apses, notwithstanding Donnelly's objections.

A little later, at the beginning of November, Donnelly wrote again to the Office of Works to object to a proposed modification of the northern end of the 'great entrance hall', which would entail the entire remodelling of that part of the building between the Science Library (now Room 41), and the Cast Courts. He suggested that the galleries to the south of the Library (Rooms 42, 44) should be made into two-storey buildings 'and arranged somewhat in the manner of the book stores of the British Museum'. (Something on these lines was carried out seventy years later.) After further proposals concerning book stacks and offices for the Library, he contested the suggestion that the staircase at the eastern end of the Library should be removed. 'It will be required', he stated, 'under any circumstances – there not

---

1. 8 August 1891.
2. PRO, Ed. 84/72.
3. Ibid., 26 November 1891, and PRO, Works 17/25/4.

being sufficient access to the galleries on the First Floor without', but he hinted that Webb's main staircase in what is now Room 43 might be dispensed with (and eventually it was).

A month later Aston Webb agreed to consider further changes to the offices, but he did not agree to make any changes to the apsidal ends to the galleries which he was 'very desirous to retain as affording a more architectural treatment to these Courts than at first shown'. H. W. Primrose, of the Office of Works, discussed these apses with both Donnelly and Festing, subsequently reassuring Webb that the Board of Works was not 'disposed to interfere with your discretion in regard to the ... treatment'.[4]

Donnelly, on receiving further revised plans, was very annoyed to find the apses undisturbed, and pointed out, justly, that these and several other curved recesses were 'quite unsuitable for a museum, where all the walls are required for exhibition spaces'.[5]

As refreshment rooms and kitchens for the office staff were at this time planned for the eastern portion of the building, Donnelly had a few comments about the arrangements in this area. 'The place marked as a Wine Cellar will serve better as a larder. A Beer Cellar will be required close to the Refreshment Rooms, and this might perhaps be under one of them.' However, it was not long before this part of the scheme was abandoned. Later, in October 1892, Webb proposed that an additional floor should be added above the offices for these rooms and kitchens. There is, in the Public Record Office, a section showing this rearrangement, which would have been facing Cromwell Road behind the parapet, with a glass roof. A good arrangement, thought Donnelly, 'no smells'.[6]

The Department of Science and Art, sticking to its past traditions and methods, expressed the view that 'a Model of the proposed buildings should be made' and Donnelly was told to 'urge strongly that steps should be taken for putting it in hand at once. Without it, it is impossible to judge the effect of the buildings, and it may be the means of considerably reducing the cost.' Aston Webb also was in favour of a model 'when the details of the façade are complete, but I suppose there is no money at present for it'.[7]

This was the crux of the matter. The competition had been held under the aegis of Lord Salis-

bury's second (Conservative) administration which resigned, on losing a vote of confidence, on 11 August 1892. It was succeeded by a Liberal government under Gladstone, which soon discovered that it could not afford to embark on building at South Kensington.

In 1892, as the Treasury estimates were being prepared for the financial year 1893–4, the Office of Works suggested that instead of planning for the construction of Webb's building in one operation, thereby entailing a heavy liability on the Treasury for an estimated seven or eight years, the building should be erected in phases, beginning with the south-east wing to provide the Department of Science and Art with its much-needed extra office accommodation. Consequently, the Office of Works asked for provision to be made in 1893–4 only for the sum of £15,000, on account of a total of £97,000. The Treasury, however, would not comply.[8]

It was the same story in 1893, when the time came to prepare the estimates for 1894–5. During 1894 an assurance was given on behalf of the Government that a vote for commencement of the works would be taken sometime during the 1895–6 session, and plans by Webb were exhibited in the Commons Tea Room. Nonetheless, in January 1895, the Treasury once again found itself short of money.[9] It had, over the three years 1893 to 1896, made available only a few small sums to pay the architect and to help clear the site.

So far as Webb was concerned, it appears that he had been more or less fully engaged upon revising his plans since the autumn of 1891, but when it was decided that no money would be forthcoming in 1893–4, he was instructed on 27 December 1892 by the First Commissioner 'to lay them aside until further orders'. 'Mr. Webb thereupon made a claim for something on account, and with Treasury sanction received £1,000, which added to the £315 paid him for the Completion Drawings, makes £1,315 which he has received in all.'[10] W. J. Downer of the Office of Works calculated that if the proposal to build at

---

4. PRO, Works 17/25/4, 11 December 1891, 1 July 1892.
5. PRO, Ed. 84/72, 19 March 1892; plan, PRO, Works 17/25/4.
6. PRO, Ed. 84/72.
7. Ibid., 22 October 1892.
8. PRO, Works 17/25/8, report by W. J. Downer.
9. Ibid., 25 January 1895.
10. PRO, Works 17/25/8.

South Kensington was abandoned, Webb would be entitled to further compensation: £1,835 if Parliament refused to vote funds for the scheme, or £2,875 if the Government did not bother to ask Parliament at all and quietly dropped the scheme.[11]

The first moves to prepare the site were taken in 1891 when H. W. Primrose instructed Donnelly to get in touch with John Taylor at the Office of Works, to arrange the surrender of the land to the builders.[12] This led to a mildly absurd wrangle over the Boilers, which would have to be demolished to make way for the new buildings. Primrose had allowed that some temporary accommodation must be provided in their place,[13] and, after considering and rejecting houses at 192 and 195 Queen's Gate, the Office agreed to put up further iron structures, one in the Museum quadrangle and another on ground in Imperial Institute Road.[14] The Treasury vouchsafed £3,250 for this purpose, and, after a copious correspondence with the Department of Science and Art, these sheds were set up during the financial year 1893–4.

The South Kensington authorities, however, made no move to get rid of the Boilers, and, when prodded in June 1895, refused to vacate them unless they were given a third temporary iron building, which would cost £1,000.

Reginald Brett, Secretary to the Office of Works, wrote to South Kensington stating that the new request had caused 'much surprise' in the Office of Works.[15] South Kensington remained firm, and in November, as neither side had given way, Taylor recommended that 'in the circumstances it appears desirable to allow the "Boilers" to remain as they are for use until the Govt. shall have decided what steps are to be taken in regard to the completion of the museum.' Brett, in a very militant mood, asked Taylor why the Office should not 'send and take down these "Boilers" at once: and merely inform the S & A Dept of our intention'.[16] Taylor, in spite of his antipathy to South Kensington – although, no doubt, privately relishing the thought of leading the attack against the Kensington Generals – counselled that the Works Office 'was not in a position to do this. The Lord President of the Council would no doubt at once step in if such a course were taken. The Treasury should be informed of the present position.'[17] The Treasury, in fact, snubbed the First Commissioner. 'If the Science and Art

Department ... do not think fit to remove their officers from the Boilers, My Lords see no objection need be raised by your Office.'[18] And so the affair temporarily was laid to rest.

A change of government

In June 1895, the Liberal Government (now under Lord Rosebery, who had taken over from Gladstone in March 1894) resigned, and the Conservatives returned to power under Lord Salisbury, with Sir Michael Hicks-Beach as Chancellor of the Exchequer. Hopes rose for renewed support for the museum building, and on 21 March 1896, the First Commissioner of Works, Aretas Akers-Douglas, announced in Parliament that Webb would be instructed to draw up revised plans. But the clouds were gathering over South Kensington.

It must be remembered that the Department of Science and Art had much else to do besides running the Art Museum. Its chief function was to promote technical education through its chain of art and science schools, and through the grants which it gave to support scientific education. The grants were awarded on a 'payment by results' system: the greater the number of pupils who passed the Department's exams, the greater the amount of money paid. The system thus had a built-in incentive towards its own expansion, and it did expand. Simultaneously, its Whitehall rival, the Education Department, was enlarging its powers: W. E. Forster's Education Act of 1870 set up the 'Board Schools', a system of state-supported compulsory elementary education. These schools were brought also into South Kensington's sphere of influence, since grants were made to support scientific classes in them, and gradually the foundations of state-aided secondary education were laid. Although, after Cole's retirement, the Education Department and the Department of Science and Art were run in tandem by Sir Francis Sandford, it was Colonel Donnelly at South Kensington who took the lead in creating

11. Ibid.
12. PRO, Ed. 84/72, 5 August 1891.
13. PRO, Works 17/25/5, March 1890.
14. Ibid., 4 March 1891.
15. Ibid., letter from Donnelly asking for an additional 4,000 square feet, 22 October; draft of Brett's reply, 29 October 1895.
16. Ibid., 20 November 1895.
17. Ibid., 23 November 1895.
18. Ibid., 21 December 1895.

the national system of scientific education. Under the second Gladstone administration (1880–5), he enjoyed the staunch support of the Vice-President of the Committee of Council on Education, A. J. Mundella, and succeeded in setting up at South Kensington a central school of science (which became the Royal College of Science and grew into Imperial College). When Sandford retired in 1884 Donnelly was made permanent head at South Kensington, which once again became free of the Education Department and pushed ahead with its scientific work.

During all this, the South Kensington Museum was run by Sir Philip Cunliffe Owen. When he retired in 1893, his job was split in two in recognition of the widening gap between the artistic and the scientific collections. General Festing, who had been at South Kensington with the Sappers since the early days, took over as Director of the Science Museum, and a new man was brought in to head the Art Museum: Professor J. H. Middleton, who had been Slade Professor at Cambridge and Director of the Fitzwilliam Museum. Although Middleton was an art historian, most of his staff were not, since Cole had preferred to appoint administrators, and the Museum was at a low ebb. A small reforming party began to agitate against an administration that seemed to them unsympathetic to art, and Middleton was caught between them and Donnelly, who, still on a rising wave, was made a Major-General in 1887 and was knighted in 1893. In the 1890s Donnelly's empire of scientific education expanded as never before, but it was too successful, especially in developing secondary education. It was not logical for the country to have two competing departments concerned with education, and the Bryce Commission on secondary education, in 1894, recommended rationalization. It seemed, therefore, that South Kensington was likely to be taken over, and Donnelly, who had served the Department for thirty-five years, threw his considerable personal prestige into a battle for survival. Just at this difficult time the agitation at the Museum (which he had been trying to suppress) blew up in his face.

The internal malcontents had been joined by influential outsiders such as Lord Balcarres and M. H. Spielmann, Editor of the *Magazine of Art*. Their campaigns in Parliament and the Press were successful when, in 1897, a Select Committee of Parliament was appointed to look into the Depart-

ment of Science and Art's museums at Kensington (and elsewhere). The strain had been too much for Dr Middleton, who died unexpectedly in 1896. He was succeeded by Caspar Purdon Clarke, a South Kensington man of long standing, who held things together skilfully through a period of tribulation.

It is not necessary here to describe in detail the deliberations of the Select Committee, which make more or less hair-raising reading. Donnelly was the first to face interrogation, which lasted throughout March and into April 1897, at the very time when he was preparing to take a leading part in an International Congress on Technical Education in London. Various scandals were displayed, and attacks were launched on the 'military element' at South Kensington, which caused Donnelly to lose his temper and the Chairman to call for the room to be cleared. Amid all the discussion of mistaken acquisition policies and corrupt staff appointments, the state of the buildings was reviewed; and later, as the Committee continued its deliberations in 1898, there was some inconclusive consideration of how the collections might be rearranged in a new building.

What chiefly alarmed the Committee about the old buildings was their susceptibility to fire; and an interim report was rushed out in May 1897 to emphasize the fire risk. This was backed up by organized lobbying, for South Kensington had a body of opinion on its side. The pressure groups by whom the Government might be assailed had been defined by W. J. Downer, in advising the First Commissioner in 1895.[19] Pressure would be brought to bear:

> By the S[cience] & A[rt] Dept. who will certainly not rest till they get what they want. It must be borne in mind that the demands of the Dept. for buildings on the *west* side of Exhibition Road for a Science Museum and for the Royal College of Science are only held in check by the obvious inability of Govt. to entertain such demands, which are powerfully backed up by the Reports of Committees and by the 'Professors' generally, so long as the half-finished Art Buildings remain for completion. The abandonment, if such a course is now practicable, or even the indefinite postponement of the latter scheme, would immediately bring the Science Buildings question to the front. If the Art

---

19. PRO, Works 17/25/8, 21 October 1895.

Buildings be completed, the Eastern Galleries (now occupied by the Indian Collection) and the North, or Cross Gallery in the Imperial Institute (to which the Persian Collections were recently removed), together with the two Temporary Buildings on the west side, would be available for the Science Division, and the Government with a good conscience could then say that the Science requirements would thereby be sufficiently met for many years to come. Members of Parliament will also want to know why the scheme is not to go on. Session after Session members have pressed for explanations as to the delay, and assurances have been repeatedly given that financial reasons only have prevented the commencement of the work. The F[irst] C[ommissioner] may expect to be heckled very considerably on the subject. Members interested in Art matters; members scientific; members who perhaps care nothing for either science or art, but who are anxious to see an end put to the discreditable appearance the unfinished and temporary buildings fronting Cromwell Road have presented for so many years; Labour members who would have Govt. build anywhere or anything in order to give employment – all of these will have to be reckoned with.

The newspapers, too, of all shades of opinion, judging from the chorus of approbation which went up from them when the scheme was resolved upon in 1891, will not be slow to condemn its abandonment. But Public Depts. are rather case-hardened against press criticism.

The Architectural world will also, it may be safely assumed, protest vigorously against any backsliding in the matter. The Competition for Designs held in 1891 excited much interest, and the selected design ... was, I think, very generally regarded as of great merit ... Mr. Webb himself may be expected to bring every kind of pressure upon Govt. not to throw him over, and his professional friends may be trusted to back him up in every way.

Two years later, Webb's friends did indeed weigh in. A petition urging the completion of the new buildings and signed by many distinguished figures from the art world was presented on 4 May 1897 by Sir Lawrence Alma-Tadema to the Duke of Devonshire, who, as Lord President of the Council, was the political chief of the Department of Science and Art. He sent it on to the Treasury;[20] with his endorsement, while a similar memorial was sent to the Chairman of the Select Committee, Sir John Gorst, and received by him as evidence on 23 July. Among the 89 signatories were Sir Edward Poynter, H. H. Armstead, Sir Edward Burne-Jones, Walter Crane, W. Holman Hunt, Sir W. B. Richmond, Sir L. Alma-Tadema, Frank Dicksee, Hamo Thornycroft, Val Prinsep, J. S. Sargent, Hubert Herkomer, George Frampton, Ernest Waterlow, James Sant, J. W. Waterhouse, J. L. Pearson, W. L. Wylie, Onslow Ford, Thomas Jackson, Stanhope Forbes, H. S. Marks, Marcus Stone, Thomas Brick, E. A. Abbey, G. P. Jacomb-Hood, H. S. Tuke, Feodora Gleichen, G. F. Watts, E. Blair Leighton, and Colin Hunter.

Although this memorandum must certainly have added momentum to the campaign in favour of a new building, its only immediate result was an instruction to demolish some of the more obviously inflammable buildings at South Kensington. One of these was the art students' common room, a temporary wooden building, perhaps one of those that had come from Marlborough House in 1857. Since the students smoked their pipes in it, it was declared too dangerous to stay; the Department of Science and Art, pointing out that the students 'have great difficulty in maintaining themselves on the small allowances they receive', besought the Treasury to provide an alternative rest room.

A more complicated problem was presented by the various official houses on the site, both in decaying old buildings and in Fowke's terracotta wing. It was felt that it was bad practice to have domestic dwellings within the Museum – they included 81 domestic fireplaces – and the residences had already been strongly criticized by Arthur Street in a report on the risk of fire in the Museum buildings, which he had prepared in 1893 but which had subsequently been withdrawn. One of the inhabitants of the residences was the warrant officer in charge of the detachment of Royal Engineers, who were responsible for fire-fighting on the site. It was feared that if this sergeant-major were deprived of his residence, the War Office might remove him, with his sergeant and eleven sappers, from South Kensington altogether. Thus the elimination of a building that was a fire risk might result in the elimination of the fire-fighting force. In any case, the sappers were valuable not only as a fire brigade: the sergeant had been set on to clerical and book-keeping

---

20. PRO, Ed. 84/57, 4 November 1897.

duties in the 'Works' office; of the sappers, two were employed as Museum photographers, two as laboratory attendants in the Science Schools, and others as 'artisans' under the Foreman of Works. Their working pay, amounting to £12 5s 9d a week, was paid by the Science and Art Department and each man was sent on a course of instruction in drawing at the Art Schools. General Festing estimated their value to the Department, from the extra labour provided, as £23 per week.[21]

The paradoxical difficulty was argued out late in 1897, and finally the Treasury put its foot down on 24 December.[22] The residences were to be abolished, the present residents were to be given allowances, so as to 'enable them to take suitable houses within 500 yards of the Museum, those houses to be connected by telephone with the Museum'; and future holders of their posts were to have salaries adjusted to the new situation.

Thus tiny steps were taken towards the commencement of a building programme. In response to the petition from the artists, the Treasury held out the prospect of a beginning in the financial year 1898-9[23] and in March 1898 the First Commissioner of Works, still Akers-Douglas, asked Parliament for £80,000 for the completion of the South Kensington buildings. But now came a new development with far-reaching implications.

The twilight of South Kensington

As has been said, the Education Department and the Department of Science and Art had both greatly expanded their influence during their half-century of existence. Whereas at the mid-century the rôle of the state in education was more or less confined to handing out modest financial assistance to voluntary bodies that organized schools, by the end of the century the state had under its control an elaborately ramifying system of schooling. The Bryce Commission, which examined secondary education in 1894, had concluded that it was time for the three state agencies that had developed the educational system – the Education Department, the Charity Commissioners, and South Kensington – to be united in one body with overall control. Sir John Gorst, Vice-President of the Committee of Council on Education in the Conservative government, was sympathetic to the educational reformers and in 1899 put through an Act establishing a new Board of Education.

In 1898 the certain prospect of the dissolution of the Department of Science and Art seemed to throw plans for the new South Kensington buildings back into the melting pot. When the bureaucrats moved away from South Kensington, they would leave some empty space: this seemed to Hicks-Beach, the Chancellor of the Exchequer, to present an opportunity for saving space in the new building.[24] (Ultimately, indeed, no offices were included in the Aston Webb building, since the Departmental office block had become available.) Furthermore, the dissolution of the Department imparted a new urgency to another problem: what to do about better accommodation for the Science Museum and the Royal College of Science. The official policy (as W. J. Downer pointed out in his minute quoted on p. 204) was to settle the fate of the art museum on its site east of Exhibition Road, before considering the possibility of expanding the science collections on land westwards of Exhibition Road. This was still the policy which the First Commissioner of Works affirmed to the House of Commons on 21 March 1898.[25]

But Hicks-Beach had scented the possibility of using Webb's new building to accommodate both science and art, and he suggested to the Duke of Devonshire that a small committee should be set up to work out how to fit everything in. The committee consisted of Caspar Purdon Clarke and General Festing, Directors respectively of the Art and Science Museums; Reginald Brett and Sir John Taylor, who were Secretary and Principal Surveyor at the Office of Works; and Aston Webb. Hicks-Beach ended his letter by airily proposing that Webb '(much of whose former design will still be of service) should be designated as Architect for all the buildings East of Exhibition Road'. Webb was no doubt grateful to have his position recognized, but must have been startled at Hicks-Beach's suggestion that more space could be gained over the Museum quadrangle and adding another storey on to the new building.

These latter proposals were contested by the Duke of Devonshire (Lord President of the Council) and the South Kensington authorities,

---

21. PRO, Ed. 84/57, Report by Festing, 3 July 1897.
22. PRO, Works 17/26/1, 24 December 1897.
23. PRO, Ed. 84/57, letter to Donnelly 4 December 1897.
24. PRO, Works 17/26/2, 18 February 1898, Hicks Beach to the Duke of Devonshire.
25. PRO, Ed. 84/58, 21 March 1898.

though Webb had obligingly conceived the notion of using a new storey for offices and work rooms.[26] The Duke agreed to the formation of a committee, but South Kensington thereupon dug its heels in. Brett tried to convene a meeting, but had to report non-cooperation from Festing and Clarke, who 'replied that they are "waiting instructions from the Lord President"'. I take this to mean that they are not to have 'full powers', but are to be limited by instructions from Sir J. Donnelly. If that be the case, we shall have a difficult negotiation.'[27]

The Committee did meet, unofficially on 30 March 1898,[28] and again on 20 April. Sir John Taylor suggested dividing the new building down the middle, with science to the west and art to the east. When it was pointed out that the Royal College of Art, in its premises at the back of the Museum, was in need of room for expansion, he suggested that it should be moved to the western side of Exhibition Road. 'We remarked', Festing reported later, 'that this would be to take Art students away from the Art Museum, and set them down near the Science Museum, while Science students would be placed alongside of the Art Museum. We then found ourselves at deadlock, and agreed that we must wait further instructions.'[29]

Next the Duke of Devonshire produced a scheme whereby the Art Museum could retain almost all of the new buildings, except for a new laboratory block which should be built beside the Royal College of Science, on Exhibition Road. Webb was instructed to draw up yet more plans to achieve this: 'It would be desirable to reduplicate the Royal College of Science, keeping to the height and general elevation of that building. You should further bear in mind that the Science Building should be kept as distinct as possible from the Art Building ... I am to add that your design, which has already been approved, should be left as far as possible unchanged.'[30] Webb sportingly agreed to try.

However, it soon became apparent that the scientists were as opposed as anyone to this revision of the earlier plan. Sir Henry Roscoe, FRS, testifying before the Select Committee of enquiry, which was still sitting, said that the site near the busy junction of Exhibition Road and Cromwell Road was 'about the most unfit place that could be found'[31] for laboratories; and an anguished

memorial from Fellows of the Royal Society, including Lord Lister, Lord Rayleigh, Lord Kelvin, W. Christie, the Astronomer Royal, General Wilson, RE, expressed their strong opinion that the expansion of the Science Buildings should not be on the east side of Exhibition Road, in contradiction to the views acknowledged by the Government since at least 1890.[32]

The Duke of Devonshire wearily concluded: 'it seems to be rather a pity that we should be absolutely committed to a plan to which for some reason or other the experts are opposed, if the original plan could be carried out at about the same cost.'[33] And when, at the end of May, Brett drew up a report for the *ad hoc* building committee, he recommended adherence to the original plan – although not without anxious deference to the superior wisdom of the Treasury.[34]

At about this time the Prince of Wales visited South Kensington. With the Duke of Devonshire, Donnelly, Festing and Clarke he went to the top of the Royal College of Science and looked down on the site over which such disputes were raging. Afterwards he wrote that 'the fights the different depts. of the Govt have with the Treasury are most difficult to get over'.[35]

South Kensington had not yet finished fighting, however. Festing and Clarke produced such strong objections to Brett's report,[36] that in June 1898 Brett concluded that his committee could not reach agreement. He lamented to the Treasury that negotiation seemed impossible with the Science and Art Department.

> Their requirements are so varying, are so largely in excess of what any Government in recent years has been inclined to grant, that I would strongly advise for your Lordships' consideration that the whole responsibility ... be thrown upon the First Commissioner of Works, as is habitually done in the

26. PRO, Works 17/26/2, 11 March 1898. PRO, Ed. 84/57, 31 March 1898.
27. PRO, Works 17/26/2, 24 March 1898.
28. Ibid., 29 March 1898, Mowatt to Brett.
29. PRO, Ed. 84/72, Festing on the Building Committee, 20 April 1898.
30. PRO, Works 17/26/2, 26 April 1898.
31. Select Committee 1898, Minutes of Evidence, para. 3138.
32. Ibid., Appendix 18.
33. PRO, Works 17/26/2, 2 May 1898.
34. PRO, Works 17/26/2.
35. Royal Archives, Add A4/57, 4 May 1898.
36. PRO, Works 17/26/2, 27 May 1898.

case of other public buildings; and that the sifting of the stated requirements of the offices of the Science and Art Department be left to Sir John Taylor and his assistants, who have had a long experience in discriminating between requirements which are alleged to be, and which are really necessary.[37]

From this moment, though, it became apparent that the original scheme must go ahead, if it could possibly be financed. So now, and only now, almost ten years after the competition, the authorities turned to consider in detail how the space in the proposed new building should be allocated;[38] and now, only now, Aston Webb announced that he would be visiting recently built continental museums – at Amsterdam, Berlin, Vienna, Dresden and Munich – to study how their interiors were arranged.[39]

The business of allocating space in the Museum might reasonably have been left to the Museum authorities, but the Duke of Devonshire and the Chancellor of the Exchequer could not resist the temptation to get involved, and at once began to dispute with each other whether plaster casts and carpets were worth exhibiting.[40] Hicks-Beach had no doubts, moreover, that 'early Victorian furniture, which no one now would desire to study except in order to avoid, may be consigned to cellars, if it must be retained at all'.[41] The Permanent Secretary at the Treasury, Sir Francis Mowatt, was soon lamenting: 'I almost despair of getting forward with this matter. The Duke and the Chancellor bandy the papers backward and forward each contributing en route some unhelpful observations which lead to nothing.'[42] But he too became involved. He called at the Museum in August to look at the space then occupied by furniture, carpets and pictures, and, in Clarke's absence, was shown round by his deputy, A. B. Skinner. He took exception to displays of Indian commercial carpets and calicoes,[43] and Clarke had to be called back from Arundel to see him at the Treasury and smooth him down.[44] Mowatt then conceded that the allocation of space was not really the Treasury's business, and suggested that, since the Office of Works had washed its hands of the matter, a committee might be formed to consider it: otherwise, 'it might take years to come to any decision'.

Some rather uninformative statistics had been compiled by Clarke, stating the existing space

occupied by the various sections of the Museum, and the amount of space needed for expansion.

	Existing Space (ft)	New Space (ft)
Sculpture	12,400	4,000
Furniture, woodwork and musical instruments	21,814	50,000
Ironwork, goldsmiths' work, ivories and enamels	14,037	50,000
Pottery and glass	13,710	25,000
Textiles	16,155	20,000
Picture galleries	15,090	5,000
Indian and oriental collections	55,819	56,000

The textiles, Clarke suggested, should be kept in a study room not open to the public. In addition he allocated 10,000 feet for plaster casts, 2,000 for the Jones Collection, and 5,000 for the Circulation department. This all added up to 217,000 square feet of extra exhibition space; and 8,000 feet more office space was needed.[45] In October the Duke of Devonshire cross-questioned Clarke on these figures, asking him whether he had given the figures to Donnelly in 'a lump or in detail', if he had given measurements, and so on, remarking that 'it was difficult to arrive at the truth'.[46]

Webb was busily at work revising his plans, and in December 1898, they were taken by Reginald Brett to Windsor for the Queen's scrutiny. Their arrival provoked a summons from the Prince of Wales to Purdon Clarke to go to Windsor to see his eldest sister, Princess Victoria (the Empress Frederick of Prussia, and mother of Kaiser Wilhelm). Clarke reported:

37. Ibid., 4 June 1898.
38. Ibid., 20 June 1898, minute from Hicks Beach to Mowatt.
39. PRO, Ed. 84/57, 23 July, 30 July 1898.
40. As for note 38.
41. Ibid., 23 June 1898.
42. PRO, Works 17/26/2, 29 August 1898.
43. PRO, Ed. 84/57, 20 August 1898, Donnelly to Clarke.
44. Ibid., 22 August 1898, Clarke to Donnelly.
45. Ibid., 9 July 1898.
46. Ibid., 17 October 1898.

PLATE XXXIII *(opposite inset) Design for the decoration of the western Cast Court, C. 1871. Watercolour*

PLATE XXXIV *(opposite) The restored western Cast Court, March 1982*

The Empress Frederick felt very strongly the want of dignity in the ornamentation of the building, and was personally of opinion that it would have been better to have arranged the Museum upon the plan adopted at Munich – one which will in future be followed by great national museums.

This system has been to construct several blocks, picturesquely arranged, each in a different style, a Gothic building to take the Gothic collections and a Renaissance building for those of the later period. At Berlin the first Museum – which was built without regard to the nature of the collections – has proved wholly unsuitable, but a new Museum has been built and is now in course of completion in which every section has been specially designed for the housing of its particular collections, and great satisfaction has been expressed by the museum authorities.

The Empress Frederick stated that she had sent for me on account of the deep interest she always felt in the South Kensington Museum – which she looked upon as the pioneer of all similar Institutions in Europe and elsewhere, and that she could not in any way publicly offer advice, but that she thought, perhaps, if I would convey her views to the Lord President, a little more consideration might be given at least to the ornamental defects in the general appearance of the building.[47]

This intervention by the Empress was very much to the point. She had observantly noted a powerful but short-lived fashion in Germany for building museums to match their contents. The pioneer example of this practice had been Alexandre Lenoir's Musée des Monuments Français in Paris, founded in 1793, which had 'period rooms', century by century through the Middle Ages. This was dismantled at the Restoration of the monarchy, but occasionally old buildings, such as the Hôtel de Cluny in Paris, were used to house art collections of corresponding antiquity. The classic example was the German National Museum in Nuremberg, set up in 1857 in a secularized medieval monastery. In the 1870s and '80s additions were made to this building in medieval revival styles until the whole complex became highly picturesque. In the 1890s several architects decided that this was the right way to

build a museum.[48] First came the Schweizerisches Landesmuseum at Zurich (1890–8), followed by the Historisches Museum at Bern (1892–6); the North Bohemian Museum in Reichenberg (Liberec), the Kaiser-Friedrich-Museum at Magdeburg, and the Märkisches Museum in Berlin continued the tradition, which reached its climax in the Bavarian National Museum at Munich (1894–9). The rising wave of architectural fashion (of which Aston Webb, starting work on his designs in 1891, could have known nothing) suddenly broke and receded. This kind of museum building, though romantically attractive, was from a practical point of view inconvenient. It reflected, however, a more fundamental conviction among museum people that museums should be arranged on historical principles. The Empress Frederick's intervention might have directed the thoughts of the South Kensington authorities to this idea. But they rejected it then, and later.

They thought she was complaining only about Webb's exterior elevations, and it was clearly too late to make changes. 'We have not yet seen the Elevations,' claimed Donnelly, in reporting the matter to the Vice-President. 'I do not know whether we shall ever see the elevations.'[49] The problem went up to the Lord President of the Council, the Duke of Devonshire, who settled it by observing, 'I do not think we must trouble ourselves about the elevations. We are not responsible for them.'

In 1899, events suddenly began to move swiftly. On 9 February, parliamentary questions elicited from Akers-Douglas, First Commissioner of Works, the information that all the buildings on the east side of Exhibition Road (with the exception of the Royal College of Science) were to be devoted to the art collections, and a separate building was to be erected for science purposes on the western side of Exhibition Road. (No extensions were provided for the Royal College of Art. Walter Crane, its head, had asked in January 1899 if the College might extend into the attics of the

---

47. Ibid., 15 December 1898.
48. See Jörn Bahns, 'Kunst- und Kulturgeschichtliche Museen als Bauaufgabe des späten 19 Jahrhunderts' in *Das Kunst- und kulturgeschichtliche Museum im 19 Jahrhundert*, ed. Bernward Deneke und Rainer Kahsnitz (Fritz Thyssen Stiftung: Studien zur kunst des neunzehnten Jahrhunderts, Band 39), Munich: Prestel Verlag, 1977, pp. 176–192.
49. PRO, Ed. 84/57, 19 December 1898.

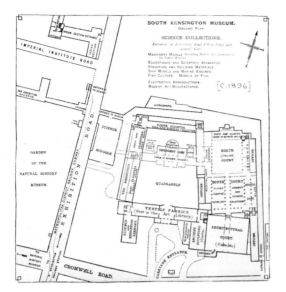

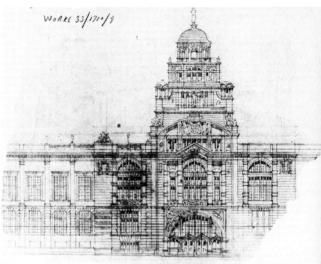

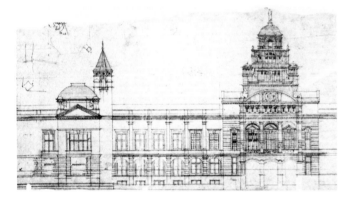

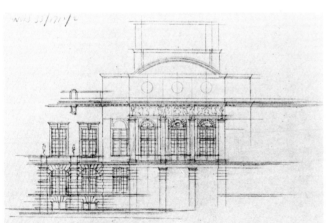

245. *(top left) Ground plan of the Museum, c. 1896.*

Sir Aston Webb's new Museum designs showing modifications made after the competition. 246. *(top right) Sketch for the elevation of the Main Entrance and dome.* 247. *(centre left) Sketch for the elevation to Cromwell Road.* 248. *(above) Sketch for the elevation of the Main Entrance*

former Residences which adjoined it, but as these were due to be gutted and rebuilt, his request was turned down.)[50]

Shortly afterwards, plans and elevations were published; they show that the Museum's design had virtually assumed its final form. The large central tower of the 1891 design had disappeared, and had been replaced by three octagonal recessed storeys, the highest surmounted by a small cupola. *The Times* approved that the 'useless towers' had been cut down.[51] It was, however, the plan of the building that had undergone the major change. Following Waterhouse's tip (p. 201), Webb now aligned the western side of the building with Exhibition Road. This led to awkward angles and spaces within the building, though they were – and are – to some extent masked. Furthermore, Webb inserted, immediately behind the galleries flanking Cromwell Road, a long gallery extending the entire length of the building, with, on the west, a large square court (eventually to become octagonal) which balanced the architectural courts of General Scott on the east. The long gallery was a feature that Webb might have picked up from the competition designs of either Belcher or

249
250

251

50. Ibid., 18, 24, 25 January 1899.

51. During the Select Committee sittings of 1897, Sir Henry Howorth asked if the Office of Works had 'done away' with some of Webb's towers. Taylor replied, 'There has been a desire to dispense with very large towers which were unnecessary, but the final plan has not yet been approved . . . There is every desire on the part of the Office of Works to avoid large towers if they possibly can, and to make a suitable and sightly building without them.' *Report*, 1897, p. 365, No. 7251.

249. *(top) Sir Aston Webb's new Museum designs: perspective view from the south-west in 1899 at the time of laying the foundation stone*

250. *(above) Sir Aston Webb's new Museum designs: elevation to Cromwell Road in 1899 at the time of laying the foundation stone*

251. *(right) Sir Aston Webb's new Museum designs: ground plan in 1899 at the time of laying the foundation stone, showing the proposed gallery across the Quadrangle*

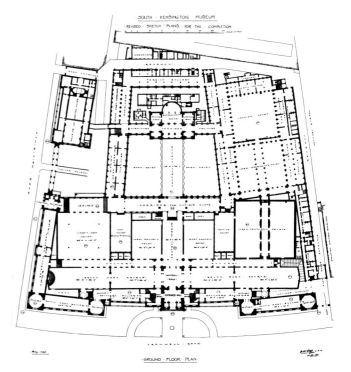

Macartney. Perhaps the latter is the more likely source, since he had combined a lateral gallery with a similar north-south corridor reaching to the Lecture Theatre, and this feature Webb also adopted in his new plan. From the main entrance there was to be a vista right through the Museum to the gilded doors leading to the Refreshment Rooms on the north side of the quadrangle. To achieve this, the architect now proposed to alter a part of General Scott's south side of the quadrangle, so as to insert a single-storey gallery cutting the quadrangle in two. Though this was opposed by the Museum authorities, the architectural journals were in favour, as it gave the old and new buildings a useful central north-south axis corridor. The Museum administration objected as it was thought the appearance of the quadrangle would be ruined. The *Builder* felt it was more a question of the staff not wanting to lose their tennis court, and considered the new gallery essential for both architectural and practical reasons.[52]

In order to make this vista even more impressive, Webb proposed to provide, along the same line, a ceremonial exterior approach to the main entrance, running through the gardens of Thurloe Square. This came to nothing, although the Museum authorities had always been concerned to preserve the open aspect of Thurloe Square, and had purchased in 1863 the triangle of land (separating Cromwell Road and Thurloe Place) that intervenes between the Museum and the Thurloe Square gardens. It had belonged to a Mr Spicer, and to prevent it being built over, the Department of Science and Art bought it with funds raised by selling off a small plot at the north-west corner of the Museum site: this accounts for the otherwise unexplained contraction of the Museum's land to the north of the College of Science.[53] The Department of Science and Art reserved the right, and presumably the Museum retains this right, to erect a monument on Spicer's land; it permitted the installation of a drinking trough by the Metropolitan Drinking Fountain and Cattle Trough Association in 1876,[54] but forbade Kensington Vestry to construct a public urinal in 1882.[55]

Although Webb abandoned his external approach to the Museum, he brought up the proposal for an internal vista again in 1911, when the Museum was under a new Director. Nothing came of it, however.[56] Another change made in his revised plans of 1899 was the abandonment of his grand staircase. In his 1891 plan, he had intended that the library should be approached by a main staircase from the central court, as the conditions of the competition required. In time this requirement had been abandoned, and one original staircase at the west end of the library was to be removed (in the present Room 74), while the other at the eastern end (Room 85) was to be retained as the means of reaching the library. However,

in April 1899 this arrangement was queried: 'We all, including the librarian, consider that the arrangement originally proposed of entering the library in the middle will be more convenient. The staircase for this can be readily provided for, as it was in a previous plan. By the other arrangement at present, all persons coming on business to the Library ... have to come through the reading room.'[57] But it was too late. These second thoughts, accompanying the realization that a mistake had been made when the grand central staircase was abandoned, were doomed to remain only regrets. A chance to put the matter right did not come until the 1960s when the central court was recast with three additional floors. Then it would have been possible to provide the library entrance on the first floor, so near the main entrance, but the opportunity was missed.

Aston Webb's designs thus emerged, comparatively unscathed and, indeed, improved, from a long period of uncertainty. Many must have felt the fears, voiced by the *Builder*,[58] that the Government wanted to cut the building down to 'a plain utilitarian structure', 'on the usual English theory in regard to public buildings, that ... all expenditure on architectural dignity and beauty is money wasted'. The *Builder* claimed that the Treasury would not succeed 'in crushing all the architecture out of the proposed building', and so it turned out.

On 1 March 1899, Reginald Brett wrote to tell the Department of Science and Art[59] that Webb's revised design had been approved, that instructions had been given for the trees to be cleared from the site, and that a foundation stone was soon to be laid by the Queen.

---

52. *Builder*, 20 May 1899, p. 486.
53. PRO, Ed. 84/35, Board minute précis, 14 June 1861; and further papers 17 October 1861, 30 January, 20 April 1862, 24 March, 15 April, 6 May 1863.
54. PRO, Ed. 84/36, 18 August 1876; The trough was demolished by a lorry in 1981.
55. PRO, Ed. 84/38, Board minute précis, 19 October 1882.
56. PRO, Ed. 84/69, 3 March 1911, W. Fisher to H. Kennedy; and 5 July 1912, from Kennedy.
57. PRO, Ed. 84/57, 18 April 1889, memo sent to the Vice-President.
58. *Builder*, 15 January 1898.
59. PRO, Ed. 84/57.

CHAPTER XIII

The new building achieved (1899-1909)

Foundation

Queen Victoria's visit to lay a foundation stone, first announced for 12 May 1899,[1] actually took place on 17 May. Because the Queen wished to perform the ceremony under cover, the Office of

Works put up a pavilion, designed by Webb and decorated with flags and a red and white striped awning.[2] The day was fine, and the visit was made a proper state occasion. Queen Victoria left Buckingham Palace at a quarter-past four in the afternoon in a semi-state open landau, accompanied by Life Guards. The journey took only fifteen minutes, and the Queen's carriage drove right into the pavilion. With her were the Duke of Connaught and the Princesses Christian and Henry of Battenberg, while waiting at South Kensington were the Prince of Wales, together with the Duke of Devonshire, Lord President of the Council; Aretas Akers-Douglas, the First

252

253
254

1. PRO, Ed. 84/57, Brett.
2. Webb's drawings are in PRO, Works 17/26/4. For a description see *Builder*, 20 May 1899, p. 486.

252. *(centre left) The temporary wooden pavilion designed by Sir Aston Webb to accommodate spectators at the laying of the foundation stone, seen from the west side of Thurloe Square*

253. *(above) Queen Victoria arriving in the pavilion to lay the foundation stone, after a drawing by S. Begg*

254. *(right) Queen Victoria receiving a bouquet from a student of the Art Schools*

Commissioner of Works; and Aston Webb. The Lord President read a speech of welcome, and was handed the written reply of the Queen:

> It is a great pleasure to me to be here to lay the Foundation Stone of the Building which will worthily contain the magnificent collection of objects illustrating the Fine and Industrial Arts which have been brought together on this site during the period of My Reign.
>
> My interest in this great Institution which in its inception and during its early days I shared with My Dear Husband has grown with its progress and development; and I rejoice that I have been able to take a personal part in the completion of a Scheme which will be not the least Distinction of My Reign, and which will, I trust, continue to be a powerful factor in the industrial enlightenment and artistic training of My People.
>
> I am pleased that the priceless collection of treasures which the munificence of private persons and the Public Spirit of Parliament have brought together will always be associated with My name and My Dear Husband.
>
> In compliance with your prayer, I gladly direct that in future this Institution shall be styled 'the Victoria and Albert Museum', and I trust that it will remain for ages a Monument of discerning Liberality and a Source of Refinement and Progress.[3]

At first the Queen had wanted to rename the institution the 'Albert Museum', but she had agreed in September 1898 to the Duke of Devonshire's request that she add her name.[4] Both Queen and Consort were included in the inscription on the foundation stone which had been submitted to the Queen on 27 March 1899, and to which she had given her approval two days later from the Hotel Regina at Cimiez.[5] The inscriptions reads:

> This stone was laid by Her Majesty Queen Victoria, Empress of India on 17th day of May 1899, in the 62nd year of Her reign, for the completion of the South Kensington Museum inaugurated by His Royal Highness the Prince Consort, and henceforth to be known as the Victoria and Albert Museum.

The stone itself, of red Argyll granite, was fashioned by Farmer & Brindley at a cost of £29 10s.[6] It can now be seen to the left of the main entrance, but this is not where the Queen laid it. Beneath it was a cavity containing a casket. This was made of copper with gold decoration, having a domed top on which was the Imperial Crown on

255. *The trowel used by Queen Victoria to lay the foundation stone*

a cushion. It was designed by Sir George Hayter Chubb, Chairman of Chubb and Sons Lock and Safe Company, who volunteered his services.[7] He urged that the 'Casket should be placed in the Stone so as to be afterwards partially visible from the outside', but in this he was disappointed. Within the casket were placed a history of the Museum and a set of current coins obtained from the Royal Mint to the value of £2 1s 4¾d. The Royal Mint asked the Office of Works to make sure that they were reimbursed.[8]

The casket was presented to the Queen after

---

3. PRO, Ed. 84/215.
4. Royal Archives, PP. Vic. 10167, 18 September 1898.
5. PRO, Works 17/26/4, 27 March 1899.
6. The costs of the ceremony were defrayed by money provided by the Public Buildings Expenses Act. PRO, Works 17/26/2, letter from Mowatt, 24 February 1909.
7. PRO, Works 17/26/4, 13 February 1899.
8. Ibid., April 1899.

she had silently transmitted her speech to the Lord President. Helped by the Prince of Wales, she placed it in the cavity beneath the foundation
255 stone. An ornamental trowel (now kept in the Museum Library) was handed to her, and assisted by Aston Webb, she completed the ritual. A madrigal composed by the Poet Laureate, and set to music by Sir Alexander MacKenzie, was sung by students of the Royal College of Music. At the end of the ceremony, the Archbishop of Canterbury said a prayer, and Queen Victoria was then trundled up Exhibition Road to Paddington Station to catch the train to Windsor.

At some stage in the ceremony, the Queen was presented with a bouquet of flowers by a female art student. This act was recorded on a primitive
254 moving picture device, the Mutoscope, now in the Museum's historic photograph collection. By peering into a viewer rather like those of 'What-the-butler-saw' machines, the observer may still behold, endlessly repeated, a part of what was Queen Victoria's last public state ceremony.

Construction begins

Once the foundation stone had been laid, Aston Webb got down to business. By 4 July 1899 he was preparing to demolish the old buildings and construct a temporary entrance.[9] It was not until February of the following year, however, that work began on the foundations. The laying of the stone had been timed to suit the Queen's convenience, and it was only on 15 December 1899 that the contract for the foundations, for £33,410, was signed with Leslie & Co., who moved onto the site in February 1910.[10]

On 8 August 1901, the First Commissioner of Works, still Akers-Douglas, replying to a Parliamentary question from the Member for Central Finsbury, Massey-Mainwaring, announced that tenders would shortly be invited for the superstructure. The contract was eventually given to Holliday and Greenwood of Brixton.

During 1901 a remarkable piece of work was *256* achieved. This was the extension of General Scott's lecture theatre block, on the north of the quadrangle, by one bay to the east; the complete rebuilding and re-alignment of the whole of the *258* east wall of the quadrangle; and the addition of *260* another storey and of two bays to the south, so as to join the former Sheepshanks Gallery to the staircase at the east end of the library. This extension had not been made in 1869 when the south court was lengthened. The new exterior walls, of

9. PRO, Ed. 84/57.
10. PRO, Ed. 84/58, 19 February 1900.

256. *The Quadrangle: the eastern wall as completed, c. 1901. The present ornamental trees were not planted until 1947*

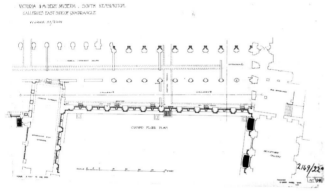

257. *(above) Mosaic panel for the decoration of the new easternmost bay of the Lecture Theatre block*

258. *(centre left)*, 259. *(below left) Sir Aston Webb's new Museum designs: plan, c. 1900, of the ground floor of the east side of the quadrangle, showing the eastern extension of the Lecture Theatre block, the re-alignment of the Quadrangle's eastern wall, and the addition of two bays at the southern end. The roof above, from the north.*

260. *(below) Sir Aston Webb's new Museum designs: elevations and plans of the first floor of the extension of the Lecture Theatre building*

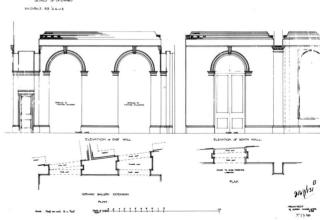

261. *The Administration of the Department of Science and Art in 1899. Sir John Donnelly is seated in the centre of the front row; at the end on the left, is Thomas Armstrong, and Major-General Festing on his left; Sir Caspar Purdon Clarke is seated second from right.*

red brick and terracotta (by Doulton) are so closely modelled on the work by Godfrey Sykes that at a casual glance they are indistinguishable. However, on close inspection, particularly at the north-east angle, where the old work is joined by the new, there is a distinct change in the colour of the terracotta, the newer work being much more yellow. Above, the north-east roof angle is a sham, supported on brackets at the rear, purely to give a unified appearance to the quadrangle. The firm responsible for some of the work, Diespeker, was asked to supply a mosaic panel (the easternmost) to match the existing five. No one had paid much attention to these until the time came to make a match. 'On looking more closely ...,' commented Webb, 'I find they are processions of figures apparently those engaged at that time in the management of the museum.'[11]

257   Webb felt that he should not duplicate one of the existing panels, but produce a new one. Consultations were therefore set on foot to choose worthy subjects for representation. General Festing, head of the Science Museum, to whom the matter was referred, suggested that these might be officials of the Science and Art Department and the Board of Education. Eventually it was decided that the portraits should be of Sir Francis Sandford (Secretary of the Education Department, 1870–84 and of the Department of Science and Art 1874–84), General Donnelly (his successor at South Kensington, 1884–99), Sir George Kekewich (Secretary of the Education Department and later the Board of Education, 1890–1902), Sir William Abney (Director for Science at South Kensington 1893–9, and Principal Assistant Secretary at the Board of Education, 1899–1903), Sir Edward Poynter and Sir Thomas Armstrong (Directors for Art at South Kensington, 1875–81 and 1881–98), Sir Philip Cunliffe Owen and Sir Caspar Purdon Clarke (Directors of the South Kensington Museum, 1873–93 and 1896–1905), Walter Crane (Principal of the Royal College of Art, 1898–9) and Aston Webb.

The new extension on the east side of the quadrangle, for the Dyce Library, was ready for occupation in December 1901.[12] The remainder of the galleries on that side of the quadrangle were available for plastering and wiring by June 1902. Leslie & Co. undertook the joinery there for

11. PRO, Ed. 84/68, 23 March 1901.
12. Ibid., 20 December 1901.

£1,913 18s 7d; the plastering was executed by a Mr Bickley for £934 0s 4d; Minton, Hollins extended the tiled floor of the Ceramic Gallery for £142 18s;[13] and there was difficulty in obtaining a wood-block floor up to the specification.[14]

The Ceramic Gallery and the gallery beneath it had elaborate painted ceilings, and the new bay would have to be decorated in keeping. Webb approached the Principal of the Royal College of Art, Augustus Spencer, and it was decided (with the agreement of Sir William Abney, and Sir Schomberg McDonnell at the Board of Works) that this new decoration should be carried out, as the rest of the ceilings had been, by College students.[15] Work began on 4 December 1902.

At the end of the following January, the students petitioned their Principal:

> We were asked by you to undertake the decoration of two ceilings in the ... Victoria and Albert Museum. We have been engaged on this work since the 4th December last and it is now well in hand, but, up to the present, we have received no notification as to any form of remuneration for the same.
>
> As the work necessitates the entire cessation of our studies during the time we were engaged upon it, and in consequence entails considerable loss to ourselves, may we ask you to permit us to withdraw from it unless our labours receive some recognition ... Edward Walker, E. E. Atkins, H. Woollen, Gordon M. Forsyth, A. E. Martin, W. W. Rawson.

No one had considered the necessity of paying the students. Spencer suggested that the student in charge should be paid 25s a week, while the remainder might make do with a pound. He settled on these figures because they were the rates at which Moody's assistants had been paid. A total of £206 5s 0d was required.[16] The Board of Works was asked to find the money, but Abney demurred, and asked Webb if something could be found in the building vote. This, however, contained no provision for decorations. An argument dragged on until May, when the Office of Works grudgingly agreed to pay the students 15s a week, with £1 for their leader. The Office ruled that 'any future employment of students should be made the subject of a further communication', and so far as is known, students have only once again been employed in the Museum, in 1913, in the Ceramic Gallery.

A much more difficult problem involving the Royal College of Art was set by the need to expand its accommodation. As we have seen, Walter Crane had tried to take over the attics of the Residences in 1899 (see p. 209), but had to make do with the assurance that the College could occupy the top floor of that wing after it had been rebuilt. A year later, on 8 June 1900, these promised premises were declared inadequate: Sir William Abney proposed to Sir George Kekewich that the College should take over the whole top floor of the new museum building, giving up in exchange the premises it currently occupied. This was regarded as a fair exchange; and Webb thought it feasible. Sir John Gorst, Vice-President of the Committee of Council on Education approved, and on 20 June was taken round the College premises by Alan Cole, Sir Henry Cole's son: he found them crowded with partitions, curtain and obsolete casts and suggested that they should be cleared up as a priority measure.[17]

Reginald Brett, now Lord Esher, told the Treasury about the Royal College proposal on 8 August 1900, asserting that 'Mr. Aston Webb ... considers that the cost of adapting the top floor next Cromwell and Exhibition Roads ... would not, as far as the requirements are at present known, affect his estimate.' As for adapting the college buildings for museum use, Webb estimated that this would cost an extra £10,000.[18] This proposal was approved.

Webb thereupon busied himself in the preparation of new plans. He proposed that the College should occupy the premises right from the Ceramic Staircase. There was to be access from the staircase at the Exhibition Road entrance, as well as from those in Rooms 124 and 128. The College Library was in Room 141, on either side of which was the Antique Room (Room 140) and the Figure and Mural Decoration Room (Room 142). From both of these rooms staircases led to additional studios above, flanking the central tower which, with a spiral staircase, was to be the Library's bookstore. Two years later, however, a Parliamentary question from Sir

264
265
266
267

---

13. PRO, Works 17/22/12, 12 May 1902.
14. Ibid., 21 April 1903.
15. PRO, Ed. 34/68, 2 December 1902.
16. Ibid., 6 February 1903.
17. PRO, Ed. 84/58.
18. Ibid.

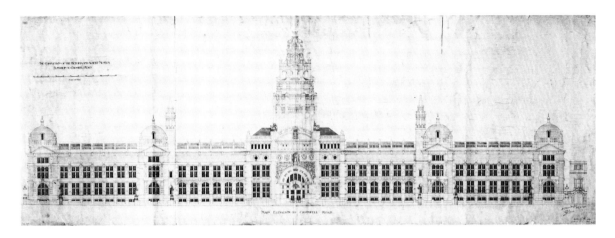

262. (above) Sir Aston Webb's new Museum designs:
elevation to Cromwell Road, 1900, showing further
modifications to the skyline

263. (below right) Detail (redrawn) of the central tower

Francis Powell to the Parliamentary Secretary to
the Board of Education, Sir William Anson,
elicited the view that allotting the top floor of the
new building to the College 'might be regarded as
prejudicial' to the arrangement of the Museum.[19]

Negotiations between the Board of Education,
the Office of Works, and the Treasury[20] eventually
led to the abandonment of the proposed change.
The top floor reverted to the Museum, and Webb
produced his finally revised plans in July 1904,[21]
in which the central tower simply became an
empty shell.

In October of that year, the Museum was
thrown into agitation when the progress of the
building works required that the Art Director,
the Science Director, the Assistant Art Director,
the clerical staff and the messengers should lose
their rooms. It was proposed that the ground floor
of the new eastern range of the quadrangle, which
had just been rebuilt and filled with exhibits,
should now be emptied again and partitioned off
to form temporary offices.[22] The Office of Works

19. PRO, Ed. 84/215, 22 June 1903.

20. PRO, Ed. 84/58, 25 November, 30 November, 3 December
1903, 9 February 1904, 22 February 1904.

21. PRO, Ed. 84/72, 5 August 1904. A plan of the second floor as
adapted for the College's use in the RIBA Drawings Collection
(OS4/21/9), together with the plan revised for the Museum (OS4/
21/10). Other related drawings in the PRO, are Works 33/2233,
2235, 2257, 2267, 2280, 2316.

22. PRO, Ed 84/58, 12 November 1904.

264. *(above) Sir Aston Webb's new Museum designs: plans and elevation to Cromwell Road, 1904, with the Tower modified to contain bookstores.*

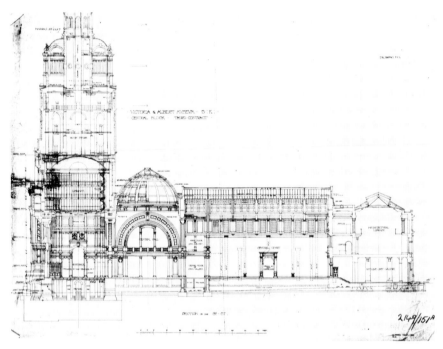

265. *(left) Sir Aston Webb's new Museum designs: section through the Main Entrance, Central Tower, Room 49, Room 43 and Library, c. 1904, showing the Tower modified to contain the Library and book stores of the Royal College of Art*

266. *(below left) Sir Aston Webb's new Museum designs: perspective view from the south-west, 1904, after a drawing by T. Raffles Davison*

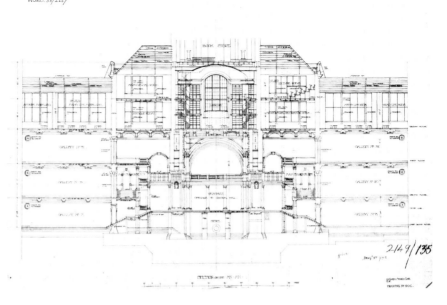

267. *(right) Sir Aston Webb's new Museum designs: section through the Entrance Hall from the south, c. 1904, showing the top floor incorporating accommodation for the Royal College of Art*

268. *Sir Aston Webb's new Museum designs: elevation of the Main Entrance and Tower, c. 1904, with variations from the published design of 1904*

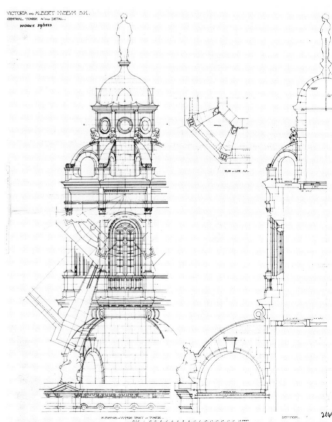

269. *Sir Aston Webb's new Museum designs: part elevation, section and plan of the lantern of the Central Tower proposed in a design of c. 1904*

sensibly quashed this idea, and the problem diminished on closer examination: only one of the old offices need be vacated for alteration at a time, and consequently only one temporary office need be found. A room was discovered off the Ceramic Gallery. It was full of music belonging to the Bach Choir, who, since 1878, had rehearsed in the Lecture Theatre on winter Tuesday evenings. The Bach Choir was evicted.[23]

In 1905 the basement was prepared, to accommodate the Circulation, Packing and Reception departments. It was the intention that these should occupy the lower ground floor of the new building: Rooms 1 to 6 were for Circulation, while the other departments would occupy Rooms 8 and 9. Between them Aston Webb was asked to provide a subway as wide and as straight as possible, so that objects and cases could easily be moved between the two areas. It was thought, also, that a trolley track would be an added convenience.[24] The sloping bed of the track can still be followed in the basement. Access to the basement for vans was by a ramp from the office entrance at the south-east corner of the site. In November an enquiry from the Geological Survey was received regarding the water levels. In excavating for the foundations it was found that there was no uniform waterline, and no tidal influence had been noted at the point where water had been encountered. This had been at the north-western portion of the site, the remainder of which was practically free from water. Under the central tower the excavations passed through gravel into London clay at about the average level of +8.00 ordnance datum, and only a trickle of water had been noticed over the surface of the clay. The tower foundations were laid at a level of +1.13 ordnance datum.

Aston Webb asked, in April 1906, if the stores under the western gallery should be lit by glass pavement lights. The storekeeper, Saltmarsh, was consulted. His reply, expressed with troglodyte humility in the third person, was:

that remembering the dark places which have hitherto been very largely the share of his section in the buildings here, he is grateful for your consideration in projecting this additional light, and that he hesitates to express an opinion in the direction of diminishing light. At the same time he does not think that the light which would be obtainable through the pavement lights would be worth the expense of securing it. Towards this view he is in

part moved by the feeling that the Museum Authorities would more than likely wish in time to place cases or objects over the lights and that, in any case, the public passing to and from over such lights as were in the gangway would so interfere with the illumination of the store below that electric light would be required in any case.

Slowly the building began to be brought into use; by the end of October 1906 the Offices on the south side of the Library were ready for occupation.[25] A few days later F. G. Ogilvie, of the Education Department, asked Aston Webb if he had any plans to 'deal in some way with the present unsightly south gable' of the office block adjacent to Brompton Oratory.[26] This had been left during the nineteenth century so that it could be incorporated into Fowke's, and later Scott's plans for the completion of the building. Ogilvie presumed that there was the intention to face it in some way, now that it was to be left exposed. He had, however, not heard of any proposals – and presumably there was none, as this southern end has to the present day retained its unfinished appearance.

The full size of the new building now began to become apparent. Webb, in a description of the building written for the first edition of the new Museum guide, recorded that it had *270*

a frontage of 720 feet to Cromwell Road and 275 feet to Exhibition Road; the total length of the perimeter of the site is occupied by three stories of side-lighted galleries; the Fourth Floor galleries being top-lighted; the remainder of the site is covered with top-lighted Courts. The total length of these galleries alone is three-quarters of a mile, but including the long gallery of two floors that runs down the centre of the building, the galleries in the new building are just one mile in length, while the top-lighted courts have a superficial area of 6,500 square yards, or nearly $1\frac{1}{2}$ acres.

Of the interior Webb remarked: *271*

The planning . . . has been laid out on as simple lines as a building of this scale will allow, and the necessity of conveniently linking it up to and adapting it to the various levels of the old building were considerations which greatly increased the difficulty of the problem.

23. November 1904.
24. PRO, Ed. 84/58, memorandum on space, 14 March 1905.
25. PRO, Ed. 84/58, letter from Office of Works, 24 October 1906.
26. Ibid., 9 November 1906.

270. *Aerial view of the Museum*

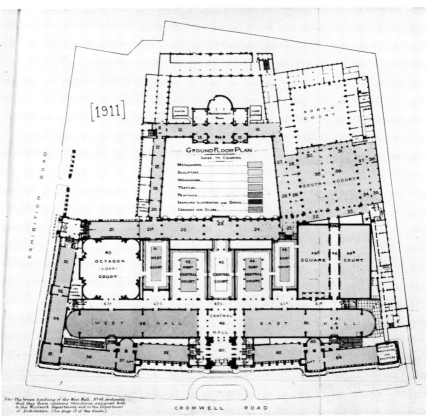

271. *Ground plan of the Museum, 1911*

272. *The Entrance Hall*

273. *(above) The east staircase adjoining the Entrance Hall, in course of construction*

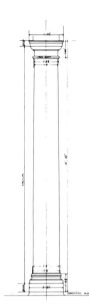

274. *(above right) Sir Aston Webb's new Museum designs: elevation of a marble column in the Entrance Hall*

272　　On passing through the entrance doors a vestibule is entered 40′ × 40′ running through two floors of the building. The walls are faced with Portland stone, while the ceiling is in teak, carved and inlaid with holly . . .

273　　To the right and left of this vestibule are the staircase leading to the three floors of side lighted-galleries. The walls of these staircases are lined with pavonazza marble in flat slabs; the columns are of brescia and the steps themselves of piastraccia. The lower part of the walls of these stairs and the entrance vestibule are the only portions of the interior not intended for the exhibition of objects. The walls of the galleries and courts, therefore, are kept perfectly plain and free from architectural features of any kind. On the other hand, an attempt has been made to prevent weariness to the visitor by avoiding galleries of undue length, by providing vistas and glimpses through the building in passing, and by varying the sizes, proportions, and design of the various courts and galleries.

The Long Gallery, again, forms an easy means of communication to all the Courts on either side, and this enables a visitor at a glance to get a general idea of the contents of the Museum and what there is to see.

All the Courts in the North side of this gallery are also themselves connected so that the visitor can pass readily through from one to the other.

Passing through the Vestibule, the visitor reaches the domed Central Hall, with the long Eastern and Western Halls, 50 feet wide, for large Architectural exhibits leading off to the right and left, and beyond is the Central Court forming the main entrance to the older portion of the Museum. On either side of this Entrance Hall are the West and East central courts, with nave and aisles divided by arcades of the Basilican type, the aisles being vaulted and the naves having flat ceilings. Further to the West of these is the great Octagon Court, 110 feet in diameter, and 65 feet high in the centre.

Webb went on to stress the even lighting of the side-lit galleries; the Plenum system of air-conditioning, which changed the air four times an hour ('so necessary to prevent lassitude to visitors'); the teak floors of the galleries; and the mosaic marble floors of the Courts, 'laid out in squares to facilitate the arrangement of cases and objects'. The marble work was entrusted to Farmer & Brindley, whose estimate for £13,699 was the lowest received. This was the firm who had recommended piastraccia to Webb for use on the treads, risers and pavings of the staircases, as being more durable than the Sicilian marble favoured by the architect. The extra cost was £297. The decorative plaster in the new building was by

PLATE XXXV *(opposite) John Flaxman, by Bertram Pegram; one of the statues of famous artists on the principal façade of the Museum*

PLATE XXXVI *(opposite) The main entrance and the central tower from Thurloe Square*

G. P. Bankart and the Bromsgrove Guild, and Hart, Son & Peard executed the metalwork.[27]

In August 1906 the building was, with the exception of the central tower, sufficiently finished for most of the scaffolding to be removed. For the first time the edifice could be seen, and, as the *Pall Mall Gazette* (21 August 1906) told its readers, 'one can now grasp its magnitude and stateliness crowned with imposing domes and cupolas.

The *Yorkshire Post* (25 August 1906) felt that, although there was still at least two years' more work, Aston Webb had succeeded in his efforts to produce a building in which dignity of style was happily blended with an airy lightness, in admirable keeping with the purpose to which the structure was to be devoted. 'The massive stonework, which affords ample scope for the exercise of the sculptor's craft, is relieved by a rich red brick frieze – an effect pleasing enough now to the eye, but which the accumulated dirt of a few years hence will doubtless modify considerably.'

The *Tribune* (12 September 1906), while informing its readers that the scaffolding had consisted of some 40,000 poles, of an average length of 35 feet, also waxed poetic:

> Those who saw the building on one of the dark evenings of last January are hardly likely to forget the splendid picture it presented when it was still draped in its network of scaffolding – a great and mysterious mass of soaring lines silhouetted against the infinite delicacy of a winter sunset. The huge derricks swung athwart the evening light, with just a wisp of steam to emphasize the shadows of the dusk. A touch of colour was added by the green screens behind which the sculptors worked, flapping to and fro in the wind.

The sculptors here referred to were engaged upon a quite ambitious programme of exterior decoration. As we have seen, Webb deliberately kept the interior plain. Even though King Edward VII had intervened in January 1905 to ask for more interior decoration,[28] the Museum authorities resisted the suggestion. Decoration in the style that Henry Cole had sponsored was no longer in fashion. But sculpture on the exterior was quite in order.

275. *Sir Aston Webb's new Museum designs: elevation, plan and sections of the Main Entrance and Central Tower, as built. Drawn by Ralph Knott*

The decorative sculpture

The question of the sculpture was broached by Webb to the Office of Works on 2 January 1905.[29] After much consideration and consultation with the Director, he had devised a scheme. The climax of the decoration was to be around the main entrance in the centre of the Cromwell Road façade. A statue of Queen Victoria was to be in the place of honour over the great arch. She was to be flanked by St George and St Michael, and below her, above the doors but within the arch, would be Prince Albert. The present King and Queen

275

---

27. PRO, Works 17/22/15, 20 February 1905.
28. Ibid., 24 January 1905.
29. PRO, Works 17/22/16.

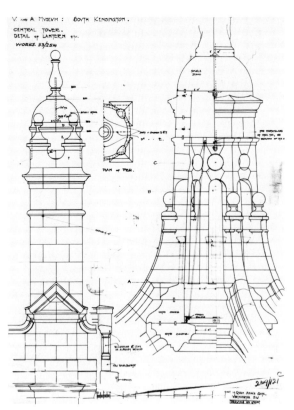

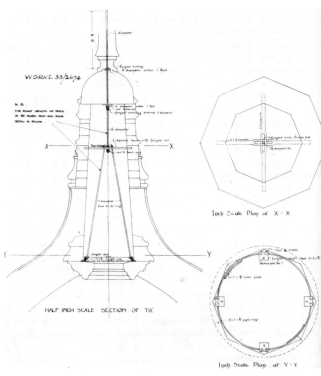

276. *Sir Aston Webb's new Museum designs: elevation of a pinnacle and the lantern of the Central Tower, c. 1906*

277. *Sir Aston Webb's new Museum designs: section and plans showing the steelwork of the lantern of the Central Tower, c. 1906.*

would occupy niches to each side of the entrance.

278 The great archway itself would be enriched with symbolic sculpture. The large bosses in the archivolt would represent various crafts; the large spandrels would have figures representing Truth and Beauty; while the two smaller niches on either side would have statues representing Imagination and Knowledge. Groups on the balustrade of the Central portion would represent Painting, Sculpture, Architecture and the Crafts; with the Royal Arms in the centre. The central dome was to be 'crowned by a bronze gilt winged figure of Fame'.

The rest of the sculpture was to consist of 'single statues, spaced out along the entire façade, in the niches between the windows on the First Floor'. Webb suggested that the statues should represent ten English painters, occupying 'the central curtains of the Cromwell Road front', while the West and East curtains of this front would accommodate, respectively, six English sculptors and six English architects. Ten English craftsmen would fill the Exhibition Road front.

Webb's suggestions, approved by Sir John Taylor and Sir Schomberg McDonnell at the Office of Works, then ascended to the King, who at this moment made his attempt (mentioned above) to divert Webb onto the interior decoration. He withdrew his objections, however, and Webb was given authority to proceed on 22 February. A month later, Webb sent in his total estimated costs, and reported that he had already commissioned several sculptors.[30]

The main ensemble around the great arch was allotted to Alfred Drury (1856–1944), who undertook to carve the Prince Consort (for £700), Queen Victoria (£600), St Michael and St George (£500), Imagination and Knowledge (£600) and nine panels in the arched entrance (£1,800). Drury had trained at the South Kensington art schools when Jules Dalou was teaching there; he subsequently worked under Dalou in Paris and Sir Edgar Boehm in London before establishing his

279
280
281

30. Ibid., 21 March 1905.

278. *(above) The Main Entrance, with the sculptured figure of* Prince Albert *by Alfred Drury in the centre, and, in the spandrels above,* Truth *(left and* Beauty *(right) by Sir George Frampton*

279. *(far left)* Queen Victoria, *a sculptured figure by Alfred Drury above the Main Entrance*

280. *(centre left)* St George, *a sculptured figure by Alfred Drury above the Main Entrance*

281. *(left)* Inspiration *a sculptured figure by Alfred Drury at the Main Entrance*

282. *(above left) Carved portraits of Queen Victoria and Prince Albert in the Entrance, probably by W. S. Frith*

283. *(left) Placing the head on the statue of* Fame *on the lantern of the Central Tower, 1906*

284. *(above right)* Fame, *a sculptured figure by Professor Lantéri and students of the Royal College of Art, on the lantern of the Central Tower*

own reputation in the 1850s. His 'quiet, contemplative art' was said to be 'always in search of the graceful, the tender, the placid',[31] and these qualities are well seen in his statues of 'Knowledge' and 'Imagination'. W. S. Frith (d. 1924), who, though primarily a teacher, specialized in architectural decorative sculpture and had worked under Webb on the Victoria Law Courts, Birmingham, undertook 'carving generally' for £8,991 11s 0d. Webb had begun to approach sculptors for the single figures along the façade (which were to be 7 feet 6 inches high): he hoped that various artists would each undertake a pair, at £150 each;

31. M. H. Spielmann, *British Sculpture and Sculptors of To-Day*, 1901, pp. 114, 109. Many of the sculptors who worked on the V&A are discussed in this work.

285. *(below) Sir Aston Webb's new Museum designs: part elevation over the Main Entrance, c. 1905, later altered and here inscribed 'All cancelled above line of Main Cornice'*

286. *(right) Sir Aston Webb's new Museum designs: elevation, section and plan of the niches for statues on the Cromwell Road and Exhibition Road façades*

INCH DETAILS of FIRST FLOOR WINDOWS of GALLERIES.

WORKS. 33/2587

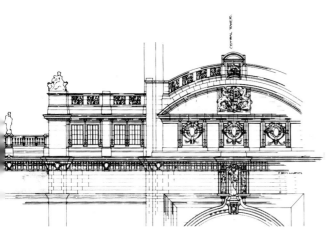

287. *(right) Four of the sculptured figures (Lord Leighton, G. F. Watts, John Constable, Sir John Millais) for the Cromwell Road façade of the Museum; a composite photograph made in 1907*

the total for 34 statues would be £5,100. He had asked Edward Lantéri, Professor of Sculpture at the Royal College of Art, to select four of his students to carve one figure each under his supervision: these students were Vincent Hill, Reginald Goulden, Sidney Boyes and J. A. Stevenson, who received £130 each, Lantéri accepting £80.

At this stage Webb had not found sculptors to undertake the spandrels of the entrance arch (£1,500), the statues of the King and Queen (£400), the crowning figure of Fame (£150), and fifteen seated figures at the feet of the domes (£1,500). These latter were never executed; nor were the figures on the central balustrade which Webb mentioned in his original plan.

Progress was most rapid with the figures on the façade, which had to be carved *in situ*. The selected Portland stone had been built into the piers, and

283
284

285
286
287

229

coursed with the rest of the masonry; this is very clearly shown in contemporary photographs. Each sculptor was asked to submit a model, of a quarter real size, placed in a model of the niche, which was supplied to him. When the figure had been approved, the artist had to make a full-size version in plaster which was then placed in its correct site on the façade in order that its effect might be judged. Not much time was allowed; the smaller model had to be ready within one month of the acceptance of the commission, and two months after that the large plaster model had to be finished. 'As soon as the full size is approved the carving on the building is to be commenced and to be completed within 3 months of that date. The Sculptor will be asked to complete the stonework of the niche when his figure is finished and to leave it all complete and perfect for the agreed sum.' By the end of 1905, therefore, all the figures in the façade niches were complete.

This array of celebrated artists was one of the last attempts to present, on a public building, a pantheon of artistic immortals. Such a scheme of decoration had been tried already at South Kensington in the mosaics of the South Court, and a sculptural version could be seen not far away around the base of the Albert Memorial, where some ninety artistic figures are joined by musicians and writers.

Other such sculptural schemes may be found at the Alte Pinakothek, Munich; the New Hermitage, Leningrad; the Royal Academy, London. There are painted schemes at both the Alte Pinakothek and the Neue Pinakothek, Munich and at the Ecole des Beaux-Arts, Paris. All these displays belong to the nineteenth century, and are a result, perhaps, of

> the particular frame of mind in which the nineteenth-century writer or historian looked both at his own period and at the past. It was perhaps the first time that the factors of eclecticism of taste, historicism of outlook and the wish to make knowledge available and accessible to a wider public than had ever been the case before, were combined with the confidence that was necessary to present a value judgement in such permanent form.[32]

The Victoria and Albert Museum's pantheon was conspicuously nationalistic.

The painters who were represented need no introduction. The sculptors who executed these

included the four students, and the other three were relatively unknown. The statues were:

William Hogarth by Reuben Sheppard
Sir Joshua Reynolds by Reuben Sheppard
Thomas Gainsborough by S. Nicholson Babb
George Romney by S. Nicholson Babb
Richard Cosway by Ernest George Gillick
J. M. W. Turner by Ernest George Gillick
John Constable by Vincent Hill
G. F. Watts by Richard Reginald Goulden
Lord Leighton by Sydney Boyes
Sir J. E. Millais by James Alexander Stevenson

The architects represented were:

William of Wykeham by John Wenlock Rollins
John Thorpe by John Wenlock Rollins
Inigo Jones by Oliver Wheatley
Sir Christopher Wren by Oliver Wheatley
Sir William Chambers by Gilbert Bayes
Sir Charles Barry by Gilbert Bayes

Of these Jones, Wren, Chambers and Barry were all classicists. The Gothic Revival is not commemorated here, though A. W. N. Pugin and Sir Gilbert Scott were admitted to the Albert Memorial. William of Wykeham (1324–1404) and John Thorpe (c. 1565–1655) were probably not architects at all. The former is associated with the building of Winchester College and New College, Oxford, as founder rather than architect. The latter left many architectural drawings of Elizabethan houses but is no longer thought to have designed them. The sculptor J. W. Rollins (born 1862) had worked on Croydon Town Hall (1894–5) and Birmingham General Hospital (1896–7), and executed a colossal statue of Queen Victoria in Belfast. Oliver Wheatley (d. after 1920) was trained at South Kensington and had worked on the interior decoration of the Royal College of Music; and Gilbert Bayes (1872–1953) was a young sculptor who had mainly worked at small scale, specializing in wax groups and low reliefs, but later created the Selfridge's clock and was President of the Royal Society of British Sculptors from 1938 to 1943.

The six sculptors represented on the façade included Alfred Stevens (1817–75), whose influence had been strong at South Kensington

---

32. Paul Hetherington, 'Pantheons in the *Mouseion*: An aspect of the history of taste', *Art History*, i (1978), 214–28 (215).

(though indirect). John Bacon (1740–97) was renowned for elaborate funerary monuments in churches from Westminster Abbey to Jamaica; while the best-known work of J. H. Foley (1818–74) was the statue of the Prince Consort in the Albert Memorial. The line of sculptors comprised:

Grinling Gibbons by W. S. Frith
John Bacon the Elder by W. S. Frith
John Flaxman by Bertram Pegram
Sir Francis Chantry by Bertram Pegram
John Foley by James Gamble
Alfred Stevens by James Gamble

The English craftsmen who were represented included some names that must have been unfamiliar to the man in the street, as he looked up at the statues along Exhibition Road.

St Dunstan by F. Lynne-Jenkins
William Torel by F. Lynn-Jenkins
William Caxton by Paul Raphael Montford
George Heriot by Paul Raphael Montford
Huntington Shaw by Abraham Broadbent
Thomas Tompion by Abraham Broadbent
Thomas Chippendale by Albert Hodge
Josiah Wedgewood by Albert Hodge
Roger Payne by Arthur George Walker
William Morris by Arthur George Walker

St Dunstan was, of course, a goldsmith and metalworker (he seized the Devil by the nose with his red-hot tongs). William Torel was another metalworker, who executed the bronze effigies of Queen Eleanor and Henry II in Westminster Abbey in the 1290s. Caxton is renowned as England's first printer. George Heriot (1563–1624) was a goldsmith in Edinburgh and later His Majesty's jeweller to James I in London. Huntington Shaw (1660–1710) was a blacksmith, reputed (on shaky evidence) to have made the famous iron screen at Hampton Court. Tompion (1639–1713) is well known as the father of English clockmaking. Roger Payne (1739–97) was a bookbinder; and Chippendale, Wedgwood and Morris are household names.

The sculptor A. G. Walker (1861–1939) produced lissom nudes, and, more memorably, the exterior sculpture on the unnerving Agapemonite Church, Stamford Hill; his best-known work must be the statue of Florence Nightingale in Waterloo Place, London. Lynn-Jenkins (1870–1927) specialized in Art Nouveau coloured friezes.

288. *(above left)* Sculpture, *a sculptured figure by Professor Lantéri and students of the Royal College of Art, on the Central Tower*

289. *(above right)* Architecture, *a sculptured figure by Professor Lantéri and students of the Royal College of Art, on the Central Tower*

The others were up-and-coming young sculptors; Montford (1868–1938) provided sculpture for the Royal School of Mines in South Kensington.

By May 1905, Webb had chosen George Frampton (1816–1928) to carve the spandrels. 'They include figures of heroic size and great importance', Webb stressed when he wrote to the Office of Works; for Frampton required £1,000 for each, and Webb had only estimated £1,500 for both. He had, however, saved some money elsewhere.[33] Frampton was one of the most original English sculptors of the *fin de siècle*, often combining stone, metal, jewels and ivory in highly decorative small sculptures with a pronounced Art Nouveau feeling. The spandrels are not his most exciting work.

Professor Lantéri and his students undertook a further commission in January 1906: to provide the three statues for the central tower for £600. 'Sculpture' and 'Architecture' were placed in niches where the tower met the roofline of the façade. 'Fame', the topmost figure, was executed in marble, not (as had been planned) in gilt bronze, and therefore worked out cheaper than expected.

33. PRO, Works 17/22/14.

290. Queen Alexandra, *a sculptured figure by Sir William Goscombe John near the Main Entrance*

Webb had intended to pay Lantéri £140; £325 was to be paid for carving and £70 'for assistance to former students of the Royal College of Art'. That £48 was estimated for casting and £17 for 'armatures, etc.' shows that a bronze statue was still envisaged in January 1906.[34]

There was by now little additional sculpture left to consider; Frith had carved the Royal Arms over the Main Entrance, the artists' dates in cartouches under the main cornice, and undoubtedly the monograms in the parapet. The artists' dates were a refinement that was really a waste of time as, being some 70 feet above the ground, they cannot be easily seen, nor would many suspect they were there.

The First Commissioner was reminded by Webb in May 1906 that statues of Edward VII and Queen Alexandra were still required, and put forward the name of Goscombe John, as he had not done anything yet for the building, and was willing to carve the figures for 'the low price named', namely £200 each. 'I fear that we can only approve', the First Commissioner sighed to McDonnell, to which the latter unenthusiastically replied, 'I suppose so'.[35] William Goscombe John (1860–1952) was responsible for public statuary, representing distinguished personages, in towns all over the country; he, like all other sculptors who had worked on the new Museum, had to agree to the same conditions, including the carving of the stone already laid in the façade.

The last phase of the sculptured work was reached in December 1906, and concerned the nine panels under the arch of the Main Entrance. The original scheme had been for figures holding scrolls, on which were to be carved the names of various crafts – goldsmith, silversmith, and so on. Now that the scheme had matured, Webb considered that these names on the scrolls 'do not seem worthy of the position'.[36] He proposed instead a passage from Reynolds's *Discourses*.[37] 'Mr. Drury I may say entirely approves of this suggestion & finds the inscription could be well accommodated on the panels'. The finished works show a woman accompanied by one or more children, together with an attribute (except two), which are, from west to east; 1. a mirror; 2. an apple tree; 3. books; 4. none; 5. an Ionic capital; 6. none; 7. an oak tree; 8. statue of Venus; 9. a rising sun. The inscription selected by Webb is adapted from Sir Joshua Reynolds, 'The excellence of every art must consist in the complete accomplishment of its purpose'.

The final touch was added to the exterior of the building – the crowning glory was literally bestowed – when in October 1908, with photographers in attendance,[38] the head of the statue of Fame on the summit of the dome was triumphantly placed in position.

Rearrangement

Faced with a mile of empty galleries and an acre and a half of empty courts, the authorities had to

34. PRO, Works 17/22/16, 3 February 1905; final payment of £172 to Lantéri approved 22 March 1907.
35. PRO, Works 17/22/16, 12 May 1906.
36. Ibid., 1 December 1906.
37. Information supplied by Charles Gibbs-Smith; see Reynolds, *Discourses*, ed. Fry, 1905, p. 269.
38. Photograph reproduced in the *Daily Graphic*, 12 October 1908.

290

decide how to fill them. As we have seen, this problem had presented itself several times already. When the brief for the new building had been drawn up in 1890, the Department of Science and Art had made perfunctory estimates of the extra space required to house the collections. Later, in 1898, when the Chancellor of the Exchequer had the idea of using the new building for science as well as art, the art museum authorities had tried to draw up a more convincing statement of what was to be accommodated in the new building. But this had ended in the Chancellor and the Lord President of the Council haggling over whether carpets and calicoes deserved to be exhibited.

The Select Committee of 1897–8 had devoted some time to considering how the Museum should be laid out. It had taken note of a much publicized letter in *The Times* (dated 26 February 1897) from Charles Yriarte, which declared that the great treasures of the Museum 'are becoming so much heaped up as to be a veritable obstacle to study'; and one of its members, Sir Henry Howorth – historian, archaeologist, orientalist and scientist – had questioned witnesses about the arrangement of galleries. He pointed out that in the great Continental museums it was now thought desirable that 'you should illustrate the art of each period in a separate room or a separate gallery, and if you could have a series illustrating the reign of Louis XIV, and another that of Louis Quinze, and a third one of Louis Seize, it is better than having enormous rooms filled with a general collection of furniture, or a general collection of sculpture, or a general collection of enamels'.[39] Most of the questions on these lines were directed upon Purdon Clarke's deputy, Arthur Banks Skinner, who had joined the Museum in 1879, and had risen swiftly to become Assistant Director in 1896. So far as it is possible to tell from the printed record of the evidence, he was simply bemused by these questions about the arrangement of the Museum. In 1905 Purdon Clarke unexpectedly accepted a new post as Director of the Metropolitan Museum in New York. It brought him more money; but it was also said that he was leaving South Kensington as 'a dignified protest'[40] against his official superiors. Skinner succeeded him as Director.

He found on his new desk a request from the Office of Works to supply some information about the allocation of space in the new building, since

it was now time to install show cases and finish the walls where appropriate. The request, dated 19 May, had to wait until 2 November for a reply, transmitted through F. G. Ogilvie. It was not very helpful. Ogilvie's minute pronounced:

> It is not possible yet to set out in detail the allocation of space in the building, or even to state generally the sections of the collections which will fall to be exhibited in the various courts and galleries. Nevertheless, a consideration of the position, form, lighting, and adaptability of these rooms yields a certain limitation in the uses and in the methods of exhibition possible in the case of each.[41]

Gnomically, it went on:

> Certain courts are conspicuously adapted for specific classes of objects for which no other courts afford satisfactory accommodation; the finishing of such courts may therefore be carried out in view of the allocation of exhibits, which is thus obviously inevitable.

In principle, the allocation of exhibits may have been inevitable, but the minute, prepared by Skinner, failed almost completely to supply any hard facts.

By 1908, with the new building almost complete, the question of rearrangement had become urgent, and it was taken in hand by the new Secretary of the Board of Education, Robert Morant (1863–1920). 'To Morant administration was a great adventure. He had a passion for making the instruments of public service more effective ... There was no intermittence in his volcanic energy. He knew no rest and enjoyed no leisure. If opportunities presented themselves he took them; if they did not he made them.'[42] Settling the Museum's difficulties was no great problem for him.

He had started his career of public service as tutor to the King of Siam (having qualified himself with a first class degree in Theology from Oxford), and was engaged in social work at Toynbee Hall in the East End, when he found his first foothold on the ladder of educational administration in the Office of Special Enquiries and Reports of the Education Department. He became private

39. Select Committee 1898, Minutes of Evidence, para. 562.
40. *Morning Post*, 24 January 1905.
41. Confidential memorandum, Art Museum Series No. 3. PRO, Ed. 84/215.
42. *Dictionary of National Biography*.

secretary to Sir John Gorst and the Duke of Devonshire, thus exercising a powerful back-room influence on the education Ministry; this he consolidated in 1902 when he was the civil servant in charge of the Education Act seen through Parliament by A. J. Balfour. In 1903 he was appointed Permanent Secretary of the Board of Education, created in 1899. The Board was now reorganized into three sections under three Principal Assistant Secretaries; the section dealing with the Museum was that devoted to Technology and Higher Education in Science and Art, and its head was (Sir) Francis Ogilvie, later Director of the Science Museum.

At the start of 1908 Morant asked Ogilvie to obtain from A. B. Skinner 'a concise memorandum setting out his views as to the main principles on which he would himself think it best that the several spaces should be allocated ... Perhaps he has already something in black and white; in any case he must be so soaked in the subject that he can readily put his opinions on paper. I should be glad therefore,' somewhat peremptorily ordered Morant, 'if I could have the Memorandum at my house on Sunday.'[43]

Skinner produced his proposals quickly, for Ogilvie sent them up to Morant two days later.[44] He began, as Morant had requested him to do, by trying to establish some general principles.

> The general scheme to be maintained throughout, as far as possible, is an arrangement according to material ... Thus I should like to see the metal work together, the textiles together, the woodwork and furniture together, and so on ... Having gathered the various items of a section together, I should then proceed to subdivide, separating the east from the west, and then subdividing again into countries.

He went on to confront the principal problem of the new building:

> ... the dimensions of the various courts and rooms provided by the architect. Some of these courts, being very large and lofty, naturally suggest themselves as suitable for specimens of large size. Take for example, the large North-West Court. It would appear to be very suitable for such objects as the Bois-le-Duc Rood Screen, the Chapel from Santa Chiara in Florence, and other architectural specimens of a large size, which could either stand on the floor or be fitted into the four large apses. Again, the East Central and West Central Courts appear

to be adapted for tapestries, owing to the extent of wall space and the protection from the sun afforded by the special form of roof. The Central Court should be a feature of the building, and should be left fairly free as far as the floor space is concerned, but should have some striking works of art on the walls. Tapestries, as I shall indicate, will suit here.

> Heavy objects, as ironwork for example, should be arranged on the ground floor ...

'In this way,' he rather weakly concluded, 'determining factors may be found which will be of considerable assistance in deciding the allocation of certain objects.'

When he came systematically to specify the contents of the various galleries, he continued to lapse into vagueness and hesitancy. For example:

> It is proposed to leave Room 8 open to the public, but it will not contain anything of great importance. The wall might be hung with various paintings, such as copies of frescoes, &c., and have statuary on the floor. In one corner is a lavatory, and with it might be arranged a counter for cloaks and umbrellas.

Some of his suggestions were at the time inescapable. The series of rooms in the lower ground floor along the Cromwell Road front had from the first been destined for reception, packing, the students' competition exhibition, and the Circulation Department, and that was the use Skinner recommended for them. It was not his fault that another use was eventually found for them. (During the period between the wars, because Rooms 1–10 were so gloomy, mirrors were placed outside, behind the low wall in Cromwell Road and Exhibition Road, in an attempt to obtain more daylight in those galleries.) Some of his suggestions prevailed: the new galleries on the top floor, which he proposed for ceramics, are so used to this day. He even added some imaginative touches.

> I should very much like to see a different setting out of the quadrangle on the lines of an old English garden. and I would suggest that the paths be laid out as at Penshurst, with a fountain in the middle and beds of flowers on the lawns. The few lead figures could stand there without much harm and would have a very pleasing effect.

43. PRO, Ed. 84/215. 23 January 1908.
44. Ibid., 25 January 1908.

His final sentence sums up the character of his report: 'In submitting these ideas, I should not like to say that the scheme set forth is in any way final.' A desire to oblige, combined with an incapacity for clear thought, cut no ice with Morant. He rejected Skinner's proposals, and from now on Skinner's fortunes were on the wane.

Almost at once Morant set up a 'Committee of Re-arrangement', which met for the first time on 20 February 1908. Its terms of reference[45] were strict. It was instructed to devise a system of arrangement

> which will provide the greatest facilities for study primarily to those interested in the commercial manufacture of objects of a kind represented in the collection – craftsmen, designers, manufacturers, and students; and secondarily to those interested in Art without regard to its relation to industrial production – artists, students of art, of history, or manners and customs.

In thus giving to technology precedence over art Morant had in mind that

> the Museum was originally founded as an instrument for stimulating the improvement in this country of such manufactures and crafts as require and admit of decorative design. In adding to the collections, however, the precise nature of its original purpose has not been throughout rigidly observed ... It has thus come about that the Museum lacks a clear definition of function ... The Board are now anxious to secure that the precise purposes intended to be fulfilled by the Museum shall be clearly realised and co-ordinated.

In the light of history, Morant may seem to have been wrong. But he made sure that his view – 'the direct practical purpose of stimulating the craftsman and manufacturer and inspiring the designer and student who is engaged in the production of objects of modern manufacture' – should prevail. He appointed to his Committee three manufacturers – W. A. S. Benson, the metalworker; H. Powell, of the stained-glass firm; J. C. Wedgwood, of the pottery firm – and Lewis Day, whom *The Times* (21 November 1908) described as 'a designer of wall-papers'. The Chairman was Sir Charles Dilke, who resigned after the first meeting owing to pressure of work; and the Committee also included Cecil Harcourt Smith, Keeper of Greek and Roman Antiquities at the British Museum, who took over as Chairman.

Smith took the initiative by providing what Skinner had conspicuously lacked; analytical method. He circulated a memorandum, recommending that the Committee should first determine.

(a) the sections into which the Museum should be divided;
(b) the system on which the collections divided into these sections should be arranged.[46]

His memorandum continues chopping logic for some time, and no doubt helped to clarify the Committee's mind. Its report, produced speedily by 29 July 1908, and drafted presumably by its Secretary, Arthur C. Richmond, was a cogent and orderly document.

The Committee had decided that, before it could embark on the classification and arrangement of the Museum collections, it must take account of the internal administration of the Museum, and of its scope in relation to other national museums. Its important recommendations on the latter score, which still to a large extent determine the Museum's operations, need no consideration in a history of the buildings. But the three points it made about administration affected the layout of the building. First, it insisted that the expert staff should have offices near their galleries (p. 7) and not, as had been envisaged, in a separate office block. Second, it recommended that the Circulation Department should be an independent entity with its own collections and that it should be accommodated in and around the North Court at the rear of the Museum (pp. 7–10): thus the loading area and trolley way in the front cellars became redundant. Third, it recommended that the collections of the India Museum should be integrated into the Museum and accommodated into its galleries (pp. 10–11).

The Committee proposed (p. 18) that the Museum's collections should be divided between eight departments:

1. Architecture and sculpture.
2. Metalwork.
3. Woodwork, furniture, and leather.
4. Textiles.
5. Ceramics, enamels, and glass.
6. Paintings.
7. The Library.
8. Engraving, illustration, and design.

---

45. Quoted in the *Report*.
46. PRO, Ed. 84/215.

235

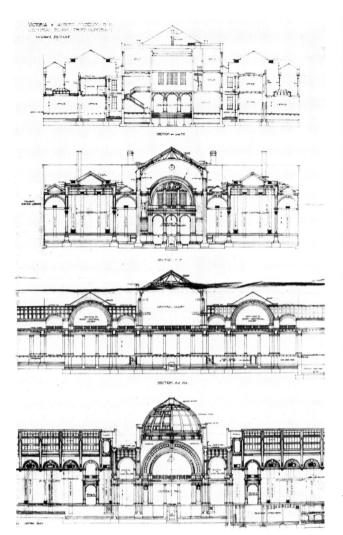

291. *(above left) Sir Aston Webb's new Museum designs: sections through the Library offices; Rooms 42, 43 and 44, from the south; Rooms 47 and 114, from the north; Rooms 48, 49 and 50 from the north.*

292. *(above right) Room 44, during construction, c. 1908*

Within these sections

1. There should be formulated for each section a reasonably logical scheme illustrating the technical and artistic development of the particular industry represented; and that scheme should, as nearly as possible, be adhered to in the arrangement of the specimens.
2. Where specimens are not available for the complete illustration of the sequence of development, attention should be drawn to the deficiencies by means of drawings and photographs, with the view of substituting for these, as time goes on, actual specimens acquired by gift or purchase.

In other words, the arrangement should be based, not so much on the existing material, as with the view to the eventual formation of series which shall illustrate in each section the complete development of process and design.

Aesthetic considerations were not entirely overlooked. The Committee concluded that the Museum was not to be simply a record of commercial practice: 'it seems to have been clearly intended that the chief aim should always be to improve the artistic quality of British design and production'. So what was inartistic must be excluded. But so also must anything that did not 'illustrate the development of technique' (p. 19).

Then the Committee began its attempt to realize its classification within the limits of the architecture. At once it encountered problems, and Morant encouraged the members to speak their mind about 'any unsatisfactory features in the ultimate scheme ... due to the structural disposition of the building'.[47]

47. Ibid.

First of all (p. 20), there were no offices in the new building. Another disadvantage was 'the enormous increase in Court accommodation, which was already in the old building too large; since for the great majority of the objects comprised in the Collections, Galleries rather than Courts offer the only suitable conditions for exhibition'. The Committee criticized also 'the absence of direct communication between the eastern and the western block of galleries on the first floor of the south front of the new building'. It further criticized 'the apparent absence of any organized principle on which the cases for the Museum were ordered (and indeed partly constructed)'. The Office of Works had endeavoured in 1905 to get some sense out of the Museum on this question, but A.B. Skinner's answers had not been helpful. As it was, 'the Committee understand that a general order for all the galleries was given for a uniform type of case, mounted on a marble plinth' (p. 24). Lastly the Committee condemned 'the same absence of any thought-out scheme adapted to modern ideas ... in the provision of lighting.' Ceiling lights were provided, but in the Committee's view, 'it is the objects on exhibition and their labels which need light, rather than the room in general' (p. 24).

These criticisms were gleefully seized on by the Press. The *Globe*, for instance, wrote on 25 November 1908:

It, indeed, furnishes food for reflection that almost before the scaffolding of the new buildings is taken down several of its structural features should be condemned, and that the experience of fifty years should be insufficient to a perfect planning. Three principal defects are pointed out, each of which would appear to the man in the street as patent defects, but which have (according to the report) been allowed to be introduced 'with the previous consent of all at the time concerned'.

The *Burlington Magazine* remarked (December 1908):

It seems rather unjust to lay these failings to the charge of Sir Aston Webb, as if he had somehow forced his design upon the nation. On the contrary, unsuitable as it has now proved, his plan was surely awarded the first place in a public competition?

And *The Times* (21 November 1908) made the fair but damaging comment:

293. *Room 50, in course of construction, c. 1908*

Most of the merits of this great and costly building are Sir Aston's own; its faults are those of the department which failed to form a clear idea at the outset of what the functions and organization of the Museum were to be and to instruct their architect accordingly.

In the placing of objects, the Committee were obliged to begin, as Skinner had, by fitting in large exhibits. They began with Webb's twin, top-lit, lengthy halls running to the right and left of the Main Entrance. In the West Hall an Indian doorway was already built in. The Santa Chiara Chapel from the North Court could neatly be inserted in the East Hall. This provided a basis for arranging other large objects: Oriental on one side, and Western on the other. No one accustomed to the topsy-turvy world of South Kensington would have noticed anything odd in the Committee's remark: 'It therefore seemed natural to place the Eastern objects in the West Hall, and the Western objects in the East Hall' (p. 25).

Webb's long corridor running east and west

294. (above) The Octagon Court, Room 40, in course of construction, c. 1908

295. (below) Sir Aston Webb's new Museum designs: sections (top) through the Exhibition Road galleries, Room 40 (Octagon Court) and Henry Scott's Room 41 (then the Science Library); and (below) through the Cromwell Road galleries, Room 48, Room 40 and the northern extension west of the Library

alongside these large halls was to be an 'architectural index' showing, in models, photographs and drawings, the development of architecture (Oriental on the west side, and Occidental on the east side, to correspond with the large exhibits). This interesting idea was never carried out.

The large central courts to the north of the corridor would have to contain large objects, which necessarily would be of various materials,

> but inasmuch as the courts form the starting point, as it were, from which the system of galleries radiates, there is nothing inconsistent in the arrangement by which the objects belonging to different sections should here converge and unite. (p. 28)

The rest of the galleries would be devoted to systematic arrangements by material: metalwork and woodwork on the ground floor, textiles on the first, ceramics on the second. For the glass gallery, the Committee attached a detailed plan of the cases. There would be three long rows

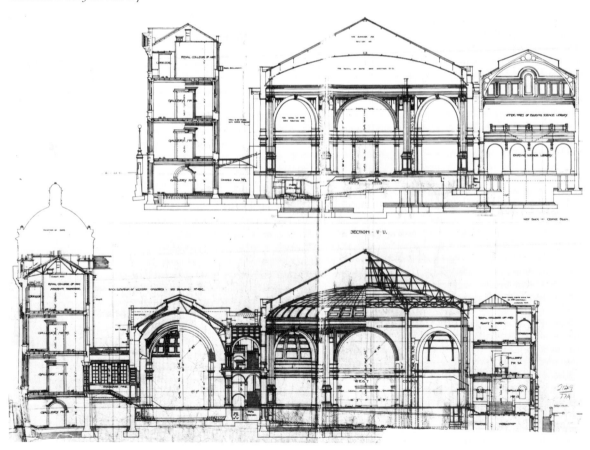

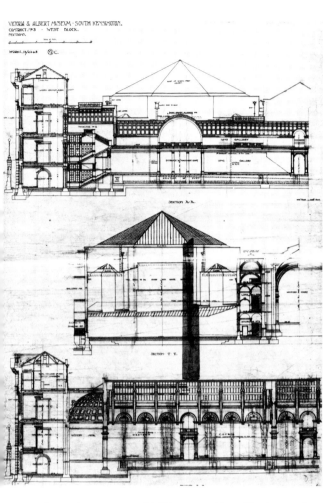

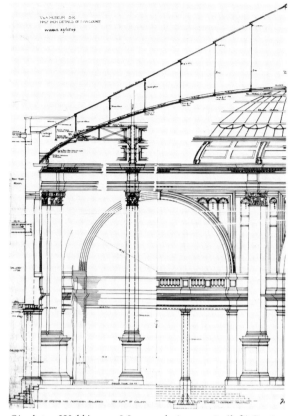

Sir Aston Webb's new Museum designs. 296. (left) Section through the galleries along Exhibition Road, and Room 47, from the south. 297. (above) Section through the Octagon Court, Room 40 and part elevation, from the south

(p. 32): one would illustrate 'ductility', another surface decorating by incision (carving, cutting, engraving, etching), the third surface decoration by enamelling, gilding and lustre. Such an arrangement seems lacking in charm.

The Committee made little of two problems. One was the presence of the Library in a suite of rooms on the first floor, blocking the way from the eastern to the western parts of the Museum. This blockage is still found annoying today. The other problem was Webb's great North-West, or Octagon, Court, which is almost useless for any purpose. The Committee hoped the problems might cancel each other out, and considered re-locating the Library in the domed Octagon Court, where it would have seemed like a younger brother of the British Museum Reading Room. But, they left it alone, and suggested that the Octagon Court should be used to display loans.

The Report of the Committee was evidently satisfactory to Morant. On 3 November 1908 he

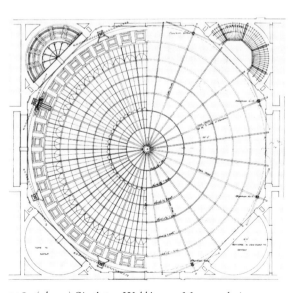

298. (above) Sir Aston Webb's new Museum designs: plan of the glass dome of the Octagon Court, Room 40, from below

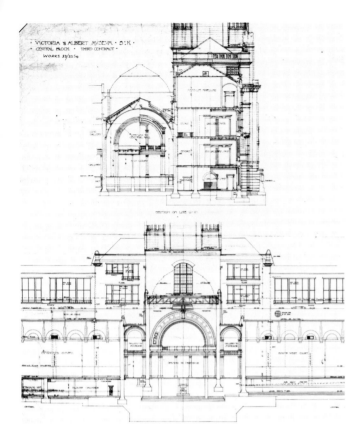

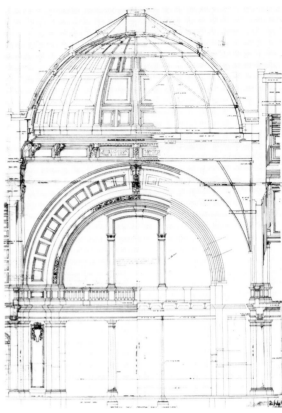

299. (above left) Sir Aston Webb's new Museum designs: sections (top) through Room 48 and the galleries along Cromwell Road from the west, and (below) through Rooms 50, 49 and 48 from the north

Sir Aston Webb's new Museum designs. 300. (above right) Section through Room 49, from the east. 301. (left) Half elevation and section of Room 49, showing plasterers' details. 302. (below) Half section of the dome of Room 49, showing plasterers' details

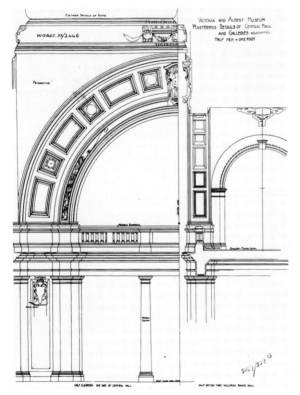

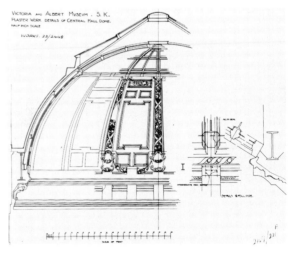

Sir Aston Webb's new Museum designs. 303. *(right) Sections (left) of the proposed rooms to the west of the Library after the removal of the staircase, and (right) through the Residences showing the proposed reconstruction of the west side.* 304. *(below) Section through the Residences, from east, showing the internal reconstruction*

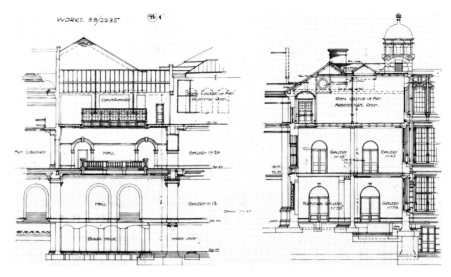

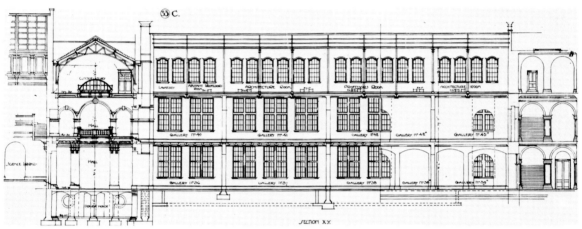

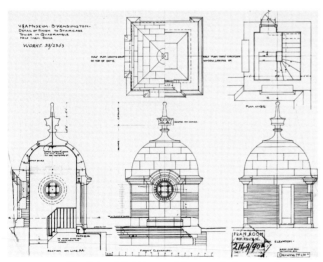

305. *Sir Aston Webb's new Museum designs: section, elevations and plans of the turret of the staircase at the south-west corner of the former Residences*

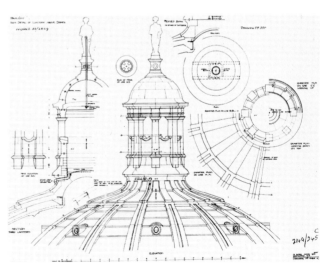

306. *Sir Aston Webb's new Museum designs: elevation, section and plans of the lanterns of the domes of the five pavilions along the façades*

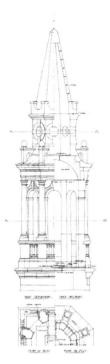

307. *(left) Sir Aston Webb's new Museum designs: half elevation, section and plans of the upper part of the lift shaft towers*

308. *(right) The Museum as built, from the south-west*

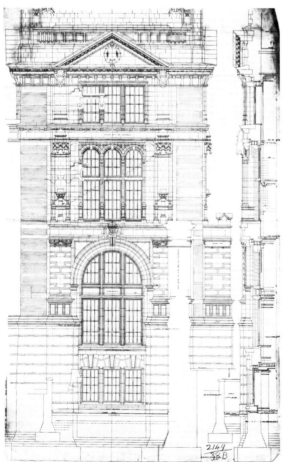

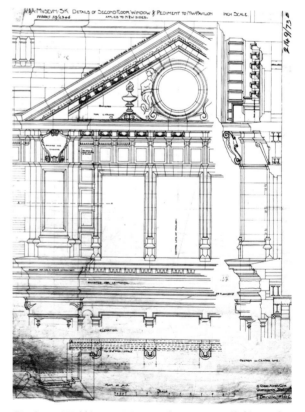

Sir Aston Webb's new Museum designs. 309. *(left) North elevation and part section of the north-west pavilion on the Exhibition Road façade.* 310. *(above) Elevation, section and plan of the window and pediment (see ill. 309)*

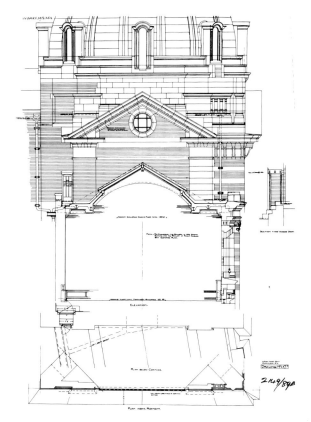

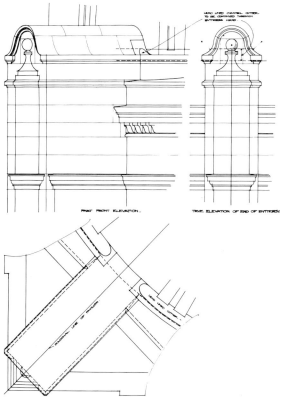

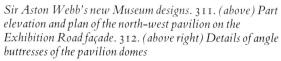

Sir Aston Webb's new Museum designs. 311. *(above) Part elevation and plan of the north-west pavilion on the Exhibition Road façade.* 312. *(above right) Details of angle buttresses of the pavilion domes*

313. *(below left) Room 143, during construction, c. 1908*

314. *(right) The corridor beneath the bridge leading from the Cast Courts gallery to Room 131, c. 1908*

315. *Room 144, c. 1908*

316. *A light fitting designed by Sir Aston Webb*

issued a circular,[48] announcing that it was to be implemented. The Museum was henceforth to enjoy greater autonomy in its affairs. Its administration would involve much greater responsibility than that called for by the 'strictly limited' duties of the existing post of Director. Consequently, this post was to be abolished, and would be replaced by a new post, 'entitled "Director and Secretary of the Art Museum"'. 'To this extremely responsible and onerous post the President [of the Council] has appointed Mr. C. H. Smith.' Skinner became Keeper of the Department of Architecture and Sculpture. Not long afterwards he died. Years later a former member of the staff, William Watts,

writing to Sir Ninian Cowper, recalled 'the case of Mr. Skinner who was deposed from being Director and died of a broken heart – "an official murder" as someone remarked at his funeral'.[49]

Cecil Smith set about his task vigorously. An official opening was in view in about six months' time, and the builder's men were still in the Museum. Smith consulted with his staff and with Webb, and undertook that, even though most of

---

48. Confidential memorandum, Art Museum series.

49. Letter from William Watts to Ninian Comper, 15 November 1942. (In the possession of the Rev. Anthony Symondson, to whom acknowledgement is made.)

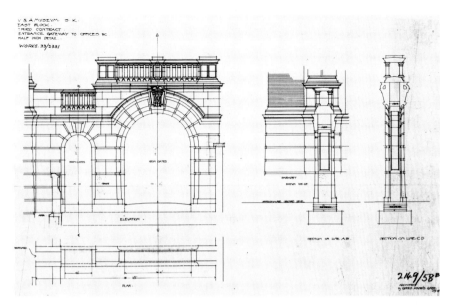

317. *(right) Sir Aston Webb's new Museum designs: elevations, sections and plan of gateway (not built) from Cromwell Road to Secretariat wing*

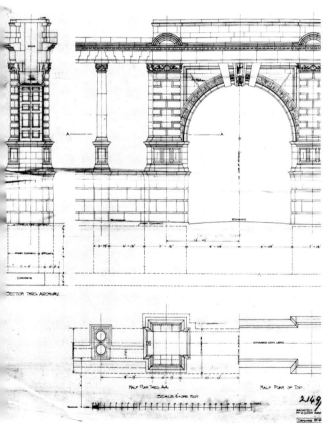

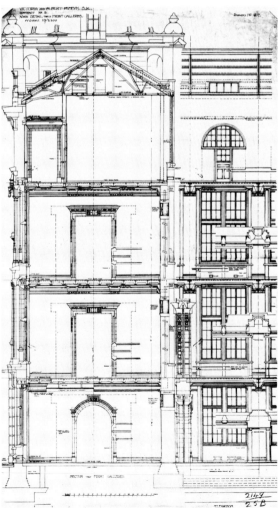

Sir Aston Webb's new Museum designs. 318. *(above) Part elevation, section and plan of the screen between the Science Schools (Henry Cole Building) and the north-west pavilion*

319. *(right) Section through the Cromwell Road galleries, from the east*

the wall cases would not be delivered until June 1909, the Museum would by then be sufficiently rearranged to justify opening the new building to the public.[50]

The newly arranged Museum proved, on the whole, disappointing. A German writer remarked that, although on the outside it was a palace, on the inside it was a warehouse, as it had been before; and he noted that King Edward VII at the official opening actually called it 'a *storehouse* of masterpieces worthy of the study of designers and manufacturers.'[51] A French writer complained about the white-painted interior ('ce blanc éclatant') and pleaded for a little pale blue or pale green to break up 'cette monotone et éblouissante blancheur'.[52] Claude Phillips, Keeper of the Wallace Collection and art critic of *The Daily Telegraph*, who had campaigned fiercely against the new system of arrangement, found himself 'overwhelmed by the vastness, the coldness, the nakedness' of the new halls. 'The general impression made by the naked, austere, too uniformly-lighted buildings themselves, and by the scientific or pseudo-scientific mode of classification and arrangement adopted is that of some immense, finely-appointed modern hospital for the analysis and dissection of applied art rather than that of a temple of the higher delight ...' The qualities of the works of art, 'the soul, the mysterious flower of spiritual beauty that is in them retires within itself, folds itself up, shrinks from contact with cold, unsympathetic surroundings.'[53] This was, perhaps, a melancholy result of years of effort, but it also offered the promise of a new beginning.

One further point remained to be settled before the opening of the new building: its name. When Queen Victoria had laid the foundation stone, she had bestowed the name 'Victoria and Albert Museum', but this had been adopted not only by the Art Museum, but by the Science Museum; above the entrance to its buildings west of Exhibition Road was a notice 'Victoria and Albert Museum, Science Collections'.

Smith[54] and Morant[55] felt that the time had come to restrict the name to the Art Museum. Anxious exegesis of the Queen's speech seemed to support this view. The King had to be consulted, of course. Morant wrote twice to his Private Secretary, Lord Knollys, but it was obvious that the Palace did not understand what was going on, and Morant had to go and explain to Lord Knollys

at Buckingham Palace on 21 June. Approval was given, and 25 June, the day before the opening, Morant issued a confidential instruction that the name 'Victoria and Albert' was not to be used by the Science Museum. Presumably to spike objections from the Science Museum, he required that: 'No steps are to be taken of a public nature ... to draw attention to the fact of this change of practice'.[56] But no one seems to have objected.

The Opening

The King agreed early in 1909 to open the Museum, and his servants embarked on the intricate task of choosing a suitable time for the ceremony. Nobody wanted to postpone it into 1910. But the autumn of 1909 was, as Cecil Smith pointed out, 'undesirable, as many people are away from London at that time'.[57] The King could not manage July. So June was chosen, and the King proposed either Saturday the 26th or Monday the 28th. The First Commissioner of Works reasoned:

> If the opening of the V. & A. Mus. is fixed for a Monday *afternoon* it makes it difficult for Peers or M.P.s to attend.
> If it is fixed for a Monday *morning* it is difficult for people to get up from the country & get into Court dress etc.
> If it was fixed for a Saturday near mid-day: it would be popular with the public, convenient for politicians and not inconvenient to week-enders. Please consider these arguments.[58]

Saturday was chosen.

In April a committee was formed to make the formal arrangements. They thought that the Brigade of Guards should form a Guard of Honour, that another formed by the Prince of Wales's Own Civil Service Rifles should be formed up inside the Museum, and yet another, outside, should be found from the local Kensington Territorial Army.

50. PRO, Works 17/26/7, 14 February 1909. Report by Smith to Morant.
51. Richard Graul, 'Zur Neuaufstellung des Victoria und Albert-Museums in London', *Kunstchronik*, xxi (1909–10), p. 86.
52. Raymond Koechlin, 'Le nouveau Musée de South Kensington', *La Chronique des Arts*, 6 November 1909, p. 273.
53. July 1909.
54. PRO, Ed. 84/215, 8 March 1909.
55. Ibid., 15 March 1909.
56. Printed memorandum, Art Museum Series No. 11, 6 July 1909.
57. PRO, Works 17/26/7, 14 February 1909. Report by Smith to Morant.
58. Ibid., 16 February 1909.

Aston Webb prepared plans for seating in the Octagon Court, and in the West Hall. The Mayor of Kensington told McDonnell that the forthcoming visit would be the first by the King since he had created the Royal Borough, and consequently the Mayor and Council would present an address when the King arrived at the main door, and asked for seats at the ceremony. He was allocated two in the Octagon Court, with an additional fifty in the West Hall for the Council.

320 It was next decided that representatives of the workmen should present an address to the King also, though there was a little disagreement about who would present it. The men composed the address themselves after Runciman had told them that neither he nor the First Commissioner 'wanted *in any way* to influence them as to the phraseology they might care to adopt ... and that they were quite free to send us a draft worded in whatever way they thought best...'[59]. After a slight alteration to this draft, it was submitted to the King for his approval, and as a result, Edward VII decided that he wanted the workmen to read it, instead of simply handing it to him. This caused a revision of the plans, and the Clerk of Works was told to 'practise his elocution before the day arrives'.[60]

321 The State Opening of the new building took place at noon on Saturday, 26 June 1909. It was a brilliant affair, with most people either in military uniform, or wearing levee or court dress. The main ceremony took place in the Octagon Court which was banked with tiers of specially constructed seats, covered with red cloth; the floor was carpeted in red, with a low dais covered with a grey eastern rug. Accommodation had been planned by Aston Webb for about 1,500 guests in the Octagon Court, and another 800 in the Western Gallery.[61] Holliday & Greenwood executed the seating and platform, which was estimated to cost £2,500. Much of the decoration had been placed in the hands of Messrs Harrods.

High up in the arch of the western recess was a choir from the Royal College of Music, who entertained during the long waiting period with songs which included Dowland's 'Awake, sweet love', Stanford's 'Shall we go dance?', and, conducted by its composer, Sir Hubert Parry, 'There tolls the deep'. The choir alternated with the band of the Irish Guards, which played suitable background music. It was not until about 11 o'clock that the more important guests began

320. *(top) Workmen employed on the building, after the opening ceremony in 1909*

321. *(above) At the official opening in 1909, Edward VII receives the key from the First Commissioner of Works*

to assemble. Among them were the Lord Mayor of London, A. J. Balfour, Winston Churchill, the Webb family, Ingress Bell, Alma-Tadema, Ernest George, the sculptors Drury, Frampton, Goscombe John, Brock, Lantéri and others; and an array of ambassadors. All the main newspapers sent representatives, but Harcourt gave instructions that there were to be 'no cameras'.[62]

The King and Queen Alexandra drove in an open carriage from Buckingham Palace, up

59. PRO, Works 17/26/9, 18 June 1909.
60. Ibid., 22 June 1909.
61. Plan in PRO, Works 17/26/7.
62. Ibid., 14 June 1909.

Constitution Hill to Knightsbridge where they passed under a triumphal arch bearing a message of welcome from the Royal Borough of Kensington and the words 'Our Borough rejoices in Your Majesty's Favour'. The crowds became more numerous along the Brompton Road, which was decorated with coloured masts and festoons of red and green. When the King and Queen arrived at the Main Entrance of the Museum, the King was handed an address by the Mayor of Kensington, Colonel W. F. Cavaye. This was in a casket decorated with the arms of the Borough, and views of the Museum in coloured enamel; it had been made by the Goldsmiths' and Silversmiths' Company of Regent Street. Queen Alexandra received a bouquet from her godson, Alexander Cunliffe Owen, the youngest grandson of the late Director, Sir Philip Cunliffe Owen. The sovereigns were received by Walter Runciman, the President of the Board of Education and Lewis Harcourt, the First Commissioner of Works.

The royal party formed up in the main hall, the King in Field Marshal's uniform, and Queen Alexandra in a dress described as 'grey-blue mauve' with a black hat trimmed with white ostrich feathers. Led by the builder, the architect, and the Secretaries to the Board of Education, together with Cecil Smith, the Director, followed by Walter Runciman, the procession moved off. Then followed the Secretary to the Office of Works carrying the ceremonial key, behind whom walked the Cabinet. Immediately after the Prime Minister, Herbert Asquith, came the King and Queen at the head of a large gathering of the royal family, among whom were the Prince and Princess of Wales, with Princess Mary, the Duke and Duchess of Connaught, the Duchess of Argyll, the Duchess of Albany, Prince Arthur of Connaught and Princess Patricia, Prince and Princess Alexander of Teck, Prince Christian, Princesses Victoria and Marie-Louise of Schleswig-Holstein, Princess Louise of Wied, and Prince Francis of Teck.

Awaiting the arrival of the King on the dais in the Octagon Court were the Archbishop of Canterbury and the Bishop of London, and members of the royal household. As the King and Queen entered through the east entrance, the Irish Guards played the National Anthem.

Then an address was read to the King. In the early planning stages for the opening ceremony, the Address was to be read by the Prince of Wales in his capacity as President of the Royal Commission for the Exhibition of 1851. The government, however, had raised an objection to this with the Lord Chamberlain, as it was their view that the 1851 Commissioners were in no way connected with the building. Consequently Walter Runciman addressed the King:

May it please your Majesty, On behalf of the Board of Education I humbly desire to thank your Majesty and her Majesty for consenting to open today the new buildings of the Victoria and Albert Museum.

As your Majesty is aware, the first object of the founders of the Museum, the most illustrious of whom was your Majesty's father, the Prince Consort, was to encourage and promote a high standard of excellence among the craftsmen, manufacturers and designers of this country. Their initial efforts, which were seconded by the generosity of private donors, and the liberality of Parliament, have resulted in an unequalled collection of objects of industrial and decorative art.

For many years lack of space has prohibited such a systematic arrangement and classification of the collections as would do justice to their educational value. The completion of the new buildings, however, now makes it possible to display the collections in a manner more worthy of the generous ambition which prompted their formation.

With this object in view, the Board of Education have formulated a complete and comprehensive scheme for the future organisation and management of the Museum. The collections are classified in eight departments. Each department will have its own expert staff, while a separate staff will have charge of the supplementary collections intended for loans to provincial museums and schools of art. These loan collections perform an increasingly important function ancillary to the main purpose of the central Museum. It is hoped that under the new organisation the influence of the Museum may be more effectively exercised, locally as well as centrally, and be of especial assistance to students and craftsmen all over the country in their efforts to study the methods and processes and to emulate the achievements of the best artists of all countries and of all ages.

It will be within the recollection of your Majesty that, on the occasion of the laying of the foundation stone of the new buildings ten years ago, her late Majesty Queen Victoria was pleased to direct that the whole block of buildings intended for the accommodation of the art collections should be known as the Victoria and Albert Museum. The collections are thus permanently associated with the names of the Sovereign under whose 'special and personal protection' the Art Museum was declared to be, and with that of her illustrious Consort, to whose suggestion and influence its foundation was so largely due. By your presence here today your Majesty and her Majesty the Queen have been graciously pleased to signify your interest in a scheme the realisation of which owes much to the favour of her late Majesty, and the prestige and influence of which is enhanced by the continued favour of the reigning Sovereign. It is therefore with feelings of the deepest gratitude that we welcome your Majesty and your gracious Consort here today, and thank you for this further proof of the profound interest you take in all that touches the welfare and the enlightenment of your people.

The King replied to the President of the Board of Education in 'a clear voice which could be heard all over the great court', there were a few prayers from the Archbishop of Canterbury, and the First Commissioner of Works handed to the King a gold key, with a stem of steel damascened with gold, designed by William Bainbridge Reynolds. (It cost £95, and, with its leather case designed and made by Douglas Cockerell, is now kept in the Museum Library.) The King took the key, and declared the building open. This crowning moment was marked by a flourish of trumpets.

The procession re-formed, and their Majesties were conducted into the western part of the long hall, where Aston Webb was presented to them, and an address was read to the King by Herbert Tanner, the Clerk of the Works, on behalf of the workmen and craftsmen who had worked on the building. This over, the Director was knighted.

A few days after the opening, the First Commissioner of Works wrote to King Edward expressing gratitude at the King's satisfaction concerning the arrangements. Harcourt was particularly pleased that everything had gone well in view of the fact that 'so few of the principal participants were able to take part in the rehearsals. During the rehearsals on the last day Mr. Harcourt represented alternately Your Majesty, the Archbishop of Canterbury, Mr. Runciman and himself.' 'He seems very much pleased with himself!', was King Edward's comment.[63]

In all the celebrations one name was conspicuously not invoked. In *The Times* of 28 June, Sir H. T. Wood, Secretary of the Royal Society of Arts, complained that Sir Henry Cole had been so completely forgotten that there had been no 'word of recognition for his memory'. So far as records could be traced, it was Cole who

first conceived the idea of a museum of industrial art having for its main object the education of industrial art workers. And he not only conceived the notion, but he carried it out. This, too, he did, not with the help of popular favour, but in the teeth of official opposition and in spite of popular ridicule and contempt ... So he went on, ignoring or overcoming opposition, till the magnificent collection the nation now owns was housed in the 'Brompton Boilers', an edifice which he hated, but which was the best that official parsimony would provide.

Now, when the treasures he collected are after more than 50 years to be honourably and fitly housed, nobody remembers who it was that provided these collections, whose existence made it worth while to erect a noble building to contain them. Probably he would not have greatly cared. As he was indifferent to personal credit, he probably would not have specially desired posthumous fame. He liked his own way, and he generally got it, though his methods were not such as endeared him either to the superiors whose orders he evaded or to the subordinates whose submission he compelled. He had many really great and many extremely disagreeable qualities. He was quite impervious to ridicule, and would collect and chuckle over the numerous caricatures of which 'Cole, C.B.' was the frequent object. He did more than any other single man to bring about the modern change of sentiment in the appreciation of industrial art, and this though he had no aesthetic judgment and no artistic power. Within his limits he was a great man, and his work deserves, especially at this moment, at least the tribute of recognition.

But Sir Henry Wood was a lone voice crying in the wilderness, as the new master, Sir Cecil Smith, and the Board of Education, wanted to forget the nineteenth century.

---

63. Royal Archives, 1035/60, 29 June 1909.

CHAPTER XIV

Changing fashions in museum decoration in the twentieth century

Large-scale additions and alterations to the Museum fabric have been impossible since the Aston Webb building filled up every corner of the site. The Museum's collections, staff and activities, however, have greatly expanded during the twentieth century, and there have been constant attempts to fit more into the existing buildings and to adapt them to new uses. At first this led to the destruction of some of the mid-Victorian decoration, which had become unfashionable in the early decades of the twentieth century. By the 1960s and '70s Victorian architecture was again in favour and planning controls were stricter, with

322

the result that much of the surviving decoration of the old buildings was rehabilitated.

A new proposal for decoration

Museum professionals in the twentieth century wanted a neutral background for exhibits. The first assertion of this view at South Kensington was in response to an offer, made to Aston Webb through Alfred East, the landscape painter, by Frank Brangwyn. Brangwyn proposed to paint a mural in the Octagon Court for nothing. Webb considered Brangwyn 'quite one of the greatest decorative Artists that we have at the present time'

323

322. (right) Room 145 in 1911, containing works from the George Salting bequest

324. (opposite) The Jones Collection of eighteenth-century French decorative art, in the former Ceramic Gallery in 1928. By that date the ceramic columns had been replaced, but the painted ceiling still survived

323. *The Octagon Court in 1920, when used for the display of objects loaned by private collectors*

and urged Cecil Smith to accept this 'splendid offer', for, in his view, there could be no better start for the decoration of the new building. He forwarded to Smith Brangwyn's ardent proposal:

> Standing in the Octagon Court ... it came to me that here was a place, a national possession, the superb lines and spacing of which would give a great chance for a decoration such as it would be a source of pride for me to do. May I suggest that if 4 of the lunettes were painted and the alternate 4 were treated with a conventional design of swags, emblems and the like, the effect would complete the decorative enhancement of about one of the greatest spacings in Modern London.
>
> If you approve of this suggestion I undertake to decorate one of the large lunettes in the Octagon Court if I can be supplied with the cost of materials and scaffolding.
>
> In making this offer on national grounds I would ask this consideration that if the work be done by me, the remainder of the lunettes should become part of my design in case they should be completed, in order to keep the cohesion of the whole and do justice to your art and to mine. I would gladly submit a sketch of this complete scheme and I would also undertake, great as would be the work, to complete the whole for some five thousand pounds in consideration of its becoming a vast public work, and as a tribute to your great achievement.
>
> Of course, as you know, it is not to me a question of money, I approach it in a national spirit. This sum is far below what I should receive for similar work or would be received by a man of my reputation. In any case I offer to paint the one great lunette for nothing ...[1]

This letter began a long haul round the various officials who were involved. The President of the

---

1. PRO, Ed. 84/68, 5 August 1909.

Board of Works, Harcourt, cannily stated that he was tempted to accept one lunette, thanked Webb for passing on the offer, and pointed out that acceptance would need the agreement of the Board and the permission of King Edward.[2] Webb urged a speedy decision, since Brangwyn had 'the Artistic temperament'.[3]

Cecil Smith was appalled at the proposal, and raised every possible objection.[4] In what medium, he asked, was the painting to be executed? Tempera would not last long in London, and as for fresco painting, the Museum had had sufficient trouble with Leighton's lunettes. He went on to assert that Brangwyn's paintings would not fit in with the exhibits in the Octagon Court: at present it contained tapestries.

> Could anything be more unsuitable and inartistic than to show fine figure tapestries of the xv or xvi centuries in immediate proximity to a modern pictorial composition, of whatever quality?
>
> At the present moment, the most prominent object exhibited on loan in this court is a colossal bronze Buddha: is it possible to devise any complete decorative scheme which will harmonise with Buddha and the tapestries?

(He dodged the question of whether the Buddha and the tapestries were congruous with each other.) He was alarmed by Webb's apparent assumption that further decoration might follow the first experiment.

> I should like to be allowed to enter a protest against any such policy. It is, I believe, generally accepted as an axiom, by those best qualified to judge, that the chief decorations of a Museum are the objects placed there for exhibition; the rooms containing these should be like the setting of a fine gem, dignified, harmonious and self-effacing; the decoration should assist the lighting where necessary, but otherwise not challenge attention. A Museum like the Victoria and Albert, stocked with countless objects to study, is apt to be confusing and wearisome to the visitor, however simple and clear the arrangement of the floor and wall space may be: we do not need to ... weary him further.

And he remarked, with admirable foresight, that 'experience shows that, as a Museum grows, radical changes of arrangement are sooner or later certain to ensue and it is a mistaken policy which would commit posterity to conditions which would hamper this natural development'.

Smith had an ally in Morant, who, in referring the matter to the President of the Board of Education, W. G. Runciman, shrewdly stirred him up against Harcourt, whom he accused of overstepping his authority.

> Though one realises that in a certain limited sense Government buildings are looked after by the Office of Works, it is certainly you, and only you, who have any right to decide a matter of such a nature as this fresco for the Museum. I refer to this because we are constantly seeing signs of attempts at very serious encroachments by the Office of Works ... Certainly Mr. Harcourt's claim to settle this fresco question; merely asking you what you happen to feel about it, is an intolerable assumption on his part.[5]

Morant revealed, incidentally, that he was still thinking of converting the Octagon Court ('a monstrosity') into a library.

Walter Runciman turned down Brangwyn's offer; Cecil Smith had won his first battle for a 'self-effacing' museum.

Some renovations and their effects

During the hectic preparations in 1908 for the opening of the new building, there were also some attempts to renovate the older galleries.

All the roofs in the Fowke buildings, that is to say the North and South Courts and the galleries that surrounded them, were at least fifty years old, and had become somewhat unreliable in wet weather – as they still are. The attention of the Office of Works was drawn to this state of affairs by Sir Robert Morant during December 1908, and the sum of £700 was taken in the estimates for 1909–10 for making a start on the roofs of the painting galleries; the work costing £700 can only have been first aid, since the total cost of the necessary repairs was estimated in excess of £5,000.

However, H. M. Cundall, Keeper of Paintings, was keen on replacing all Fowke's roofs by 'factory roofs' with north lights, so as to reduce sunlight in the painting galleries. At the same time he wanted slight structural alterations to the various rooms, and complete redecoration. The Office of Works decided that since it was of steel the roof

2. Ibid., 7 August 1909.
3. Ibid., 19 August 1909.
4. Ibid., 15 September 1909.
5. PRO, Ed. 84/215, 17 September 1909.

of the then Raphael Cartoon gallery (Room 94) did not need renovating. The Office of Works also had to consider a big reconstruction of walls in Rooms 96–99, which was due to the provision of chimney flues for the Office of the Department of Circulation on the ground floor below. Basil Long, of the Department of Engraving, Illustration and Design, wanted all the walls between rooms 96 and 98 removed so as to create one long room, girders being used to carry the roof instead of the walls.[6]

However, when the matter was referred to A. P. Oppé, the Deputy Director, he reacted quite strongly:

> The original proposal was, I gather, to keep the dimensions of the rooms as they are, but to strip them of all decoration, to flatten the doors and to replace the roofs by 'factory roofs' ... The greater length of the room would only emphasise its extreme lowness ...
>
> I feel as convinced as an amateur can be, that the proposed long low room would be unsightly and unsuitable for pictures. Further the present rooms are well proportioned and both in their general design and in their decoration they are excellent and typical specimens of a particular period of English Art. That period may be just at this moment in disrepute, but it is of historical interest to this Museum which owes its own existence to it. Moreover it is very nearly the period of the pictures hung in the rooms. When they (as a whole) come to be regarded as being of interest, the rooms will also come in for their share of admiration.

A scheme of reconstruction was devised by Reavell of the Office of Works who declared: 'I do not consider the architecture is of such a character as to be worth preserving.'[7] Oppé headed this off by discovering that he was obliged to refer it to the President of the Board of Education,[8] who was induced by Morant to agree to the repair only of the South Court roof.[9] The Office of Works, however, had no money and was still looking for some in July 1912.[10] In March 1913 the question of the 'factory roofs' was referred to the newly formed Advisory Council of the Museum (one of Morant's reforms), who pronounced against it. When money became available in September 1914 new plans were drawn up and approved on September 29. These made no alterations to the structure: a satisfactory outcome entirely due to Oppé's opposition to the original scheme.

During this period, other works of a relatively minor nature were arranged. These included the transfer of the Dyce and Forster libraries from Rooms 83 and 86, to the floor above, and the removal of a spiral staircase, which then necessitated an access being made above the cove of the library staircase.[11] The vacated rooms were converted into exhibition galleries and an extra opening was made between Room 83 and 91. The protracted renovation of the South Court roof was continuing,[12] while redecoration of the Raphael Cartoon gallery was agreed, and certain galleries were proposed to be floored with wood blocks in place of ceramic tiles; although in 1911 the Office of Works said that there were no funds for such work, money was found at the end of that year.

There were complaints early in 1911 that the new revolving doors at the main entrance might be defective, as they kept collapsing, especially in high winds. The doorkeepers were told not to put things right themselves, but to send immediately for the Clerk of the Works. That things did not improve immediately is shown by a minute of 13 January 1911: 'It is an interesting commentary on our letter ... that the very next day the doors should have collapsed again and then again on the next day (today): whether the sequence will continue we shall learn tomorrow.'[13]

The Ceramic Gallery and West Staircase

Having resisted Brangwyn's proposal to decorate the new building, Cecil Smith next turned to an attempt to efface some of the decoration in the old building. In October 1910 he sent a long memorandum[14] to the President of the Board of Education, suggesting alteration to the Ceramic Gallery and the West Staircase which adjoined it. He re-asserted 'the Board's view that the decorations ... of a Museum should be as unobtrusive as possible, and should in no way overpower the effect of the objects exhibited'. The decoration of the Ceramic Gallery, he continued, 'belonged to a bygone age when a different view was held'.

6. PRO, Ed. 84/69, 3 April 1911.
7. Ibid., 22 May 1911.
8. Ibid., 13 June 1911.
9. Ibid., 1 September 1911.
10. PRO, Ed. 84/71, 5 July 1912.
11. PRO, Ed. 84/68, 12 December 1910.
12. The postponement of half the work until 1913 was lamented by Oppé in May 1912. PRO, Ed. 84/71.
13. W. Fisher to A. Kennedy. PRO, Ed. 84/69.
14. PRO, Ed. 84/68, 2 October 1910.

325. (above) The Jones
Collection in 1910, housed
in Room 104 (now Room
100), before its transfer to
the former Ceramic Gallery

326. (right) A view of the
present galleries of
Continental eighteenth-
century decorative art
(Rooms 5–7), where the
Jones Collection is now
displayed

He disliked five features: the ceiling, the columns, the windows, the tiled floor and the frieze around the top of the walls.

The ceilings, painted 'mostly in a greyish-blue monochrome on a white ground' with 'decorative patterns and figure objects, conceived in a classical style', he considered 'not in themselves objectionable': and although a portion at the west end was 'totally destroyed by the action of damp', and in most of them large circular gas-holders would have to be replaced with electrical light fittings, he was willing that they should be retained and cleaned.

The ten columns, which were encased in 'slabs of glazed terra-cotta with high relief', he found 'most obtrusive and objectionable'. He suggested that these should have their terracotta casing removed, and be re-covered 'with fibrous plaster so as to form a simple classical shape', at an expense of £120.

> The windows on the north side are glazed with an old-fashioned type of yellowish fluted glass, on which designs are drawn chiefly in black, illustrative of the processes of pottery-making throughout the ages and centuries beginning with China, Egypt and Greece. These drawings were executed at the order of the Science and Art Department by William Bell Scott in 1869. Scott was an engraver and painter, who frequently exhibited at the Academy, and who was also an examiner at South Kensington, but he is best known perhaps for his connection with the pre-Raphaelite Brotherhood. There are 18 windows in all of varying sizes, and Mr. Scott appears to have been paid at the rate of £55 a window, making a total for the whole of not far short of £1,000.

Smith judged Scott's designs 'crude and amateurish', and he asked that the windows be replaced with 'obscured glass of a modern kind'.

The floors were covered with Minton tiles, which 'dazzle the eye and absorb light', and would have to be disturbed for a new heating system. Smith suggested that they should be replaced with parquet flooring or covered with linoleum.

As for the frieze, which was

> decorated with the names of a large number of places which have been known to produce ceramic fabrics and the dates of these fabrics arranged in alphabetical order, beginning with Adria, Italy, A.D.100, and ending with Zurich, Switzerland, A.D.1715,

327. *The 1914–18 War Memorial by Eric Gill*

Smith requested that it should be painted over.

He believed that the same objections applied to the decoration of the West Staircase. The removal of the stained-glass windows on the landing would, he thought, improve the lighting in a dark corner. As it would be almost impossible to remove the applied terracotta decoration, he suggested that it should be partly covered up 'with plain removable panelling on which engravings from the Museum Collection could, if necessary, be exhibited'.

On the half-landing of the staircase was the monument to Sir Henry Cole: his portrait in mosaic within a Della Robbia ware frame. Boldly sacrilegious, Smith wanted this out of the way too. 'I suppose that we are bound to exhibit it somewhere,' he grudgingly conceded; but 'it certainly should not be allowed to occupy its present place', which, he disingenuously claimed, would be valuable as space for exhibition'.

With this memorandum, entirely unsympathetic to the nineteenth-century decoration, Sir Cecil Smith started a train of events that turned out to be exceedingly controversial and was not properly concluded for a number of years. The President of the Board of Education approved Smith's proposals but warned that there might be violent criticism, and was, as Morant told Smith, 'very strong on the point that we must in no sense seem to insist'.[15]

Nothing further was done to affect the decoration in question for over a year, but decoration did begin to disappear below the Ceramic Gallery, in the series of rooms between the Quadrangle and the Refreshment Rooms, where there were painted ceilings by Hugh Stannus. During December 1911, John Eyre, RBA, ARCA wrote to the Secretary of the Imperial Arts League complaining that Stannus's ceilings had recently been covered with whitewash. He presumed that the next thing to disappear would be the ceilings designed by Frank Moody, 'in what was formerly the Ceramic Gallery. Critics may differ as to their merit, but it may be well to remember that they were designed by students, who were at the time studying in the Art Schools, and were much admired. It seems almost as though the present authorities desired to get rid of all the works of their predecessors.'[16]

Eyre hoped that the League would publish his letter, but it was diplomatically referred to Smith, and at the Museum, Oppé was able to head off criticism by pointing out that Stannus's ceilings had decayed beyond the possibility of restoration.[17] Cecil Smith put on record that Stannus's ceiling 'had very little importance as a design' and that since 1909 only two other ceilings had been obliterated, one of which was that of the Prince Consort Gallery (Room 110).

In the spring of 1912, the walls of the West Staircase were boarded over for a display of prints and drawings, and this did arouse opposition.

A correspondent to the *Daily Mail*, signing himself as 'A Friend of Frank Moody', complained that he had

learnt of the intention on the part of the authorities ... to dismantle the staircase, the decoration of which was designed and executed by the late F. W.

Moody, and also to strip the Keramic Gallery columns of their decorative covering of glazed earthenware. I should have imagined such a thing impossible; but the rumour has reached me from so many different sources, that I fear it may have a basis of fact.

It is possible that those now responsible for the destinies of the museum are not in sympathy with the art traditions which were handed on from Alfred Stevens by Godfrey Sykes, Frank Moody, James Gamble and Reuben Townroe; but they constituted the creed of that little band of artists who found at South Kensington, a place for their embodiment. These men left a definite achievement as their record, and that record, it would appear, is now to be obliterated. I have always viewed with sadness those rows of tombstones removed from the graves they once covered and ranged in a grim series around a churchyard which has become a recreation ground. They at least are preserved; but we are now threatened with the indecent destruction of works which should stand as an abiding illustration of an interesting phase of British Art and as memorials of those who are, alas! no longer able to speak on their own behalf. I trust that their living brother artists will join me in my emphatic protest against this act of vandalism.

This brought the Office of Works down to the Museum to find out what was going on,[18] and provoked Sir Henry Cole's son Alan to write in protest to L. Selby-Bigge at the Board of Education.[19] It also elicited a question in the House of Commons from James Grant, MP for West Cumberland, on 1 April. In preparing the reply to this, Smith admitted that the stained-glass windows on the staircase had been removed since they were damaged, but would be put back.[20] The President of the Board of Education instructed Smith that no further alterations were to be made without his knowledge,[21] and on 4 April assured Grant in the Commons that no decorations were to be destroyed.

Alan Cole was not convinced: 'I have been to the Museum,' he wrote to Selby-Bigge on 1 May, 'to see what is going on as regards the windows.

15. Ibid., 14 October 1910.
16. PRO, Ed. 84/69.
17. Ibid., 29 December 1911, 4 January 1912.
18. PRO, Ed. 84/71, Memorandum by Sir Cecil Smith, 2 April 1912.
19. Ibid., 1 April 1912.
20. Ibid., 2 April 1912.
21. Ibid., 3 April 1912.

I may be wrong but it looks as though they were *not* to be put back ...'[22] He got no reply. Grant too was dissatisfied and on 2 May fired off a fusi-lade of Parliamentary questions, asking the President of the Board of Education

> ... whether he will now give instructions for the removal of the boarding recently erected over a considerable part of the permanent decorations of the north-western staircase in the Victoria and Albert Museum, which thereby destroys the unity of that decoration?
> ... if he will give instructions for the drawings &c., which are at present hung upon the north-western staircase of the Victoria and Albert Museum to be removed to a more suitable exhibiting space in one or other of the better lighted rooms, now increasingly occupied by minor examples and purely experimental sketches?
> ... if he will explain why the two stained glass windows which existed on the north-western staircase at the Victoria and Albert Museum have been removed, thereby destroying the unity of the scheme of decoration; and whether he can see his way to nullify such an act of vandalism by ordering the windows to be replaced?
> ... if he will give instructions for making good and for the repainting of the dilapidation of a small part of the ceiling in the lecture theatre gallery in the Victoria and Albert Museum, as well as for the walls of that gallery to be cleaned of the accumulation of many years dirt, so that they may be repainted in a tint corresponding with that used when the scheme of decorating this gallery was originally carried out?

Selby-Bigge, having visited the Museum, felt some apprehension and advised the President to set up a Committee to advise on the matter.[23] This consisted of Sir Reginald Blomfield, architect and Visitor of the Royal College of Art, Selwyn Image, Slade Professor at Oxford and a member of the Advisory Council of the Museum, and Gerald Moira, painter and Professor at the RCA. Aston Webb had been suggested, but was vetoed by the President because of his support for Brang-wyn's proposal for mural decoration.[24] The Museum was not represented on the Committee, which met on 4 and 25 June.[25]

Meanwhile Alan Cole had got up a petition to the Prime Minister, Herbert Asquith. It stated:

> Many parts of the older buildings of the Victoria and Albert Museum, South Kensington, were decorated between the years 1859 and 1879 by Artists of distinction, several of whom were pupils and brother workers of the late Alfred Stevens ... That it is due to the memory of such men and to the interests of the general Student of the 19th Century British decorative work to preserve these characteristic examples. That some of them have been subject lately to removal, some to obliteration by being boarded over, and others to damage during the passage of the last thirty years. Your memorialists therefore pray that enquiries be made forthwith, in order that the necessary restitutions, repairs, etc., may be made, and the future careful guardianship of these architectural and decorative works may be secured.

Among the 118 signatories were Hubert von Herkomer, Aston Webb, Sir W. B. Richmond, Sir George Birdwood, James McBey, P. Wilson Steer, Alfred Drury, F. W. Pomeroy, F. R. Fowke, C. M. Q. Orchardson, W. Russell Flint, C. F. A. Voysey, Alfred Gilbert, William Reynolds-Stephens and Walter Crane. Most of the signatures were those of members of the Chelsea Arts Club and the Royal Institute of Oil Painters. Cecil Smith dismissed the petition on the grounds that many 'gave their names without having the remotest idea of the real points at issue'.[26]

At the end of June, the committee reported. They ordered that the boarding over the staircase should be taken down. But they approved the removal of the stained-glass windows on the staircase, and recommended that those in the Ceramic Gallery should also go. Furthermore they backed Cecil Smith in recommending the removal of the columns and the tiled floor, while allowing that the ceiling should remain.

This took the wind out of the sails of the protestors. Alan Cole circulated a printed description of the Museum decorations, to little effect. Grant demanded that the committee's report should be debated in the Commons, but no one took any notice. Selby-Bigge suggested to his President that the Board might safely commit itself to 'the principle that it is very desirable that worthy and interesting specimens of the Decorative Arts of 19th Century Artists should be preserved', since it could then shift the debate to the question: 'what

22. Ibid., 1 May 1912.
23. PRO, Ed. 84/70, 6 May 1912.
24. Ibid., 8 May 1912.
25. Ibid., 4 June 1912, letter from Blomfield; memorandum by Sir Cecil Smith, 4 June 1912.
26. Ibid., 29 July 1912.

are interesting and worthy specimens?' He drafted a long letter for the President to send to Grant, decrying the decorations as the unplanned product of numerous unharmonious hands. Grant riposted as best he could.[27]

By the middle of the following month, the boarding on the staircase had been removed, and the stained glass had been cleaned, ready to be replaced in the two windows – albeit only temporarily. But Cecil Smith was quite definitely determined to get rid of Bell Scott's glass, and its substitution by clear glass was put into the estimates for 1913, as also was the removal of the floor tiles.

The Museum authorities were by now resigned to keeping Moody's painted ceiling in the Gallery, so Sir Cecil Smith wrote to the headmaster of the Royal College of Art, A. Spencer, asking if he had any students who would undertake the restoration of the painting, how much it would cost, and when the work might be done, if indeed anyone could be found to do it.[28] Spencer replied[29] that he had students who had served their apprenticeships in such work, and thought that they could probably begin after 17 January 1913, at a rate of twenty-five shillings each week, which would be in addition to their scholarship allowance. Eventually Spencer found one student, Ivor Beaumont, who agreed to carry out the painting for £12; but for various reasons the work was not sanctioned until August of that year.[30] Ivor Beaumont, the student who took it on, finished his task on 28 August. Much of the decoration was painted out shortly after 1950, and hope of eventually uncovering it vanished when, in about 1970, RCA students, working immediately above, flooded their studio and brought the plaster ceiling crashing down into the gallery. In 1977 a storm producing over an inch of rain broke through the roof and another portion of the ceiling collapsed.

In March 1913 the newly formed Advisory Council took a hand. They discussed the housing of the Jones Collection of eighteenth-century French furniture and works of art, which was then placed in the Ceramic Gallery. It had, by the terms of the bequest, to be kept altogether, and the Council, after considering various places to put it, decided that it must stay where it was, but that the alterations in the Gallery should go ahead so as to make a more suitable setting. They suggested that the ceramic columns should be removed altogether but the Office of Works architect informed

Cecil Smith that the iron stanchion within the ceramic covering was load-bearing and must stay, though it might be reclothed.[31]

Cole and Grant soon got wind of the new moves, and arrived at the Museum on 1 May 1913 for another inspection.[32] In July Grant asked another Parliamentary question, and later that month Selby-Bigge and his President descended on the Museum in Smith's absence and issued some inapposite instructions as to the re-creation of the stained glass from the staircase.[33] In the end Smith did get rid of this; it was discovered in 1974 in store in a ruinous condition.

The battle for the Ceramic Gallery was not yet over, however, and a new combatant entered the lists: Frank Moody's daughter Fanny, Mrs King. She wrote on 25 November 1913 to remind Cecil Smith that he had promised her, when she visited the Museum the previous year, that the columns and ceiling in the Gallery would be left intact.[34] Smith twice denied that he had given her any such assurance,[35] so she triumphantly quoted at him the notes she had made at their meeting. 'This enables me to say with certainty . . . that a definite assurance of the preservations of the Columns . . . was given and that if these matters no longer remain within the recollection of Mr. Strange and yourself, it illustrates the value which a written record possesses over fallible memories'.[36] Alas, Civil Servants were not to be caught out by this, and the Museum did no more than acknowledge her letter.

Alan Cole made another visitation on 27 November. As the Director was out, a subordinate, H. Fass, held Cole in conversation and eventually induced him 'to admit that it was, after all, a question of sentiment, and I explained that there would be at any rate the columns in the Refresh-

27. Ibid., 18, 23 October, 2 November 1912.
28. Ibid., 16 December 1912.
29. Ibid., 19 December 1912.
30. Ibid., 21 January 1913, 31 July 1913.
31. Ibid., 27 March, 2 April 1913.
32. PRO, Ed. 84/71, 2 May 1913.
33. PRO, Ed. 84/70, 8 August 1913, Smith to Selby-Bigge; 13 August 1913, Sir Joseph Pease to Smith; 21 August 1913, Smith to Pease.
34. Ibid., 25 November 1913.
35. Ibid., 28 November 1913. On receiving another letter from Mrs King, 4 December 1913, Smith sent her a note by personal messenger on 12 December, in which he repeated that he had given her no assurance.
36. Ibid., 18 December 1913.

ment Rooms available for anyone who wished to see work of that period'.[37]

Fass concluded that 'Mr. Cole went away feeling that it was too late to start another agitation about the Columns'. Nonetheless, controversy broke out briefly in the Press. Accusations of 'vandalism' were levelled at the Museum by a writer in *The Times* on 8 December, and in the ensuing correspondence Cole and Grant raised their voices. From the *Architects' and Builders' Journal*, however, on 17 December 1913 came the dismissive comment that the 'old crockeryware columns are so many memorials of the unequalled depths of inanity to which "art" had descended at the period at which they were perpetrated'. Articles of an opposite tendency ('Destruction at South Kensington' and 'Halt!') appeared on 9 January 1914 in the Letchworth *Citizen* ('Non-Sectarian, Non-Partisan, open to All'). All this was of no avail; nor did another salvo of Parliamentary questions from Grant early in 1914 achieve anything.

Alan Cole slipped in one last blow below the belt, against Robert Morant, who had courted controversy too recklessly at the Board of Education and had been transferred to work on Lloyd George's insurance scheme. Cole, in an article on the Museum decoration in the *Journal* of the Royal Society of Arts (Vol. LIX, 1913–14, pp. 270–2) recalled meeting Morant in 1908,

> He told me that in his opinion it would be an advantage if all of us formerly on the South Kensington staff were 'cleared out' . . . In spite of his removal to the Chairmanship of the National Insurance Commission the germs of Sir Robert's virus had been sufficiently nurtured for them to maintain a powerful influence, to which I think the present method of dealing with the old decorations can be traced.

Work had been proceeding in the Ceramic Gallery through the autumn of 1913 (the floor was ripped up to remove the old heating system, which forced the Royal College, on the same heating circuit, to abandon nude models for a time) and the columns were removed and replaced with plain plaster columns in February 1914. These nondescript replacements were the subject of careful aesthetic and scholarly consideration. Sir Reginald Blomfield, on seeing the Office of Works drawings, had criticized the proportions[38] – for he was learned in architectural precedent – and when he saw the finished columns he crossly pointed out that the caps were an inch too large, the necking an inch too low, and the base an inch too wide.[39] To modern eyes this hardly seems to matter, but Cecil Smith felt obliged to refer it to the President of the Board of Education.[40]

As the columns were being destroyed, the Director of the Weston Park Museum, Sheffield, wrote to ask for some surviving pieces, since James Gamble had been a Sheffield boy, and his brother had been Mayor of the town. Smith snubbed him: 'unfortunately we found it necessary to leave untouched the core of the columns . . . and it proved impossible, owing to the peculiar hardness of the cement in which they were set, to get them away in sections'.[41] This was not strictly true. In reply to a protest letter of 19 May 1914 from the Association of Old Students of the Royal College of Art, the Museum admitted, for the first time, and only for internal purposes, that although the ceramic casing to the first column was destroyed by the Office of Works, the other decorations had been preserved. A recent search through the Museum's stores revealed under a pile of empty packing cases, several crates filled with column material, and behind them, unprotected and dirty, but surprisingly mostly undamaged, William Bell Scott's painted glass windows.

A final ironic twist was added to this story when in February 1914, as the columns were being dismantled, the Department of Circulation wrote to Stoke-on-Trent asking if Minton still had the original moulds of the staircase and columns, so that examples could be acquired as museum specimens of modern majolica for inclusion in travelling exhibition sets.

---

37. Ibid., 28 November 1913, memorandum by H. Fass.
38. Ibid., 1 December 1913.
39. Ibid., 19 February 1914.
40. Ibid., 3 March 1914.
41. Ibid., 18 December 1913.

CHAPTER XV

Settling in

The subway

When planning the new Exhibition Road entrance, Aston Webb took advantage of a subway which had been under the road, and the Museum's land, for many years, but which, as a result of bureaucratic argument, had remained blocked. It had been as long before as 1870 that General Scott, acting in his capacity as Secretary to the 1851 Commissioners, asked the Treasury to join the Commissioners, together with the Metropolitan Railway, to construct a tunnel from the South Kensington station to the junction of Exhibition and Cromwell Roads, to serve the proposed International Exhibitions.[1] The Treasury, however, did not feel that any public money should be spent on anything to do with the exhibitions.[2] Although the Commissioners then proposed that they would undertake the tunnel at their own risk if the Treasury agreed (1) to all the 6d admission fees to the South Kensington Museum above an agreed average figure calculated on the attendances since 1857 going to the Commission, (2) that these fees should pay off the capital expenditure (plus 5% interest) on the tunnel, and (3) when paid for, the Commissioners would present the tunnel to the Department of Science and Art, the Treasury still refused its permission,[3] in spite of an appeal from the Department.

During the next few years other schemes were put forward as private ventures. For instance, in 1872, T. W. Rammell proposed a pneumatic railway from South Kensington station to the Albert Hall, together with a pedestrian subway to the Museum.[4] Although the Board gave its blessing, provided it incurred no expenditure,[5] nothing more was heard of the proposal. Professors of the Royal College of Science opposed other suggestions for underground railways to Paddington beneath Exhibition Road, on the grounds that there would be electrical interference on their experiments.

Approaches from both the Metropolitan and the Metropolitan District Railway companies for a foot tunnel were favourably considered by the Department.[6] The District Railway received Parliamentary approval in the autumn of 1884 and during December, J. Wolfe Barry informed Donnelly that he had written to the Office of Works suggesting an exit from the subway into the Museum's grounds; Donnelly's response was that this plan would be 'most desirable',[7] and the Office of Works decided 'not to withhold' permission.[8]

In January 1885, Wolfe-Barry was told by A. B. Mitford that the Board of Works was:

prepared to consent to the proposed access being made where a prolongation of the central line of the present Art Library Building would cut the line of the subway subject to the following conditions:
(1) That the Company will enter into an agreement to pay a nominal rent of £1 per annum;
(2) That the Company will agree to complete and maintain at their own expense the requisite communication between the cross subway and the Museum Buildings;
(3) That the Company will also undertake to remove the cross subway at their own expense to a distance not exceeding 20 feet north or south of the position now sanctioned in case the erection by the Government of any new buildings should render such a change ... necessary;
(4) That the Government shall have the right of making at any time ... a subway from the South Kensington Museum and Schools on the east side of Exhibition Road to the Science Museum

---

1. PRO, Ed. 84/78, 15 February 1870.
2. Ibid., 24 February 1870.
3. Ibid., 30 May 1870.
4. PRO, Ed. 84/79, 12 February 1872. In 1864, Cole with Hennie, Isabella and Fowke had visited the Crystal Palace 'to inspect the first experiments of the Pneumatic Railway. Abt a quarter of a Mile. We were blown thro' successfully.' Cole, diary, 26 August.
5. Ibid., minute, 22 February 1872.
6. PRO, Ed. 84/80, 17 December 1883.
7. Ibid., 6 December 1884.
8. Ibid., 11 December 1884.

on the west side ... and that they shall be at liberty to cross the Company's subway without toll or charge of any kind.[9]

The subway was almost complete by the end of April 1885, in spite of a campaign by local residents objecting to the ornamental street refuges, and on the 23rd of the month Wolfe-Barry 'ventured to suggest' that as it had been agreed by the Museum that it would provide the building at the subway's entrance, now was the time to start work.[10] While the Department was pondering over this surprise news, Wolfe-Barry wrote again to state that he was mistaken as he had noticed in a draft agreement that a small piece of the Museum's land was to be leased to the railway company which would erect the building to connect the subway entrance to the Museum building.

This was the start of the trouble that caused the project to be abandoned for a quarter of a century.

Festing knew nothing about the new agreement, and Donnelly told the Office of Works that it was inadvisable for any private building to be put on government land, or that such land should be leased; in his view the Office of Works should build the corridor 'of a very cheap and temporary character'.[11] The Office of Works was undecided as it was still negotiating the lease, and ran into further trouble in August.

The railway company wished to install a ticket office at the entrance to the Museum subway, but the Office of Works, thinking of the future Science Museum, preferred the railway to agree that museum staff and visitors going from one museum to the other could do so without any charge. This was not cordially received by the railway authorities, as it 'would be to greatly damage the Company's control of its own property and to seriously complicate the working of the subway', but agreed to grant a concession to Museum staff.[12]

9. Ibid., 5 January 1885.
10. Loc. cit.
11. Ibid., 30 April 1885.
12. Ibid., 26 August 1885.

328. *Pneumatic railway between South Kensington and the Royal Albert Hall, proposed in 1872*

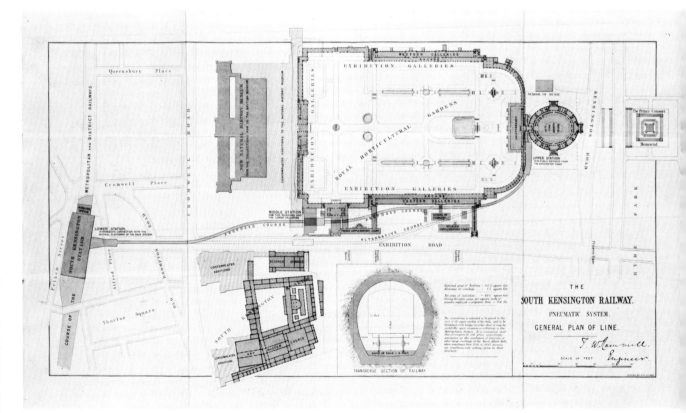

However, by April 1886, the Office of Works had been instructed by the Treasury that agreement could not be given to any proposed covered corridor. The Department of Science and Art, in an attempt to break the deadlock, suggested that, as £300 had been allowed for repairing tiled floors in the Museum, this money might be diverted to paying for the building, but were told that this could not be done as the Treasury objected in principle to the covered way. The Department asked the Treasury for the reason.

Sir Reginald Welby told Donnelly that the Treasury had learned of the provisional agreement with the railway which stated that 'the Government will make and maintain a covered corridor not less than 10 feet wide ... into the South Kensington Museum and will (if asked to do so by the Railway Company) collect the tickets of the Company without charge, and will provide and maintain a booking office about 15 feet × 10 feet near the end of the Company's cross subway for the use of the Company's booking clerks, and for the issue of the Company's tickets during such times as the Museum is open to the public.' As these proposals were new ones, 'Their Lordships must object to this change of arrangement which involves a considerable charge to the Public Exchequer.'[13]

The Department of Science and Art let the Treasury know that it was not a party to this surprising agreement and, although it wanted the subway entrance, was opposed to leasing any land as this would be 'certain to lead to friction and misunderstanding'.[14] The clause was deleted from the agreement, with the result that there was left only an entrance from the subway into the grounds of the new Natural History Museum.

Quite understandably, the railway company was huffy and complained that it had gone to considerable expense in burrowing needlessly, it now appeared, beneath Exhibition Road. Donnelly was asked if he had any suggestion to make which might resolve the *impasse*, but he had none.

As the Treasury refused to reconsider its decision, the railway company eventually proposed that it should put up the money for the connection into the Museum. Yet even this offer did not help to reach a settlement, for Richard Thompson stated[15] that the Museum would still have to find at least £380 a year for two doorkeepers and two policemen. Still the railway went on trying, and

still the Treasury refused to allow 'what may be a convenience, but certainly cannot be called a necessity, for my Lords believe that the subway is now open ... to a point in Exhibition Road, nearly opposite the Museum ... Economies ... are imperatively required.'[16] That, so far as the Treasury was concerned, was that.

In 1894, a member of the Museum's staff intrepidly asked General Donnelly if the subject could be revived, because

In consequence of the extra-ordinary development of the vehicular traffic and the inefficient lighting of the roadway, it is positively dangerous to cross the roadway after dark – especially when the weather is at all inclement ... To know that one could arrive here without a soaking would be worth something on the rates.[17]

General Festing, when consulted, reminded Donnelly that an entrance into the subway would mean the construction of steps and a police house. As, however, plans were still being worked on for Aston Webb's postponed new building, Festing thought that an entrance might be incorporated, but this suggestion was turned down by the Office of Works.[18] The matter was shelved until the end of 1899 when work on Webb's building had at last started. Donnelly, Festing and Caspar Purdon Clarke considered asking for the link,[19] Webb prepared a scheme, but this was eventually turned down by the Treasury.[20]

During 1906, the Metropolitan District Railway sought parliamentary sanction to extend the tunnel – which then ended at Imperial Institute Road – as far as the Albert Hall, a scheme received favourably by the 1851 Commissioners. The Office of Works did not think that any of the buildings under its control would be affected as the extension would be in the area of buildings of London University.[21] Although the extension did not materialize, Aston Webb was, at long last, allowed to plan for a subway entrance in 1907,

13. Ibid., 13 May 1886.
14. Ibid., 27 May 1886.
15. Ibid., 16 October 1886.
16. Ibid., 30 December 1886.
17. E. Harris, PRO, Ed. 84/87, 26 October 1894.
18. *Loc. cit.*, 5 January 1895.
19. PRO, Ed. 84/81, 22 November 1899.
20. Ibid., 5 November 1902.
21. Ibid., 11 May 1906.

but all was not straightforward, for negotiations were then resumed with the railway company. Up to this date, the subway appears to have been kept closed except when there were 'special attractions' at the Albert Hall. The underground railway authorities told the Office of Works on 22 May 1908 that they would be prepared to open the subway whenever South Kensington Station was open and to allow free public access. There was a drawback, however. The company would thus be put to 'considerable expense' and suggested that the Office of Works contributed £500 as grant-in-aid. The principal architect to the Office of Works, Sir Henry Tanner, queried whether such a privilege was worth paying for and brought to light an agreement whereby the railway would have an area of 900 square feet inside the Museum for a booking office, which Aston Webb thought was 'quite unpleasant'.[22]

(Sir) Francis Ogilvie's opinion was that a single grant of £500 was worthwhile, but it was out of the question if the railway company was hoping for this payment annually. The booking office, too, was unacceptable, but the Board of Education would not object to 'a booking clerk with a portable ticket box being stationed within the Museum door on such few special occasions in any year as there was reason to believe would involve a very large number of visitors leaving the Museum and desiring to book there for railway journeys.'[23] The argument continued for a considerable time, starting with a report by Tanner (according to the autocratic Robert Morant, Permanent Secretary to the Board of Education, badly drafted and its meaning indecipherable), in which he stated that the Office of Works was under an obligation to provide both a ticket office and ticket collectors' boxes.

Morant, on 31 August, told the Office of Works that the Board of Education did not 'look upon the subway as of any *great* value in enhancing the value of the Art Museum' and that there was no question of an annual grant to the company. Although the Board could not agree to any booking office, there was no objection to the occasional temporary, removable box for issuing tickets on those special occasions to be decided by the Board.

Eventually Morant heard that the railway company considered that it should decide when the box should be in use, and proposed extra iron doors to close the subway when the Museum was shut. The Office of Works hoped that the Board of Education would agree, although they naïvely stated that the Board might feel that it 'should have some voice as to the occasions when the movable Booking Office is to be brought into use.[24] Morant replied that the Board, and only the Board, should be the deciding authority and would 'never exercise their veto in unreasonable ways; but they cannot undertake to allow the box to be placed and used by the Company in the premises of the Museum whensoever the Company think fit.'[25]

The matter remained unresolved and on 9 June, just before Edward VII was due to open the new building, W. J. Downer, of the Office of Works, wrote expressing his fear that there was no hope of a settlement being reached for some while. The matter was in the hands of the Treasury Solicitor. Three days later, however, he sent over a draft agreement[26] which Morant ordered should be 'carefully scanned', as it seemed to contain certain differences on conditions upon which the Board had already expressed its views. Meanwhile, it was decided that after the official opening, the subway entrance would stay closed.

The draft was not explicit and there was a difference in opinion about the location of the booking office. Ogilvie thought that it was within the Museum, whereas Sir Cecil Smith gave his view that as there was ample room in the passage extending from the subway, under Exhibition Road, the question of the ticket office being brought into the Museum 'seems hardly to arise'.[27] In November 1909 an amended draft was received. The Company agreed to pay the First Commissioner of Works an annual rent of £1, erect iron doors and keep them open whenever the Museum was open, and be at liberty to erect a booking office outside the Museum's premises. Agreement, at last, and the entrance was opened in 1910.

The Victoria and Albert Museum is the only Museum to have very useful direct access to the South Kensington station, but unfortunately after sixty years had gone by, the doors were closed for security reasons in 1970.

22. Ibid., 18 June 1908.
23. Ibid., 18 July 1908.
24. Ibid., 30 November 1908.
25. Ibid., 4 December 1908.
26. *Loc. cit.*
27. Ibid., 24 September 1909.

The catalogue stall

Although the Museum had been selling catalogues and other of its publications since the Marlborough House days of 1852, it was not until after Edward VII had opened the new building in 1909 that any thought seemed to have been given to a catalogue stall. A temporary counter had been put up immediately inside the main doors, which did not meet with the architect's approval. There was some internal discussion about a more suitable location. In addition, something had to be provided for umbrellas. Eventually, Sir Cecil Smith wrote to Webb:

> We are in need of 2 counters at the Main Entrance of the Museum, one for the purpose of a Catalogue Stall and the other for the reception of Umbrellas. It has occurred to me that you might be so good as to give us the benefit of your advice as to the form they should take, so that there should be no danger of detracting from any of the architectural features. I think the balance of advantage is in favour of putting one counter in the corner immediately to the left of the Entrance and a corresponding one in the corner to the right, and it would really be a great favour if you would let me know whether you see any insuperable objection from an architectural point of view. I did wonder if you would go so far as to let me have a design for such a counter; if you could I need hardly say how much we should appreciate such assistance.[28]

The rather embarrassed tone of this letter must reflect the Director's thoughts that Sir Aston Webb ought to have had the subject mentioned in his brief several years earlier. Certainly the architect's design left little scope. Indeed, it is hardly surprising that Webb's reply was somewhat testy:

> I am now asked to provide a plan showing the counters &c at the main entrance for the sale of catalogues. I understand that you have now formulated your wishes in the matter. Should I meet you one morning at the building to discuss it?[29]

A little thought had been given to the problem. Fisher had found a 'Heating Apparatus & recess convenient for a Chair and a little Table for the Attendant', which Arthur Richmond, Secretary to the Advisory Council feared 'wd. be very draughty'.

Sir Cecil and Sir Aston met in the main entrance,[30] to review the situation. They decided that the catalogue stall should also have provision for the albums of official photographs for sale, and that for this purpose the space immediately to the left of the doors was 'altogether inadequate' and badly lit. A suggestion that there should be a separate counter for the photographs was turned down as being too inconvenient for the public. They rejected an umbrella stand between the two sets of revolving doors as 'offering obstruction to visitors'.

The Arcade on the left flank of the Vestibule [? Room 49] was then considered & in view of its length & good light & proximity of Storeroom and heating apparatus was approved & Sir Aston Webb promised to prepare a Plan. It was agreed that there shd be flanking glass screens to avoid draughts & a direction board easily seen by Visitors on entering.

The Arcade on the opposite side was then considered for Coats & Umbrellas & a smaller counter was agreed to providing for wet umbrellas in a stand so that they may easily dry in a ventilated space than in a confined room & dry coats on shelves just inside the Counter, and for wet coats & (if need be) dry umbrellas inside the Attendants Room. It was arranged that the Doorkeepers must attend to this except on busy days when an extra attendant cd. be provided.

The Western Entrance [Exhibition Road] was then considered & Sir Aston promised Plans for this. It was understood that a set of Photo Guard Books wd. be exhibited at both Entrances.

Webb sent in drawings for these counters, a year later, 'for your observations before obtaining estimates for them'.[32] Democratically, the plans were circulated, probably the most sensible comment being from H. A. Kennedy, 'I suppose a square counter either close to pillars or under the dome in the central hall is not possible? I am afraid we may lose some customers if the stall is tucked away at the side.' W. Fisher proposing detail amendments to Webb's counter designs, commented, concerning the cloakroom, 'I think the plan is open to question in principle; it seems questionable whr. the separation of umbrellas and

---

28. PRO, Ed. 84/152. Draft by W. Fisher, 10 November 1909. To this is added 'I think we sh. limit ourselves to Umbrellas & Sticks & so avoid all the difficulty of hanging up Coats.'

29. *Loc. cit.* All other papers on this subject have the same P.R.O. reference.

30. 10 December 1909.

31. Memorandum by W. Fisher, 10 December 1909.

32. 4 November 1910.

cloaks & the shutting of them up in 2 separate rooms will work. Where is the Cloakroom man to stand ... ?'

However, there was no rush for a decision, as it turned out, because in January 1911, Sir Cecil Smith heard that the Office of Works had no money to do the work for at least a year.[33]

A temporary stall in the proposed location was suggested by Sir Cecil Smith, but it was decided that anything so temporary would not be worthwhile. Fortunately, the Office of Works found the money during the 1912–13 financial year, and by the end of July, the cataloge stall was completed.

The cloakroom counter was not so lucky. The passage of time seems to have taken Sir Cecil Smith away from Aston Webb's scheme. In the 1913–14 estimates appears 'Counters for the reception of cloaks near the Main Entrance are required as forming part of the necessary equipment of the Museum. It is suggested that teak counters running from the pillars on either side of the Vestibule to the revolving doors would meet the purpose. At a meeting with G. Reavell, ARIBA, of the Office of Works,[34] the Director explained that he thought of a semi-circular counter running from each door to the first archway. But still nothing was done, the First World War passed, and in 1925 a plea went to the Office of Works stating that the temporary counter was 'quite unworthy of the building' and that the need for a teak counter in keeping with the rest of the structure 'has been emphasized several times in communications to your Board since the new portion of the building was opened'.[35] This did the trick; by 7 May there had been a visit from the Surveyor's Office; by 29 May, plans had been received and approved, and the new counter was finished on 23 November 1925.

33. W. A. Kerr, 31 January 1911.
34. 18 November 1912.
35. 22 April 1925.

CHAPTER XVI

Space!

The underlying theme of the Museum since its earliest days had been the need for space and still more space. When Aston Webb's four-storey extension was on the point of completion, the still limited capacity of the entire 12-acre complex was appreciated. Cecil Smith's Committee of Re-arrangement in 1908 stated that 'even with the large increase of accommodation afforded by the new buildings ... the amount of room now available is not more than suffices for present requirements with reasonable regard to expansion'.[1] But before that, in 1897, Major-General Sir John Donnelly told the Select Committee on Museums of the Science and Art Department, that the Library, opened only some fifteen years earlier, had just about run out of space.[2]

After 1909, there followed several years of comparative calm, while the Museum settled into the new galleries. Sir Cecil Harcourt-Smith retired in 1924 and was succeeded as Director by Eric Maclagan, the Keeper of Architecture and Sculpture. Not many years later he was formally telling the Advisory Council that the Museum had a problem. The only building during this time was the workshops erected on a triangular piece of land north of the North Court in 1925–6.

The Advisory Council had been created as a result of the Select Committee of 1897 and 1898, which had recommended that a Board of Visitors should be appointed. Nothing was done immediately, but in 1904, Robert Morant resurrected the matter and, following the resignation in 1905 of the Director, Sir Caspar Purdon Clarke, Lord Liverpool, President of the Board of Education, minuted the Prime Minister, A. J. Balfour, putting the proposition that the Museum might benefit if 'its Directors were ... cut free from the existing control of Officers and Political Heads of the Board of Education, and were placed under the control of a Body of Trustees ...'[3] The Prime Minister favoured the trustee system, but Lord Liverpool, influenced by Morant, decided that

there would be no major changes, except for the appointment of a Council to advise the President of the Board of Education on matters relating to the Museum, particularly on purchases, but precluded from most matters concerning staff. The first meeting of this new Advisory Council was held during 1913.

At the time of the economic crisis of 1931, the purchase grant of the Museum was reduced from £16,000 to only £2,000, which Sir Eric Maclagan decided was to be used solely for buying books for the National Art Library. In January 1932, therefore, Maclagan circulated a memorandum to the Council;[4] which is worth quoting in full:

It seems inevitable that acquisitions should be slowed down to a very considerable extent by the cutting short of the purchase grant, and this ought to provide an opportunity for considering some of the more insistent general problems with which we are faced with regard to the existing collections. Nearly all of these turn ultimately on the lack of space for expansion. Many members of the Council are no doubt aware that there was every hope of a considerable accession of space for the Museum by the removal of the Royal College of Art to new buildings on the other side of Cromwell Road.[5] This scheme, which had for long been under consideration, was actually before the Treasury a year or more ago but was indefinitely postponed even at that date owing to the expense involved. It is clearly unlikely that it will be taken up again for some years to come. And as when it is taken up the first step will be the building of new premises for the College, and we shall be unable to start work on the reconstruction of the existing buildings now occupied by the College until the new buildings are completed and the move

---

1. *Report of the Committee of Re-arrangement*, 1908, p. 18.
2. *First Report* from the Select Committee, 1897, Question No. 549, '... it is cramped for space, or will be very soon, for the storage of books'.
3. Victoria and Albert Museum, Advisory Council file.
4. PRO, Ed. 84/114. Minutes of the Advisory Council.
5. On the land now occupied by the Ismaili centre, and for many years the intended site of the National Theatre.

has been made, the likelihood of any fresh space being readily available for the Museum collections lies only in the relatively distant future. The same is no doubt true with regard to the practical possibility of the foundation of a Museum of Oriental Art, to which parts of our existing collections might have been transferred. It seems necessary therefore to face the fact that extra space will somehow have to be found within the existing buildings.

In some Departments there are possibilities in the way of withdrawing objects into accessible storage, and on a small scale this has already been done. Unfortunately the provision of suitable storage space (either by cases with glass topped drawers or by partitioning off parts of the existing Galleries) is in itself somewhat expensive and can only be proceeded with slowly in the absence of a special grant of money for the purpose. In other Departments, such as Woodwork, accessible storage presents almost insuperable difficulties. In others, such as the Library and the Department of Engraving, Illustration and Design, the material is already stored and additional storage space has somehow to be found.

The problem is particularly acute in the Department of Woodwork, where it is hardly an exaggeration to say that each new acquisition made now involves the withdrawal of an existing exhibit, and in the Library, where we reckon that storage space is only available to meet the normal acquisitions of another year or so. A third Department in which the congestion is particularly acute is that of Circulation.

There are two pieces of territory in the Museum which are not occupied departmentally; the Loan Court [Room 40] and the North Court. Until the new buildings of the Museum were occupied in 1909, loans had normally been shown in the Departments to which they appertained with the exception of the Salting and Morgan Loans. It was, I imagine, the existence of these two very large and important loans which dictated the allocation of a special Court to loans when the new arrangement was made. The Loan Court still contains certain important loans occupying in each instance a number of cases with more or less similar objects. But I have always felt that the whole policy of extensive loans belongs rather to the earlier stages in a Museum's history, and of late years we have been extremely chary of accepting fresh loans except in cases where the loan was believed to be a preliminary stage towards a gift or bequest.

It is difficult to see how the existing loans could be incorporated in the Departments (particularly in the case of Ceramics, the territory of which is already desperately congested). But if such an arrangement could be devised, a fairly large although unfortunately most inconvenient Court would be set free for departmental use.

The North Court provides a large amount of valuable and conveniently handled space. Since 1909 it has been reserved for Temporary Exhibitions; and I cannot help feeling that the amount of time during which it has been occupied for such purposes during some fifteen years is regrettably small. It would be a grave loss to the Museum if the possibility of Temporary Exhibitions on a large scale were put an end to. But it has become a serious question whether we can justify the loss of this space during the greater part of the year (space might, so far as I can see, be nearly doubled at a relatively small expense by the provision of a second floor) in order as at rare intervals to organise Exhibitions like those of the Treasures belonging to the City Companies and of English Medieval Art; and to provide space fairly frequently free of cost for institutes like the Sketch Club of the Royal College of Art, the Civil Service Arts Association and the British Institute of Industrial Art.

Apart from the Loan Court and the North Court, the only other direction in which there seems any possibility of setting free any considerable amount of space is the Cast Court. Members of the Advisory Council will remember the interesting and carefully considered memorandum on this subject which was put forward some years ago[6] by Sir Reginald Blomfield, involving the removal of the existing Cast Collection to the Crystal Palace. But apart from the objections which were expressed elsewhere to this proposal, it seems at the moment out of the question for financial reasons, and I do not think that the liberation of the Cast Court can actually be considered as a practical possibility.

It will, I am sure, be of the greatest possible assistance to me if I can have the advice of the Council on these urgent and important questions. They might perhaps be divided into five.

(a) The policy of the Museum with regard to loans and the future of the Loan Court;

(b) The policy of the Museum with regard to Temporary Exhibitions and the future of the North Court;

(c) The provision of fresh space for the Department of Woodwork;

(d) The provision of fresh space for the Department of Circulation; and

(e) The provision of fresh storage space for the Library (and the Department of Engraving, Illustration and Design).

6. 1928. Blomfield was also against the acquisition of 'architectural features', but admitted that he 'seemed to be flogging a dead horse'.

329, 330, 331. *Removing and safeguarding the exhibits in the Second World War*

Very little was eventually decided. The extra floor over the North Court was approved, but in 1934, the Director had to tell the Advisory Council that the Office of Works was not able to do anything for the moment.[7] A temporary measure was decided upon for Room 40, the Octagon or Loan Court. Mr Ormsby-Gore stated that his architectural advisers had let him know that 'no drastic structural alterations should be contemplated ... in view of the fact that the needs of the Museum as a whole would inevitably have to be considered before long'.[8] A model of the Octagon was exhibited to the Council, with partitions which 'would at least make a background for a certain amount of furniture'. Lord Harewood, the Chairman, proposed that Lord Ilchester, Sir Reginald Blomfield, Sir Ambrose Heal, Mr Ormsby-Gore and Lady Lytton should form a subcommittee to consider the matter. So far as the loans were concerned, Sir Eric Maclagan proposed that those which could be dispensed with

should be returned to their owners, while the remainder should be taken over by the Departments concerned. In May, the subcommittee reported to the Council.[9] There were two schemes: (a) four structures to be placed parallel with the apses and (b) four structures to be placed at right angles to the apses. The first was supported by the Director and by all the subcommittee except one member, but the second had the blessing of Sir Ambrose Heal and the Department of Woodwork. The Council supported the Director and the subcommittee. By September, the Council was able to inspect the new arrangement.[10] As Eric Maclagan was considering rearrangements in display, such as 'period' galleries, the Second World War broke out, which changed everything.

---

7. The scheme has (1982) been revived.
8. 49th meeting, 25 January 1934.
9. 50th meeting, 5 May 1934.
10. 52nd meeting, 21 September 1934.

332. *Transferring the Raphael cartoons to a bomb-proof shelter in the Second World War*

Up to August 1939, things were normal. On 24 July Queen Mary attended an evening reception in connection with the 15th International Congress of the History of Art. But one month later, on Thursday 24 August, because of the preparations for the coming war, the Museum was closed to the public, and many of the exhibits were packed and put in storage, some in the Aldwych train tunnel.

The Library re-opened on 13 November and provided a limited service for British Museum Library and National Art-Collections Fund ticket holders. Certain Museum galleries were re-opened to Royal College of Art Students, and two days later these galleries were re-opened to the public as well. Because of bomb damage, the Museum was forced to close again Sunday, 20 April 1941 until the following Wednesday. It was not until Monday, 3 July 1944, that this happened again, this time because a VI flying bomb had fallen on houses in Exhibition Road just north of the Science Schools. A very restricted Library service was provided in the Board Room for some weeks, but it was not until 11 October that sufficient of the glass roofs had been repaired to allow the public into a few of the galleries. From then onwards things slowly improved, although most of the collection was in an underground quarry in Wiltshire or at Montacute House, Somerset. The

Raphael cartoons, too large to remove from the building, were bricked up in a specially constructed shelter outside the refreshment rooms in Gallery 14, where they remained until about 1950.

Between 1941 and 1944 certain galleries became a school for children evacuated from Gibraltar and the South Court was transformed into a canteen, at first for the Royal Air Force, and later for Bomb Damage Repair Squads.[11]

By 1948, most of the collections had returned to London, although only 40 or so rooms were open to the public.[12] Bethnal Green Museum fared rather worse. It closed in 1939 and from 1941 became a restaurant for the London Meals Service, and also served as a kitchen providing school meals. It was not re-opened to the public until 6 May 1950.

When the war ended, Sir Eric Maclagan retired in 1945 and was succeeded by Leigh Ashton of the Department of Ceramics, and Secretary to the Advisory Council. It fell to him to reorganize the gallery display. Sir Leigh had the advantage of an enormous, almost empty building, so that he could stand back, as it were, take an objective view, and replace all the objects where he wanted them to go.

---

11. *Third Report* of the Standing Commission on Museums and Galleries, 1948, pp. 10, 11.

12. There is a persistent rumour, told to the author by Charles Gibbs-Smith, that 'hush-hush' activities took place in the northern portion of the Museum, and that there was a special, secret, entrance made from Prince's Gate Mews.

333. *'Britain can Make It' crowds, September 1946*

334. *The restaurant c. 1958, showing paintings by students of the Royal College of Art*

Virtually nothing, eventually, was left where it had been before the war, with the exception of the ceramics on the top floor, and certain large architectural features. Progress at first was slow, however, because of the Council of Industrial Design's 'Britain Can Make It' exhibition of 1946 which took over most of the ground floor. Opened by King George VI on 24 September, the exhibition proved enormously successful and for weeks large crowds queued along Cromwell Road and up Exhibition Road towards Hyde Park, patiently waiting to see what the 'brave new world' promised them in the future.[13]

In 1944, Sir Leigh had told the Advisory Council that he proposed that the galleries should be reorganized into two groups. There would be the Primary Galleries in which all the best and most important exhibits would be displayed together by period, in a series of rooms starting from the Main Entrance.[14] Everything else, the study collections, would be kept together in their groups by material, mainly on the upper floors. However, none of this reorganization was destined in any way to solve the basic and chronic problem of space – in fact, the situation was aggravated by fashionable, space-consuming methods of display. More and more, as a result, was squeezed into storage that was incapable of expansion. At the same time, staff numbers began to increase, leading to a need for additional offices and workshops in a building that was from its beginning inadequately

provided with such accommodation. There was, therefore, bound to be a crisis, but when it came, it came from an entirely unexpected quarter, thereby making a bad situation, in a listed building on a finite site, practically insoluble; a problem which faced Sir Trenchard Cox, who had succeeded Sir Leigh Aston in 1956.

In 1953, the Government had announced that there was to be a massive expansion of Imperial College. As is well known, this involved the controversial demolition of not only the Imperial College, but the remains of the International Exhibition eastern and western galleries, and Waterhouse's City and Guilds College. This meant that the Indian collection of the Museum in the eastern and cross galleries had to be rehoused.

The Committee of Re-arrangement of 1908 had proposed that this collection should be put in the newly completed western portion of the Museum, but there had not been sufficient space, so it had remained where it was. Now, the Museum's hand was forced. Only very limited room was made available. An additional first floor was created in 1957 round the perimeter of the North Court for paintings, which released Room

13. The exhibition closed at the end of the year, when it had been seen by 1,432,546 visitors (*2nd Report* of the Council of Industrial Design, 1946–1947, p. 4.

14. C. H. Gibbs-Smith, 'Revolution at the V. and A.' *Sphere*, 14 February 1953, pp. 229–232.

335. *(above left) The new paintings galleries, designed by Christopher Firmstone and installed in Rooms 8 and 9 in 1978*

336. *(above right) The paintings galleries in Rooms 103–106, over parts of the North Court in 1957*

337. *(left) The North Court in 1929. Where the blank wall runs round the court above the arcade, the new galleries (Rooms 103–106) were built out in 1957; the middle of the court was left open to the roof*

41 for the Indian material.[15] The remainder of the collection has, since then, led a nomadic existence between Burlington Gardens, Perivale and Battersea. The demolition of the Indian Museum meant that most of its collections disappeared from public view, only adding to the Victoria and Albert Museum's overall display and storage problems.[16]

Shortly afterwards, in 1960–2, a free-standing circular platform, providing a first-floor gallery of 3,650 square feet, was built in the Octagon Court at a cost of £30,000 or so, providing a partial

15. *Museums Journal*, Vol. 57, February 1958, pp. 264–266. These galleries were never satisfactory. Although beneath the North Court roof, they were in fact built against the exterior walls of 1860, in which were embedded pipes to take rainwater from Fowke's glass roof with an area of more than 10,000 square feet. There was constant trouble as the walls were, more often than not, saturated.

16. 'The largest problem that confronts the authorities of the Victoria and Albert Museum (and one that will certainly haunt my successors) is the amazingly unsuitable building in which the collections are housed. In spite of its colossal cubic capacity the floor space is entirely inadequate', Sir Trenchard Cox, 21 January 1960, V&A.M. file 60/259. (See also Robert Skelton, 'The Indian Collections: 1798 to 1978, *Burlington Magazine*, Vol. cxx, 1978, pp. 297–304.

338. *(above) A view in the Continental baroque galleries (Rooms 1–3), re-opened in 1978 after reconstruction*

339. *(right) Room 1c in 1973 before reconstruction*

340. *(below left) Reconstruction and the installation of air-conditioning in progress in Room 3 in 1974*

341. *(right) Room 42 in 1951: one of Aston Webb's 'basilica' courts, adapted for the display of Islamic art*

solution for more economical use of the huge volume of the Court. Care was taken not to obscure or destroy any of the existing architectural features. The marvellous echo, at least, has disappeared.[17]

While this work was in progress, covetous eyes were looking at the open area, the Kitchen, or Schools, Court behind the Lecture Theatre. A preliminary scheme was drawn up which would have meant the demolition of the Lecture Theatre, and the Morris, Gamble and Poynter Rooms. As two of these rooms were still in use as stores and the revival of interest in High Victorian design had not gained its full momentum, the Ministry of Public Building and Works proposed that portions of the decoration of these rooms could be preserved and exhibited in the galleries.[18] The scheme was vetoed by Sir Trenchard Cox.

The most controversial of the projects to create extra space that were actually realized was undertaken during 1966–7, in order to provide what was expected to be adequate shelf storage for Library books for the foreseeable future, an aim that was quickly seen to be too optimistic, even though it gave 27,500 lineal feet of shelves. These were soon filled up.

In spite of being right in the heart of the Museum, it was decided to insert three floors into Room 43, Aston Webb's 60-feet high Central Court, thereby reducing the height of the ground floor gallery to 18 feet. It was stated at the time that this conversion brought to an end 'the visual

242
243

conflict between the character of the museum exhibits – early medieval art – and the Victorian renaissance detail of the original room design.'[19]

The foundations of Webb's existing walls were found to be inadequate, so a steel frame was inserted together with two rows of four columns.[20] The scheme was designed by the Directorate General of Works (Superintending Architect, W. Kendall; Architect, H. G. Yexley), cost £115,000, and was completed during 1967.

The concentration of books from outlying areas of the Museum, following the completion of this work, allowed the Director to plan for a mezzanine in the former attics of the residences on the east side of the quadrangle, for offices and improved storage facilities for the Department of Prints and Drawings (completed in 1964), as well as for a minor modification to the similar area

17. Peter Thornton, Keeper of Furniture and Woodwork, then Assistant Keeper of Textiles, devised the scheme for the display of the dress collection and later, for musical instruments as well.

18. 'There was no question that the Morris Room must be preserved, though not necessarily in situ; the larger refreshment room was a more doubtful matter. Tentatively we thought that the best plan would be to reconstruct the Morris Room elsewhere in the building where it would be preserved in a suitable context; that a section of the larger room might be preserved (in the Architecture Court?) as an example of the period and as a part of the Museum's history, and the rest allowed to go . . .' Minutes of a meeting between the Museum and the Ministry of Public Building and Works, 1 December 1961.

19. Press notice 154/67, Ministry of Public Building and Works, dated 8 June 1967.

20. During the excavations, the roots of the great plane tree were unearthed (information from Charles Gibbs-Smith).

342. *Room 43, Aston Webb's Main Hall (see ill. 225), after a three-storey bookstore had been erected in its upper part. The ground floor, re-opened in 1967, contained a re-arranged display of early medieval art*

343. *The top floor of the new bookstore in Room 43, showing Aston Webb's cornice and barrel-vaulted roof*

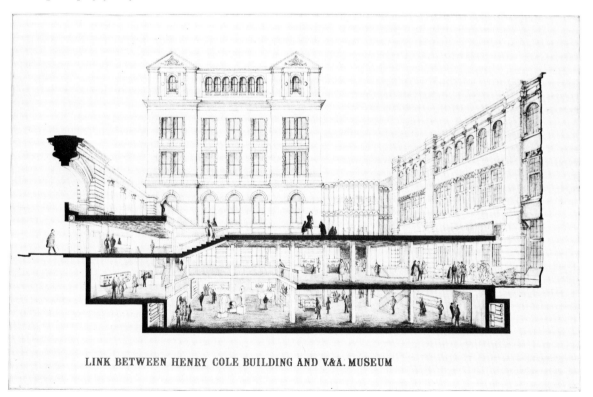

LINK BETWEEN HENRY COLE BUILDING AND V.&A. MUSEUM

344. *A linking gallery and exhibition room between the Museum and the Henry Cole building, on the site of Aston Webb's boiler house, proposed in 1976, and designed by David Church and John Sansom for the Department of the Environment*

345. *(above) Restoration: Godfrey Sykes's railings on the Lecture Theatre roof were repainted and regilded in 1977*

346. *(above right) Restoration: the floor of the Centre Refreshment Room was repaired in 1976*

347. *(centre right) The start of work on the Link building, July 1979*

348. *(below right) The Link on 8 April 1981*

created by Aston Webb in 1900 on the west side of the garden, above the Sheepshanks Gallery, as offices for the Department of Metalwork.

Other minor schemes were undertaken during this period, but none was comprehensive enough to solve the underlying problem of providing the enormous area of extra space that was really necessary. However, for some time there was the promise of the Royal College of Science (Huxley) Building, which Sir John Pope-Hennessy hoped would house the Indian and other Oriental collections.[21]

The Huxley Building (now renamed the Henry Cole Building) is extremely deceptive. In spite of being the tallest in the museum area, it consists of, at the north end, only a massive staircase, and at the south end, a single quite large room on each floor. These are connected by what are no more than corridors about 12 feet wide and 24 feet high. From outside it appears vast, but the centre was a large open space above a glass-roofed lecture theatre, which occupied the core of the building.

It was not until 1974, immediately following

21. *10th Report, 1973–1977,* Standing Commission on Museums and Galleries, 1978, pp. 10, 11, 243.

276

349. The new gates in Exhibition Road designed by the Royal College of Art (Christopher Hay and Douglas Coyne), completed 1982

the appointment of Dr Roy Strong as Director, that the Department of Mathematics moved out, and detailed planning got under way. To accommodate the Oriental collections, David Church, architect in the Department of the Environment, considered that most of the interior would have to be gutted, and that the large northern staircase should be removed and replaced by something less wasteful of space. The plans were made public during 1975, and immediately objections were raised, particularly from the Greater London Council Historic Buildings Division.[22] As a result, the Director decided that as much of the interior as possible was to be preserved, and the building was consequently replanned to house the Department of Prints, Drawings & Photographs, and Paintings, together with exhibition galleries. Architectural work did not begin until 1978 and was completed in 1981. It was hoped that it would

be opened to the public in 1982. The conversion, in which David Church was assisted by John Sansom, and which was undertaken by Messrs Jarvis, cost £2,682,000. As there was only a minor link from the main museum to the Henry Cole Building, as a continuation of the Ceramic Staircase in Room 11, Sir Roy Strong asked for something more substantial in Exhibition Road, providing there was sufficient money. A simple concrete ground-floor and basement structure was found to be possible within the cash limits, which would also provide a new Exhibition Road entrance. Iron gates for this were designed by Christopher Hay and Douglas Coyne[23] of the

349

---

22. Victoria and Albert Museum, *Review of the Years 1974–1978*, 1981, p. 137.

23. The designers' model was exhibited at the Summer Exhibition at the Royal Academy, 1982.

350. *(above left)* 351. *(above right) Perspectives of the 'Space-Rig', a free-standing structure proposed for Room 46b, the eastern Cast Court, in 1978, and designed by Leonard Manasseh & Partners*

352. *Repair: erecting scaffolding over Room 40 in order to rebuild the roof, 3 October 1980*

353. *The temporary roof in position over Room 40, 8 January 1981*

354. *(above left) Interior of the Henry Cole Building, above the Lecture Theatre, April 1979*

355. *(above right) The infill floors to provide accommodation for the Department of Prints, Drawings and Photographs, and Paintings, May 1979*

356. *(right) The main entrance, Blythe Road*

Royal College of Art, and made by Messrs Bingham Smith & Sons of London. The Link and Entrance will support a first-floor gallery, should one be decided upon in future.

In order to create space for galleries devoted to the twentieth century, Leonard Manasseh and Partners drew up plans on behalf of the Department of the Environment for an open, steel frame, called a 'Space-Rig', intended to create extra floors in the immense volume of the eastern Cast Court.[24] The Advisory Council approved the proposal to exhibit bronze, ivory and alabaster sculpture among plaster casts, provided that the latter were clearly labelled as reproductions. However, there were objections to this scheme, not the least among them were the problems which would have been caused, firstly, by the need to investigate the Court's foundations, and secondly, by the actual construction work. There was simply no room anywhere to provide space for everything that would have to be moved. Moreover, the roofs of the Cast Courts were in an extremely

350
351

24. Roy Strong, 'The Victoria and Albert Museum – 1978', *Burlington Magazine*, 1978, Vol. CXX, p. 276.

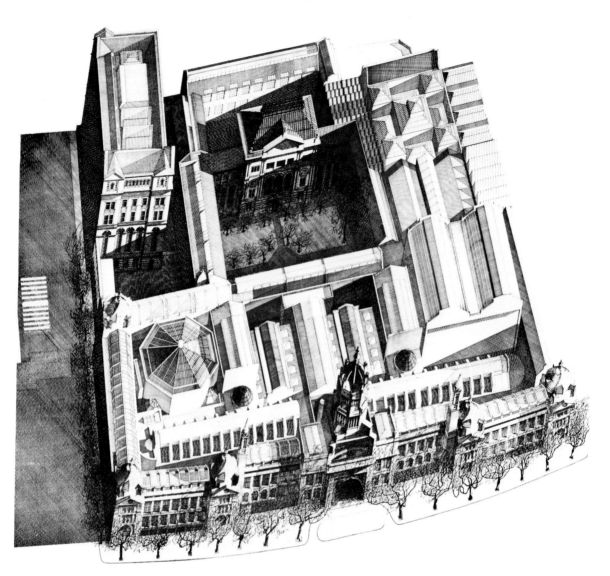

357. *Birds-eye view by Ron Sanford for Mobil Oil*

unsafe condition and they had to be rebuilt urgently. During the several years that this work required, the decision was taken that the Courts should remain internally unobstructed.

The transfer of the Department of Prints and Drawings to the Henry Cole Building during 1982 will allow a certain amount of rearrangement in the rest of the Museum, but the congestion and inadequate amount of storage space should be solved during the mid-1980s by the acquisition of more than 100,000 square feet in the former Post Office Savings Bank building at Blythe Road, West Kensington, beside Olympia, which is an exact contemporary of Aston Webb's extension to the Museum, and was designed by the government architect, Sir Henry Tanner.[25]

356

25. *Building News*, Vol. LXXVI, 23 June 1899, p. 841, together with plan, perspective and elevation, following p. 842.

APPENDIX I

Specification of the Iron Museum

'The building would be in form, 266 feet long, and 126 feet broad and about 30 feet high to the eaves. The floor would be raised 2 feet off the ground, and be supported by joists resting on main foundation frames, or on dwarf walls, as may be deemed most advisable.

'The building would cover an area of 3,700 square yards, making an entire space for exhibition of 6,400 square yards or 1⅓ acres. The walls of the building would be composed of cast-iron uprights or standards placed 7 feet apart, and tottled to a foundation frame of timber, or rest on concrete foundations, as the nature of the ground may render it expedient. The spaces between the columns would be filled up with corrugated sheets, and the interior of the walls lined with boarding, tongued and grooved.

'The lower story would be lighted by windows, filling up the spaces between each alternate standards, the runners which stiffen the wall forming the lintel of the same.

'The building would be covered by three segmented roofs, each 42 feet span, supported on the outside walls, and in two intermediate rows of columns. The trusses would be of malleable iron, 7 feet asunder and covered with corrugated sheets. A sky-light 12 feet wide, and raised 18 inches from the surface, would run along the entire ridge of each roof, the sides being fitted with moveable wrought-iron louvres.

'Galleries 42 feet wide would be constructed down each side of the building, and fill up the whole space beneath two of the roofs. They would be connected at the ends by cross galleries 21 feet wide. And these galleries would be carried by a system of longitudinal and cross girders – the longitudinal girders being placed 14 feet apart, and at an equal distance from the outside walls, and supported by columns placed 14 feet asunder. The cross girders spring from each of the standards of the outside walls, and, the intermediate ones being tottled to the longitudinal girders. Joists are fixed between the cross girders, and the flooring spikes to them. The galleries are fenced by a light trussed railing, and lighted by the skylights in roof.

'There would be six flights of stairs leading up from the ground floor, one 7 feet wide at each angle, and two in the middle of the nave 14 feet wide. The water off the roof would flow into cast gutters beneath the eaves, which would discharge down the main column of the building and be carried off by a system of pipes beneath the floor.

'A pair of cast ventilators, sufficiently large would be placed in the walls between the windows on both floors, and the vitiated air escape by the louvres under the sky-light.

'The entrance and exit to the building is effected by the doors placed beneath the verandah, within the recess at each end.

'The whole of the iron work would be covered, within and without, with three coats of oil paint, and the interior wood casing varnished two coats.

'The cost of the building as above specified, and shown in accompanying drawings would be about nine thousand eight hundred pounds (£9,800); if with an architectural front of cast-iron from £1,000 to £1,400 additional, according to design.

'Heating with a system of hot-water pipes giving a radiating surface of not less than 16,000 superficial feet, will cost from 900 *l.* to 1,000 *l.*

General Remarks.

'The building would be constructed in bays of 14 feet square, or a multiple of that number. By adopting this principle, we obtain greater economy in first construction, facility of extension, or removal and re-erection.

'In the absence of any instructions to the contrary, the whole building is calculated to be of the strongest and most substantial character, and the various materials the best of their respective kinds.

'The building is calculated to sustain a moving load of 100 lbs. to the superficial foot, both in gallery and ground-floor.

'The interior casing renders the wall double, within which there would be a constant current of air, securing comparatively an equable temperature within the building both in summer and winter, and greatly facilitating the ventilation and heating.

'The estimate of prices are to be received as proximate, but they may be assumed as tolerably near the amounts stated, the circumstances of ground and foundations being of an ordinary character.'

Statement sent by Henry Cole on 7 January 1871, to the First Commissioner of Works, on the Museum's space requirements (PRO, Ed. 84/15)

	SUPERFICIAL SPACE IN OCCUPATION	ADDITIONAL SPACE FOR PRESENT OBJECTS	ADDITIONAL SPACE FOR COMPLETE COLLECTION	TOTAL SPACE REQUIRED
Administration				
Offices	20,953			20,953
Official residences	24,277			24,277
Art Work Rooms	6,876			6,876
Stores, offices, and lavatories	34,914		16,026	50,940
Workshops and stores	7,000			7,000
Sappers' Quarters	5,248			5,248
Art Training Schools	19,401			19,401
Science Schools	5,136		51,419 (building)	56,555
Lecture Theatre	3,876			3,876
Refreshment Rooms and kitchens	6,964			6,964
Staircases, entrances and gateways	3,547		5,892	9,439
	138,192		73,337	211,529
Art Division				
Sculpture	5,850	1,000	6,000	12,850
Terra-cotta and Della Robbia Ware	3,210	1,000	3,500	7,710
Ivories	777	500	500	1,777
Furniture	5,900	2,500	5,500	13,900
Mosaics	972	500	1,000	2,472
Pottery	5,524	2,000	3,500	11,024
Glass	1,250	1,250	500	3,000
Metal Work	4,828	1,500	2,500	8,828
Goldsmiths' work	3,300	2,000	1,500	6,800
Musical Instruments	2,064	500	1,500	4,064
Carriages	1,780	1,000	2,000	4,780
Textile fabrics	2,316	1,250	3,750	7,316
Oriental objects	4,428	600	1,000	6,028
Paintings in oil	5,900	2,000	13,000	20,900
Water Colour drawings	5,000	2,500	2,500	10,000
Engraved national portraits	2,878	2,000	3,000	7,878
Circulation	1,391	1,000	3,000	5,397
Reproductions	7,750	2,000	9,500	19,250
Loans	5,311	2,500	7,200	15,011

	SUPERFICIAL SPACE IN OCCUPATION	ADDITIONAL SPACE FOR PRESENT OBJECTS	ADDITIONAL SPACE FOR COMPLETE COLLECTION	TOTAL SPACE REQUIRED
Art Division [continued]				
Special exhibitions			5,000	5,000
Competition drawings		5,000		5,000
	70,429*	32,600	75,950	178,979
Modern British pictures of National Gallery	14,435			14,435
				193,414

*These quantities change relatively with every addition.

Science and Art Divisions				
Gibbs Request of Roman Antiquities		1,000		1,000
Art Library	3,600	2,000	6,400	12,000
Dyce Bequest	1,680	500	2,180	4,360
Education Library, Reading Rooms and Museum	8,150	4,000	12,850	25,000
Structure and Building	8,550	1,000	1,500	11,050
Art Examination Rooms		5,000		5,000
Science Examination Rooms		5,000		5,000
Art Preparation Rooms	800	800		1,600
	22,780	19,300	22,930	65,010

Science Division				
Naval Models	15,770	5,000	5,000	25,770
Food Museum	3,000			3,000
Fish Collections	2,724	500	1,500	4,724
Reception and Packing Rooms	1,120	1,200		2,320
War Materials	4,590		500	5,090
Machine Models	1,800		18,200	20,000
Forestry and Entomology		250	750	1,000
	29,004	6,950	25,950	61,904

Summary

Total Space required when Museum, according to present view, is completed:–

Administration	211,529
Art	193,414
Science and Art	65,010
Science	61,904
	531,857

Total exhibiting Space in present permanent and proposed additional buildings:–
492,392 feet.

Submitted, Henry Cole, Director, 16 December 1870.

ILLUSTRATION SOURCES

Photographs of the building for which no sources are mentioned are from the Victoria and Albert Museum's series of official photographs; prints of these are preserved in guard books in the Photographic Sales Section. Some of the plans and drawings are also reproduced from photographs in the guard books, as is noted in the list below. PRO indicates Public Record Office

Colour plates

PLATE I V & A Print Room, No. 7279
PLATE II V & A Print Room, No. 2813 A.L.
PLATE III V & A Print Room, No. 2811 A.L.
PLATE IV V & A Print Room, No. 2816
PLATE V V & A Print Room, No. 7851
PLATE VI V & A Print Room, No. E.391–1943
PLATE VII V & A, Department of Paintings, No. 752–1870
PLATE VIII V & A, Department of Paintings, No. 127–1885
PLATE IX V & A Print Room, No. 8060
PLATE X V & A, Department of Paintings, No. 992–1873
PLATE XI V & A, Department of Paintings, No. 993–1873
PLATE XII V & A Print Room, E.3608–1931
PLATE XIII V & A Print Room, E.1708–1931
PLATE XIV V & A Print Room, No. 1112 A.L.
PLATE XVI V & A Print Room, E.924–1976
PLATE XVII V & A Print Room, E.1026–1927
PLATE XVIII V & A Print Room, E.1025–1927
PLATE XX V & A Print Room, No. 7356.1
PLATE XXIII V & A Print Room, E.5096–1960
PLATE XXX V & A, Department of Sculpture, A.12–1973
PLATE XXXI V & A Print Room, D.738–1905
PLATE XXXIII V & A Print Room, D.564–1905

Black and white illustrations

FRONTISPIECE Astral Aerial Surveys Ltd
3. V & A Print Room, No. 2780
4. *Illustrated London News*
6. From the *Guide*, 1853
7. From *3rd Report* of The 1851 Commissioners, 1856
8. V & A guard books (contemporary photograph)
9. *Builder*, 10 May 1856
12. V & A Print Room, No. 2816 A.L.
14. V & A Print Room, Photograph Collection, No. 98–1958
15. V & A Print Room, No. 2817 A.L.
17. V & A Print Room, No. 2815 A.L.
20. V & A Print Room, No. 2814
21. *Queen*, 29 June 1861
23. From *5th Report* 1857 (1858)
24. From *5th Report* 1857 (1858)
26. From *5th Report* 1857 (1858)
29. V & A Print Room, Photograph Collection, No. 1959–1938
30. *Punch*, 17 April 1869
32. From Select Committee 1860
34. From *The South Kensington Museum: a handbook guide*, published by H. A. Clarke, 1860
35. *Illustrated London News*, 4 February 1860
37. V & A guard books (contemporary photograph)
38. V & A guard books (contemporary photograph)
39. V & A Print Room, No. E.1048–1927
43. Photograph by Miss Elizabeth Aslin
44. *Illustrated Times*, 25 June 1864
46. Acquired by the Department of Science and Art from the 1862 Exhibition
47. V & A guard books (contemporary photograph)
48. V & A Print Room, No. E.1048–1927
52. V & A Print Room, No. E.353–1956
53. V & A Print Room, No. E.1017–1965
55. Photographed in 1968
56. Photographed in 1954
58. *Building News*, 24 February 1865
59. V & A Print Room, No. 1117.3 A.L.
60. V & A Print Room, No. 1117.1 A.L.
62. *Illustrated London News*, 21 September 1867
63. *Illustrated London News*, 30 March 1867
64. V & A Department of Paintings, No. 752–1870
65. V & A Print Room, No. 8089.I.
66. V & A Print Room, No. D.85A–1887
67. V & A Print Room, No. 8089.L.
69. V & A Print Room, No. E.2946–1911
73. V & A Department of Paintings, No. P.14–1934
74. V & A Print Room, No. 219
75. V & A Department of Paintings
76. V & A Department of Paintings
77. V & A Print Room, No. 8142
78. V & A Print Room, No. E.377–1943
79. V & A Department of Paintings, No. S.K.M. 20
80. V & A Department of Paintings, No. S.K.M. 19
81. V & A Department of Paintings, No. S.K.M. 19
82. V & A Print Room, No. 8089.C.
83. V & A Print Room, No. 8089.K.
84. V & A Print Room, No. E.4546–1909
86. V & A Print Room, No. E.2984–1911
87. *Magazine of Art*, XVI (1892–3), 406
90. V & A Print Room, No. E.1048–1927
93. V & A Print Room, Photograph Collection, No. 60762
94. V & A Print Room, No. 14.648
95. From Select Committee 1860
96. PRO, Works 33/2744
100. V & A Print Room, No. E.1049–1927
102. V & A Print Room, No. E.1048–1927
104. From *11th Report 1863* (1864)
105. V & A Print Room (neg. no. GE 1774)
106. V & A Print Room (neg. no. GE 1773)
107. V & A Print Room, No. E.924–1976
108. V & A Print Room, No. E.1049–1927
109. V & A Print Room, No. E.1049–1927
111. *Illustrated London News*, 5 March 1870
113. V & A Print Room, No. D.930–1899
115. V & A Print Room, Photograph Collection, No. 76531
117. V & A Print Room, No. 8133
119. V & A Print Room, No. 1115.7
120. V & A Print Room, No. 1118 A.L.
123. Photographed by Sgt B. Spackman, Royal Engineers, 1868
124. V & A Print Room, No. E.5878–1910
125. *Building News*, 3 March 1876
127. V & A Print Room, No. 8135.4
130. V & A Print Room, No. 1115.2 A.L.
132. Photographed in 1865 before erection
139. V & A Print Room, No. 8099.11
140. V & A Print Room, No. 8099.4
141. V & A Print Room, No. E.2897/2898/2899–1927
143. National Monuments Record
145. V & A Print Room, No. E.4551–1909
148. Photograph by C. Thurston Thompson (Original design : V & A Print Room, No. 729)
153. *Graphic*, 26 February 1870
157. V & A Print Room, No. E.1055–1927
158. V & A Print Room, No. 8125 A.L.
161. *Magazine of Art*, XVI (1892–3), 407
162. V & A Print Room (neg. no. GE 1778)
166. *Building News*, 18 February 1876
167. *Building News*, 10 March 1876
168. V & A Print Room, No. 8134.1
172. V & A Print Room, No. E.1049–1927
173. V & A Print Room, No. E.4552–1909
175. *Magazine of Art*, XVI (1892–3), 404
176. *Magazine of Art*, XVI (1892–3), 405
177. V & A Print Room, No. E.4550–1909
178. PRO, Works 33/1663
180. V & A Print Room, No. E.2033–1921
181. V & A Print Room, No. E.2034–1921
182. V & A Print Room, No. E.1048–1927
183. V & A guard books (contemporary photograph)

INDEX